ENERGY AND ENVIRONMENT
The Four Energy Crises Second Edition

G. TYLER MILLER, JR.
St. Andrews Presbyterian College

WADSWORTH PUBLISHING COMPANY
Belmont, California
A Division of Wadsworth, Inc.

Science Editor: Jack C. Carey

Designer: Cynthia Bassett

Developmental Editor: Autumn Stanley

Copy Editor: Don Yoder

Illustrators: John Dawson, Florence Fujimoto

Cover Photo: Carol Simowitz

© 1980 by Wadsworth, Inc.

Printed in the United States of America

1 2 3 4 5 6 7 8 9 10—84 83 82 81 80

Library of Congress Cataloging in Publication Data
Miller, George Tyler, date
  Energy and environment.

  Bibliography: p.
  Includes index.
  1. Energy policy—Environmental aspects.
2. Power resources.   3. Environmental policy.
I. Title.
HD9502.A2M54   1980   333.79   80–10872
ISBN 0–534–00836–4

Preface

Ecologist Garrett Hardin has stated that the basic principle of ecology is: everything is connected to everything. We are slowly beginning to realize that energy and its flow through all living things is the primary common denominator that connects everything to everything. Thus, understanding some of the basic principles of energy and the consequences of its use and misuse must be a prime requisite for understanding what we can and cannot do on this planet.

This book is a nontechnical introduction to energy and environment—it can be used as a basic text for short courses on energy and environment or as a supplement for introductory courses in biology, geography, chemistry, and environmental studies.

The purpose of this book is to look at the two basic energy laws—you can't get something for nothing, and you can't even break even—and use them to evaluate our energy options. Reams of words have been written about the energy crises. I shall not dwell on the details of these crises nor engage in the "find the villain" game that is our first response to most crises. Instead this book is designed to evaluate our future options for the energy crises coming during the next few decades.

The book's tone is neither gloom-and-doom pessimism nor technological optimism, both of which encourage or allow inaction or withdrawal. We live on an exciting "hinge of history" with many alternatives and hopeful choices still available. Indeed, I believe that during the next fifty years we must and can make the transition to an earthmanship society, one that recognizes (in the words of Rolf Edberg) that "the earth does not belong to us, but we to the earth." Such a transition can happen only if we accept and act according to the realities of energy and ecology.

Major Features

Emphasis on Basic Concepts The second edition develops basic energy principles in a nontechnical manner early in the text and then uses them to connect many of the complex and seemingly unrelated energy facts, problems, and possible options.

Guest Editorials Seven prominent scientists have written short guest editorials for this book (see the list of guest editorialists at the end of this preface). The second edition includes three new guest editorials. To avoid breaking up the logical flow of the chapter, guest editorials are boxed and appear at the end of each chapter in a different typeface from the text.

Documentation The second edition has over 1400 references—many more than the first edition—to back up the textual material and to provide students with starter references for term papers, reports, or further study of any topic.

Extensive Manuscript Review Because of the complexity of energy issues, no author or small group of authors can provide the necessary expertise. Thus, we have used some fifty-eight reviewers to improve the quality and accuracy of the book and to ensure that it is up-to-date. Each chapter has been reviewed in detail by at least two recognized experts in that area and by at least nineteen reviewers who teach environment-related courses in colleges and universities (see the list of reviewers at the end of this preface).

Balanced Treatment The second edition continues to discusss opposing sides of major energy issues and to examine both the merits and the demerits of proposed alternative solutions to problems. Specific proposals for action are integrated throughout the text, and the major principles that should be used in developing a detailed energy plan are emphasized.

Illustrations I have tried especially hard to find or commission attractive and useful illustrations, designed to simplify complex relationships. In the second edition, most figures have been modified to make them even more useful, photographs that served no specific functional purpose have been eliminated, and new figures have been added.

As you and your students deal with the crucial and exciting issues discussed in the book, I hope you will take the time to correct errors and suggest improvements for future editions.

Acknowledgments   I wish to thank all of the teachers who responded to the detailed questionnaires evaluating the first edition. My thanks go also to the students and teachers who responded so favorably to the first edition and offered suggestions for improvement. I am deeply indebted to the prominent environmentalists who wrote guest editorials for this book and to the reviewers (see the list at the end of this preface) who pointed out errors and suggested many important improvements. Any deficiencies remaining are mine, not theirs. My sincere thanks also go to Mrs. Ruth Y. Wetmore for her skill in typing the manuscript despite my almost illegible handwriting and for the improvements she suggested. I also wish to thank Peggy S. O'Neal and Anne Morgan for helping me check and assemble the new references for the second edition.

One of the pleasures of writing both editions of this book has been the opportunity to work with the talented people at Wadsworth Publishing Company. I am particularly indebted to Autumn Stanley for reading the entire manuscript and making many improvements; to Mary Arbogast for coordinating the editing and publishing activities with her usual dedication, talent, and good humor in times of stress; to Darwen Hennings, Vally Hennings, and John Waller for their innovative artwork in the first edition; to John Dawson and Flo Fujimoto, the artists who continued and improved this tradition of excellence in the second edition; and to Cynthia Bassett, the designer of the book.

Above all, I wish to thank Jack Carey, Science Editor at Wadsworth. Besides designing and managing a superb reviewing system, he has provided many key ideas for the overall organization and format of both editions of this book. It has been a rare pleasure to work closely with such a talented, creative, and dedicated editor and to count him as one of my closest personal friends.

G. Tyler Miller, Jr.

Reviewers

Kenneth B. Armitage University of Kansas
Virgil R. Baker Arizona State University
Ian G. Barbour Carleton College
Albert J. Beck California State University, Chico
Jeff Bland University of Puget Sound
Arthur C. Borror University of New Hampshire
Patrick E. Brunelle Contra Costa College
Lynton K. Caldwell Indiana University
Richard A. Cellarius The Evergreen State University
Preston Cloud University of California, Santa Barbara
Bernard C. Cohen University of Pittsburgh
Richard A. Cooley University of California, Santa Cruz
John D. Cunningham Keene State College
Allan Fitzsimmons University of Kentucky
George L. Fouke St. Andrews Presbyterian College
Dr. Paul Grogger University of Colorado
Raymond E. Hampton Central Michigan University
Ted L. Hanes California State University, Fullerton
Harry S. Hass San Jose City College
Denis A. Hayes Worldwatch Institute
David L. Hicks Whitworth College
Eric Hirst Oak Ridge National Laboratory
C. S. Holling University of British Columbia
Donald Holtgrieve California State University, Hayward
Marilyn Houck Pennsylvania State University
David R. Inglis University of Massachusetts
David I. Johnson Michigan State University
Nathan Keyfitz Harvard University
Edward J. Kormondy The Evergreen State University
William S. Lindsay Monterey Peninsula College
Valerie A. Liston University of Minnesota
Ruth Logan Santa Monica City College
T. Lovering University of California, Santa Barbara
Dr. Ralph Morris Brock University, Canada
William W. Murdoch University of California, Santa Barbara
Brian C. Myres Cypress College
C. A. Neale Illinois State University
Jan Newhouse University of Hawaii, Manoa
John E. Oliver Indiana State University
Harry Perry Library of Congress
Robert B. Platt Emory University
Grace L. Powell University of Akron

James H. Price Oklahoma College
Marian E. Reeve Merritt College
Robert A. Richardson University of Wisconsin
C. Lee Rockett Bowling Green State University
Richard G. Rose West Valley College
Stephen Schneider National Center for Atmospheric Research
H. F. Siewert Ball State University
Patricia M. Sparks Glassboro State College
John E. Stanley University of Virginia
Mel Stanley California State Polytechnic University, Pomona
William L. Thomas California State University, Hayward
Donald E. Van Meter Ball State University
John D. Vitek Oklahoma State University
Kenneth E. F. Watt University of California, Davis
John C. Williams College of San Mateo
George M. Woodwell Brookhaven National Laboratory

Contributors of Guest Editorials

Richard A. Falk
Albert E. Milbank Professor of International
Law and Practice, Princeton University

David Rittenhouse Inglis
Emeritus Professor of Physics, University of
Massachusetts

Howard T. Odum
Graduate Research Professor of Environmental Engineering
Sciences and Director of the Center for Wetlands,
University of Florida

Stephen H. Schneider
Deputy Head of the Climate Project, National Center
for Atmospheric Research

Glenn T. Seaborg
University Professor of Chemistry and
Associate Director of the Lawrence Berkeley Laboratory,
University of California, Berkeley

Kenneth E. F. Watt
Professor of Zoology, University of California, Davis

Alvin M. Weinberg
Director, Institute for Energy Analysis

Contents

Prologue

Passengers on *Terra I*, the only true spacecraft, it is time for the annual State of the Spaceship report. As you know, we are hurtling through space at about 107,200 kilometers (66,600 miles) per hour on a fixed course. Although we can never take on new supplies, our ship has a marvelous life-support system that uses solar energy to recycle the chemicals needed to provide a reasonable number of us with adequate water, air, and food.

Let me briefly summarize the state of our passengers and of our life-support system. There are over 4.4 billion passengers on board, distributed throughout 161 nations that occupy various sections of the ship. One-quarter of you in the developed nations occupy the good to luxurious quarters in the tourist and first-class sections. You used about 80 percent of all supplies available this past year.

I am saddened to say that things have not really improved this year for the 75 percent of you in the so-called developing nations traveling in the hold of the ship. Over one-third of you are suffering from hunger, malnutrition, or both, and three-fourths of you have inadequate water and shelter. More people starved to death or died from malnutrition-related diseases this year than at any time in the history of our voyage. This number will certainly rise as long as population growth continues to wipe out gains in food supply and economic development.

With the limited supplies and recycling capacity of our craft, many of you are now wondering whether you will ever move from the hold to the tourist and first-class sections. Even more important, many of you are asking why you had to travel in the ship's hold in the first place.

The most important fact molding our lives today is that we have gone around the bend on a curve in the shape of the letter J of increasing population and pollution. Population growth rates have decreased slightly in recent years, partially because of tragic increases in death rates for the billion of you living in the desperately poor countries. At the present growth rate, our population will double to over 8 billion passengers in the next 48 years. But we don't have to maintain our present rate of population growth. We must come to grips with an important question: What is the population level that will let all passengers live with freedom, dignity, and a fair share of *Terra I's* resources? Some experts put this ideal level at about 2 billion passengers, a figure that we reached in 1930.

But the overpopulation of the hold, serious though it is, may be less of a threat to our life-support system than the overpopulation in the tourist and first-class sections. Both consumption and pollution rise sharply with even a slight increase in these wealthier populations. For example, the 220 million Americans, who make up only 5 percent of our total population, used about 35 percent of all our supplies and produced over one-third of all our artificial pollution last year. Each tourist and first-class passenger has about 25 times as much impact on our life-support system as each passenger traveling in the hold. The tourist and first-class passengers must continue to reduce their rate of population growth and at the same time change their patterns of consumption, which squander many of our limited supplies. Failure to do so will continue to strain and damage the life-support system for everyone. Efforts to conserve resources in the rich nations are still grossly inadequate. Pollution control in these nations, however, continues to improve, although there is a long way to go.

In spite of the seriousness of the interlocking problems of overpopulation, dwindling resources, and pollution, the single greatest human and environmental threat is that of war—especially a nuclear holocaust. It is discouraging that so little progress has been made in reducing the extravagant waste of resources and human talent devoted to the arms race. During the past year we spent 170 times more on military expenditures than on international cooperation for peace and development. Each year more nations develop the ability to produce nuclear weapons.

Some say that our ship is already doomed, while other technological optimists see a glorious future for everyone. Our most thoughtful experts agree that the ship's situation is serious but certainly not hopeless. They feel that if we begin now, we have 30 to 50 years to learn how to control our population and consumption and to learn how to live together in cooperation and peace on this beautiful and fragile lifecraft that is our home. Obviously, more of us must start to act like members of the crew rather than like passengers. This particularly applies to those of you traveling tourist or first class, who have the most harmful impact on our life-support system and who have the greatest resources to correct the situation.

Just what is spaceship *Terra I?* Where are we going? What problems and opportunities do we face? What is our individual responsibility for the other passengers and for preserving our life-support system? We must look more deeply into these complex questions so that we may convert our understanding into effective individual and group action.

1. Two college students spending the weekend at a Colorado ski resort caught the State of the Spaceship report on the lodge's color TV. "I'm sick of hearing about the environmental crisis," said John as he ripped the tab from his third can of beer. "It's already too late. My motto is 'Eat, drink, and have a good time while you can.' What's the world done for me?"

"I don't think it's too late at all," observed Susan. "If we can put astronauts on the moon, we can certainly solve our pollution problems. Sure it's going to cost some money, but I'm willing to pay my share. The whole thing is just a matter of money and technology. John, during Christmas break let's fly to Switzerland to ski. There are too many people here. We always have to wait in line, and all these hideous new ski lodges have spoiled the view. Besides, I want to shop for a new ski outfit."

2. In a rotting tenement room in Harlem, Larry angrily switched off the TV, even though he usually kept it on to drown out the noises around him—particularly the rats scratching. A high school dropout, he'd given up looking for work. "This ecology crap is just another whitey trick to keep us from getting a piece of the action. Every summer some liberal college kids come down to help the social workers show us blacks how to use IUDs. Sounds like a new way to keep us down. What do I care about pollution when my little sister was bitten by a rat last night, my ma's got emphysema, and we haven't had any heat in this firetrap for months? Tell it to my uncle in Florida who's paralyzed from the waist down from some chemical they used on the fruit he was picking. Give me a chance to pollute and then I might worry about it."

3. In Calcutta, Mukh Das, his wife, and their seven children did not hear the broadcast in the streets where they lived. As Mukh, who is 36, watched his 34-year-old wife patting dung into cakes to be dried and used for fuel, he was glad that 7 of his 12 children were still alive to help now that he and his wife were in their old age. He felt a chill, and he hoped his children would soon be returning from begging and gathering dung and scraps of food. Perhaps they had been lucky enough to meet another rich American tourist today.

4. In a Connecticut suburb, Bill and Kathy Farmington and their three children, David, Karen, and Linda, were discussing the broadcast. David, a college senior, turned away from the TV in disgust. "This ecology thing is just a big cop-out by people who don't really know what it's all about. In the commune I'm moving into we're going to get back to nature and away from this plastic, racist society of people who don't care."

"That's the biggest cop-out of all," said Karen, a college sophomore. "The only reason you have the freedom to drop out is that you live in a rich country. Why don't you help rather than trying to escape? The real problem is with the poor Americans in the ghetto who keep having all those children. Why don't you work on family planning in the slums this summer like I'm going to do? I'm even going to get college credit for it."

Bill Farmington, chief engineer for Monarch Power Company, looked with irritation at his children. "The problem with all you back-to-the-woods dropouts and misguided liberals is that you don't understand what hard work it takes to keep the world going. If you're so fired up about pollution, David, why don't you walk to your commune rather than driving the car I gave you? Karen, you might consider turning in that snowmobile you use to recuperate from your hot summer in the ghetto. How do you think I paid for all those things you wanted? I'm all for clean air and water, but we can't stop the economic progress our American way of life is built on. Remember last year when we had a lot of ecofreaks and liberal professors trying to stop us from building the new nuclear power plant? In spite of all this talk about conservation, Americans are using more and more energy, and we have to give our customers the power they want. You're as bad as those college professors who go around making speeches and writing books on ecology, but don't change their own life-styles and don't know what hard physical work is all about. David, cut off that TV and the one in the kitchen, too. I'm sick of hearing about pollution, corruption in government, and rioting in India. Linda, it's getting hot in here. Would you please turn up the air conditioning?"

Kathy, Bill's wife, was slowly shaking her head. "I just don't know. This ecology crisis is bad and we have to do something. The problem is I don't know what to do. One scientist says we shouldn't build nuclear power plants, another says we should. One says ban DDT and another says if we do many will die from diseases and starvation. How can we know what to do when experts disagree? I recognize that the population problem is bad in India, Africa, and South America. Remember how horrid it was in Calcutta on our trip last summer? I just couldn't wait to leave. I'm glad we don't have an overpopulation problem in the United States. At least we can afford to have children."

As Linda, a college freshman, got up, she was thinking that no one really listened to the speech. "Don't they realize that we are all connected with one another and with our life-support system? Can't they see that everyone on *Terra I* is a unique human being entitled to a share of our ship's basic resources? I'm afraid for all of us too, but I really don't think it's too late. When I become a public service lawyer, I plan to devote my life to environmental reform."

This book is dedicated to the growing number of Lindas on Terra I *and to Larry, the Das family, and others whose right to human dignity, freedom, and a fair share of the world's resources must be respected.*

1

The Four Energy Crises

Turn off the lights; in the silence of your darkened home you can hear a thousand rivers whispering their thanks.

Clear Creek

1–1 Energy Resources and Energy Crises

A Preview of the Age of Scarcity   Energy is the lifeblood of the ecosphere and of human society everywhere. The amounts and types of useful energy available shape not only individual life-styles but also the entire economic system of a country and of the world. Today we live in a petroleum era with oil providing over one-third of the energy used in the world each year and about one-half of the energy used in industrialized nations. Until 1973 most nations, rich and poor, assumed that an ample and relatively cheap supply of oil would always be available to fuel economic growth and more energy-intensive life-styles. In 1973 this dream was shattered. The 1973 Arab oil embargo and the subsequent fivefold increase in the price of oil by mid-1979 by the Organization of Petroleum Exporting Countries (OPEC)[1] marked the end of the cheap oil energy era for all nations.

During 1973 Americans were shocked to find themselves turning down their thermostats and waiting in long lines for gasoline. By 1979 they were jolted even more to find gasoline costing about 26¢ a liter ($1.00 a gallon), but this was still cheap compared to the 53¢ a liter ($2.00 a gallon) many Europeans had to pay.

But the sharp rise in oil and gasoline prices was only the beginning. Consumers throughout the world learned an obvious but often forgotten lesson—energy is needed to manufacture, grow, or move anything. In a world that runs on oil, when oil becomes more expensive so does food, fer-

tilizer, clothing, antifreeze, electricity, medicine, steel, tires, and almost everything else. In many developing countries crop yields dropped because poor farmers could no longer afford fertilizer or fuel for their irrigation pumps to help grow food.

Even though the 1973 oil embargo did not represent a true shortage of oil, it gave the oil-dependent industrialized nations a preview of the age of scarcity that lies ahead for finite and nonrenewable energy resources such as oil (and perhaps natural gas and uranium) and for various nonrenewable nonfuel mineral resources. If the industrialized world takes this important warning seriously and begins a 50-year program of massive energy conservation and searching for energy alternatives to oil, natural gas, and uranium, then the temporary oil energy crisis of the mid-1970s could be a blessing in disguise. If not, we face disaster.

Types of Energy Resources   Energy resources can be classified as nonrenewable, renewable, and derived, as summarized in Table 1–1. The limit on a nonrenewable resource is the *quantity* available—the total amount that can be found, converted to a useful form, and used at an affordable cost and with an acceptable environmental impact. Theoretically the supply of a renewable resource has no limit. Here the limiting factor (besides cost) is the *rate* at which the resource is used. If a renewable resource (such as wood) is used faster than it is replenished, then it can become depleted and, for all practical purposes, nonrenewable.

Types of Energy Crises   Strictly speaking, we will never run out of energy. But energy can be used to cook, to heat our dwellings, to move us from one place to another, and to perform other services only if we can get it in a useful or concentrated form at an affordable price and without unacceptable environmental disruption. Thus, the term **energy crisis** refers either to a shortage, or to a catastrophic price rise for one or more forms of useful energy, or to a situation in which energy use is so great that the resulting pollution and environmental disruption threaten human health and welfare.

---

[1]At present, OPEC consists of 13 nations, which account for over half of the world's output of oil and about 90 percent of all oil exports. These nations are Algeria, Ecuador, Gabon, Indonesia, Iran, Iraq, Kuwait, Libya, Nigeria, Qatar, Saudi Arabia, United Arab Emirates, and Venezuela.

Table 1–1 Classification of Energy Resources

Nonrenewable	Renewable	Derived Fuels

Fossil fuels
  Petroleum
  Natural gas
  Coal
  Oil shale (rock containing solid hydrocarbons that can be distilled out to yield an oil-like material called shale oil)
  Tar sands (sand intimately mixed with an oil-like material)
 	
Nuclear energy
  Conventional nuclear fission (uranium and thorium)
  Breeder nuclear fission (uranium and thorium)
  Nuclear fusion (deuterium and lithium)*
 	
Geothermal energy (trapped pockets of heat in the earth's interior)†
	Energy conservation‡
	
	Water power (hydroelectricity)
	
	Tidal energy
	
	Ocean thermal gradients (heat stored in ocean water)
	
	Solar energy
	
	Wind energy
	
	Geothermal energy (continuous heat flow from earth's interior)†
	
	Biomass energy (burning of wood, crops, food and animal wastes)
		Synthetic natural gas (SNG) (produced from coal)
		
		Synthetic oil and alcohols (produced from coal or organic wastes)
		
		Biofuels (alcohols and natural gas produced from plants and organic wastes)
		
		Hydrogen gas (produced from coal or by electrical or thermal decomposition of water)
		
		Urban wastes (for incineration)

*The supply of deuterium (a form of hydrogen) produced from seawater would be so large if nuclear fusion becomes feasible that this resource could be reclassified as a renewable resource.
†The high-temperature geothermal energy trapped in underground pockets is a nonrenewable resource, but the slow to moderate flow of heat from the interior of the earth is a renewable resource.
‡Technically, conservation is not a source of energy. Instead of providing energy itself, it reduces the use and waste of energy resources.

On a short-, intermediate-, and long-term basis it is useful to distinguish among four closely related, present and projected energy crises (see the summary box). Three of these are *energy shortage crises* due to an actual or projected shortage of one or more widely used energy resources or to price rises that prevent widespread use of a useful source of energy. The fourth one is an *energy policy crisis* based on the urgent need to develop and implement world and national energy policies that will conserve energy and find substitutes for nonrenewable petroleum, natural gas, and uranium energy resources as affordable supplies are depleted over the next 40 to 80 years.

1–2 Some Urgent Questions

Today, with the exception of food and firewood, the world faces no serious shortage of any widely used energy resource. But we do face an energy policy crisis. Somehow we must develop and carry out comprehensive short-, intermediate-, and long-term plans that will allow us to make the transition to a new earthmanship energy era built on energy conservation and the use of a mix of environmentally acceptable energy sources. *Making a relatively smooth transition to a new earthmanship energy era is the single most important, complex, and difficult problem the world faces.*

The critical nonrenewable resource in this transition is time. Some new oil, natural gas, and uranium deposits may be found and developed to buy us a few more years; we can learn how to depend more on a mix of renewable energy sources such as solar, wind, geothermal, and biofuel energy; and per capita energy use and waste in the developed nations can be decreased without lowering living comfort (Boretsky 1977, Demand and Conservation Panel of the Committee on Nuclear and Alternative Energy Systems, National Academy of Sciences 1978, Hayes 1976a, Hirst 1976a, Lovins 1976, 1977c, 1978a, Mazur & Rosa 1974, Ross & Williams 1976). But all of these changes will take time. Fortunately, we appear to have about 50 years to make this transition to a new energy era. Past history indicates that it takes about 50 to 75 years to shift to new energy sources and energy life-styles (Cook 1976b). We have enough time, but only if we begin now.

In order to see how the world might make a successful transition to a new earthmanship energy era, we need to look at several questions:

1. How much energy do we use and waste?

2. What are our present and future energy alternatives? How long will each alternative last, and what is its net useful energy yield, relative cost, and environmental impact?

3. How can energy demand and waste (especially in developed nations) be reduced?

4. What are the major principles of a short-, intermediate-, and long-term plan for making a relatively smooth transition to a new earthmanship energy era?

The Four Energy Crises

Today's Food and Firewood Energy Shortage Crisis

At least one-fourth and perhaps three-fourths of the people in developing nations do not have an adequate daily intake of food energy, and the 90 percent of the people in poor countries who rely on firewood as their principal fuel are finding increasing difficulty in getting an adequate supply (Eckholm 1975, 1976).

Today's Energy Policy Crisis

There is an urgent need to develop and carry out short-, intermediate-, and long-term energy plans over the next 50 years. These plans will allow the world to replace dwindling supplies of petroleum, natural gas, and uranium with a new mix of environmentally acceptable energy sources and to emphasize energy conservation so that excessive energy use won't overpollute the environment.

The Oil Energy Shortage Crisis of 1985 to 2000

If oil use continues to grow at present rates, then sometime between 1985 and 2000 the world demand for oil will probably exceed the rate at which it can be supplied (Central Intelligence Agency 1977, Flower 1978, Organization for Economic Cooperation and Development 1977, Wilson 1977). As oil supplies drop, prices will rise catastrophically. Even nations that can afford to buy oil will face economic ruin, and international tensions will increase as industrialized nations compete for available oil.

The Energy Shortage and Environmental Disruption Crisis of 2020 to 2060

Affordable supplies of oil, natural gas, and uranium will probably begin running out between 2020 and 2060. By this time, if the world has not instituted a stringent energy conservation program and shifted to a new mix of affordable and environmentally acceptable energy sources, it faces massive economic disruption along with a population crash. Even if world energy consumption rises sharply and the world somehow manages to avoid any serious energy shortages after 1980, sometime between 2020 to 2060 human health and welfare could be threatened by massive water pollution, air pollution, land degradation, and global climate change, caused by too many people using too much energy.

There is little doubt that these and related questions will dominate our lives over the coming decades—whether we like it or not.[2] In this chapter and the next we will examine these questions, emphasizing the second, third, and fourth energy crises.

[2]For more details on energy problems, resources, supplies, and alternatives, see the following: Alfvén 1972, Anderson et al. 1974, Anthrop 1974, Askin 1978, Basile & Sternlight 1977, Bent 1977, Brown 1971, 1976a, 1978a, 1978b, Brubaker 1975, Carr 1976, Central Intelligence Agency 1977, Cheney 1974, Clark 1974a, Committee on Interior and Insular Affairs 1972, Commoner 1976, Commoner et al. 1975, Cook 1972, 1976b, Council on Environmental Quality 1973, Council on Environmental Quality, *Environmental Quality,* 1976, Daly 1977, Demand and Conservation Panel of the Committee on Nuclear and Alternative Energy Systems, National Academy of Sciences 1978, Doolittle 1978, Dorf 1978, Ehrlich et al. 1977, Energy Policy Project 1974, Energy Research and Development Administration 1976c, Executive Office of the President 1977, Exxon Company 1976, Federal Energy Administration 1974a, 1976, Fisher 1974, Flower 1978, Fowler 1975a, 1975b, Freeman 1974, Garvey 1972, Georgescu-Roegen 1976, Gordon & Meador 1977, Grenon 1977, Häfele 1974, Häfele & Sassin 1977, Halacy 1975, 1977, Hammond 1973b, Hammond et al. 1973, Hannon 1977a, Hayes 1976a, 1977, Healy 1974, Holdren 1975a, Holdren & Herrera 1971, Hollander & Simmons 1976, Hollander et al. 1977, 1978, Hottel & Howard 1972, Hubbert 1962, 1969a, 1971, 1973, 1974, Inglis 1973, Institute for Energy Analysis 1976, Joint Committee on Atomic Energy 1973, Landsberg 1974b, Large 1973, League of Women Voters Education Fund 1977a, 1977b, 1977c, Lenihan & Fletcher 1976, Lovins 1974, 1975, 1976, 1977b, 1977c, 1978a, Lovins & Price 1975, Luten 1971, Maddox 1975, Martin & Pinto 1978, McLean 1972, McMullan et al. 1978, Meador 1978, Mervine & Cawley 1975, Miles 1976, Miller et al. 1975, Moody & Geiger 1975, National Petroleum Council 1972, Odum 1971a, 1973, Odum & Odum 1976, Office of Emergency Preparedness 1972, Office of Science and Technology 1972, Ophuls 1977, Organization for Economic Cooperation and Development 1977, Peach 1973, Policy Study Group of the M.I.T. Energy Laboratory 1974, Portola Institute 1974, Priest 1975, Reddy 1978, Reed 1975, Rose 1974a, Rouse & Smith 1975, Ruedisili & Firebaugh 1975, Schanz 1978, Schipper 1976a, Schneider 1977, Schurr 1971, Science and Public Policy Program, University of Oklahoma 1975, *Scientific American* 1971, Shell Oil Company 1973, Sporn 1974, Starr 1971, 1973, Steinhart & Steinhart 1974a, Stoker et al. 1975, Tavoulareas & Kaysen 1977, *Technology Review* 1972, Theobald et al. 1972, Udall 1973, Udall et al. 1974, United Nations 1976, U.S. Atomic Energy Commission 1973a, U.S. Department of the Interior 1975, U.S. Senate, Select Committee on Small Business and Committee on Interior and Insular Affairs 1977, Warren 1978, Weinberg 1972, Widmer & Gyftopoulos 1977, Williams 1975, Willrich 1976, Wilson 1977, Wilson & Jones 1974, Woodwell 1974.

1–3 Energy Use and Waste

How Did We Get into This Mess?   Although the present energy predicament in the developed nations is enormously complex, it results from the interaction of five major factors: (1) nearly complete dependence on nonrenewable fossil fuel energy resources (especially oil) because of their relatively high net energy yields as well as their relatively low costs; (2) greatly increased per capita energy use since 1950; (3) increased dependence of many industrialized nations on oil imports either because increased demand has outstripped domestic supplies or because vast and easily accessible oil deposits in the Middle East and Venezuela could be extracted at lower cost than most remaining deposits in importing countries; (4) little concern for energy conservation and for developing alternative energy sources (such as sunlight, wind, biofuels, geothermal energy, and nuclear fusion) because of the mistaken belief that abundant and relatively cheap supplies of nonrenewable fossil fuels and uranium would always be available; and (5) stimulation of high energy use and waste by keeping fossil fuel energy prices at artificially low levels by not including environmental, health, and social costs in energy prices and by government subsidization and regulation of energy prices in some countries, including the United States.

The common thread among these factors is economics. Any useful and presumably abundant energy resource that consumers can buy at a relatively low price will be widely used with little concern either for reducing energy waste and pollution or for finding alternatives. In other words, the developed nations got into the present predicament by using good sense. Oil was cheap and readily available, so they began using it in larger and larger quantities. Now that the end of the oil energy era is in sight, these nations will hopefully have the good sense to plan for an orderly transition to a new earthmanship energy era.

The J Curve   One of the most important facts affecting our lives today is that we have gone around the bend on a **J curve,** or *exponential curve,* of rising energy use. What is a J curve? Any system that grows by doubling, that is, 1, 2, 4, 8, 16, 32, and so on, grows **exponentially** or *geometrically.* If you graph these numbers, you get a curve shaped like the letter J: For a few doublings, nothing much seems to happen. Then suddenly the bend in the J is rounded and the curve takes off.

Let me take you around the bend on a J curve. Let us start doubling the thickness of a page of this book. If we assume that the page is about 0.1 millimeter (about 1/254 inch) thick, after the first doubling the thickness is 0.2 millimeter, then 0.4, 0.8, 1.6, 3.2, and so on. After 8 doublings, the paper is 25.6 millimeters (about 1 inch) thick. After 12 doublings it is about 410 millimeters (1.34 feet) thick, and

after 20 doublings about 105 meters (340 feet). Still very little has happened; we are on the lower part, or the *lag phase,* of the J curve.

However, if we double our page slightly over 35 times, its thickness would equal the distance from New York to Los Angeles. Double the page 42 times and we would create a mound of paper reaching from the earth to the moon, some 386,400 kilometers (240,000 miles) away. Double it just over 50 times and the thickness reaches to the sun, 149 million kilometers (93 million miles) away.

Energy Use in the World and the United States   At the primitive level of survival, energy use is limited to the food one eats, about 2,000 kilocalories a day (Figure 1–1).[3] Each stage of human cultural evolution thereafter has involved a dramatic increase in supplementing food energy with energy from animals, the burning of wood and fossil fuels, and more recently nuclear fission (Figure 1–1). Today people in most industrial nations have an average per capita energy consumption of about 125,000 kilocalories a day—a 63-fold increase over the primitive survival level (Cook 1976b). The average American, however, consumes—or, more accurately, degrades—an average of 250,000 kilocalories per day—a 125-fold increase over the survival level. This means that each American directly and indirectly uses an amount of energy equivalent to that in 41 kilograms (91 pounds) of coal each day or 15,000 kilograms (16.5 tons) of coal each year.

Around 1850 wood was the primary fuel used in the world (Cook 1976b), and it is still burned today as a fuel by 90 percent of the people in poor nations. But 80 percent of the energy used in the world today comes from fossil fuels (oil, coal, and natural gas), with oil the leading fuel (Figure 1–2).

---

[3]Unfortunately, a bewildering array of different units and conversion factors are used to express energy values. The most widely used units are kilojoules (kJ), joules (J), kilocalories (kcal), calories (cal), British thermal units (Btu), kilowatt-hours (kWh) and quads. The following is a summary of the relationships between these units and their energy equivalents in terms of the energy content of crude oil, natural gas, and coal:

$1 \text{ kJ} = 10^3 \text{ J} = 0.239 \text{ kcal} = 239 \text{ cal} = 0.9485 \text{ Btu} = 2.78 \times 10^{-4} \text{ kWh}$

$1 \text{ kcal} = 10^3 \text{ cal} = 4.184 \text{ kJ} = 4,184 \text{ J} = 3.968 \text{ Btu} = 1.16 \times 10^{-3} \text{ kWh}$

$1 \text{ kWh} = 3,600 \text{ kJ} = 860 \text{ kcal} = 3,413 \text{ Btu}$

$1 \text{ quad} = 1.054 \times 10^{15} \text{ kJ} = 2.52 \times 10^{14} \text{ Btu} = 2.93 \times 10^{11} \text{ kWh}$

$1 \text{ Q} = 1,000 \text{ quads} = 1.054 \times 10^{18} \text{ kJ} = 2.52 \times 10^{17} \text{ kcal}$
$= 10^{18} \text{ Btu} = 2.93 \times 10^{14} \text{ kWh}$

Crude oil equivalent: 1 barrel (159 liters, or 42 gallons)
$= 6.1 \times 10^6 \text{ kJ} = 1.5 \times 10^6 \text{ kcal} = 5.8 \times 10^6 \text{ Btu} = 1.7 \times 10^3 \text{ kWh}$

Natural gas equivalent: 1 cubic foot (0.0283 cubic meters)
$= 1,088 \text{ kJ} = 260 \text{ kcal} = 1,032 \text{ Btu} = 0.302 \text{ kWh}$

Coal equivalent: 1 ton (909 kilograms) $= 2.3 \times 10^7 \text{ kJ}$
$= 5.5 \times 10^6 \text{ kcal} = 2.2 \times 10^7 \text{ Btu} = 6.4 \times 10^3 \text{ kWh}$

Figure 1-1 Average daily per capita energy use at various stages of human cultural evolution. (Data from Cook 1971, 1976b)

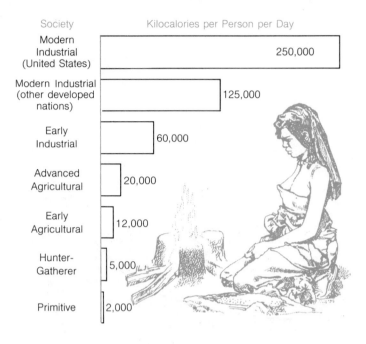

Society	Kilocalories per Person per Day
Modern Industrial (United States)	250,000
Modern Industrial (other developed nations)	125,000
Early Industrial	60,000
Advanced Agricultural	20,000
Early Agricultural	12,000
Hunter-Gatherer	5,000
Primitive	2,000

Figure 1-2 World energy sources in 1975. (Data from Cook 1976b. Staff report 1976a, United Nations 1976)

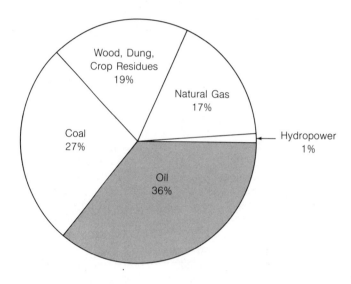

Wood, Dung, Crop Residues 19%

Natural Gas 17%

Coal 27%

Hydropower 1%

Oil 36%

The shift to new energy sources since 1850 occurred primarily in the developed nations and has taken place in several phases. For example, America's economic growth and increased energy use during this time have been fueled by a succession of primary energy sources—first wood, then coal, and today oil and natural gas (Figure 1-3). However, the switch from coal to oil and natural gas did not occur be-

cause of a shortage of coal, which was and is still the most abundant fossil fuel in the United States. Instead it took place because oil and natural gas were cleaner, easier, and safer to extract, transport, and burn. In addition, oil could be converted to gasoline to power America's growing dependence on the automobile. Today about 42 percent of all oil used in the United States each year is refined into gasoline. In 1850 about 91 percent of America's energy came from wood—a renewable energy source. By 1977, however, nonrenewable fossil fuels supplied 94 percent of all energy used in the United States (Figure 1-3).

Figure 1-3 Changing patterns in the use of energy resources in the United States. Circle size represents relative amount of total energy used. (Data from U.S. Bureau of the Census, Resouces for the Future, and U.S. Federal Energy Administration)

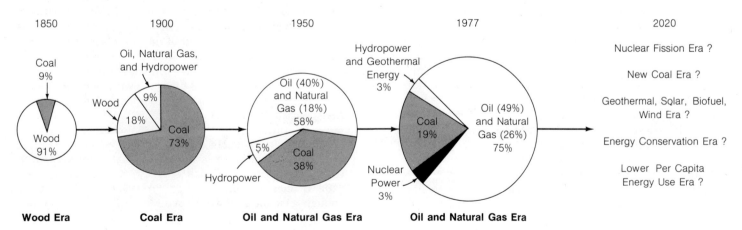

1850

Coal 9%

Wood 91%

Wood Era

1900

Oil, Natural Gas, and Hydropower 9%

Wood 18%

Coal 73%

Coal Era

1950

Oil (40%) and Natural Gas (18%) 58%

Hydropower 5%

Coal 38%

Oil and Natural Gas Era

1977

Hydropower and Geothermal Energy 3%

Coal 19%

Oil (49%) and Natural Gas (26%) 75%

Nuclear Power 3%

Oil and Natural Gas Era

2020

Nuclear Fission Era ?

New Coal Era ?

Geothermal, Solar, Biofuel, Wind Era ?

Energy Conservation Era ?

Lower Per Capita Energy Use Era ?

Primarily because of the increased availability of relatively inexpensive oil and natural gas, world energy consumption tripled and average annual energy consumption per person doubled between 1950 and 1975 (Staff report 1976a). As a result, most of the fossil fuels ever used have been consumed since 1950. Oil has been pumped out of the ground for over 100 years (since 1869), but over half of the total amount extracted was consumed between 1960 and 1978. Today the rate of energy use is so high that the world's oil and natural gas era could come to an end within 40 to 80 years, as discussed in more detail later in Chapter 5.

Most of the world's increase in energy consumption per person since 1900 has taken place in the developed nations, and the gap in average per capita energy use between rich and poor nations has been widening (Figure 1–4). In 1975 the developed nations, with only 25 percent of the world's people, used about 80 percent of the world's energy (Brown 1978a). Between 1975 and 2000 total world energy demand may triple, and average per capita energy demand may double (Population Reference Bureau 1977). But these projected demands for more energy may not be met, especially in the developed nations. Decreasing supplies and rapidly escalating prices of oil, natural gas, and uranium and the increased pollution that automatically results from increased use of any type of energy may change the J curve of increasing per capita energy use in the developed nations to an S curve (Figure 1–4).

People who think that major oil or natural gas discoveries will solve the problem simply do not understand the arithmetic and the consequences of the J curve. Saudi Arabia, with the world's largest known oil deposit, could supply the world's total oil needs for only 5 years at the 1978 rate of consumption (Staff report 1978f). The recent petroleum find in Mexico (Metz 1978a), which may equal the deposit in Saudi Arabia, will merely add another 5 years of oil at present use rates. The oil under Alaska's North Slope—the largest American find ever—would meet current world demand for only about 6 months and U.S. demand for only 2½ years. Even if Atlantic Ocean drilling off New Jersey meets the most optimistic estimates, the resulting oil could meet world oil needs for only 1 week, U.S. oil needs for less than 3 months, and U.S. natural gas needs for about 5 months. The recently developed North Sea oil reserves would satisfy current world oil demands for only about 1½ years. We need to search the world vigorously for more oil. But according to former U.S. Secretary of Energy James R. Schlesinger, anyone who tells us that new discoveries will solve world oil supply problems is really saying that we need to discover the equivalent of a new Mexico or Saudi Arabia oil deposit *every 5 years* merely to maintain our present level of energy use (Staff report 1978f).

The United States is a prime example of greatly increased energy use since 1900 and especially since 1950

Figure 1–4 Past (solid lines) and projected (dotted lines) average per capita annual energy consumption in the world. (Data from Keyfitz 1976, United Nations 1976)

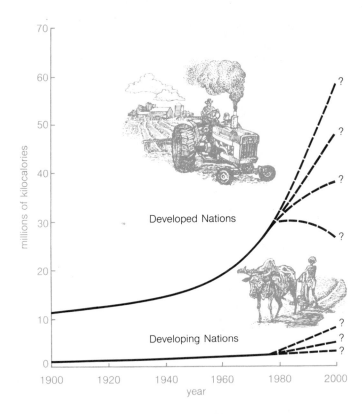

(Figure 1–5). Between 1900 and 1975, U.S. population increased less than threefold, while national energy consumption increased sevenfold, and per capita energy use doubled (Council on Environmental Quality, *Environmental Quality*, 1976). In 1976, with about 5 percent of the world's population, the United States accounted for over 30 percent of the world's energy consumption, including 49 percent of all natural gas, 30 percent of all oil, and 20 percent of all coal (Population Reference Bureau 1977). In comparison, India, with about 15 percent of the world's population, consumed only about 1.5 percent of the world's energy in 1975 (Reddy 1978, Revelle 1976). In 1975 the average energy consumption per person in the United States was 34 times that in India (Reddy 1978), 8 times the world average (Goldstein 1978), and 2 to 3 times that of other industrialized nations such as Sweden, Great Britain, West Germany, and Japan (Darmstadter et al. 1977, 1978, Schipper & Lichtenberg 1976). In 1974, 214 million Americans used more energy for air conditioning alone than 800 million Chinese used for all purposes (Udall et al. 1974). According to the Federal Energy Administration, in 1976 Americans used enough gasoline *each day* to send 1.6 million automobiles (each getting an average of 6.3 kilometers per liter, or 15 miles per gallon) from New York to Los Angeles.

U.S. Dependence on Imported Oil
By the late 1960s most low-cost oil deposits in the United States had been depleted. For example, in the early 1960s the cost of producing 159 liters (1 barrel) of Middle East oil was 16¢, compared with $1.73 for production in the United States (Lappé & Collins 1977). By 1973 oil production in the United States had peaked and began to fall (Figure 1–6). As a result, the nation began to depend more on imported oil, which was then cheap (Figure 1–6). After the sharp price rises in 1973, most industrialized nations began to reduce their oil consumption, but demand in the United States continued to rise. In 1973 America imported about 35 percent of its oil. By 1978, 5 years after the OPEC embargo, the United States imported about 43 percent of its oil with about 85 percent of it coming directly or indirectly from OPEC nations (Goldstein 1978, Petroleum Economics Ltd. 1978). The staggering $45 billion cost of imported oil in 1978, compared with $8.4 billion in 1973, created a massive trade deficit and seriously undermined the strength of the American dollar throughout the world. During 1978 each American paid an average of $200 to oil-exporting nations—enough money to have created 5 million new jobs or to build over 900,000 new $50,000 homes. The annual flow of money into OPEC nations from the United States and other nations is hard to comprehend. This income for 1978 alone was enough to buy the entire U.S. farm crop or all the stock in the 30 biggest American industrial corporations. And this is only 1 year's income!

But this is only the beginning. According to the Department of Energy, if the United States does not curb its appetite for oil, then by 1985 the nation could be importing at least 50 percent of its supply (Figure 1–6). By 1990 the imported oil bill could quadruple to $180 billion per year with each American paying an average of $750 per year to oil-exporting nations. Even if world supplies are adequate, the United States could probably not afford such a large annual financial drain without disrupting its entire economy. However, the economy could also be disrupted without enough oil if present demands continue. It seems clear that over the next decade the United States must learn how to kick its addiction to larger and larger amounts of oil. Unfortunately, many Americans have yet to take the warning of the 1973 oil embargo seriously. In 1978 a Gallup poll indicated that only 40 percent of the American public felt that the U.S. energy situation was "fairly serious," and about 40 percent didn't even know that the nation imported oil, despite massive publicity between 1973 and 1978.

Figure 1–5 Past (solid line) and projected (dotted lines) average per capita annual energy consumption in the United States. (Data from Demand and Conservation Panel of the Committee on Nuclear and Alternative Energy Systems, National Academy of Sciences 1978)

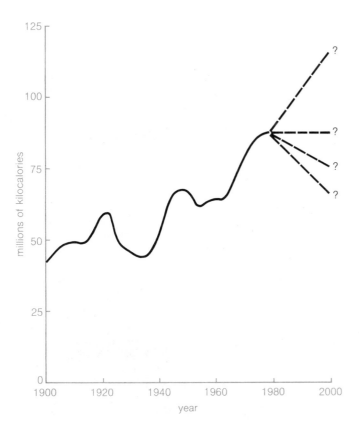

Figure 1–6 Past (solid lines) and projected (dotted lines) daily domestic oil supply and demand in the United States. (Data from Central Intelligence Agency 1977, Council on Environmental Quality, *Environmental Quality*, 1976, Exxon Company 1976, Petroleum Economics Ltd. 1978)

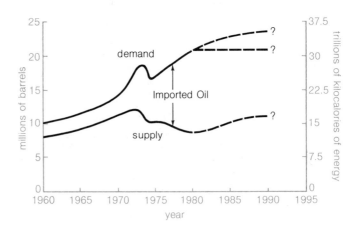

Energy Waste in the United States In addition to being the world's largest energy user, America is also the world's largest energy waster. About 85 to 90 percent of all the energy used in the United States each year is wasted (American Physical Society 1975). In 1975 alone Americans wasted more fossil fuel than was used by two-thirds of the world population (Hayes 1976a).

Japan and most industrialized European nations with standards of living (as measured by average per capita GNP) equal to or greater than that in the United States use only one-third to one-half as much energy per person (Darmstadter et al. 1977, 1978, Schipper & Lichtenberg 1976). National energy use patterns vary so that some types of energy savings in one nation can't always be used in other countries (Darmstadter et al. 1977, 1978). Typically about 40 to 75 percent of all energy used each year will automatically be degraded to low-temperature waste heat as a result of the second law of energy (see Section 2–3; Ross & Williams 1976). But there is strong evidence that average per capita energy use in the United States could be cut by 25 to 50 percent without decreasing the quality of life (American Physical Society 1975, Boretsky 1977, Demand and Conservation Panel of the Committee on Nuclear and Alternative Energy Systems, National Academy of Sciences 1978, Hayes 1976a, Hirst 1976a, Hirst & Moyers 1973, Lovins 1976, 1977c, 1978a, Makhijani & Lichtenberg 1972, Mazur & Rosa 1974, Office of Emergency Preparedness 1972, Ross & Williams 1977b).

The United States can no longer be a society that uses 5,000 pound [2,273 kilogram] automobiles for half-mile [0.8 kilometer] round trips to the market to fetch a six-pack of beer, consumes the beer in buildings that are overcooled in summer and overheated in winter, and then throws the aluminum cans away at an energy loss equivalent to one-third of a gallon [1.3 liters] of gasoline per six-pack.

John Holdren

Guest Editorial: The Role of Energy in Our Future Growth and Change

Glenn T. Seaborg

Glenn T. Seaborg is one of America's most distinguished scientists, administrators, and proponents of nuclear energy as our major energy source. He discovered element 94 (plutonium) and eight other transuranium elements. In 1951, at the age of 39, Dr. Seaborg was awarded the Nobel Prize in Chemistry. From 1958 to 1961, he was Chancellor of the University of California, Berkeley, and then served as Chairman of the U.S. Atomic Energy Commission until 1971. He is one of the strongest and most eloquent supporters of nuclear energy as evidenced in his book with W. R. Corliss, Man and Atom *(1971).*

In 1972 he served as President of the American Association for the Advancement of Science and is now University Professor of Chemistry and Associate Director of the Lawrence Berkeley Laboratory at the University of California, Berkeley. He is also an ardent conservationist.

There is no doubt that energy—how much of it we have and the ways we produce and use it—will have a significant effect on our future. In meeting the challenge of the future, we do not have the choices of "energy or no energy," or of "energy or environment." Energy is the essential underpinning of almost all of our society. Industrial production, transportation, communication, population, knowledge for improving the quality of life—the growth of these and many other aspects of civilization is related to and supported by energy growth.

Our choices for the future rest in how we perceive and use our resources. We are seeing—or should be seeing—our total energy reserves as a huge, versatile energy pool. We must treat it with a vastly expanded rationale—expanded beyond the needs of this spot, these short-term economics, this point of time, to total global reserves on a very long-term scale. We must determine which resources could serve us best for what purposes and the effects of their various uses on both our natural and human-made environment. In short, we must begin to think, plan, and act as we have never done before in making energy work for us without its inadvertently working against us.

This will require some enormous changes in our society, nationally and internationally. The longer-term energy resource problem and the shorter-term environmental crises due to the misuse of such resources now challenge individuals, nations, and the entire international community to undertake serious energy policy planning. If we are not thoroughly to deplete many of our irreplaceable natural resources in a few generations, and at the same time put those generations in environmental jeopardy by the misuse of those resources, we must begin to use those resources rationally.

One of the most difficult challenges we face is to find ways to ensure that all peoples of the world share more equitably the vast human benefits that energy can bring. If we want to see our children live in a world of peace based not on terror or suppression but on the fulfillment of human needs and the recognition of human dignity, we must over the coming years make every effort to narrow the energy gap.

Contrary to the notion that our use of energy must necessarily deplete our planet's resources or despoil nature, I believe that our wise use of energy—and considerably more than we are using now—can restore nature and rejuvenate humankind.

Guest Editorial Discussion

1. What "enormous changes in our society" do you believe must be made to deal with the energy problem? How will these affect you personally?

2. What constitutes rational use of our energy resources?

3. Debate the proposition that the United States should reduce its consumption of energy by one-third.

4. How would you implement Dr. Seaborg's suggestion that all peoples in the world share more equitably the world's energy resources and the benefits energy can bring?

2

Some Matter and Energy Laws

Look at a beautiful flower, drink some water, eat some food, or pick up this book. The two things that connect these activities and other aspects of life on earth are matter and energy. **Matter,** or anything that has mass and occupies space, is of course the stuff you and all other things are made of. **Energy** is a more elusive concept. Formally it is defined as the ability or capacity to do work by pushing or pulling some form of matter. Energy is what you and all living things use to move matter around and to change it from one form to another. Energy is used to grow your food, to keep you alive, to move you from one place to another, and to warm and cool the buildings in which you work and live. The uses and transformations of matter and energy are governed by certain scientific laws, which unlike legal laws cannot be broken. In this chapter we begin our study of ecological concepts with a look at one fundamental law of matter and two equally important laws of energy. These laws will be used again and again throughout this book to help you understand many environmental problems and to aid you in evaluating solutions to these problems.

2–1 Law of Conservation of Matter: Everything Must Go Somewhere

We always talk about consuming or using up matter resources, but actually we don't consume any matter. We only borrow some of the earth's resources for a while— taking them from the earth, carrying them to another part of the globe, processing them, using them, and then discarding, reusing, or recycling them. In the process of using matter, we may change it to another form, such as burning complex gasoline molecules and breaking them down into simpler molecules of water and carbon dioxide. But in every case we neither create nor destroy any measurable amount of matter. This results from the **law of conservation of matter:** In any ordinary physical or chemical change, matter is neither created nor destroyed but merely changed from one form to another.

This law tells us that we can never really throw any matter away. In other words, there is no such thing as either a consumer or a "throwaway" society. *Everything we think we have thrown away is still here with us in some form or another.* Everything must go somewhere and all we can do is to recycle some of the matter we think we have thrown away.

We can collect dust and soot from the smokestacks of industrial plants, but these solid wastes must then go somewhere. Cleaning up smoke is a misleading practice, because the invisible gaseous and very tiny particle pollutants left are often more damaging than the large solid particles that are removed. We can collect garbage and remove solid wastes from sewage, but they must either be burned (air pollution), dumped into rivers, lakes, and oceans (water pollution), or deposited on the land (soil pollution and water pollution if they wash away).

We can reduce air pollution from the internal combustion engines in cars by using electric cars. But since electric car batteries must be recharged every day, we will have to build more electric power plants. If these are coal-fired plants, their smokestacks will add additional and even more dangerous air pollutants to the air; more land will be scarred from strip mining, and more water will be polluted from the acids that tend to leak out of coal mines. We could use nuclear power plants to produce the extra electricity needed. But then we risk greater heat or thermal pollution of rivers and other bodies of water used to cool such plants; further, we also risk releasing dangerous radioactive substances into the environment through plant or shipping accidents, highjacking of nuclear fuel to make atomic weapons, and leakage from permanent burial sites for radioactive wastes.

Although we can certainly make the environment cleaner, talk of "cleaning up the environment" and "pollution free" cars, products, or industries is a scientific absurdity. The law of conservation of matter tells us that we will always be faced with pollution of some sort. Thus, we are also faced with the problem of *trade-offs.* In turn, these frequently involve subjective and controversial scientific, political, economic, and ethical judgments about what is a dangerous pollutant level, to what degree a pollutant must be controlled, and what amount of money we are willing to pay to reduce a pollutant to a harmless level. Now let's look at energy and the two energy laws that tell us more about what we can and cannot do on this planet.

2–2 First Law of Energy: You Can't Get Something for Nothing

Types of Energy You encounter energy in many forms: mechanical, chemical, electrical, nuclear, heat, and radiant (or light) energy. Doing work involves changing energy from one form to another. In lifting this book, the chemical energy stored in chemicals obtained from your digested food is converted into the mechanical energy that is used to move your arm and the book upwards and some heat energy that is given off by your body.

In an automobile engine the chemical energy stored in gasoline is converted into mechanical energy used to propel the car plus heat energy. A battery converts chemical energy into electrical energy plus heat energy. In an electric power plant, chemical energy from fossil fuels (coal, oil, or natural gas) or nuclear energy from nuclear fuels is converted into mechanical energy that is used to spin a turbine plus heat energy. The turbine then converts the mechanical energy into electrical energy and more heat. When this electrical energy passes through the filament wires in an ordinary light bulb, it is converted into light and still more heat. In all of the energy transformations discussed in this section, we see that some energy always ends up as heat energy that flows into the surrounding environment.

Scientists have found that all forms of energy can be classified either as potential energy or kinetic energy, as shown in Figure 2–1. **Kinetic energy** is the energy that matter has because of its motion. Heat energy is a measure of the total kinetic energy of the molecules in a sample of matter. The amount of kinetic energy that a sample of matter has depends both on its mass and its velocity (speed). Because of its higher kinetic energy, a bullet fired at a high velocity from a rifle will do you more damage than the same bullet thrown by hand. Similarly, an artillery shell (with a larger mass) fired at the same velocity as the bullet will do you considerably more harm than the bullet.

Stored energy that an object possesses by virtue of its position, condition, or composition is known as **potential energy.** A rock held in your hand has stored or potential energy that can be released and converted to kinetic energy (in the form of mechanical energy and heat) if the rock is dropped. Coal, oil, natural gas, wood, and other fuels have a form of stored or potential energy known as chemical energy. When the fuel is burned, this chemical potential en-

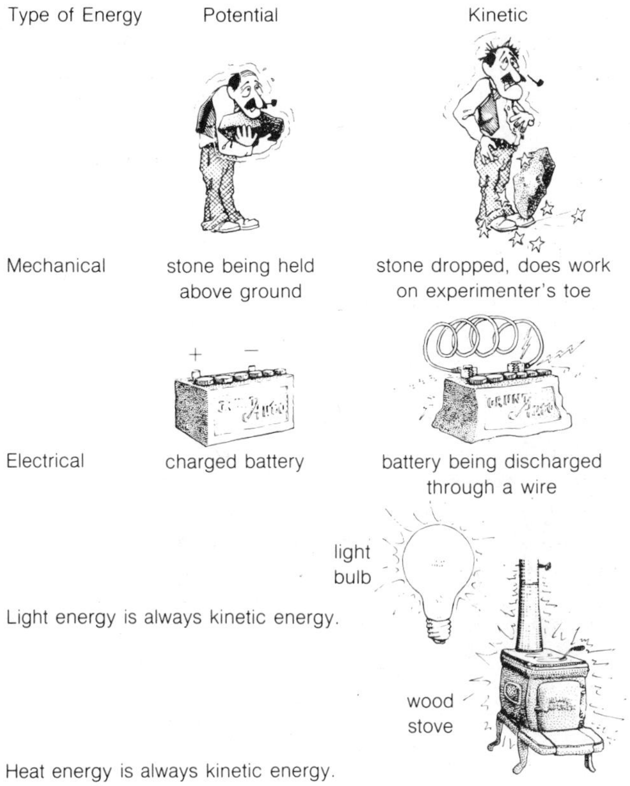

Figure 2–1 Potential and kinetic energy are the two major types of energy.

ergy is converted into a mixture of heat, light, and the kinetic energy of motion of the molecules in the air and other nearby materials.

With this background on the types of energy, we are now prepared to look at the two scientific laws that govern what happens when energy is converted from one form to another.

First Energy Law What energy changes occur when you drop a rock from your hand to the floor? Because of its higher position, the rock in your hand has a higher potential energy than the same rock at rest on the floor. Has energy been lost, or used up, in this process? At first glance it seems so. But according to the **law of conservation of energy,** also known as the **first law of thermodynamics,** in any ordinary physical or chemical process, energy is neither created nor destroyed but merely changed from one form to another. The energy lost by a *system* or collection of matter under study (in this instance the rock) must equal the energy gained by the *surroundings,* or *environment* (in this instance the air).

Let's look at what really happens. As the rock drops, its potential energy is changed into kinetic energy (energy of motion)—both its own kinetic energy and that of the air molecules through which it passes. This causes the air molecules to move faster so that their temperature rises. This means that some of the rock's original potential energy has been transferred to the air as heat energy. The energy lost by the rock (system) is exactly equal to the energy gained by its surroundings. In studying hundreds of thousands of mechanical processes (such as the rock falling) and chemical processes (such as the burning of a fuel), scientists have found that no detectable amount of energy is created or destroyed.

Although most of us know this first energy law, we sometimes forget that it means in terms of energy quantity we can't get something for nothing; at best we can only **break even. In the words of environmentalist Barry Commoner (1971), "There is no such thing as a free lunch."** For example, we usually hear that we have so much energy available from oil, coal, natural gas, and nuclear fuels (such as uranium). The first law of thermodynamics, however, tells us that we really have much less energy available than these estimates indicate. *It takes energy to get energy.* We must use large amounts of energy to find, remove, and process these fuels. The only energy that really counts is the *net energy* available for use after we have subtracted from the total energy made available to us the energy used to obtain it. In Chapter 4 we will use the first energy law to help us evaluate various options for dealing with present and future energy crises.

2–3 Second Law of Energy: You Can't Break Even

Second Energy Law and Energy Quality Energy varies in its *quality* or ability to do useful work. The chemical potential energy concentrated in a lump of coal or liter of gasoline, and concentrated heat energy at a high temperature, are forms of high-quality energy. Because they are concentrated, they have the ability to perform useful work in moving or changing matter. In contrast, dispersed heat energy at a low temperature is low-quality energy, with little if any ability to perform useful work. In investigating hundreds of thousands of different conversions of heat energy to useful work, scientists have found that some of the energy is always degraded to a more dispersed and less useful form, usually heat energy given off at a low temperature to the surroundings, or environment. This is a statement of the *law of energy degradation,* also known as the **second law of thermodynamics.**

Let's look at an example of the second energy law. In an internal combustion automobile engine, the high-quality potential energy available in gasoline is converted into a combination of high-quality heat energy, which is converted to the mechanical work used to propel the car, and low-quality heat energy. Only about 20 percent of the energy available in the gasoline is converted to useful mechanical energy, with the remaining 80 percent released into the environment as degraded heat energy. In addition, about half of the mechanical energy produced is also degraded to low-quality heat energy through friction, so that 90 percent of the energy in gasoline is wasted and not used to move the car. Most of this loss is an energy quality tax automatically extracted as a result of the second law. Frequently the design of an engine or other heat-energy conversion device wastes more energy than that required by the second law. But the second law always ensures that there will be a certain waste or loss of energy quality.

Another example of the degradation of energy involves the conversion of solar energy to chemical energy in food. Photosynthesis in plants converts radiant energy (light) from the sun into high-quality chemical energy (stored in the plant in the form of sugar molecules) plus low-quality heat energy. If you eat plants, such as spinach, the high-quality chemical energy is transformed within your body to high-quality mechanical energy, used to move your muscles and to perform other life processes, plus low-quality heat energy. As shown in Figure 2–2, in each of these energy conversions, some of the initial high-quality energy is degraded into low-quality heat energy that flows into the environment.

The first energy law governs the *quantity* of energy available from an energy conversion process, whereas the second energy law governs the *quality* of energy available. In terms of the quantity of energy available from a heat-to-work conversion, we can get out no more energy than we put in. But according to the second law, the quality of the energy available from a heat-to-work conversion will always be lower than the initial energy quality. Not only can we not get something for nothing (the first law), we can't even break even in terms of energy quality (the second law). As Robert Morse put it, "The second law means that it is easier to get into trouble than to get out of it."

The second energy law also tells us that high-grade energy can never be used over again. *We can recycle matter but we can never recycle energy.* Fuels and foods can be used only once to perform useful work. Once a piece of coal or a tank of gasoline is burned, its high-quality potential energy is lost forever. Similarly, the high-quality heat energy from the steam in an underground geothermal well is gone forever once it is dispersed and degraded to low-quality heat energy in the environment. This means that the net useful, or high-quality, energy available from coal, oil, natural gas, nuclear fuel, geothermal, or any concentrated energy source is even less than that predicted by the first energy law.

net high-quality   total high-quality
    energy   =   energy available

              − high-quality energy needed to find,

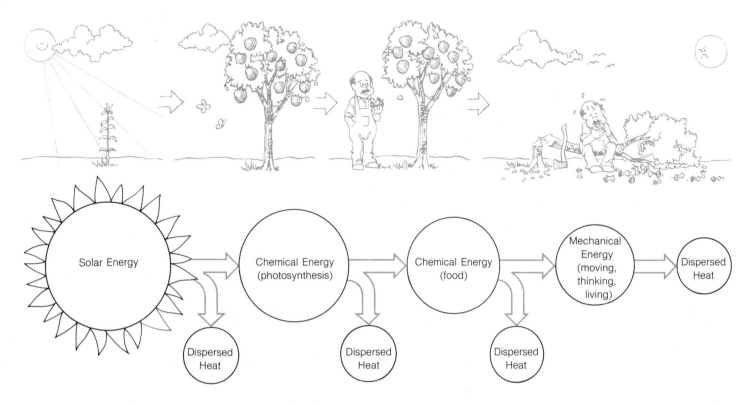

Figure 2–2 The second energy law. In all energy changes some energy is degraded to low-quality heat energy that is dispersed in the environment.

get, and process the energy (first law)
— energy quality lost in finding, getting, and processing the energy (second law)

From this we see that both the first and second energy laws must be used to evaluate our energy options, as discussed further in Chapter 4.

Second Energy Law and Increasing Disorder The second energy law can be stated in a number of ways. Another way of looking at this law is to realize that energy tends to flow or change spontaneously from a compact and ordered form to a dispersed and random, or disordered, form. Heat always flows spontaneously from hot to cold. You learned this the first time that you touched a hot stove. A cold sample of matter has its heat energy dispersed in the random, disorderly motion of its molecules. This is why heat energy at a low temperature can do little if any useful work.

Let's look at other spontaneous changes in the world around us. A vase falls to the floor and shatters into a more disordered state. A dye crystal dropped into water spon-

taneously dissolves, and the fact that color spreads is evidence that its molecules spontaneously tend toward a more dispersed and disordered state throughout the solution. A woman dies and the highly ordered array of molecules in her body decays to many smaller molecules that are dispersed randomly throughout the environment. Your desk and room seem spontaneously to become more disordered after a few weeks of benign neglect (Figure 2–3). Smoke from a smokestack and exhaust from an automobile disperse spontaneously to a more random or disordered state in the atmosphere. Pollutants dumped into a river or lake tend to spread spontaneously throughout the water. Indeed, until we discovered that the atmosphere and water systems could be overloaded, we assumed that such spontaneous dilution solved the problem of pollution.

These observations all suggest that a *system* of matter spontaneously tends toward increasing randomness, or disorder. But is this hypothesis valid? You may have already thought of some examples that contradict this hypothesis. As its temperature decreases to 0°C, liquid water spontaneously increases its order and freezes into ice. What about living organisms with their highly ordered systems of molecules and cells? You are a walking, talking contradiction to the idea that systems tend spontaneously toward disorder. We must look further.

Figure 2–3 The spontaneous tendency toward increasing disorder of a system and its surroundings.

Most of the examples cited concern an apparent increase in disorder in matter. Since we are looking for an energy law, perhaps we should focus on energy. Any change in matter requires either an input of energy or a release of energy. When water freezes and goes to a more ordered state, heat energy is given off to the surroundings. In changing from liquid water to solid ice, the order in the system increases. But the heat given off during this change increases the disorder in the surroundings. Measurements reveal that this increase in disorder in the surroundings is greater than the order created in the system.

The way out of our dilemma then is not to look at changes in disorder or order in the system only, but to look at such changes in both the system *and its environment.* Look at your own body. To form and preserve its highly ordered arrangement of molecules and its organized network of chemical reactions, you must continually obtain energy and raw materials from your surroundings. This means that disorder is created in the environment—primarily in the form of low-quality heat energy. Just think of all the disorder in the form of heat that is added to the environment to keep you alive. Planting, growing, processing, and cooking foods all require energy inputs that add heat to the environment. The breakdown of the chemicals in food in your body gives off more heat to the environment. Indeed, your body continuously gives off heat equal to that from a 100-watt light bulb—which explains why a closed room full of people gets hot. Measurements show that the disorder, in the form of low-quality heat energy, that is added to the environment to keep you alive is much greater than the order maintained in your body. This does not even count the enormous amounts of disorder added to the environment when concentrated deposits of minerals and fuels are extracted from the earth and burned or dispersed to heat the buildings you use, to move you around in ve-

hicles, and to make the clothes, shelter, and other things that you use.

In considering the system and surroundings as a whole, scientists find that there is *always* a net increase in disorder with any spontaneous chemical or physical change. For any spontaneous change, either (1) the disorder in both the system and the environment increases, (2) the increase in disorder in the system is greater than the increase in order created in the environment, or (3) the increase in disorder in the environment is greater than the order created in the system. Experimental measurements have demonstrated this over and over again. Thus, we must modify our original hypothesis to include the surroundings or environment. *Any system and its surroundings as a whole spontaneously tend toward increasing randomness or disorder,* or in other words, if you think things are mixed up now, just wait. This is another way of stating the second energy law, or **second law of thermodynamics.**

Scientists frequently use the term **entropy** as a measure of relative randomness or disorder. A random, or disorderly, system has a high entropy, and an orderly system has a low entropy. Using the entropy concept, we can state the second energy law as follows: Any system and its surroundings as a whole spontaneously tend toward increasing entropy.

No one has ever found a violation of this law. In most apparent violations, the observer fails to include the greater disorder (entropy) increase in the surroundings when there is an increase in order in the system.

2–4 Matter and Energy Laws and the Environmental Crisis

As we shall see throughout this book, the law of conservation of matter and the first and second laws of energy (see summary box) give us keys for understanding the environmental crisis and for dealing with it. These laws tell us why any society living on a finite planet like earth must eventually become an *earthmanship society* based on recycling and **reusing matter and reducing the rate at which matter and energy are used.** Energy flows to the earth from the sun and then goes back into space, but for all practical purposes little matter enters or leaves the earth. We have all of the supply of matter that we will ever have. Romantic and technological dreams that we can get new supplies of matter from space and other planets fail to consider that these efforts, even if the supplies were available on inhospitable planets, might require more of the earth's resources than we could bring back. Since we won't get any large amounts of new matter from beyond the earth, and since the law of conservation of matter tells us that no breakthrough in technology will create any new matter, we must learn to live with the matter we now have.

Our present one-way or "throwaway" society is based on using more and more of the earth's resources at a faster and faster rate (Figure 2-4). To sustain such growth rates requires an essentially infinite and affordable supply of mineral and energy resources. Technology can help us stretch these supplies and perhaps find substitutes, but sooner or later we must face up to the finiteness of the earth's supplies. The present environmental crisis and rising prices of key resources are warnings that these limits to growth may be closer than we like to think.

Some say we must become a *matter recycling society* so that growth can continue without depleting matter resources. As high-grade and economically affordable matter resource supplies dwindle, we must, of course, recycle more and more matter. But there is a catch to such a recycling society. In using resources such as iron, we dig up concentrated deposits of iron ore (because they are the cheapest). Then we disperse this concentrated iron over much of the globe as we fashion it into useful products, discard it, or change it into other chemical substances. To recycle such widely dispersed iron, we must collect it, transport it to central recycling centers, and melt and purify it so that it can be used again. This is where the two energy laws come in. *Recycling matter always requires energy.* However, if a resource is not too widely scattered, recycling often requires less energy than that needed to find, get, and process virgin ores. In any event, a recycling society based on ever increasing growth must have an essentially inexhaustible and affordable supply of energy. And energy, unlike matter, can never be recycled. Although experts disagree on how much usable energy we have, it is clear that supplies of fossil fuels and nuclear fuels are finite. Indeed, affordable supplies of oil, natural gas, and nuclear fuel may last no longer than several decades.

"Ah," you say, "but don't we have an essentially infinite supply of solar energy flowing into the earth?" The laws of energy help us to evaluate this option. Sunlight reaching the earth is dispersed energy. In order to use it to heat water to high temperatures, to melt metals, or to produce electricity, this dispersed energy must be collected and concentrated. This requires energy—lots of it. This means that we must have an almost infinite supply of some other energy source, such as nuclear or fossil fuels. We are apparently in a vicious circle.

For the moment, however, let's assume that nuclear fusion energy (still only a faint technological dream) or some other energy breakthrough comes to our rescue. Even with such a technological miracle, the *second energy law tells us why continued growth on a finite planet is not possible. As we use more and more energy to transform matter into products and then recycle these products, the disorder in the environment will automatically increase.* We will have to disrupt more and more of the earth's surface and add more and more low-quality heat energy and matter pollutants (many of which are small gaseous molecules created by breaking down larger, more ordered systems of matter) to the environment. Low-quality heat energy flows back into space, but if we create it at a faster rate than that at which it can flow back, the earth's atmosphere could heat up and create unknown and possibly disastrous ecological and climatic changes, as discussed later on in Chapter 9. Thus, paradoxically, the more we try to order, or "conquer," the earth, the greater the stress we put on the environment. From a physical standpoint, the environmental crisis is a disorder, or entropy, crisis, and the second energy law tells us why. Failure to accept the fact that no technological breakthrough can repeal the second energy law can only result in more and more damage to the quality of life on this planet.

Why do many think we can ignore or repeal the second energy law? Part of the problem is ignorance. Most people have never heard of the second law, let alone understood its significance. In addition, this law has a cumulative rather than individual effect. You accept the law of gravity because it limits you and everyone else on a personal level. However, though your individual activities automatically increase the disorder in the environment, this individual impact seems small and insignificant. But the cumulative impact of the disorder-producing activities of billions of individuals trying to convert all of the world's resources to trash and garbage as fast as possible can have a devastating

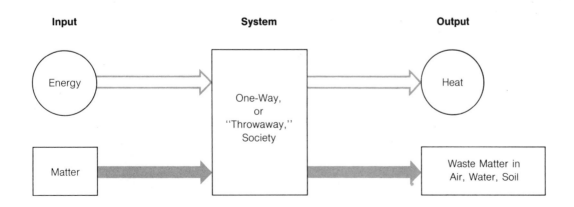

Input   **System**   **Output**

Energy → One-Way, or "Throwaway," Society → Heat

Matter → One-Way, or "Throwaway," Society → Waste Matter in Air, Water, Soil

Figure 2-4 Today's one-way, or "throwaway," society is based on maximizing the rates of energy flow and matter flow in an attempt to convert the world's mineral and energy resources to trash, pollution, and waste heat as fast as possible. It is sustainable only with essentially infinite supplies of mineral and energy resources and an infinite ability of the environment to absorb the resulting heat and matter wastes.

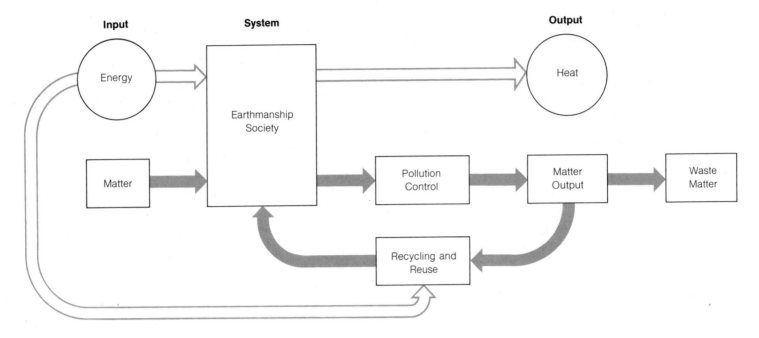

Input   **System**   **Output**

Figure 2–5 An earthmanship society is based on energy flow and matter recycling. It requires reusing and recycling finite mineral resources, conserving energy (since it can't be recycled), increased pollution control, and deliberately lowering the rate at which we use matter and energy resources so that the environment is not overloaded and resources are not depleted.

impact on the life-support system that sustains us all. *The second energy law tells us that we are all interconnected whether we like it or not.*

This may seem like a rather gloomy situation, but it need not be. The second energy law, along with the first energy law and the law of conservation of matter, tells us what we *cannot* do. But even more important and hopeful, these laws tell us what we *can* do. They show us that the way out is to shift to an *earthmanship society* (Figure 2–5), which is based on a deliberately reduced rate of use of matter and energy so that the entropy or disorder limits of the environment are not exceeded and resources are not depleted. This requires matter recycling, but more important it requires reuse of matter (which takes less energy than recycling), making products that last, increased pollution control, and emphasizing conservation of matter and energy (which cannot be recycled). Only by conserving and not wasting matter and energy supplies can we conserve and preserve life and life quality. This is the key to earthmanship.

To make the exciting and necessary transition to an earthmanship society, we must stop thinking of earth as a spaceship that we can pilot—and resupply—at will. Far from "seizing the tiller of the world," as Teilhard de Chardin would have us do, we must stop trying to steer completely. Somehow we must tune our senses and hearts to nature, though we will never completely understand its marvelous

complexity. We must learn anew that we belong to the earth and not the earth to us. As part of nature, we will always attempt to shape it to some extent for our own benefit, but we must do so with ecological wisdom, care, and restraint.

Matter and Energy Laws

Law of conservation of matter: In any ordinary physical or chemical change, matter is neither created nor destroyed but only transformed from one form to another.

or

We can never really throw matter away.

or

Everything must go somewhere.

First law of energy or thermodynamics (law of conservation of energy): In any ordinary physical or chemical change, energy is neither created nor destroyed but merely changed from one form to another.

or

You can't get something for nothing in terms of

energy quantity; you can only break even.

or

There is no such thing as a free lunch.

Second law of energy or thermodynamics (law of energy degradation): In all conversions of heat energy to work, some of the energy is always degraded to a more dispersed and less useful form, usually heat energy given off at a low temperature to the surroundings, or environment.

or

You can't break even in terms of energy quality.

or

Energy can never be recycled.

or

Any system and its surroundings (environment) as a whole spontaneously tend toward increasing randomness, disorder, or entropy.

or

If you think things are mixed up now, just wait.

The law that entropy increases—the second law of thermodynamics—holds, I think, the supreme position among laws of nature. . . . If your theory is found to be against the second law of thermodynamics, I can give you no hope; there is nothing to do but collapse in deepest humiliation.

Arthur S. Eddington

Discussion Topics

1. Explain why we don't really consume anything and why there is no such thing as a throwaway society.

2. A tree grows and increases its mass. Explain why this isn't a violation of the law of conservation of matter.

3. Explain why removing odors and large particles from the smoke emitted from smokestacks could be a misleading and even dangerous long-term pollution control strategy. Does this mean it shouldn't be done? Explain.

4. Discuss the line in Genesis 3:19 "You are dust and to dust you shall return" in relation to the law of conservation of matter and the second law of thermodynamics.

5. Describe the energy transformations involved in the flow of water over a dam. How could some of the energy released be used to generate electricity?

6. List six different types of energy that you have used today and classify each as either kinetic or potential energy.

7. Use the first and second energy laws to explain why the usable supply of energy from coal, oil, natural gas, and uranium (nuclear fuel) is considerably less than that given by most official estimates.

8. What does it mean to say that electricity is high-quality energy and that sunlight is low-quality energy?

9. Use the second energy law to explain why a barrel of oil can only be used once as a fuel.

10. Criticize the statement "Any spontaneous process results in an increase in the disorder of the system."

11. Criticize the statement "Life is an ordering process, and since it goes against the natural tendency for increasing disorder, it breaks the second law of thermodynamics."

12. Explain how the environmental crisis can be considered an entropy crisis.

13. Using the first and second energy laws and the law of conservation of matter, explain the idea "To exist is to pollute." Does this mean that increasing pollution is inevitable? Why or why not? Does it apply to all types of pollution or only to some?

14. **a.** Use the law of conservation of matter to explain why a matter recycling society is necessary.

b. Use the second energy law to explain why there must be more emphasis on reusing than on recycling matter and why we must move to an earthmanship society.

c. Use the second energy law to explain why energy can never be recycled.

Further Readings

Angrist, S. W., and L. G. Hepler. 1967. *Order and Chaos.* New York: Basic Books. Excellent nontechnical introduction to thermodynamics emphasizing its fascinating historical development.

Bent, Henry A. 1971. "Haste Makes Waste: Pollution and Entropy." *Chemistry,* vol. 44, 6–15. Excellent and very readable account of the relationship between entropy (disorder) and the environmental crisis.

Boulding, Kenneth E. 1964. *The Meaning of the 20th Century.* New York: Harper & Row. Penetrating discussion of our planetary situation by one of our foremost thinkers. See especially Chapters 4, 6, and 7 on the war, population, and entropy (disorder) traps.

Cook, Earl. 1976. *Man, Energy, Society.* San Francisco: Freeman. Superb discussion of energy and energy options.

Cottrell, F. 1955. *Energy and Society.* New York: McGraw-Hill. Survey of our development of energy sources.

Miller, G. Tyler, Jr. 1971. *Energetics, Kinetics and Life: An Ecological Approach.* Belmont, Calif.: Wadsworth. My own attempt to show the beauty and wide application of thermodynamics to life. Amplifies and expands the material in this chapter at a slightly higher level.

Odum, Howard T. 1971. *Environment, Power and Society.* New York: Wiley-Interscience. Important and fascinating higher-level discussion of human energy use.

Odum, Howard T., and Elisabeth C. Odum. 1976. *Energy Basis for Man and Nature.* New York: McGraw-Hill. Outstanding discussion of energy principles and energy options at a somewhat higher level.

Priest, Joseph. 1973. *Problems of Our Physical Environment: Energy, Transportation, Pollution.* Reading, Mass.: Addison-Wesley. Slightly more technical but highly readable treatment of energy principles.

Steinhart, Carol E., and John S. Steinhart. 1974. *Energy: Source, Use, and Role in Human Affairs.* North Scituate, Mass.: Duxbury Press. Excellent treatment of energy principles and options.

Thirring, Hans. 1958. *Energy for Man.* New York: Harper & Row. Informative overview of our use of energy.

3

Some Ecological Concepts

Earth and water, if not too blatantly abused, can be made to produce again and again for the benefit of all. The key is wise stewardship.

Stewart L. Udall

Walk into a forest on a warm summer day and look, listen, smell, and feel. A gentle breeze flows over your skin and the air feels cool and slightly damp. The sounds of the urban world you just left are masked out by magnificent oak and hickory trees that surround you with their beauty. Glimmering sunlight cascades through the canopy of leaves to reveal a varied tapestry of shrubs and herbs growing at your feet. A squirrel scampers noisily up a tree trunk. Looking down you see the tracks of a deer. Turning over a rotting log in your path, you uncover a frenzy of activity as worms, beetles, ants, termites, centipedes, cockroaches, and other unidentifiable insects move in all directions to escape your intrusion into their world. You pick up a handful of soil looking for further signs of life. But you can only imagine that it teems with countless millions of bacteria and other microorganisms.

What types of plants and animals live in this forest? How do they get the matter and energy that they need to stay alive? How do these plants and animals interact with one another and with their physical environment? What changes will this dynamic system of life undergo with time? Ecology is the branch of science that attempts to answer such questions. Ernest Haeckel coined the term *ecology* from two Greek words: *oikos*, meaning "house" or "place to live," and *logos*, meaning "study of." Literally, then, **ecology** is a study of organisms in their home; it is a study of the structure and function of nature (Odum 1962, 1971b, 1972, 1975), or of what organisms and groups of organisms are found in nature and how they function or interact with one another and with their environment. Ecologists call the forest just described and other dynamic systems of living things and their environment *ecosystems*.

3-1 Ecosystem Structure: What Is an Ecosystem?

Levels of Organization Looking at earth from space, we see mostly a blue sphere with irregular green, red, and white patches on its surface. As we zoom closer these colorful patches become deserts, forests, grasslands, mountains, seas, lakes, oceans, farmlands, and cities. Each subsection is different, having its own characteristic set of organisms and climatic conditions. Yet, as we shall see, all of these subsystems are related. As we move in even closer, we can pick out a wide variety of living organisms. If we could magnify these plants and animals, we would see that they are made up of cells, which in turn are made up of molecules, atoms, and subatomic particles. All matter, in fact, can be viewed as being organized in identifiable patterns, or levels of organization, ranging in complexity from subatomic particles to galaxies (Figure 3-1).

The Realm of Ecology As Figure 3-1 shows, ecologists are concerned with five levels of organization of matter—*organisms, populations, communities, ecosystems,* and the *ecosphere* (Sutton & Harmon 1973, Whittaker 1975, Wiens 1972). A group of individual organisms (squirrels, oak trees) of the same kind (species) is called a **population.** A population may be local or global, depending on the size of the geographic system under study. It may include all of the squirrels and oak trees on earth or all of the squirrels and oak trees in the oak-hickory forest described in the opening of this chapter.

In nature we find several populations of different organisms living in a particular area. The populations of plants and animals living and interacting in a given locality are called a **community,** or *natural community.* Each organism in such a community has a **habitat,** the place where it lives. Habitats vary widely in size from an entire forest to the intestine of a termite. A community, such as an oak-hickory forest, is not just a collection of squirrels, trees, plants,

Figure 3–1 Levels of organization of matter.

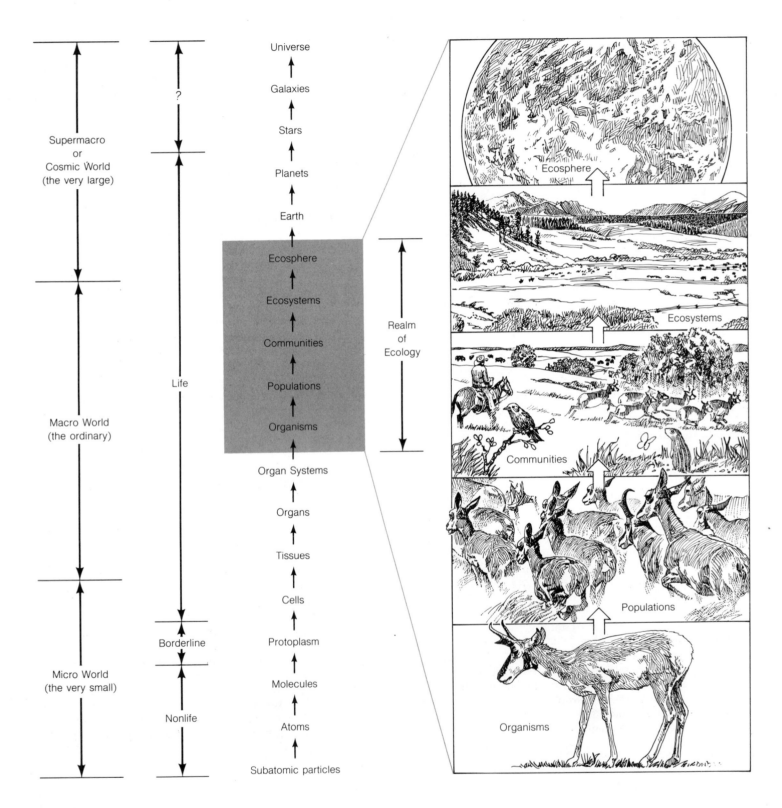

Supermacro
or
Cosmic World
(the very large)

Macro World
(the ordinary)

Micro World
(the very small)

?

Life

Borderline

Nonlife

Universe

Galaxies

Stars

Planets

Earth

Ecosphere

Ecosystems

Communities

Populations

Organisms

Organ Systems

Organs

Tissues

Cells

Protoplasm

Molecules

Atoms

Subatomic particles

Realm
of
Ecology

Ecosphere

Ecosystems

Communities

Populations

Organisms

bacteria, and other populations living together in the same place. The importance of a natural community is that its animals and plants are interacting with one another. In many communities one or two organisms dominate. For example, in an oak-hickory forest community, oak and hickory trees are the dominant species. They provide habitats and protection from the harsh sun so that certain plants and animals can survive. They also serve as the largest single source of food for a number of organisms, such as squirrels and small rodents.

Any natural or biological community also has an environment. A community of living things interacting with one another and with their physical environment (solar energy, air, water, soil, heat, wind, and various essential chemicals) is called an *ecological system* or **ecosystem,**[1] a term first introduced by A. G. Tansley (1935). An ecosystem can be a planet, a tropical rain forest, a pond (Deevey 1951), an ocean, a fallen log, or a puddle of water in a rock. An ecosystem is any area with a boundary through which an input and output of energy and matter can be measured and related to one or more environmental factors. The boundaries drawn around ecosystems are arbitrary and are selected for convenience in studying each system. It is easy to think of a pond, lake, desert, or forest as an ecosystem, because each tends to have recognizable geographic boundaries. But it is often just as useful to treat a patch of an oak-hickory forest or a clump of grass in a field as an ecosystem. Just as a community is not merely a collection of plants and animals, an ecosystem is not merely a group of plants and animals plus their environment. In studying an ecosystem, we are interested in the interactions between the organisms and between the organisms and their environment.

All of the various ecosystems on the planet, along with their interactions, make up the largest life unit, or planetary ecosystem, called the **ecosphere,** or **biosphere** (Cole 1958, Hutchinson 1970, *Scientific American* 1970; see Figure 3–1). The ecosphere includes all forms of life and every relationship that binds these various forms of life together. The earth can be divided into three interconnected spherical regions—the **atmosphere** (air), the **hydrosphere** (water), and the **lithosphere** (soil and rock). The ecosphere, or sphere of life, is found within these three spherical areas. It consists of three life zones: (1) above us, a thin layer of usable atmosphere no more than 11 kilometers (7 miles) high; (2) around us, a limited supply of life-supporting

water in rivers, glaciers, lakes, oceans, and underground deposits as well as in the atmosphere; and (3) below us, a thin crust of soil, minerals, and rocks extending only a few thousand meters into the earth's interior. This intricate film of life contains all of the water, minerals, oxygen, carbon, phosphorus, and other chemical building blocks necessary for life. Because essentially no new matter enters or leaves the earth (Section 2–4), these vital chemicals must be recycled again and again for life to continue.

If the earth were an apple, the ecosphere would be no thicker than the skin on the apple. Everything in this skin of life is connected and interdependent: Air helps purify water and keep plants and animals alive, water keeps plants and animals alive, plants keep animals alive and help renew the air, and the soil keeps plants and many animals alive and helps purify the water. The ecosphere is a remarkably effective and enduring system—and endure it must, or life will become extinct. We are beginning to understand that disrupting or stressing the ecosphere in one place can often create unpredictable and sometimes undesirable effects elsewhere in the system. This ecological backlash effect has been eloquently summarized by the English poet Francis Thompson: "Thou canst not stir a flower, without troubling of a star." *The goal of ecology is to find out just how everything in the ecosphere is connected.* Using this knowledge, humans can **work as partners within nature rather than as conquerors of nature.**

Let's take a look at the structure or components of an ecosystem. As mentioned earlier, an ecosystem always has two major parts or components: nonliving and living. The *nonliving,* or **abiotic,** part includes an outside energy source (usually the sun), various physical factors such as wind and heat, and all of the chemicals essential for life. The *living,* or **biotic,** portion of an ecosystem can be divided into food **producers** (plants) and food **consumers.** Consumers are usually further divided into *macroconsumers* (animals) and **decomposers,** or *microconsumers* (chiefly bacteria and fungi), as shown in Figure 3–2.

Is an Urban System an Ecosystem? A number of ecologists and urban experts treat cities and urban regions as ecosystems (Detwyler & Marcus 1972, Ehrlich et al. 1976, Foin 1976, George & McKinley 1971, Havlick 1974, Hawley 1971, Meier 1976, Richardson 1977, Stearns & Montag 1973, Sudia 1971). Other ecologists argue that while an urban system has some characteristics of a natural ecosystem, it is not a true ecosystem (Holling & Orians 1971, Odum 1971b, Smith 1976).

Much of this disagreement depends on how we define an ecosystem. In this section an ecosystem is defined as a community of plants and animals interacting with one another and with their environment. Technically, a city meets the requirements of this definition. But there are some important differences between natural ecosystems and urban ecosystems.

---

[1]The ecosystem approach is not the only way of studying ecology. Some ecologists (such as Colinvaux 1973, Emlen 1973, Pianka 1974, Ricklefs 1973, 1976) prefer to approach ecology from the standpoint of biological evolution. Because the evolutionary approach requires a fairly detailed and technical background in biology, we will use the ecosystem approach. For more details on the ecosystem approach see Commoner 1970a, Darling & Darling 1968, Darnell 1973, Emmel 1973, Kormondy 1976, McHale 1970, Metillo 1972, Miller 1972, Odum 1962, 1969, 1971b, 1972, 1975, Reid 1970, Richardson 1977, Smith 1974b, 1976, Southwick 1976, Sutton & Harmon 1973, Watt 1973.

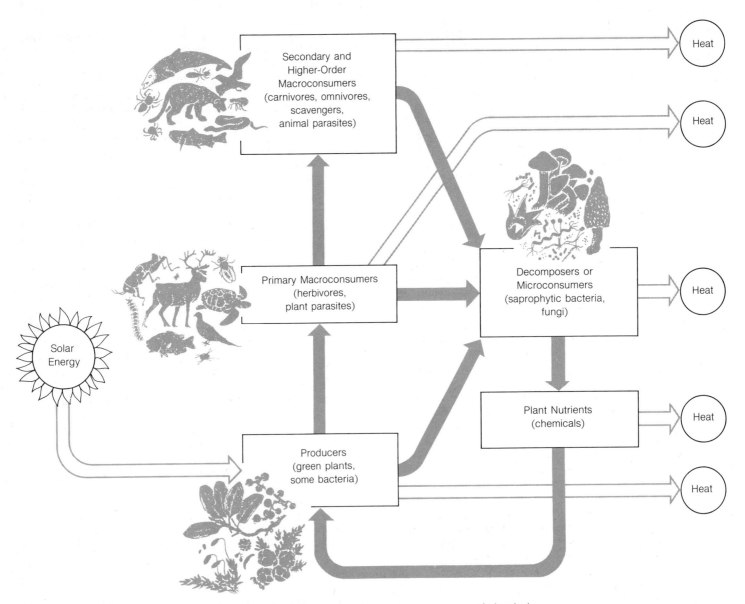

Figure 3–2 The basic components of an ecosystem. Solid lines represent the cyclical movement of chemicals through the system, and unshaded lines indicate one-way energy flows.

Unlike natural ecosystems, cities do not have enough producers (green plants) to support their inhabitants. Cities may have a few trees, lawns, and parks, but these are not used as food for humans. As an unknown observer remarked, "Cities are places where they cut down the trees and then name the streets after them." Some cities are even replacing their shrubs and grass with plastic plants and Astroturf. This is unfortunate, since urban plants, grasses, and trees absorb some air pollutants, give off oxygen, help cool the air by evaporating water from their leaves, muffle noise, and satisfy an important psychological need for urban dwellers, whose artificial environment cuts them off from nature (Robinette 1972). The lack of producers in cities also means that the input of solar energy is largely wasted, in sharp contrast to its use for photosynthesis in natural ecosystems.

Cities also lack animals or consumers that can be used as food for their human population. Without enough producers and consumers, urban systems survive only by importing food from external plant-growing ecosystems located throughout the world (Darling & Dasmann 1969, Ehrlich et al. 1977, Mines 1971, Strange 1969).

Cities must also obtain fresh air, water, minerals, and energy resources from outside areas. At the same time, they must export their solid, liquid, and gaseous waste products and waste heat to outside areas (Figure 3–3) (Marquis 1968, Wolman 1965). Without such inputs and outputs of matter and energy a city collapses, as shown by occasional electrical power failures and air pollution alerts in New York City and water shortages in San Francisco. In exchange for such life supports, cities provide goods, services, information, manufacturing, technology, and entertainment for outlying towns and farms (Figure 3–3). Future shortages of energy and matter resources (especially water and some metals) may force cities to use matter more efficiently, to make better use of solar energy, and to reduce the flows of matter and energy through them (Meier 1976, Richardson 1977).

Urban systems can be classified as self-sustaining ecosystems only if we expand their boundaries to include (1) the farmlands, forests, mines, watersheds, and other areas throughout the world that provide their input materials and (2) the air, rivers, oceans, and soil that absorb their massive output of wastes. This should remind us that *practically none of the world's cities can sustain themselves.* In the words of Theodore Roszak (1972):

> The supercity . . . stretches out tentacles of influence that reach thousands of miles beyond its already sprawling perimeters. It sucks every hinterland and wilderness into its technological metabolism. It forces rural populations off the land and replaces them with vast agroindustrial combines. Its investments and technicians bring the roar of the bulldozer and oil derrick into the most uncharted quarters. It runs its conduits of transport and

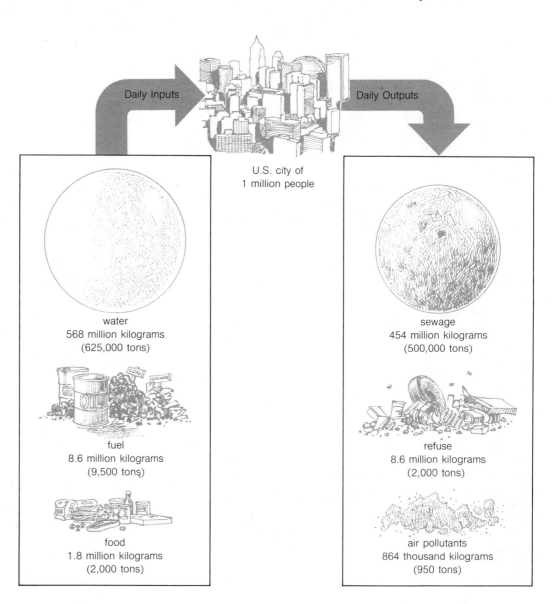

Daily Inputs

Daily Outputs

U.S. city of
1 million people

water
568 million kilograms
(625,000 tons)

fuel
8.6 million kilograms
(9,500 tons)

food
1.8 million kilograms
(2,000 tons)

sewage
454 million kilograms
(500,000 tons)

refuse
8.6 million kilograms
(2,000 tons)

air pollutants
864 thousand kilograms
(950 tons)

Figure 3–3 Typical daily inputs and outputs for a U.S. city of 1 million people. (Modified after Lockwood 1969 and Wolman 1965)

communication, its lines of supply and distribution through the wildest landscapes. It flushes its waste into every river, lake, and ocean or trucks them away into desert areas. The world becomes its garbage can.

3-2 Ecosystem Function: How Do Ecosystems Work?

Energy Flow and Chemical Cycling What keeps you, an oak tree, a squirrel, a termite, and other living organisms alive on this relatively small planet hurtling through space at about 107,200 kilometers (66,600 miles) per hour? To survive, you or any other form of life must have an almost continuous *input* of both energy and matter, or chemicals. An oak tree gets its energy directly from the sun, while you and other animals get energy from certain chemicals in your food supply. Merely receiving energy and matter, however, will not keep an organism alive. An *output* of degraded energy (heat) and waste matter must flow from an organism—otherwise it will be drowned in its own waste heat and waste matter. To remain alive, the input and output of energy and matter must be in balance. Thus, *life at the organism level depends on a balanced flow of both matter (chemicals) and energy through the organism.*

Organisms, however, don't live in isolation, as we saw in the previous section on ecosystem structure. To get the matter and energy they need, living things must interact with their physical environment and with other organisms. For animals like you this is called breathing, drinking, eating, and reproducing. At the ecosystem and ecosphere levels (Section 3–1) life still depends on energy flow, because according to the second law of energy (Section 2–3) *energy can never be recycled.* As energy flows through an organism, community, ecosystem, or the ecosphere, it is always degraded in quality to less useful heat energy.

Life at the ecosystem and ecosphere levels depends on matter or chemical cycling, not on one-way matter flow. The one-way flow of energy through the ecosystem and ecosphere is used to cycle these essential chemicals, as summarized in Figure 3–4. Thus, *while life at the organism level depends on energy flow and matter flow, at the ecosystem and ecosphere levels it depends on energy flow and matter cycling.*

Chemicals must cycle in the ecosphere because no significant amounts of matter enter or leave the earth and because, according to the law of conservation of matter (Section 2–1), we cannot create any new matter or destroy what we have. This means the overall survival of the collection of species in an ecosystem and in the ecosphere requires that certain essential forms of matter, such as water, carbon, oxygen, nitrogen, and phosphorus, be converted from one form to another and thus be cycled and recycled.

At the ecosphere level, the chemicals essential for life must be completely recycled. But since the various ecosystems on earth are connected, some matter flows from one ecosystem to another. Considerable chemical cycling, however, must occur in any ecosystem for it to survive. Indeed, in an ecosystem there is almost no such thing as waste matter. One organism's waste or death is another organism's food. If vital chemicals in an ecosystem and in the ecosphere are not recycled or if they are recycled at rates that are too fast or too slow, then individual organisms, groups of organisms, or even all organisms will die.

Thus, we can generally answer the question "What happens in an ecosystem?" by saying that energy flows and matter (chemicals) cycles. These two major ecosystem functions connect the various structural parts of an ecosystem (Section 3–1) so that life is maintained. This relationship between ecosystem structure and ecosystem function is summarized in Figure 3–5.

In the remainder of this chapter we will look more closely at these two functional processes occurring in ecosystems. We will examine energy flow first at the ecosphere level and then at the ecosystem level.

3-3 Solar Energy and Global Energy Flow

A Nuclear Fusion Reactor The source of the energy that sustains all life on earth is the sun, a star located about 150 million kilometers (93 million miles) from the earth. The sun warms the earth and provides energy for photosynthesis in plants, which in turn provides the carbon compounds that feed all life.

The sun is composed mostly of the chemical element hydrogen. Its temperature is over 100 million degrees Celsius. Under such high temperatures (and also high pressures) four nuclei of hydrogen atoms can be combined or fused together to form one heavier helium nucleus. In this thermonuclear process, called **nuclear fusion,** some of the mass of the hydrogen nuclei is converted to energy. This vast amount of energy travels through space in all directions. The amount of energy released by this gigantic thermonuclear reactor is about 100,000,000,000,000,000,000,000,000 (or 10^{26}) joules[2] of energy per second. This means that the sun converts about 3.8 billion kilograms (4.2

---

[2]The joule (abbreviated J and pronounced *jool*) is the standard unit of heat in the metric system of measurement. Other widely used energy units are the kilojoule (kJ), calorie (cal), and kilocalorie (kcal), shown below:

$$1 \text{ kJ} = 1,000 \text{ or } 10^3 \text{ J}$$

$$1 \text{ cal} = 4.186 \text{ J}$$

$$1 \text{ kcal} = 1,000 \text{ or } 10^3 \text{ cal} = 4,186 \text{ J}$$

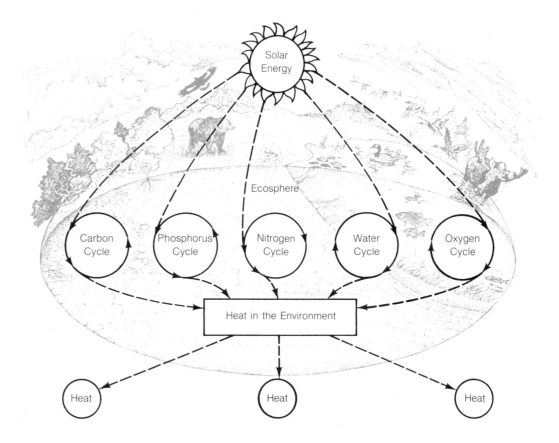

Figure 3–4 Life on earth depends on the cycling of critical chemicals and the one-way flow of energy through the ecosphere. Dotted lines represent energy flow and solid lines represent chemical cycling.

million tons) of its mass into energy every second. But don't worry about the sun running out of fuel. In the normal life cycle of stars, the sun is entering middle age. It has probably been in existence for at least 6 billion years, and there is enough hydrogen left to keep it going for at least another 5 billion years.

Solar Electromagnetic Spectrum Only about half of one-billionth of the sun's total radiated energy is intercepted by the earth, a minute target in the vastness of space. The sun's energy comes to us as *radiant energy*, traveling through space at a speed of 300,000 kilometers (186,000 miles) per second. At this speed the light striking your eyes made the 150-million-kilometer (93-million-mile) trip from the sun to earth in about 8 minutes. The visible light we call sunlight is only a tiny part of the wide range, or spectrum, of energies given off by the sun, which is known as the **electromagnetic spectrum** (Figure 3–6). This spectrum of energy ranges from high-energy gamma rays, X rays, and ultraviolet radiation to lower-energy visible, infrared (heat), and radio waves. Each different type of energy in the spectrum can be treated as a wave with a different **wavelength,** the distance between the crest of one wave and the next. High-

energy radiation has a short wavelength, whereas low-energy radiation has a long wavelength. The higher-energy, shorter-wavelength rays—gamma rays, X rays, and most ultraviolet rays—are harmful to living organisms. Luckily, most of this harmful radiation is screened out by chemicals in the atmosphere, such as ozone and water vapor. Without this screen almost all life on this planet would be destroyed.

Global Energy Flow Let's see what happens to the tiny fraction of the sun's total energy output that is intercepted by the earth. As shown in Figure 3–7, about 30 percent of the incoming solar radiation is immediately reflected back to space by clouds, chemicals in the air, dust, and the earth's surface (Gates 1971). This reflectivity of the earth and its atmosphere is called the planetary **albedo.** The remaining 70 percent of the incoming radiation is absorbed by the atmosphere, lithosphere, hydrosphere, and ecosphere systems of the earth.

About 47 percent of the incoming solar energy is used to heat the land and warm the atmosphere. Another 23 percent regulates the cycling of water through the ecosphere. Solar energy evaporates water on land, in lakes and rivers, and in the ocean. As this warm, moist air rises in the atmo-

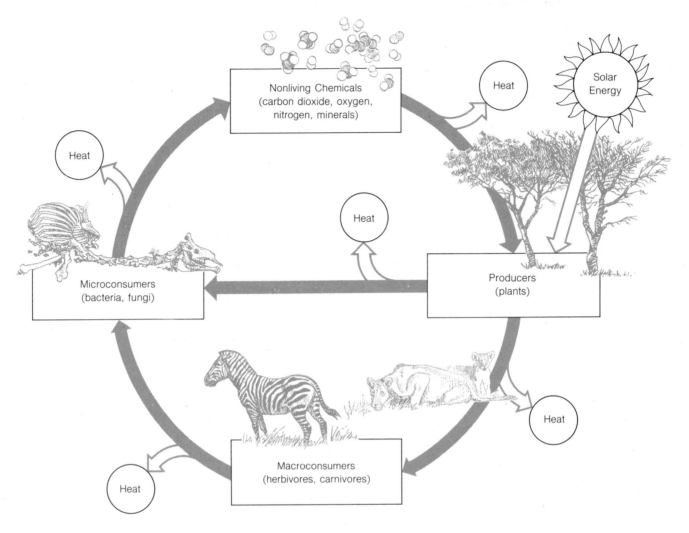

Figure 3–5 A summary of ecosystem structure and function. The major structural components (energy, chemicals, and organisms) of an ecosystem are connected through the functions of energy flow (unshaded lines) and chemical cycling (solid lines).

sphere, it expands and cools. This forms clouds, which can release their water as rain, snow, or hail. A tiny fraction (0.2 percent) of the incoming solar energy is used to generate air currents or winds, which in turn move the clouds and form waves in the ocean. An even tinier fraction of only 0.0023 percent is captured by green plants and converted by photosynthesis to chemical energy in the form of carbohydrates, proteins, and other molecules needed for life.

Almost all of the 70 percent of the solar energy entering the earth's atmosphere, hydrosphere, lithosphere, and ecosphere is degraded into longer-wavelength heat or infrared radiation, in accordance with the second law of thermodynamics (Section 2–3). This heat flows back into space and the total amount returning to space is called the **emis-**

sivity of the earth. Emissivity is affected by various chemical molecules (such as water and carbon dioxide) in the atmosphere. These molecules act as gatekeepers either to allow heat energy to flow back into space or to absorb and reradiate some of the heat back toward the earth's surface.

Usually the amount of heat or infrared radiation emitted by the earth is approximately equal to the 70 percent of incoming solar energy absorbed by the earth. This balance, along with the albedo of the earth, determines average global temperatures. Should something change either the albedo or the emissivity of the earth, the average global temperature would drop or rise to correct the imbalance. For example, a rise of only 2°C in the average global temperature could cause major changes in global weather patterns, and a 3° to 6°C rise could eventually melt the polar

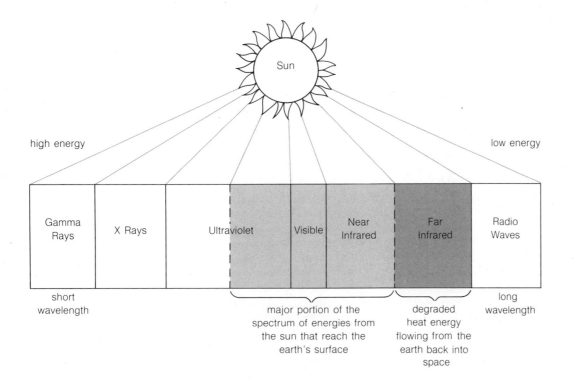

Figure 3–6 The electromagnetic spectrum. The sun radiates a wide range of energies with different wavelengths. Much of this incoming radiation is reflected and absorbed by the earth's atmosphere so that mostly moderate- to low-energy radiation actually reaches the earth's surface.

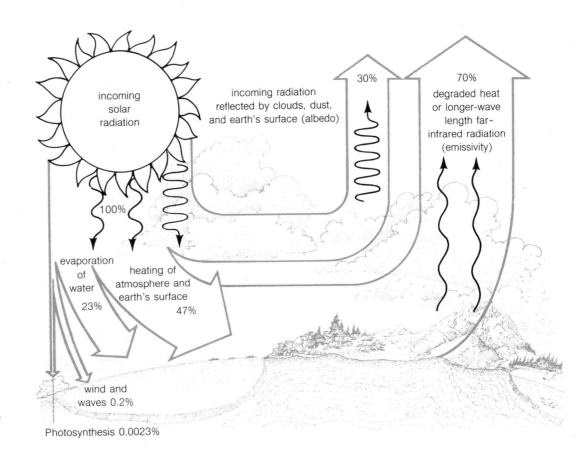

Figure 3–7 The flow of energy to and from the earth.

ice caps, thus flooding a large portion of the world (SCEP 1970, SMIC 1971). Similarly, a drop of only a few degrees in the average global temperature could trigger an ice age (Budyko 1969).

Increasing the albedo of the atmosphere could lead to global cooling, whereas decreasing the atmosphere's emissivity could lead to global heating. We know that volcanic eruptions and dust storms can disturb the albedo by injecting tiny particles into the atmosphere. Such particles normally increase the reflectivity of the atmosphere and lead to a drop in average global temperature. There is concern that land-clearing activities and smoke-emitting power and industrial plants may be adding significant amounts of dust and soot particles to the atmosphere.

The atmosphere's emissivity is affected by a number of factors, including the total amount of carbon dioxide gas in the atmosphere. There is concern that the large amounts of carbon dioxide that we add to the atmosphere by burning wood and fossil fuels (oil, coal, and natural gas) could lead to a gradual warming of the atmosphere (the greenhouse effect). A more detailed discussion of whether human activities may be altering global climate is given in Chapter 9.

In the mid-1970s some scientists suggested that we may also be changing the type of solar energy reaching the earth by decreasing the amount of ozone in the stratosphere. Ozone levels could be decreased by the upward diffusion of fluorocarbon molecules used in aerosol sprays and as air conditioner refrigerants, by nitrogen oxide gases released from nitrogen fertilizers, or by direct injection of nitrogen oxide gases into the layer of ozone by supersonic airplanes (SSTs). Since ozone is a key molecule in filtering out harmful ultraviolet radiation, any decrease in the amount of ozone in the stratosphere could increase cases of human skin cancer, damage some forms of plant life (including some food crops), and possibly alter global climate patterns.

With this overview of global energy flow, we are now ready to look more closely at how energy flows through ecosystems.

3–4 Energy Flow in Ecosystems

Food Chains and Food Webs In general, the flow of energy through an ecosystem is the study of who eats or decomposes whom (Gosz et al. 1978, Woodwell 1970b). The general sequence of who eats or decomposes whom is called a **food chain,** or *energy chain.* A food chain involves the transfer of food energy from one organism to another when one organism eats or decomposes another (Figure 3–8). The various levels of producers (plants) and consumers (herbivores, carnivores, and decomposers) in a food chain are called **trophic levels** (from the Greek *trophikos* for "nourishment," or "food").

The first trophic level in an ecosystem always consists of *producers,* or green plants (and some photosynthesizing bacteria). *Herbivores,* or plant eaters, represent the second trophic level. Because they are the first organisms to feed on other organisms, they are sometimes called *primary consumers.* The third trophic level is composed of *carnivores,* who feed on herbivores. They are often called secondary consumers. The *top carnivores* in a food chain are animals that feed on other carnivores. They represent the fourth and sometimes even the fifth trophic levels and are often called *tertiary* and *quaternary consumers,* respectively. When plants and animals at all trophic levels die, their bodies are broken down by *decomposers,* or *microconsumers.* The early stages of decomposition may be accomplished by millipedes, earthworms, woodlice, and other invertebrates, but the final breakdown of organic compounds into inorganic compounds is accomplished by microorganisms and fungi, such as bacteria and yeast. Some organisms eat from more than one trophic level and are called *omnivores.* When you eat a bacon, lettuce, and tomato sandwich, you are eating three types of producers (lettuce, wheat, and tomato) and one consumer (pig).

The food-chain concept is a very convenient tool for tracing out who eats or decomposes whom in an ecosystem. By itself, however, it gives an inaccurate picture of what is really happening in an ecosystem. Many animals feed on several different types of food at the same trophic level. In addition, omnivores, such as humans, bears, and rats, can eat several different kinds of plants and animals at several trophic levels. For example, birds that normally eat seeds may switch to insects in the spring. Foxes may gorge themselves on mice when they are abundant, go after rabbits when mice become scarce, eat berries when they are ripe, and switch to grasshoppers and fallen apples in the fall.

Because of these more complex feeding patterns, different food chains intertwine. When we diagram these more complex feeding relationships in an ecosystem, we get a **food web** instead of a series of linear food chains lying side by side.

Food Chains and the Second Energy Law Because of the second law of thermodynamics (Section 2–3), no transfer of energy from one trophic level to another is 100 percent. In fact, *only about 10 percent of the chemical energy available at one trophic level gets transferred and stored in usable form in the bodies of the organisms at the next trophic level.*[3] *In other words,*

---

[3]Actual percentages vary with species. Some sulfur bacteria have an energy transfer of only 2 percent. Typically, only 10 percent of the energy entering the plant population is available to herbivores. For warm-blooded carnivores, the conversion efficiency is usually lower than 10 percent, whereas for cold-blooded ones it may be 20 or 30 percent. Ten percent seems a fair average.

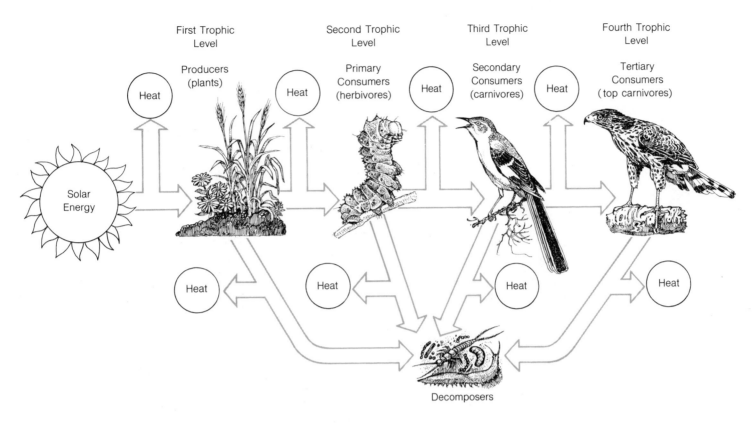

First Trophic Level

Second Trophic Level

Third Trophic Level

Fourth Trophic Level

Producers (plants)

Primary Consumers (herbivores)

Secondary Consumers (carnivores)

Tertiary Consumers (top carnivores)

Heat

Solar Energy

Decomposers

Figure 3–8 A food chain. The arrows show how energy in food chemicals flows through various trophic levels with some of the energy being degraded to heat in accordance with the second law of thermodynamics.

about 90 percent of the chemical energy is degraded and lost as heat to the environment (Figure 3–9). The percentage transfer of useful energy from one trophic level to another is called **ecological efficiency** or *food-chain efficiency* (Phillipson 1966).

Two important principles emerge from the food-chain concept. First, all life and all forms of food begin with sunlight and green plants. Second, the shorter the food chain, the less the loss of usable energy. This means that a larger population of humans (or other organisms) can be supported by a shorter plant-based food chain, such as rice ⟶ human, than by a longer meat-based food chain, such as grain ⟶ steer ⟶ human. An overpopulated country or world will be better off, at least in terms of total energy intake, by eating wheat or rice than by feeding such plants to herbivores (with a 90 percent energy loss) and then eating the herbivores (with another 90 percent energy loss). But a diet based on only one or two plants lacks some of the proteins essential for good health.

3–5 What Can Go Wrong in an Ecosystem?

Ecosystem Adaptability Many people think "balance of nature" means that ecosystems do not change. Nothing could be further from the truth. *Ecosystems are dynamic.* They contain organisms that, by their very presence, change local conditions. The organisms may then be forced to change or die in response to the new conditions that they themselves have created. Or their environment may change because of fires, floods, drought, volcanic eruptions, erosion, climatic shifts, earthquakes, or human influences (farming, industrialization, pollution, or urbanization). Although ecosystems are always changing, they do show a certain stability—the ability to tolerate or resist changes by outside influences or to restore themselves after an outside disturbance. If Robin Hood were alive today, he would still find a Sherwood Forest (though much smaller), and he would still recognize most if not all of the kinds of plants and trees growing there. This ability to adapt but at the same time maintain an overall stability if not pushed too far is truly a remarkable feature of ecosystems. Indeed, if most ecosystems were not so adaptable we would not be here today.

Effects of Environmental Stress Since mature ecosystems are self-maintaining and self-repairing, why not just drop all of our wastes into the environment and let nature take care of them? By now you should realize that there are

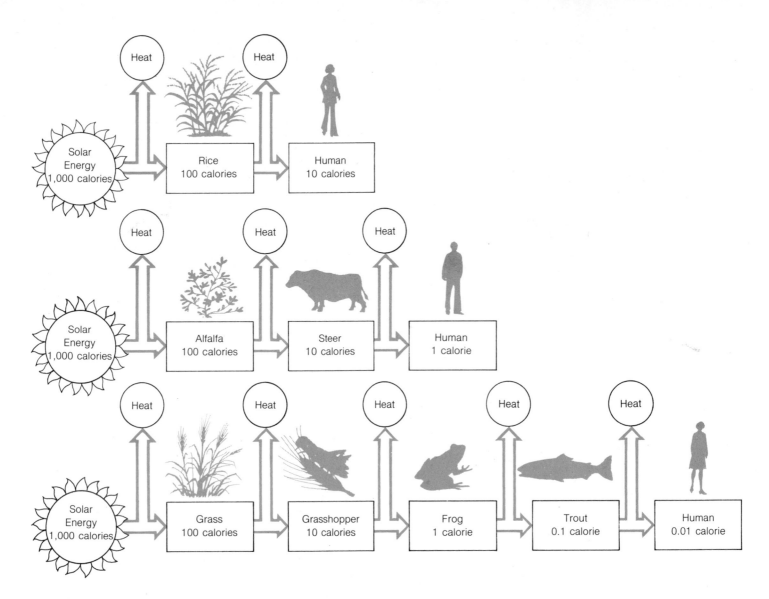

Figure 3–9 In a food chain only about 10 percent of the energy available is transferred from one trophic level to another. Because of the second law of energy, the other 90 percent of the energy is degraded to heat and lost to the environment. (Actual energy transfer values vary somewhat from the average values shown.)

serious problems with this idea. First, we must note that organisms, populations, and ecosystems all have certain limits of tolerance. Second, ecosystems do not have the decomposers and other mechanisms for coping with many of the synthetic chemicals produced by humans. Third, populations could evolve so that ecosystems could digest these new chemicals and absorb many of today's environmental insults—but for most populations (especially the human population) these evolutionary changes would take hundreds of thousands if not millions of years, and many people would have to die.

Thus we are left with the problem of trying to understand just how various environmental stresses affect ecosystems. Table 3–1 summarizes what can happen to organisms, populations, and ecosystems if one or more limits of tolerance are exceeded (Darnell 1973, Loucks 1972, Stumm 1977, Woodwell 1970a).

The stresses that can cause the changes shown in Table 3–1 may result from natural or geological hazards, such as earthquakes, volcanic eruptions, hurricanes, tornadoes, drought, floods, and forest or brush fires ignited by lightning. Stresses also come from human activities such as industrialization, urbanization, transportation, agriculture, and other land-clearing activities.

Humans and Ecosystems In modifying ecosystems for our own use we simplify them. Every dam, cornfield, highway, pipeline and irrigation project, and use of insecticides makes ecosystems simpler. We bulldoze fields and forests containing thousands of interrelated plant and animal species and cover the land with buildings, highways, or fields containing single crops of wheat, rice, or corn that sometimes stretch as far as the eye can see. Modern agriculture consists of deliberately keeping ecosystems in early or immature states of succession, where net productivity of one or only a few plant species (such as corn or wheat) is high. But due to their simplicity, such fast-growing, single-crop systems (monocultures) are highly vulnerable. Weeds and just a single disease or pest can wipe out an entire crop unless we protect the crop with chemicals such

as pesticides (pest-killing chemicals) and herbicides (weed-killing chemicals) and support the crop's growth with chemicals such as water and synthetic fertilizers. Modern agriculture also requires large amounts of fossil fuel energy to make fertilizers, pesticides, and other agricultural chemicals and to run the tractors and other machines used to plant, protect, and harvest the crops (Figure 3–10). When quickly breeding insects develop genetic resistance to some pesticides, we often use stronger and stronger pesticides. This can kill other species that prey on the pests, thus simplifying the ecosystem even further and allowing the pest population to grow even larger and to become more genetically resistant.

It is not only cultivation that simplifies ecosystems. The sheep rancher doesn't want bison competing with the sheep for grass, so the bison must be eliminated. So must the wolf, coyote, eagle, and any other predator that occasionally kills sheep. We also tend to overfish and overhunt some species to extinction or near extinction. A living species is a nonrenewable resource that carries valuable genetic information developed through thousands or millions of years of evolution. Once extinct it is gone forever. Species become extinct naturally, but we often deliberately or accidentally kill off species. Since 1600, humans have exterminated over 300 different species of mammals and birds (Dasmann 1970, Utetz & Johnson 1974). Today at least 900 animal and 20,000 plant species are endangered, and the lists are growing (Ehrenfeld 1970, Fisher et al. 1969, IUCN *Red Data Books,* Olsen 1971, Simon & Geroudet 1970).

There is nothing wrong with converting a reasonable number of mature ecosystems into immature ecosystems in order to provide food for the human population. But the price we must pay for simplifying mature ecosystems includes matter and energy resources, time, and money needed to maintain and protect these vulnerable systems, as summarized in Table 3–2.

Table 3–1 Some Effects of Environmental Stress

Organism Level

Physiological and chemical changes
Psychological disorders
Fewer or no offspring
Genetic defects (mutagenic effects)
Birth defects (teratogenic effects)
Cancers (carcinogenic effects)
Death

Population Level

Population decrease
Excessive population increase (if natural predators are eliminated
   or reduced)
Change in age structure (old, young, and weak may die)
Natural selection of genetically resistant individuals
Loss of genetic diversity and adaptability
Extinction

Community-Ecosystem Level

Disruption of energy flow
  changes in solar energy input
  changes in heat output
  changes in food webs and patterns of competition

Disruption of chemical cycles
  leaks (shifts from closed to open cycles)
  introduction of new synthetic chemicals

Simplification
  lower species diversity
  loss of sensitive species
  fewer habitats and ecological niches
  less complex food webs
  lowered stability
  partial or total collapse of structure and function of the ecosystem
  return to an earlier stage of succession

Achieving a Balance between Simplicity and Diversity
The comparison in Table 3–2 does not mean we should not simplify complex ecosystems. But there is the danger that as the human population grows, we will convert too many of the world's mature ecosystems to young, productive, but highly vulnerable ecosystems. These immature systems depend on the existence of nearby mature ecosystems. For example, simple farmlands on the plains must be balanced by diverse forests on nearby hills and mountains. These forests hold water and minerals and release them slowly to the plains below. If the forests are cut for short-term economic gain, then the water and soil will wash down the slopes in a destructive rush instead of a nourishing trickle. Thus forests must not be valued only for their short-term production of timber but also for their vital long-term

Figure 3-10 Industrialized agriculture uses energy from fossil fuels to supplement solar energy. This increases crop yields and productivity per worker, but it also increases pollution and the heat load on the environment because of energy losses required by the second law of energy (Section 2-3).

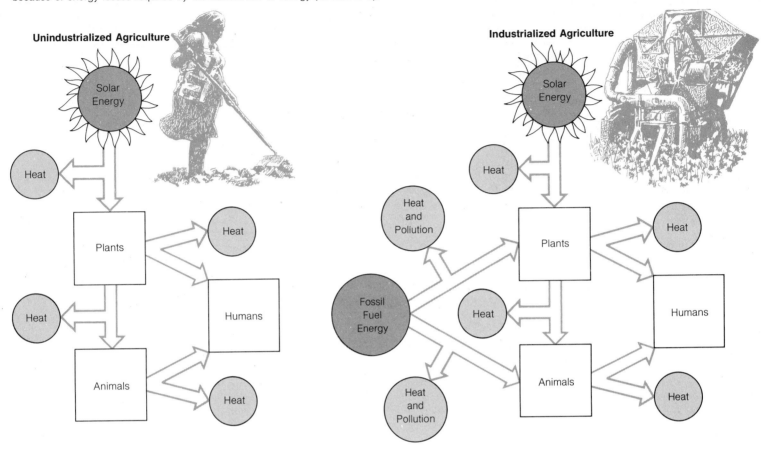

Table 3-2 Comparison of Some Properties of a Mature Natural Ecosystem and a Simplified Human System

Mature Ecosystem (marsh, grassland, forest)	Human System (cornfield, factory, house)
Captures, converts, and stores energy from the sun	Consumes energy from fossil or nuclear fuels
Produces oxygen and consumes carbon dioxide	Consumes oxygen and produces carbon dioxide
Creates fertile soil	Depletes or covers fertile soil
Stores, purifies, and releases water gradually	Often uses and contaminates water and releases it rapidly
Provides wildlife habitats	Destroys wildlife habitats
Filters and detoxifies pollutants and waste products free of charge	Produces pollutants and waste materials, much of which must be cleaned up at our expense
Capable of self-maintenance and self-renewal	Requires continual maintenance and renewal at great cost

After Rodale 1972.

role in maintaining the young productive ecosystems that supply our food. If every forest is cut down, what will carry out these vital functions?

What we must do then is to preserve a balance between young and mature ecosystems (Odum 1969). Deciding on this balance is difficult, however, since we still know so little about how ecosystems work. Biologist Paul Ehrlich has likened the ecosphere to a massive and intricate computer cross-linking a vast array of transistors and other electrical components. Even though we do not really understand it, and even though our lives depend on it, we are busy simplifying this complex network by randomly pulling out transistors and by overloading and disconnecting various parts and circuits. Slowly we are beginning to realize that we are playing an ecological Russian roulette, hoping that the computer whose workings we don't understand will not break down as we tinker with it.

In addition to preserving biological diversity, we also need to preserve human cultural diversity to help maintain our mental health and to keep life from being boring (Dasmann 1970, Watt 1972a). Think what life would be like if everyone on the planet looked alike. As Lewis Mumford put it most eloquently at a conference in 1965:

> When we rally to preserve the remaining redwood forests or to protect the whooping crane, we are rallying to preserve ourselves, we are trying to keep in existence the organic variety, the whole span of natural resources upon which our own future development will be based. If we surrender this variety too easily in one place, we shall lose it everywhere; and we shall find ourselves enclosed in technological prison, without even the hope that sustains a prisoner in jail—that someday we may get out.

Some Lessons from Ecology   What can we learn from the brief overview of ecological principles presented in the past few chapters? It should be clear that ecology forces us to recognize three major features of all life: *interdependence, diversity,* and *limits.* Its message is not that we should avoid change, but that we should recognize that human-induced changes can have far-reaching and often unpredictable consequences and that there are important limits to what we can and cannot do to ecosystems. Ecology is a call for wisdom, care, and restraint as we alter the ecosphere.

What has gone wrong, probably, is that we have failed to see ourselves as part of a large and indivisible whole. For too long we have based our lives on a primitive feeling that our "God-given" role was to have "dominion over the fish of the sea and over the fowl of the air and over every living thing that moveth upon the earth." We have failed to understand that the earth does not belong to us, but we to the earth.

Rolf Edberg (1969)

Discussion Topics

1. **a.** How would you set up a self-sustaining aquarium for tropical fish? Suppose you had a balanced aquarium with a transparent glass top used to seal it.

   b. Can life continue in the aquarium indefinitely as long as the sun shines regularly on it?

   c. Which of the following will probably be the limiting factor—the oxygen supply in the air above the water, the original oxygen supply dissolved in the water, or the supply of nitrogen in soil at the bottom?

2. A friend cleans out your aquarium and removes all of the soil and plants, leaving only the fish and water. What will happen?

3. **a.** A popular bumper sticker asks, "Have you thanked a green plant today?" Give two reasons for thanking a green plant.

   b. Trace back the materials comprising the sticker and see whether the sticker itself represents a sound application of the slogan.

4. Why can't energy be recycled in an ecosystem?

5. Would you rather be exposed to electromagnetic radiation with a short or long wavelength? High or low frequency? Explain why people who spend a lot of time getting suntans may get skin cancer.

6. Using the second law of thermodynamics, explain why there is such a sharp decrease in usable energy along each step of a food chain. Doesn't an energy loss at each step violate the first law of thermodynamics? Explain.

7. Using the second law of thermodynamics, explain why people in the poorer nations of the world must exist primarily on a vegetarian diet.

8. Describe how urban systems and natural ecosystems are similar and how they differ.

Further Readings

Billings, W. D. 1970. *Plants, Man, and the Ecosystem.* 2nd ed. Belmont, Calif.: Wadsworth. See especially the discussion of biomes in Chapter 7.

Clapham, W. B., Jr. 1973. *Natural Ecosystems.* New York: Macmillan. Excellent introduction to ecology at a slightly higher level.

Colinvaux, Paul A. 1973. *Introduction to Ecology.* New York: Wiley. Excellent basic text using the evolutionary approach.

Commoner, Barry. 1970. "The Ecological Facts of Life." In H. D. Johnson, ed., *No Deposit—No Return.* Reading, Mass.: Addison-Wesley. Excellent simplified summary of ecological principles.

Darling, Lois, and Louis Darling. 1968. *A Place in the Sun.* New York: Morrow. Beautifully done, simple introduction to ecology.

Darnell, Rezneat M. 1973. *Ecology and Man.* Dubuque, Iowa: Wm. C. Brown. Outstanding introduction to ecological principles. Highly recommended.

Ehrlich, Paul R., Anne H. Ehrlich, and John P. Holdren. 1977. *Ecoscience: Population, Resources and Environment.* San Francisco: Freeman. Superb, more detailed text at a higher level.

Emlen, J. M. 1973. *Ecology: An Evolutionary Approach.* Reading, Mass.: Addison-Wesley. Very good higher-level text using the evolutionary approach.

Kormondy, Edward J. 1976. *Concepts of Ecology.* 2nd ed. Englewood Cliffs, N. J.: Prentice-Hall. First-rate introduction at a slightly higher level.

McHale, John. 1970. *The Ecological Context.* New York: Braziller. Highly recommended. Superb diagrams and summaries of ecosphere data.

Metillo, Jerry M. 1972. *Ecology Primer.* West Haven, Conn.: Pendulum Press. Very readable introduction.

Miller, G. Tyler, Jr. 1979. *Living in the Environment.* 2nd ed. Belmont, Calif.: Wadsworth. My own more detailed introductory text discussing ecological concepts and environmental problems and possible solutions.

Odum, Eugene P. 1975. *Ecology.* 2nd ed. New York: Holt, Rinehart and Winston. Superb short introduction.

Odum, Eugene P. 1971. *Fundamentals of Ecology.* 3rd ed. Philadelphia: Saunders. Probably the outstanding textbook on ecology by one of our most prominent ecologists.

Reid, Keith. 1970. *Nature's Network.* Garden City, N.Y.: Natural History Press. Beautifully done introduction to ecology. See Chapter 8 on succession and Appendix 1 on biomes.

Richardson, Jonathan L. 1977. *Dimensions of Ecology.* Baltimore: Williams & Wilkins. Excellent brief introductory text.

Ricklefs, Robert E. 1976. *The Economy of Nature.* Portland, Ore.: Chiron Press. Beautifully written introduction to ecology at a slightly higher level.

Scientific American. 1970. *The Biosphere.* San Francisco: Freeman. Excellent introduction to chemical cycling and energy flow.

Smith, Robert L. 1974. *Ecology and Field Biology.* 2nd ed. New York: Harper & Row. An excellent basic text in ecology using the ecosystem approach.

Smith, Robert L. 1976. *The Ecology of Man: An Ecosystem Approach.* 2nd ed. New York: Harper & Row. Probably the best collection of selected ecological articles with excellent introductory commentaries.

Southwick, Charles H. 1976. *Ecology and the Quality of the Environment.* 2nd ed. New York: Van Nostrand Reinhold. Very readable introduction to human ecology.

Sutton, David B., and N. Paul Harmon. 1973. *Ecology: Selected Controls.* New York: Wiley. Superb self-study guide for the material in this chapter and Chapters 5 and 6.

Watt, Kenneth E. F. 1973. *Principles of Environmental Science.* New York: McGraw-Hill. Outstanding discussion of ecological principles at a higher level.

4

Present and Future Energy Options: An Overview

4–1 Applying Energy Concepts: Energy Quality and Energy Efficiency

Energy Quality   Since we cannot create or destroy energy (Section 2–2), we never really consume energy. Instead we consume **energy quality,** the ability of a form of energy to do useful work for us. According to the second law of energy (Section 2–3), whenever we use any form of energy it is automatically degraded to a lower-quality or less useful form of energy—usually low-temperature heat energy that flows into the environment. As shown in Table 4–1, different forms of energy vary in their energy quality. High or very high quality energy (such as electricity, oil, gasoline, uranium, and high-temperature heat) is concentrated. By contrast, low-quality energy (such as sunlight and low-temperature heat) is dispersed, or dilute. Note that the usefulness of a form of energy is determined by its quality, not its quantity. A kilocalorie of dispersed heat energy at room temperature or a kilocalorie of dispersed solar energy cannot do much (if any) work. But a kilocalorie of high-temperature heat energy released when a fossil fuel is burned or when the nuclei of uranium atoms undergo nuclear fission is a concentrated form of very useful energy.

Unfortunately, many of the best forms of high to very high quality energy (such as high-temperature heat, electricity, hydrogen gas, concentrated sunlight, synthetic oil, and synthetic natural gas) do not occur naturally. We must use other forms of high-quality energy (such as fossil or nuclear fuels) either to produce them or to upgrade their quality. Other forms of very high to high quality energy (such as nuclear energy from fission, nuclear fusion, and burning of fossil fuels) take large quantities of high-quality energy to find and extract the fuels and to build and run environmentally acceptable power plants.

It is wasteful to use high or very high quality energy to perform a task that only requires low- or moderate-quality energy. Thus, *an important way to reduce energy waste is to supply energy only in the quality needed for the task at hand* (Berg 1974b, Commoner 1976, Lovins 1976, 1977a, 1977c, 1978a). For example, using very high quality electrical energy merely to heat a home to 20°C (68°F) or to provide hot water at 60°C (140°F) is extremely wasteful. First, at a power plant, high-quality fossil fuel or nuclear energy is converted to high-quality heat energy at several thousand degrees with an automatic loss of some of the heat to the local environment, as required by the second energy law, or "heat tax." Then the remaining high-quality heat is used to spin turbines to produce very high quality electrical energy, with a further loss of heat. More degraded energy or heat is lost when the electricity is transmitted to a home. There the high-quality electrical energy is converted back to low-quality heat energy to heat the home or provide hot water. According to energy expert Amory Lovins (1977a), "This is like using a chain saw to cut butter."

We can save some energy by burning fossil fuels directly in a home furnace or hot water heater rather than at a power plant to make electricity. But even this process wastes large amounts of energy by burning the fuels at about 2,000° to 3,000°C to heat a house to 20°C or water to 60°C. Instead it will be less wasteful and cheaper in the long run (if fossil fuel energy prices are not kept artificially low) to heat a home or water by collecting solar energy at normal outside temperatures (typically 0°C to 19°C) and concentrating or upgrading its quality to slightly higher temperature heat energy that can be used directly or to help drive a heat pump (Berg 1974a, Derven 1976, Gilmore 1978).[1]

First Law Energy Efficiency   Another way to cut energy waste and save money (at least in the long run) is to use an

---

[1]A heat pump is essentially an air conditioner run in reverse. The device extracts heat from a low-temperature reservoir (the atmosphere or body of water) and uses energy (which can be supplied by electricity, natural gas, or concentrated solar or wind energy) to inject this heat into a higher-temperature reservoir (a home or hot water heater). A refrigerator is a well-known example of a heat pump.

Table 4–1 Energy Quality of Different Forms of Energy

Form of Energy	Energy Quality	
	Relative Value	Average Energy Content (kilocalories per kilogram)
Very high temperature heat (greater than 2,500 °C)	Very high	—
Electricity	Very high	—
Nuclear fission (uranium)	Very high	139,000,000*
Nuclear fusion (deuterium)	Very high	24,000,000†
High-temperature heat (1,000°–2,500 °C)	High	—
Hydrogen gas	High	30,000
Natural gas (mostly methane)	High	13,000
SNG (synthetic natural gas made from coal)	High	13,000
Gasoline (refined crude oil)	High	10,500
Crude oil	High	10,300
LNG (liquefied natural gas)	High	10,300
Coal (bituminous and anthracite)	High	7,000
Synthetic oil (made from coal)	High	8,900
Highly concentrated sunlight	High	—
Wind (high-velocity flow)	Moderate	—
Geothermal (high-velocity flow)	Moderate	—
Water (high-velocity flow)	Moderate	—
Moderate-temperature heat (100°–1,000 °C)	Moderate	—
Concentrated sunlight	Moderate	—
Dung	Moderate	4,000
Wood and crop wastes	Moderate	3,300
Assorted garbage and trash	Moderate	2,900
Oil shale	Moderate	1,100
Tar sands	Moderate	1,100
Peat	Moderate	950
Sunlight (normal)	Low	—
Wind (low-velocity flow)	Low	—
Water (low-velocity flow)	Low	—
Geothermal (low-velocity flow)	Low	—
Low-temperature heat (air temperature to 100 °C or lower)	Low	—

Sources: American Physical Society 1975, Berg 1974b, Cook 1976b, Dyson 1971, Hammond & Baron 1976, Odum 1971a, Odum & Odum 1976, Ross & Williams 1976, 1977b.
*Per kilogram of uranium metal containing 0.72% fissionable uranium-235.
†Per kilogram of hydrogen containing 0.015% deuterium.

energy conversion device (such as a light, home heating system, or automobile engine) that is as efficient as possible. We can define two types of energy efficiency, one based on the first energy law (Section 2–2) and the other on the second energy law (Section 2–3).

The **first law energy efficiency** is the ratio of the useful energy (or work) output to the total energy (or work) input for an energy conversion device or process. Normally this energy ratio is multiplied by 100 so that the efficiency can be expressed as a percentage:

first law energy efficiency (%)

$$= \frac{\text{useful energy (or work) energy output}}{\text{total energy (or work) input}} \times 100$$

For any conversion of heat to work, the first law efficiency will always be less than 100 percent, partly because of the automatic heat loss imposed by the second law of energy and partly because of imperfections and unnecessary waste in energy conversion devices and systems. Conversion of electrical energy to heat or mechanical work is not governed by the second energy law; thus, energy efficiencies can be 100 percent for electric motors and as high as 300 percent for an electric heat pump that merely moves heat from outside air to inside air without having to convert it from one energy form to another.

Improved technology has greatly increased the energy efficiency of many devices, but there is considerable room for improvement. When energy was cheap, industrialized nations often found it cheaper to use inefficient devices that were less costly. For example, the incandescent light bulb is only 5 percent efficient. For every 100 kilocalories of electrical energy supplied to the bulb, 95 kilocalories are degraded to low-quality heat and only 5 percent is converted to light.

first law efficiency of incandescent light bulb
$$= \frac{5 \text{ kcal of light energy}}{100 \text{ kcal of electrical energy}} \times 100 = 5\%$$

At present, the incandescent light bulb—which should really be called a heat bulb—is used for 95 percent of all home lighting in the United States. A fluorescent light bulb has a first law efficiency of about 22 percent—over 4 times that of the incandescent bulb—but its long length and bulky starting equipment have prevented it from being widely used. This could change, however, with a new type of fluorescent light bulb called the Litek, which became available in 1979. It looks like an ordinary screw-in incandescent bulb and doesn't have the bulky starting equipment of conventional fluorescents. A 75-watt Litek costs about $7.50 to $10.00, compared with about 75¢ for a 75-watt incandescent bulb, but a Litek will last about 10 years or more compared with about 6 months for the incandescent. This much longer life plus its use of 70 percent less electricity than the incandescent bulb means that the Litek will be cheaper to use over a 10-year period. If all homes in the United States switched to these more efficient bulbs, the resulting energy savings would be equivalent to 80 million liters (500,000 barrels) of oil *each day* (Staff report 1976b).

To evaluate total energy efficiency, obtaining the efficiency of the energy device alone is not sufficient. We must also evaluate the whole system of energy conversion steps—from finding and processing a fuel to transporting it, upgrading it to a more useful form, and finally using it. Figure 4–1 compares the net first law energy efficiencies for entire home heating systems. From this figure we see that in terms of first law efficiency, heating a home with electricity from a hydroelectric plant is the best choice, but unfortunately most homes are not near a fast-flowing river that can be dammed. Using electricity made from natural gas to drive a home heat pump is the next best choice, but natural gas is too scarce to burn in an electric power plant. This leaves us with either using electricity made from coal to drive a heat pump or burning natural gas directly in a home furnace. Another possibility not shown in Figure 4–1 is a solar heating system, but in many areas it has to be backed up with another conventional system or a large energy storage system to allow for a string of cloudy days. Another choice would be a solar-assisted heat pump; in this system solar energy provides much of the heat, and an electric heat pump kicks in when there is not enough sunshine. Note that the poorest choices for home heating systems in terms of net first law efficiency are electric heating based on oil-burning or nuclear power plants or home oil furnaces.

Figure 4–2 shows a similar comparison for automobiles with various types of engines. Note that the overall first law efficiency for a car powered with a conventional internal combustion engine is only about 2 percent. In other words, about 98 percent of the energy in crude oil is wasted by the time it is converted to gasoline and then burned to move a car. Most other engine systems are only about 1 to 3 percent efficient except for the 12 percent efficiency of an electric engine recharged by electricity from a hydroelectric power plant. But as mentioned before, hydroelectric power plants cannot serve most areas. In addition, present batteries limit electric cars to low speeds and allow only a short range before recharging.

Heat pumps, solar heating systems, and appliances and automobile engines with high-energy efficiencies tend to be more expensive than conventional and less efficient systems. But over their lifetimes most energy efficient devices end up saving both energy and money. *In buying any energy conversion device, it is the lifetime (or life cycle) cost—not the initial cost—that determines whether it is a bargain:*

lifetime cost = initial cost + lifetime operating cost

The average first law efficiency for all energy used in the United States in 1976 was about 31 percent (Cook 1976b, Staff report 1977d) (Figure 4–3). In other words, almost two-thirds of all the energy used in 1976 was lost to the environment as low-quality heat without performing any useful function. Part of this loss resulted from the automatic "heat tax" imposed by the second energy law, part from using unnecessarily wasteful energy systems, and part from not using well-known energy conservation techniques, such as insulation, natural ventilation, reduced lighting levels, and aligning buildings to take advantage of sunlight (as discussed in more detail in Section 5–1). The most visible symbol of energy waste, an all-glass office building lit by windows that cannot be opened, heated and cooled by blowers rather than by nature, and ablaze with light throughout the night, is now recognized as an ecological and economic disaster.

Second Law Energy Efficiency The concept of first law energy efficiency does not distinguish between the automatic losses imposed by the second energy law and those that result from using wasteful or imperfect energy systems. To get a better picture of energy loss and waste, we can use the **second law energy efficiency** (American Physical Society 1975, Commoner 1976, Metz 1975, Ross & Williams 1976, 1977b, Study Group on Technical Aspects of Efficient Energy Utilization 1975). It is the ratio of the minimum amount of useful energy (or work) theoretically needed to perform a task to the actual amount needed.

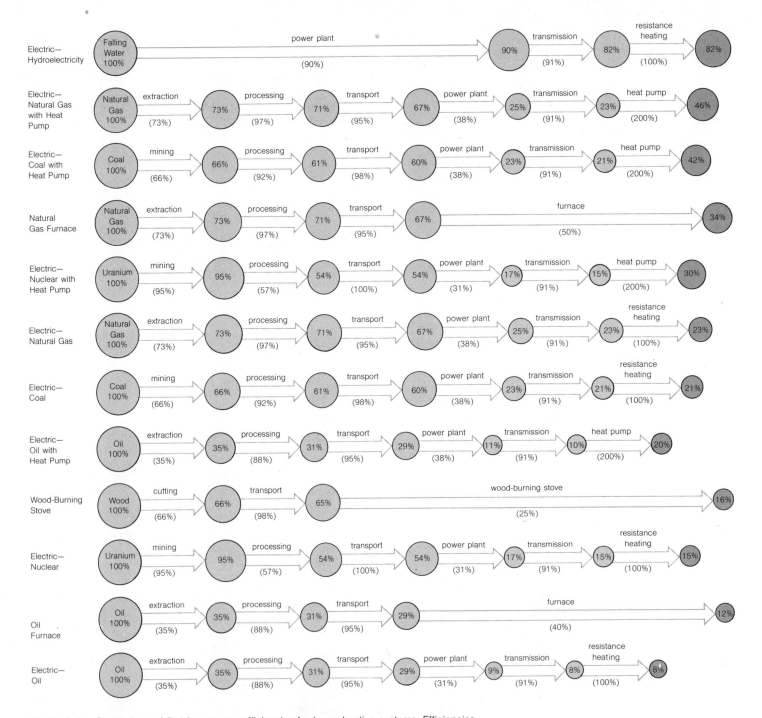

Figure 4–1 Comparison of first law energy efficiencies for home heating systems. Efficiencies between steps are shown in parentheses, and cumulative net efficiencies for the system are shown inside the circles. Each step having an efficiency less than 100% loses low-quality heat energy to the environment. (Data from Cook 1976b, Council on Environmental Quality 1973)

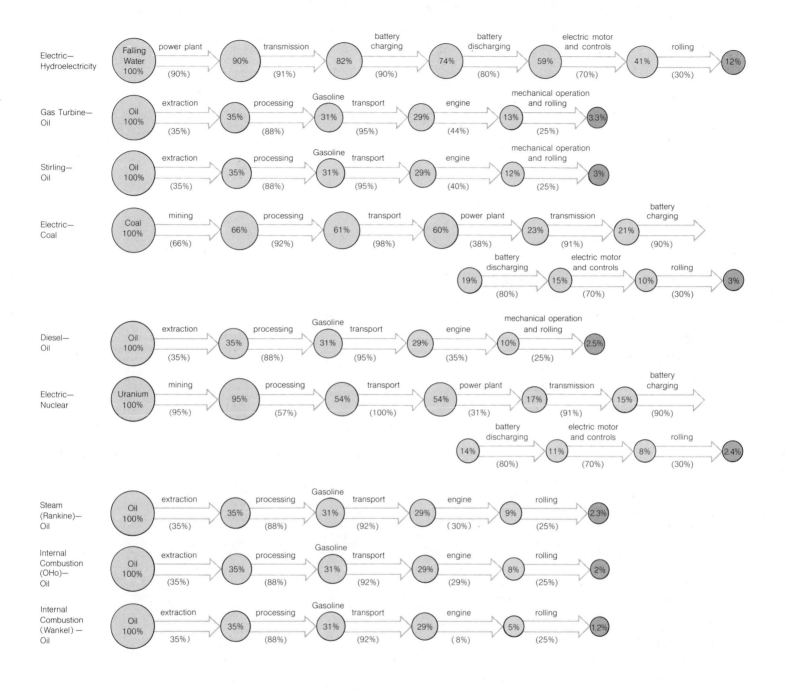

Figure 4–2 Comparison of first law energy efficiencies for automobile engine systems. Efficiencies between steps are shown in parentheses, and cumulative net efficiencies are shown inside the circles. At each step low-quality heat energy is lost to the environment. (Data from Cook 1976b, Wilson 1978)

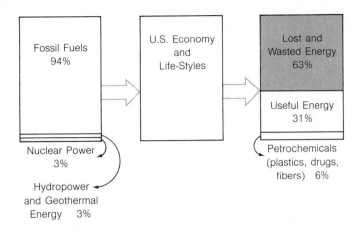

Figure 4-3 Energy flow in the United States during 1976 based on overall first law energy efficiency. (Data from Cook 1976b, Staff report 1977d)

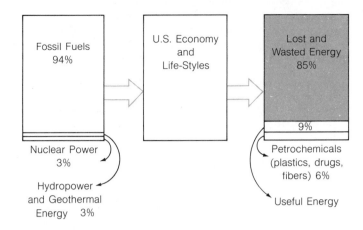

Figure 4-4 Energy flow in the United States during 1976 based on overall second law energy efficiency. (Data from American Physical Society 1975, Ross & Williams 1977b)

This ratio shows how far the performance of an energy device or system falls short of what is theoretically possible according to the second energy law.

second law energy efficiency (%)

$$= \frac{\text{minimum amount of useful energy (or work)}}{\substack{\text{actual amount of useful energy} \\ \text{(or work) needed to perform a task}}} \times 100$$

Table 4-2 shows estimates of second law energy efficiencies for various energy systems in the United States. The overall second law efficiency for annual energy use in the United States is about 10 to 15%, with about 90 to 85 percent of all used energy lost or wasted (Figure 4-4). In other words, the efficiency of energy systems in the United States can be improved significantly. Of course, some improvements in efficiency are too expensive, even when lifetime costs are taken into account (Berndt 1978). But it is estimated that about 25 to 45 percent of the present energy waste in the United States could be eliminated with no major changes in the standard of living (American Physical Society 1975, Hayes 1976a, Ross & Williams 1976, 1977b, Schipper 1976a, 1976b).

4-2 Net Useful Energy: It Takes Energy to Get Energy

The two energy laws, which can't be repealed, tell us that the only energy that really counts is *net* useful energy—not *gross* or *total* useful energy (Clark 1974b, Georgescu-Roegen 1971, 1975, 1976, Gilliland 1975, Odum 1971a, 1973, Odum & Odum 1976, Price 1974, Robertson 1975, Wilson 1977). **Net useful energy** is the total useful energy of a resource as it is found in nature *minus* the useful energy used to find, extract, and process it, to upgrade energy quality, to meet

environmental and safety requirements, and to deliver the energy to the user and *minus* the useful energy lost as a result of the second energy law and the use of unnecessarily inefficient and wasteful energy systems.

net useful energy

$$= \substack{\text{total useful} \\ \text{energy} } - \substack{\text{useful energy to find,} \\ \text{prepare, upgrade, and} \\ \text{deliver the energy in} \\ \text{a useful form}} - \substack{\text{useful energy} \\ \text{lost and wasted}}$$

Net useful energy is like net profit. If you have a business with a total annual income of $100,000 but it costs you $90,000 a year to operate, then your net profit is only

Table 4-2 Estimated Second Law Energy Efficiencies for U.S. Energy Systems

Use	Second Law Energy Efficiency (percent)
All uses	10-15
Space heating	
Heat pump	9
Furnace	5-6
Electric resistance	2.5
Water heating	
Gas	3
Electric	1.5
Air conditioning	4.5
Refrigeration	4
Automobile	8-10
Power plants	33
Steel production	23
Aluminum production	13
Oil refining	9

Sources: American Physical Society 1975, Metz 1975, Ross & Williams 1977b.

$10,000 a year. With operating expenses of $110,000 a year, you would have a net loss of $10,000 a year. If you had $200,000 in savings, you could use this capital to subsidize your losses. Within 20 years, however, you would go bankrupt and have no capital left to invest in a more profitable business.

We can apply a similar analysis to energy use. The remaining fossil fuels are our useful energy capital or savings account—deposited for us free by nature over millions of years. At present rates of use we will probably use up our oil and natural gas energy capital within 40 to 80 years and deplete our coal energy capital within 200 to 400 years. At present we are spending (burning up) all this capital at a high rate to provide us with a daily supply of high-quality energy. But we must also invest some of this irreplaceable energy capital to subsidize the development and use of new energy sources before our fossil fuel energy capital is gone. If we use most of our remaining fossil fuel (and monetary) capital to develop energy alternatives that have a low or negative yield of net useful energy, then we will have squandered the source of useful energy capital that we need to make the transition to a new earthmanship energy era.

For example, if we must use 9 units of fossil fuel (or other high-quality energy) to deliver 10 units of nuclear, solar, or additional fossil fuel energy (perhaps from a deep oil well at sea or in the Arctic or from oil shale), then our net useful energy gain is only 1 unit—a poor long-term energy and financial investment of fossil fuel capital. Putting in 11 units of useful fossil fuel energy to get back 10 units of higher-quality energy (such as electricity) may be desirable to satisfy social needs. But it is an energy and economic disaster if the supplies of fossil fuel energy capital that are used to subsidize this net energy loss system run out.

This situation is much worse if we look at the entire food system in the United States. If one counts the fossil fuel energy input used to grow, process, package, transport, refrigerate, and cook all plant and animal food in the United States, *it takes about 9 calories of fossil fuel energy to put 1 calorie of food energy on the table*—an energy loss of 8 calories per calorie of food energy (Hirst 1974, Pimentel et al. 1973, Steinhart & Steinhart 1974a, 1974b). To feed the entire world using the same energy-intensive agriculture practiced in the United States would greatly increase environmental pollution, consume 80 percent of all energy used in the world each year (Pimentel et al. 1973), and deplete the world's known oil reserves in only 13 years (Pimentel et al. 1975). Nevertheless, without fossil fuels the present agricultural system in industrialized nations would collapse, precipitating a sharp drop in food production and population size.

Concentrating and upgrading dispersed solar energy slightly to heat homes and hot water is desirable from a net energy standpoint, compared with more wasteful alternatives such as electric resistance heating. But the concept of net energy explains why large-scale electric power plants powered by solar energy may not be feasible. Solar energy is abundant and free, but it is so widely dispersed that collecting and concentrating it to create high-quality heat will be very costly and probably involve a net energy loss (Odum 1973, Odum & Odum 1976). There is also controversy over the net energy yield of conventional nuclear fission energy. Because of the fossil fuel energy inputs used for (1) mining uranium ore, (2) processing and upgrading uranium fuels, (3) building and operating very costly nuclear power plants, (4) meeting complex safety and environmental costs, (5) transporting, reprocessing, and storing nuclear fuels and radioactive wastes, and (6) decommissioning the highly radioactive plants after their 30-year lifetime, the net useful energy yield for the entire system (not just the plant itself) over the plant's lifetime is probably low (Lovins 1975, 1978a, Lovins & Price 1975, Odum 1973, Odum & Odum 1976). Some estimates, however, indicate that the net useful energy yield is moderate to high (Ott 1976, Rotty et al. 1975, Wright & Syrett 1975), but it is not clear whether these estimates evaluated the entire system.[2]

Some additional high net energy yield deposits of fossil fuels, such as Middle East oil, will be found in the future. But most of the accessible and richer deposits have already been found and are being rapidly depleted (Cook 1976b). To find the remaining oil and natural gas, we have to drill and dig deeper into the earth or into the sea bottom, tap into more diluted deposits, and develop deposits in areas (such as Alaska and the Arctic) that are far from where the energy is needed. As a result, even though total and per capita energy use in the world (Figure 1–4) and the United States (Figure 1–5) are increasing, the total and per capita net useful energy yields are decreasing (Dupree & West 1972, Odum 1973). We are having to use more and more of the remaining high-quality fossil fuel energy (and money) to find and deliver new deposits of fossil fuel and other types of energy (Figure 4–5). In 1978 about one-fourth of the energy consumption in the United States was used to mine, extract, concentrate, and transport fuels, and by the year 2000 this figure could rise to more than a third (Brown 1978a). As a result, more of the available money will be used to pay for lower net useful energy yields, so that inflation will increase (Figure 4–5) and average per capita well-being will decline.

---

[2]At present, different and often conflicting estimates of net energy yields of energy systems occur primarily because people making the estimates have not consistently used a recommended set of guidelines (International Federation of Institutes for Advanced Study 1974) that define what energy inputs shall be included or omitted. Also, people disagree on estimates of some of the inputs. As net useful energy analysis improves in coming years, many of these difficulties and conflicting claims will be resolved.

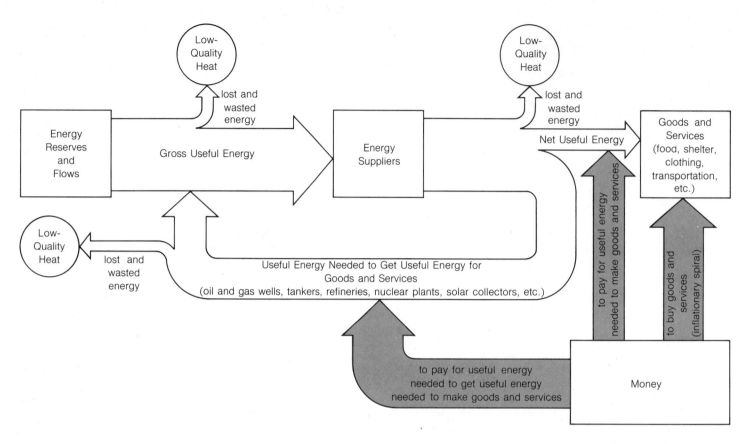

Figure 4-5 Net useful energy and money. Because we can't beat the first and second laws of energy, as energy supplies become harder to find, process, and deliver, the net useful energy yield decreases. As a result, more and more dollars are used to get the useful energy needed for basic goods and services, so that inflation increases and average per capita well-being decreases.

At present, the estimated supplies of nonrenewable energy resources are calculated as proven or expected *total energy* supply (Figure 6–4), not as the more realistic *net useful energy* supply. Thus, reserves that are supposed to offer so many years of supply will be gone sooner than present estimates show (Odum 1973).

Net useful energy analysis, if done under a consistent set of guidelines, is a very important tool in helping us to evaluate possible energy alternatives and to invest our limited fossil fuel and monetary capital wisely, as discussed in Howard T. Odum's Guest Editorial at the end of this chapter. But it is not a panacea. The most efficient use of energy in terms of physical laws may not always match up with what people and governments consider to be the most efficient social or economic use of an energy resource (Boulding 1977, Huettner 1976). For example, homeowners may find electric heating so convenient and maintenance free (at least at the home site) that they exert political pressure to maintain electricity at artificially low prices and have the losses made up by government subsidies.

4–3 Energy Alternatives: An Overview

Overall Evaluation In evaluating possible energy alternatives, we have to think and plan in three time frames: the short term (1980 to 1990), the intermediate term (1990 to 2005), and the long term (2005 to 2030). For each alternative we need to know the total estimated supply available in each time frame, the estimated net useful energy yield, projected costs for development, and potential environmental impact for the entire energy system.[3] Table 4–3 gives an overall evaluation of energy alternatives for the world, and Table 4–4 provides a slightly more detailed evaluation of energy alternatives for the United States.

---

[3]It may not be possible to prevent or control some of the adverse environmental impacts that result from developing and using an energy resource. Those controls that are possible, however, will add to the cost and cause some decrease in net useful energy yields.

Figure 4–6 The environmental effects of resource use.

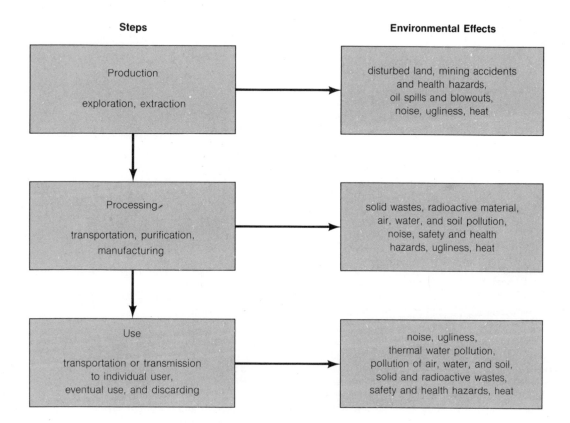

We can draw three important conclusions from Tables 4–3 and 4–4:

1. The best short-, intermediate-, and long-term alternative for the United States (and other industrialized nations) is energy conservation. It extends the supplies of fossil fuels, buys time to develop other energy alternatives, saves money, and reduces environmental impact by decreasing energy use and waste. Indeed, it is estimated that the United States could meet all of its energy needs between 1980 and 2005 by implementing a strong and comprehensive energy conservation program (Hayes 1976a).

2. Total systems for future energy alternatives in the world and the United States will probably have low to moderate net useful energy yields and high to very high development costs. Since there may not be enough capital available to develop all alternative energy systems, they must be carefully chosen now so that capital will not be depleted on systems that will yield too little net useful energy or prove to be environmentally unacceptable (Lovins 1976, 1977c, 1978a). Even if there is no shortage of capital, lending institutions may be unwilling to make loans to energy companies for investment in risky long-term energy development schemes (Pelley et al. 1976).

3. In the future, energy should be provided by a diverse mix of alternative sources based on local availability and conditions rather than relying primarily on one resource (such as our present primary dependence on oil).

4–4 Environmental Impact of Energy Alternatives

In accordance with the second law of energy, using any form of energy or nonrenewable metal or mineral resource has some environmental impact (Figure 4–6), and the faster the rate of energy use or flow, the greater the impact (Figure 2–4). This is why energy use permeates almost every phase of the environmental crisis and is directly or indirectly responsible for most land disruption, water pollution, and air pollution. For example, nearly 80 percent of all U.S. air pollution is caused by fuel combustion in cars, furnaces, industries, and power plants (Stoker et al. 1975). Electric power plants (mostly coal burning) account for more air pollution than any other source except cars; this pollution includes 55 percent of the nation's sulfur oxides, 25 percent of the soot (particulates), and 25 percent of the nitrogen oxides. Electric power plants (coal and nuclear) are

Table 4-3 Evaluation of Energy Alternatives for the World

Energy Resource	Advantages	Disadvantages
Nonrenewable Resources		
Fossil fuels Petroleum	1. Can be used in stationary (power plants) and mobile (cars) systems 2. Technology well developed 3. Relatively cheap (but prices rising rapidly) 4. Fairly easy to transport within and between nations 5. High net useful energy yield 6. Moderate environmental impact	1. Supply may be depleted within 40 to 80 years 2. Net useful energy yield will decline and prices will rise as more accessible deposits are depleted 3. Production of carbon dioxide when fuel is burned could alter global climate
Natural gas	1. Technology well developed 2. Fairly easy to transport within nations 3. Relatively cheap (but prices rising rapidly) 4. High net useful energy yield 5. Low environmental impact	1. Supply may be depleted within 40 to 80 years 2. Net useful energy yield will decline and prices will rise as more accessible deposits are depleted 3. Difficult and expensive to transport from one country to another as liquefied natural gas (LNG) 4. Production of carbon dioxide when fuel is burned could alter global climate
Coal	1. Technology well developed 2. Fairly easy to transport within and between nations 3. Large supplies (several hundred years) 4. High net useful energy yield 5. Relatively cheap (but prices rising rapidly) 6. May be burned in the future (20 to 50 years) with lower pollution and less waste by fluidized-bed firing and magnetohydrodynamic (MHD) generators 7. Can be converted to cleaner burning synthetic natural gas (coal gasification) or synthetic oil (coal liquefaction)	1. Very harmful environmental impact 2. Not useful for powering vehicles in solid form (but conversion to electricity can be used to recharge batteries in electric cars) 3. Net useful energy yield will decline and prices will rise as rich and accessible deposits are depleted and extensive pollution controls are implemented 4. Net useful energy yield declines and prices rise sharply when coal is converted to synthetic natural gas or oil 5. Requires large amounts of water for coal processing and cooling of power plants 6. Carbon dioxide produced when fuel is burned could alter global climate
Oil shale	1. Very large supplies if developed (100 to several hundred years) 2. Can be used in stationary and mobile systems	1. Technology not fully developed 2. High cost 3. Low to moderate net useful energy yield 4. Harmful environmental impact 5. Requires large amounts of water for processing 6. Carbon dioxide produced when fuel is burned could alter global climate
Tar sands	1. Very large supplies 2. Can be used in stationary and mobile systems	1. Technology not fully developed 2. Very high cost 3. Low net useful energy yield 4. Moderate to high environmental impact 5. Requires large amounts of water for processing 6. Carbon dioxide produced when fuel is burned could alter global climate
Nuclear energy Conventional fission (uranium and thorium)	1. Technology well developed 2. Low environmental impact on air and water and moderate impact on land if entire system operates normally	1. Uranium supplies could be depleted within 40 to 80 years 2. Costs have been rising so rapidly (even with government subsidies) that in recent years orders for most new nuclear power plants have been cancelled or scaled back 3. Low to moderate net useful energy yield, which will decline as rich and accessible uranium deposits are depleted and stricter safety and environmental standards are applied 4. Potentially very serious and long-lasting (hundreds to thousands of years) environmental impact if an accident or sabotage should melt

Table 4–3 Evaluation of Energy Alternatives for the World (continued)

Energy Resource	Advantages	Disadvantages
Conventional fission (uranium and thorium)		down nuclear plant and release deadly radioactive material or if radioactive wastes are not stored in almost absolute safety for thousands of years 5. Requires large amounts of water for cooling power plants 6. Commits future generations to storing radioactive wastes and protecting radioactive power plants for thousands of years, even if nuclear power is abandoned as an energy source 7. Cannot be used to power vehicles unless electricity is used to produce hydrogen gas or to recharge batteries
Breeder fission (uranium and thorium)	1. Extends uranium supplies to several hundred years 2. Low environmental impact on air and water and moderate impact on land if entire system operates normally	1. Technology not fully developed 2. Very high cost even with extensive government subsidies 3. Net useful energy yield unknown but probably at best moderate 4. Potentially very serious and long-lasting (thousands of years) environmental impact if an accident or sabotage should melt down nuclear plant and release deadly radioactive material, if fuel shipments are hijacked or diverted by countries to make atomic bombs, or if wastes are not stored in almost absolute safety for thousands of years 5. Requires large amounts of water for cooling power plants 6. Commits future generations to storing radioactive wastes and protecting radioactive power plants for thousands of years, even if nuclear power is abandoned as an energy source 7. Cannot be used to power vehicles unless electricity is used to produce hydrogen gas or to recharge batteries
Fusion (deuterium and lithium)	1. Almost unlimited supply of energy if fusion of deuterium (extracted from water) can be developed 2. Probably moderate environmental impact 3. Less dangerous than conventional and breeder fission because reactor meltdown could not occur, problem of theft of bomb material fuels is eliminated, and smaller quantities of radioactive wastes would be produced 4. Could be used as an almost infinite source of electricity to produce hydrogen gas for use as a fuel in vehicles when petroleum and natural gas supplies are depleted 5. Might eventually be used as a fusion torch to vaporize automobiles, bottles, and other solid wastes and convert them back to their basic elements for reuse	1. Technology extremely difficult and in very early stages of development 2. Would not supply large amounts of energy for 50 to 100 years and may never be developed 3. Development costs very high 4. Operating costs unknown but probably high 5. Net useful energy yield unknown 6. Radioactive wastes that are produced must be stored in absolute safety 7. Requires large amounts of water for cooling power plants 8. May depend on expensive or rare elements, such as helium and lithium
Geothermal energy (trapped pockets)	1. Technology fairly well developed and relatively simple 2. Low overall supply but very high in selected areas near deposits 3. Moderate environmental impact 4. Moderate cost and moderate net useful energy yield for easily accessible and large deposits	1. Only useful in selected areas 2. Must be converted to electricity at the site 3. Cannot be used to power vehicles unless electricity is used to produce hydrogen gas or to recharge batteries 4. High cost and low net useful energy yield for less accessible and small deposits 5. Requires large amounts of water for processing and cooling
Renewable Resources		
Conservation	1. Can be implemented fairly quickly 2. Technology fairly simple and well developed 3. Saves money 4. Reduces energy waste	1. Probably requires mandatory regulations since it is very hard to implement by preaching and voluntary action 2. Requires individuals to consider more complex life cycle energy costs of all energy systems and devices rather than just initial costs

Table 4–3 Evaluation of Energy Alternatives for the World (continued)

Energy Resource	Advantages	Disadvantages
Conservation	5. Reduces environmental impact by requiring less use of other energy alternatives 6. Extends useful supplies of petroleum, natural gas, and other nonrenewable energy resources 7. Very high net useful energy yield 8. Decreases heat buildup in the atmosphere from energy use	
Water power (hydroelectricity)	1. Source of energy (falling water) is free 2. Relatively low operating and maintenance costs 3. Technology well developed 4. Can be operated automatically from remote locations 5. Low overall supply but plentiful in selected areas near rivers that can be dammed 6. High net useful energy yield 7. Has a long life (50 to 300 years) 8. Low environmental impact on air and moderate impact on water 9. Decreases heat buildup in the atmosphere	1. Available in only a few selected areas 2. Most rivers near large population centers have already been dammed 3. Dams tend to fill up with silt 4. Lake destroys land ecosystems behind dam and alters those below dam 5. Moderate to very high development costs 6. Cannot be used to power vehicles unless electricity is used to produce hydrogen gas or to recharge batteries
Tidal energy	1. Source of energy (tides) is free 2. Very small overall supply, but plentiful in selected areas with very high daily tidal flows 3. Low environmental impact on air 4. Net useful energy yield unknown but probably moderate 5. Decreases heat buildup in the atmosphere from energy use	1. Available in only a few selected areas 2. Technology in early stages of development 3. Development and operating costs unknown but probably moderate to high 4. Ecology of bays and estuaries could be drastically changed and probably damaged 5. Cannot be used to power vehicles unless electricity is used to produce hydrogen gas or to recharge batteries
Ocean thermal gradients	1. Energy supply free (heat stored in the ocean) 2. Almost infinite supply in selected areas if ever developed 3. Low environmental impact on air and land 4. Decreases heat buildup in the atmosphere from energy use	1. Technology in early stages of development 2. Sites with sufficient temperature difference between surface and deep water may be limited 3. Net useful energy yield unknown but probably low to moderate 4. Development costs probably high 5. Could disrupt ocean ecosystems and affect regional and perhaps global climate 6. Cannot be used to power vehicles unless electricity is used to produce hydrogen gas or to recharge batteries
Solar energy Low-temperature heating (for homes and water)	1. Energy supply free and readily available on a sunny day 2. Technology for heating individual homes and hot water heaters is fairly simple and available and could be installed quickly if mass production lowers prices 3. Moderate net useful energy yield 4. Low environmental impact 5. Very safe energy source 6. Decreases heat buildup in the atmosphere from energy use	1. Usefulness depends on average number of days of sunlight each year 2. Supply not available at night or on cloudy days, so that fairly expensive storage systems or conventional furnaces or other backup systems must also be used 3. Production and installation costs high but should decrease with mass production 4. Cannot be used to power vehicles
High-temperature heating and production of electricity	1. Energy supply free and readily available on a sunny day 2. Moderate environmental impact 3. Very safe energy source	1. Technology in early stages of development 2. Useful only in areas with plentiful year-round sunlight 3. Supply not available at night or on cloudy days, so that very large and expensive storage systems and other backup energy systems must be used

Table 4–3 Evaluation of Energy Alternatives for the World (continued)

Energy Resource	Advantages	Disadvantages
High-temperature heating and production of electricity	4. Decreases heat buildup in the atmosphere from energy use	4. Very high development costs and probably moderate to high operating costs 5. Low net useful energy yield because dispersed solar energy must be highly concentrated 6. May use panels of photovoltaic cells made of expensive or rare elements (silicon, gallium, cadmium) 7. Disruption of desert ecosystems 8. Cannot be used to power vehicles unless electricity is used to produce hydrogen gas or to recharge batteries 9. Requires large amounts of water for cooling
Wind energy Home and neighborhood turbines	1. Free and readily available energy supply on a windy day 2. Technology fairly well developed 3. Very low environmental impact 4. Moderate net useful energy yield 5. Decreases heat buildup in the atmosphere from energy use	1. Insufficient wind in many places 2. Requires conventional backup electrical system or fairly expensive storage system 3. Production and installation costs are high (but should decrease with mass production) 4. Cannot be used to power vehicles unless electricity is used to produce hydrogen gas or to recharge batteries
Large-scale power plants	1. Free and readily available energy supply on a very windy day 2. Low environmental impact 3. Decreases heat buildup in the atmosphere from energy use	1. Continuous high wind levels only available at a few sites 2. Technology in early stages of development 3. Requires backup by conventional electric power plants or a very expensive storage system 4. Development cost very high and operating costs probably moderate to high 5. Low net useful energy yield 6. Cannot be used to power vehicles unless electricity is used to produce hydrogen gas or to recharge batteries 7. Requires large amounts of water for cooling power plants
Geothermal energy (continuous heat flow)	1. Moderate overall supply 2. Moderate environmental impact	1. Technology needs further development 2. Only useful in selected areas and may be limited because rate of use exceeds low to moderate rate of renewal 3. Must be converted to electricity on site 4. Low net useful energy yield 5. Development and operating costs probably high 6. Requires large amounts of water for processing and cooling 7. Cannot be used to power vehicles unless electricity is used to produce hydrogen gas or to recharge batteries
Biomass (burning of wood, crop, food, and animal wastes)	1. Technology well developed 2. Low to moderate net energy yield 3. Moderate development costs but may be high depending on location and system	1. Large amount of land required 2. May be limited because rate of use exceeds rate of renewal and sufficient land not available in some areas 3. Moderate to high environmental impact from ecosystem disruption and simplification, erosion when land is cleared, water pollution from runoff of fertilizers and pesticides, and air pollution when fuel is burned
Derived Fuels		
Synthetic natural gas (SNG) from coal	1. Fairly easy to transport within nations 2. Low environmental impact on the air 3. Technology in late stages of development	1. Accelerates reduction in supply of coal 2. Low to moderate net useful energy yield 3. High development and operating costs 4. High environmental impact on land and water because of increased production of coal 5. Difficult and expensive to transport from one country to another as liquefied SNG 6. Not presently used in vehicles (but motors could be adapted) 7. Requires large amounts of water for processing

Table 4-3 Evaluation of Energy Alternatives for the World (continued)

Energy Resource	Advantages	Disadvantages
Synthetic oil and alcohols from coal and organic wastes	1. Can be used in stationary and mobile energy systems 2. Fairly easy to transport within and between nations	1. Accelerates reduction in supply of coal 2. Supply of organic wastes widely dispersed and somewhat limited in supply 3. Hinders recycling of organic wastes back to land as fertilizer 4. Technology needs further development 5. Low to moderate net useful energy yield 6. High environmental impact on land and water because of increased production of coal
Biofuels (alcohols and natural gas from plants and organic wastes)	1. Technology in late stages of development 2. Can be used in stationary and mobile energy systems 3. Alcohols fairly easy to transport within nations and between nations 4. Moderate development costs but could be high depending on system used	1. Large land requirements 2. May be limited because use exceeds rate of renewal 3. Moderate to high environmental impact from ecosystem disruption and simplification, soil erosion, water pollution runoff of fertilizer and pesticides, and air pollution 4. Production of carbon dioxide when fuel is burned could alter global climate
Urban wastes (for incineration)	1. Moderate to large supplies in heavily populated areas 2. Technology well developed 3. Decreases solid waste disposal 4. Low environmental impact on the land	1. Supply limited in nonurban areas 2. Supply could be limited if matter recycling and reuse programs are put into effect 3. High development and operating costs 4. Low to moderate net useful energy yield 5. Moderate to high environmental impact on air and water 6. Production of carbon dioxide when fuel is burned could alter global climate 7. Cannot be used to power vehicles 8. Burns paper and other organic wastes rather than recycling them
Hydrogen gas (from coal or water)	1. Very low environmental impact from burning of fuel 2. Does not produce carbon dioxide when burned 3. Fairly easy to transport 4. Technology in later stages of development 5. Good alternative for heating homes (by using fuel cells) and powering vehicles when oil supplies run out 6. Fairly easy to transport within countries by pipeline	1. Requires an essentially infinite source of heat or electricity (such as fusion, breeder fission, or wind or solar energy) to produce hydrogen gas from coal or water 2. Development and operating costs will probably be high to very high depending on source of heat or electricity 3. Net useful energy yield will be low to moderate depending on source of heat or electricity 4. Environmental impact of entire system could be low to very high depending on source of heat or electricity

Sources: Based on data and projections in the references listed in footnote 2, Chapter 1.

the biggest thermal water polluters, responsible for 80 percent of all discharges of hot water. Table 4-5 provides more details about the potential environmental effects of the different energy alternatives.[4]

---

[4]For more details on the environmental impacts of energy alternatives, see Berkowitz & Squires 1971, Budnitz & Holdren 1976, Cambel 1970, Comar & Sagan 1976, Council on Environmental Quality 1973, Council on Environmental Quality, *Environmental Quality,* 1975, 1976, Environmental Protection Agency 1974, Federal Energy Administration 1974a, Harte & Jassby 1978, Karam & Morgan 1976, Lave & Silverman 1976, McBride et al. 1978, Mills et al. 1971, Neyman 1977, Perry & Berkson 1971, Starr et al. 1976.

4-5 Paths to a New Energy Era

Hard versus Soft Energy Paths At present there is vigorous debate over whether the intermediate- and long-term energy strategy for the United States should follow a "hard path" or a "soft path," as summarized in Table 4-6 (Lovins 1977c, 1978a, Staff report 1977e, U.S. Senate, Select Committee on Small Business and Committee on Interior and Insular Affairs 1977, Weinberg 1978). In the conventional strategy, or hard path, major emphasis would be placed on building a number of huge, centralized coal-burning and conventional nuclear fission power plants between 1980 and 2000. After 2000 the use of coal-burning power plants

Table 4–4 Evaluation of Energy Alternatives for the United States

Energy Resource	Estimated Availability*			Estimated Net Useful Energy of Entire System[†]	Projected Cost of Entire System	Actual or Potential Environmental Impact of Entire System[‡]
	Short Term (1980–1990)	Intermediate Term (1990–2005)	Long Term (2005–2030)			
Nonrenewable Resources						
Fossil fuels						
Petroleum	High (with imports)	Moderate (with imports	Low	High but decreasing[§]	High for new domestic supplies	Moderate
Natural gas	High (with imports)	Moderate (with imports)	Low	High but decreasing[§]	High for new domestic supplies	Low
Coal	High[‖]	High[‖]	High[‖]	High but decreasing[§]	Moderate but increasing	Very high
Oil shale	Low	Low to moderate?	Low to moderate?	Low to moderate	High	High
Tar sands	Low	Fair? (imports only)	Poor to fair (imports only)	Low	High	Moderate to high
Nuclear energy						
Conventional fission (uranium and thorium)	Low to moderate	Low to moderate	Low to moderate	Low to moderate?	Very high	Very high
Breeder fission (uranium and thorium)	None	None to low	Low to high?	Unknown	Very high	Very high
Fusion (deuterium and lithium)	None	None	None to low (if developed)	Unknown	Very high	Unknown (probably moderate)
Geothermal energy (trapped pockets)	Poor	Poor	Poor	Low to moderate	Moderate to high	Moderate
Renewable Resources						
Conservation	High	High	High	Very high	Low	Decreases impact of other sources
Water power (hydroelectricity)	Low	Low	Very low	High	Moderate to very high	Low to moderate
Tidal energy	None	Very low	Very low	Unknown (moderate?)	Moderate to high?	Low to moderate
Ocean thermal gradients	None	None to low	Low to moderate (if developed)	Unknown (probably low to moderate)	Probably high	Unknown (probably moderate)
Solar energy						
Low-temperature heating (for homes and water)	Moderate	Moderate to high	High	Moderate	Moderate to high	Low
High-temperature heating and production of electricity	None	Very low	Probably low	Low	Very high	Low to moderate
Wind energy						
Home and neighborhood turbines	Very low	Moderate	Moderate to high?	Moderate	Moderate to very high	Low

Table 4-4 Evaluation of Energy Alternatives for the United States (continued)

Energy Resource	Estimated Availability*			Estimated Net Useful Energy of Entire System†	Projected Cost of Entire System	Actual or Potential Environmental Impact of Entire System‡
	Short Term (1980)–1990	Intermediate Term (1990)–2005	Long Term (2005–2030)			
Large-scale power plants	None	Very low	Probably low	Low	Very high	Low to moderate?
Geothermal energy (continuous heat flow)	Very low	Very low	Low to moderate	Low	High	Moderate
Biomass (burning of wood, crop, food, and animal wastes)	Low	Low to moderate?	Low to moderate?	Moderate	Moderate to high	Moderate to high
Derived Fuels						
Synthetic natural gas (SNG) from coal	Low	Low to moderate?	Low to moderate?	Low to moderate	High	High (increases use of coal)
Synthetic oil and alcohols from coal and organic wastes	Low	Poor to fair?	Low to moderate?	Low to moderate	High	High (increases use of coal)
Biofuels (alcohols and natural gas from plants and organic wastes)	Low to moderate?	Moderate?	Moderate to high?	Low to moderate?	Moderate to high?	Moderate to high
Urban wastes (for incineration)	Low	Low	Low	Low to moderate	High	Moderate to high
Hydrogen gas (from coal or water)	None	None	Moderate?#	Unknown (probably low to moderate)#	Unknown (probably high)#	Variable#

Note. Shading indicates favorable conditions.
*Overall availability based on supply and technological, net useful energy, economic, and environmental impact feasibility.
†Rough estimates only. Better and less conflicting estimates will be available when standard guidelines for net energy analysis are adopted by all investigators.
‡See Table 4–3 for more details.
§As accessible high-grade deposits are depleted, more and more energy and money must be used to find, develop, upgrade, and deliver remote and low-grade deposits.
‖Assuming that coal's very high environmental impact can be reduced to an acceptable level.
#Depends on whether an essentially infinite source of heat or electrical energy (such as fusion, breeder fission, wind, or the sun) is available to produce hydrogen gas from coal or water. Net useful energy, costs, and environmental impact will depend on source of heat or electricity.

would continue to increase, coupled with a shift from conventional fission to breeder fission nuclear power plants (Weinberg 1978). After 2020 (or perhaps later) there would be a gradual shift to almost complete dependence on centralized nuclear fusion power plants, if this energy alternative should ever prove to be technologically, economically, and environmentally acceptable.

In sharp contrast to this strategy, energy expert Amory Lovins (1975, 1976, 1977a, 1977b, 1978a) has suggested that the United States follow a "soft path" to a new earthmanship energy era. In this approach emphasis would be placed on energy conservation, cogeneration (using industrial waste heat to generate electricity), and a crash program to greatly increase the use of renewable and more environmentally benign energy flows—sunlight, wind, and vegetation (biomass). Effective conservation efforts could cut energy waste in half, reduce the need to build additional coal-burning and nuclear power plants, decrease the environmental impact of energy use, and buy precious time to phase in a diverse and flexible array of decentralized soft energy technologies. Oil and natural gas would continue to be used but at a slower rate because of energy conservation. Coal use would increase slightly between 1980 and 2000 but would be burned primarily in intermediate-sized fluidized gas turbine power plants with the electricity fed to home heat pumps. Conventional nuclear fission power

Table 4–5 Actual and Potential Environmental Impacts of Alternative Energy Systems

Energy System	Air Pollution	Water Pollution	Land Disruption	Possible Large-Scale Disasters
Nonrenewable Resources				
Fossil fuels				
Petroleum	Sulfur oxides, nitrogen oxides, and hydrocarbons; global climate change from carbon dioxide (Section 9–2)	Oil spills from well blowouts, tanker accidents, pipeline ruptures (Section 6–5); excess heat (Section 9–4); brines	Subsidence (caving in over wells); estuary pollution	Massive spills on water from tanker accidents and offshore well blowouts; massive spills on land from pipeline breaks; refinery fires
Natural gas	Global climate change from carbon dioxide	Excess heat	Subsidence	Pipeline explosions; liquefied natural gas (LNG) tanker explosions
Coal	Sulfur oxides, particulates, nitrogen oxides; global climate change from carbon dioxide; radioactive emissions	Acid mine drainage; acid rain; dissolved solids from washing coal; excess heat	Underground and strip mining (Section 6–6); subsidence; slag disposal; erosion	Mine accidents; landslides; sudden subsidence in urban areas; depletion and contamination of water resources in arid regions
Oil shale	Sulfur oxides, particulates, hydrogen sulfide, nitrogen oxides, hydrocarbons; global climate change from carbon dioxide; odor	Dissolved solids (salinity) and heavy metals from processed shale rock; sediment; groundwater contamination	Disposal of processed shale rock; subsidence	Depletion and contamination of water supplies in arid regions where most shale is found; massive oil spills from pipeline breaks; earthquakes if nuclear blasts are used for underground processing; depletion and contamination of water resources in arid regions
Tar sands	Sulfur oxides, hydrogen sulfide, hydrocarbons, nitrogen oxides; global climate change from carbon dioxide	Possible contamination of underground water supplies if extracted and processed underground	Surface mining (for some deposits); subsidence; loss of wildlife habitats	Massive oil spills from pipeline breaks; earthquakes if nuclear blasts used for underground extraction and processing; depletion and contamination of water resources in arid regions
Nuclear energy				
Conventional fission (uranium and thorium)	Radioactive emissions	Radioactive mine wastes; excess heat; radioactive effluents	Open pit and underground mining (Section 6–6); storage of radioactive wastes	Release of radioactive materials from meltdown of reactor core, sabotage, and shipping accidents; hijacking of fuel shipments to make nuclear bombs
Breeder fission (uranium and thorium)	Same as above	Same as above except fewer radioactive mine wastes	Same as above	Same as above except potential radioactive releases more deadly
Fusion (deuterium and lithium)	Same as above	Excess heat		Release of radioactive materials from meltdown or explosion of reactor
Geothermal energy (trapped pockets)	Hydrogen sulfide and ammonia; global climate change from carbon dioxide; radioactive materials; noise; local climate change; odor	Dissolved solids (salinity); boron runoff; excess heat	Subsidence	Depletion and contamination of water resources in arid regions

Energy System	Air Pollution	Water Pollution	Land Disruption	Possible Large-Scale Disasters
Renewable Resources				
Conservation	Decreased	Decreased	Decreased	None
Water power (hydroelectricity)	Negligible	Disruption of aquatic ecosystems	Flooding of areas to form lake; ecosystem disruption; loss of wildlife and human habitat; disruption of estuary into which river flows	Dam breaks
Tidal energy	Negligible	Estuary disruption	Very little	None
Ocean thermal gradients	Local climate change	Ocean ecosystem disruption; marine life disruption	Estuary disruption	None
Solar energy 　Low-temperature heating (for homes and water)	Negligible	Negligible	Negligible	None
High-temperature heating and production of electricity	Negligible except for moderate amount from materials needed to make collectors (cement, steel, glass)	Negligible	Requires land for large farms of solar collectors; disruption of desert ecosystems	Depletion of water resources in arid regions
Wind energy 　Home and neighborhood turbines	Negligible except for some noise and aesthetic degradation	Negligible	Negligible	None
Large-scale power plants	Possible local or regional climate changes	Negligible	Negligible	None
Geothermal energy (continuous heat flow)	Hydrogen sulfide and ammonia; global climate change from carbon dioxide; radioactive materials; noise; local climate change; odor	Dissolved solids (salinity); runoff; excess heat	Subsidence	Depletion and contamination of water resources in arid regions
Biomass (burning of wood, crop, food, and animal wastes)	Particulates and hydrocarbons; global climate change from carbon dioxide	Runoff of fertilizers and pesticides; sediment from erosion	Large use of land; soil erosion; loss of habitat for wildlife	None
Derived Fuels				
Synthetic natural gas (SNG) from coal	Similar to coal but somewhat less	Same as coal plus increased pollution from heavy metals, phenols, hydrocarbons	Same as coal	Same as coal, earthquakes from blasts for underground coal gasification; pipeline explosions
Synthetic oil and alcohols from coal and organic wastes	Similar to coal but less	Same as coal except increase in pollution from heavy metals, phenols, hydrocarbons	Same as coal	Same as coal; pipeline spills
Biofuels (alcohols and natural gas from plants and organic wastes)	Global climate change from carbon dioxide	Runoff of fertilizers and pesticides; sediment from soil erosion	Large use of land; soil erosion; soil salinity and waterlogging from irrigation; ecosystem simplification; loss of wildlife habitats	None

Table 4–5 Actual and Potential Environmental Impacts of Alternative Energy Systems (continued)

Energy System	Air Pollution	Water Pollution	Land Disruption	Possible Large-Scale Disasters
Urban wastes (for incineration)	Sulfur oxides, particulates (especially heavy metals), nitrogen oxides, hydrogen chloride, hydrocarbons, hydrogen sulfide; global climate change from carbon dioxide; odor	Leaching of dissolved solids and heavy metals from ash	Decreases solid waste disposal	Fire or explosion in incinerator
Hydrogen gas (from coal or water)	Depends on source of electricity or heat to make hydrogen. Large-scale disasters also possible from pipeline explosions.			

Source: Based on references in footnote 4.

plants would be phased out by 2005 and breeder fission and nuclear fusion would not be developed because of their potentially serious and irreversible environmental impacts (Table 4–5) and because of a lack of enough capital to develop them along with soft energy technologies.

Of course, the hard and soft energy paths are not mutually exclusive. The United States could and probably will have a blend of both approaches (Lovins 1978a, Weinberg 1978). The real debate is over which approach should be emphasized and over how much of the nation's limited financial capital should be devoted to each approach.

The First and Second Thermodynamic Revolutions The developed nations have engineered what might be called the *first thermodynamic* or *energy revolution*. It consists of a dramatic increase in material goods, political participation, and education for a high percentage of their citizens by means of a large increase in total and per capita energy use. It has been based, however, on improving human well-being at the expense of the environment and by depleting low-cost, high net useful energy yield resources. The thermodynamic debt required by the first and second energy laws is now coming due.

Table 4–6 Comparison of Hard and Soft Energy Strategies for the United States

Hard Energy Plan	Soft Energy Plan
Increase the supply of energy to meet greatly increased total and per capita energy demand.	Emphasize energy conservation to reduce waste and to provide ample energy without large increases in total and per capita energy use.
Greatly increase the use of electricity to provide energy for both high-quality and low-quality energy needs.	To conserve energy quality, use electricity only for appropriate high-quality energy needs.
Depend primarily on nonrenewable energy resources (energy capital)—oil, natural gas, coal, and uranium.	Greatly increase the use of renewable energy flows (energy income)—sunlight, wind, and vegetation (biomass).
Continue to increase the use of oil and natural gas.	Increase the use of oil and natural gas only slightly to prevent rapid depletion of domestic supplies and more dependence on imports.
Greatly increase the use of large, complex, centralized coal-burning and nuclear fission power plants, followed by a shift to centralized breeder fission power plants, and then a shift to centralized nuclear fusion power plants (if they become feasible).	Greatly increase the use of a diverse array of intermediate, relatively simple, small-scale, dispersed energy production facilities using sunlight, wind, and vegetation, depending on local availability. Slightly increase the use of coal by burning it in intermediate-sized fluidized gas turbine power plants coupled with home heat pumps. Phase out the use of conventional nuclear fission power by 2005, and do not develop breeder fission and nuclear fusion energy.
Minimize pollution by building complex safety and pollution control devices into energy production facilities and assume that global climate changes from increased production of carbon dioxide and heat (Section 9–2) either won't be serious or can be dealt with by some technological breakthrough.	Minimize pollution by using energy sources that have relatively low environmental impacts and that decrease the possibility of changing global climate.

But two-thirds of the world's population have yet to participate in this first thermodynamic revolution. People talk glibly about countries becoming developed by following the present American approach to industrialization. But if the present level and pattern of American industrialization and energy use were employed throughout the world, within a short time the planet would be uninhabitable. The atmosphere would contain about 200 times more sulfur dioxide and 750 times more carbon monoxide and carbon dioxide than it now does. The world's lakes, rivers, and oceans would be loaded with 175 times more chemical wastes, and thermal pollution could completely disrupt aquatic ecosystems. Two-thirds of the world's forests would be eliminated, and each year 121,000 square kilometers (30 million acres) of vital farmland would be converted to cities and highways. The earth's supplies of fossil fuels, nonfuel minerals, and uranium would be depleted within a very short time.

The real hope for all countries lies in our ability to halt population growth and, in addition, to bring about a *second thermodynamic* or *earthmanship revolution* over the next 30 to 50 years. It would be an ecological revolution that involves taking seriously the eventual limits imposed by demography, resource supplies, and thermodynamics. It means a life-style based on the thrifty use of energy and matter and on accepting the responsibility to control population growth and to distribute the world's resources more equitably.

We are witness to the end of an era. As much as we hate to face up to it, the joyride of cheap energy is really over. But that does not mean that we are on the road to a Spartan life, nor does it mean that we cannot in coming years develop transportation systems, cities, and indeed life styles that are superior to what we must leave behind. To fashion a new America will involve a whole lot more than an energy policy. But since energy is the life blood of modern society, it might provide the focal point.

S. David Freeman

Guest Editorial: Energy Analysis and the Dynamic Steady State

Howard T. Odum

Howard T. Odum is the graduate research professor of environmental engineering sciences and director of the Center for Wetlands at the University of Florida. During his distinguished career as a research scientist, lecturer, and writer he has received a number of awards, including the George Mercer Award of the Ecological Society, the Award of Distinction from the International Technical Writers Association, the Distinguished Service Award of the Industrial Development Research Council, and Prize of the Institute de la Vie of Paris. He is internationally known for his work in systems ecology and his important pioneering work in making net useful energy analysis a part of energy planning in an increasing number of countries. Among his important books are Environment, Power and Society *(1971a) and* Energy Basis for Man and Nature *(1976, with Elisabeth C. Odum).*

The growth in the production of net useful energy in the United States and much of the industrial world has almost stopped. Consequently, economic growth has also leveled off. Since 1973 the American economy has produced enough to maintain national assets and to exchange money and goods for energy imports but not enough for significant further growth. U.S. natural gas and older oil reserves were yielding about 10 units of useful energy for each unit used in processing until the gas crisis of the winter of 1977. Now most energy sources yield 6 units of useful energy for each unit put directly and indirectly into the work of acquisition (either through foreign exchange or through exploration and processing). Nuclear energy yields only 3 to 4 units of net useful energy for each unit of useful energy put into the system. The net useful energy that can be obtained by importing fuels depends on the availability of fuel reserves in the United

States to keep the prices of foreign fuels down. As yield ratios for the primary energy sources of America fall below 6 to 1, the net useful energy drops, and with it drops the amount of useful work that can be accomplished (the real GNP). The average standard of living may hold steady for a while as emphasis shifts to eliminating waste, but eventually it may drop as net useful energy yields decline (Figure 4–5). Here are some suggestions for adaptation to these new times.

1. A 10 percent cut in salary for everyone in the United States may be needed so that unemployment can be reduced without a change in GNP, net energy use, or inflation. This action will allow each American to eliminate what is less essential or less productive. Unions might take the lead, emphasizing employment for all instead of high wages for the few.

2. If U.S. money flow can be adjusted to energy flow each year (annual use of fossil fuels plus renewable productivities), the buying power of the dollar in real value will hold constant and the dollar will then be on an energy standard. This protects the individual and prevents unwise attempts to expand the economy when such attempts will fail. This is the reverse of the deficit financing that is used in growth times.

3. It is useful to use energy costs to estimate net energy value. The unit of measure is kilocalories of solar energy to develop a kilocalorie of useful energy. Good energetics suggest items should not be used for less effect than their energy cost. Because they are at the end of a chain of energy transformations, wildlife, people, and information have high energy costs and thus are valued.

4. In planning and judging what energy alternatives and uses will be economical, purchased energy should be matched with the free resources of the sun, rain, and land. The national ratio of matching is about 2.5 kilocalories purchased to 1 supplied free (both measures in solar equivalents). The basis for money flow is 38 million kilocalories of solar equivalents per dollar (1975 dollars).

5. In all considerations of the realm of environment, economics, and energy, a basic energy analysis is needed to show the interactions of money, energy, materials, and information. Drawing and numerically evaluating energy analysis diagrams, as discussed in more detail in Odum (1971a) and Odum and Odum (1976), is a starting procedure that can be understood from the grammar school to the graduate school. Rather than being interdisciplinary, energy analysis is a new discipline that realigns knowledge and principles. We may need to institutionalize courses and degrees using energetic holism as a key to understanding the systems of humans and nature.

Guest Editorial Discussion

1. Explain how overall energy use continues to rise whereas the growth in net useful energy has leveled off in most industrial nations and may begin to decline.

2. What are the advantages and disadvantages of relating energy flow in a society to dollar flow?

3. Explain how unemployment could be reduced without a change in GNP, energy use, or inflation if everyone in the United States took a 10 percent cut in salary. Debate the pros and cons of this suggestion.

Discussion Topics

1. List the following forms of energy in order of increasing energy quality: heat from nuclear fission, normal sunlight, oil shale, air at 500°C.

2. Give three examples of the use of high-quality energy for tasks requiring low-quality energy.

3. Distinguish among first law energy efficiency, second law energy efficiency, and net useful energy, and give an example of each. Explain how net useful energy is related to dollar flow and inflation.

4. How can one estimate indicate that 63 percent of all energy used in the United States each year is wasted and a second estimate indicate 85 percent?

5. You are about to build a house. What energy supply (oil, gas, coal, or other) would you use for space heating, air conditioning, the stove, the refrigerator, the dryer, and the hot water heater? Consider long-term economic and ecological factors.

6. List the major U.S. energy alternatives for the short term (1980 to 1990), intermediate term (1990 to 2005), and long term (2005 to 2030).

7. List the major advantages and disadvantages of each of the following energy alternatives: (a) coal, (b) petroleum, (c) natural gas, (d) conventional nuclear fission reactors, (e) nuclear breeder reactors, (f) oil shale, (g) geothermal energy, (h) wind energy, (i) solar energy, (j) coal gasification, (k) nuclear fusion, and (l) biomass.

Further Readings

American Physical Society. 1975. *Efficient Use of Energy*. New York: American Institute of Physics. Superb summary of energy waste and opportunities for energy conservation based on second law energy efficiencies in the United States.

Bent, Henry A. 1977. "Entropy and the Energy Crisis." *Journal of Science Teaching,* vol. 44, no. 4, 25–29. Very readable introduction to implications of second energy law. Highly recommended.

Carr, Donald E. 1976. *Energy & the Earth Machine.* New York: Norton. Very readable introduction to energy problems and alternatives. Highly recommended.

Cheney, Eric S. 1974. "U.S. Energy Resources: Limits and Future Outlook." *American Scientist,* January-February, pp. 14–22. Excellent overview of options.

Clark, Wilson. 1974. *Energy for Survival: The Alternative to Extinction.* New York: Anchor. Very useful analysis of energy use and evaluation of alternative energy resources. Highly recommended.

Cook, Earl. 1976. *Man, Energy, Society.* San Francisco: Freeman. One of the best introductions to energy concepts, problems, and alternatives. Try to read this one.

Demand and Conservation Panel of the Committee on Nuclear and Alternative Energy Systems, National Academy of Sciences. 1978. "U.S. Energy Demand: Some Low Energy Futures." *Science,* vol. 200, 142–152. Very useful analysis showing how the United States could get along with much less energy without affecting life-styles.

Dorf, Richard C. 1978. *Energy, Resources, and Policy.* Reading, Mass.: Addison-Wesley. Excellent textbook.

Energy Policy Project. 1974. *A Time To Choose: The Final Report of the Energy Policy Project of the Ford Foundation.* Cambridge, Mass.: Ballinger. Superb overview by a high-level task force. Highly recommended. Also see the debate over this report in Tavoulareas & Kaysen 1977.

Environmental Protection Agency. 1974. *Control of Environmental Impacts from Advanced Energy Sources.* Washington, D.C.: Environmental Protection Agency. Very useful information on environmental impacts of energy use.

Fowler, John W. 1975. *Energy and the Environment.* New York: McGraw-Hill. Excellent summary of energy problems and alternatives at a slightly higher level than this text. Highly recommended. See also Fowler 1975b.

Hammond, Allen L., et al. 1973. *Energy and the Future.* Washington, D.C.: American Association for the Advancement of Science. One of the best evaluations of our energy options. At a slightly higher level than this text.

Hayes, Denis. 1977. *Rays of Hope: The Transition to a Post-Petroleum World.* New York: Norton. Outstanding analysis of energy problems and alternatives. Try to read this important book.

Hollander, Jack M., et al., eds. 1978. *Annual Review of Energy.* Vol. 3. Palo Alto, Calif.: Annual Reviews. Excellent series of detailed review articles. Published annually. See also Hollander et al. 1977, Hollander & Simmons 1976.

Lovins, Amory B. 1977. *Soft Energy Paths.* Cambridge, Mass.: Ballinger. Superb analysis of energy alternatives. Try to read this very important book. See also Lovins 1978a.

Maddox, John. 1975. *Beyond the Energy Crisis: A Global Perspective.* New York: McGraw-Hill. Attack on environmentalist approach to energy problems. Optimistic view that we can solve the problems by finding more fossil fuels and using nuclear energy. Compare with Lovins 1977c.

Odum, Howard T., and Elisabeth C. Odum. 1976. *Energy Basis for Man and Nature.* New York: McGraw-Hill. Superb introduction to energy concepts and alternatives with emphasis on net useful energy analyses. Highly recommended. See also Odum 1971a, 1973.

Wilson, Carroll L., ed. 1977. *Energy: Global Prospects 1985–2000.* New York: McGraw-Hill. Superb overview of potential energy supplies by a team of experts.

Woodwell, G. M. 1974. "Success, Succession and Adam Smith." *BioScience,* vol. 24, no. 2, 81–87. Outstanding overview of energy crisis and its ecological implications.

5

Energy Conservation

How quickly we can poison the earth's lovely surface—but how wondrously it responds to the educated caress of conservation.

Donald E. Carr

5-1 Our Most Important Energy Alternative

We have three basic approaches for dealing with the present and future energy crises (Section 1-1): (1) develop new sources of energy; (2) waste less energy in our present life-styles; and (3) adopt new life-styles using less energy. As Chapter 4 (Tables 4-4 and 4-5) shows, some combination of the latter two approaches is the best energy alternative (and also the largest potential source of energy) available to the United States.[1]

Without a massive energy conservation program and some changes in life-style, the United States can scarcely create, much less sustain, and earthmanship energy society. Yet we seem reluctant to begin, partly because some people think energy conservation means hardship. Not so. The United States wastes so much energy each year (see Fig-

ures 4-3 and 4-4) that enormous amounts of energy can be saved without cutting off any vital services (Hayes 1976a). For instance, energy conservation means an efficient heating system and a well-insulated house, not a cold house. Energy conservation means driving a car that gets 6.6 kilometers per liter (40 mpg) instead of 2.5 kilometers per liter (15 mpg), not giving up your car altogether (Hayes 1976a).

To see how to waste less energy, we must first see how we use energy. Figure 5-1 shows how Americans use energy in four basic sectors: transportation, residential, commercial, and industrial. In the rest of this chapter, we will look at some specific ways to save energy in each of these four sectors.

5-2 Energy Savings in Transportation

Transportation Options People in urban systems move from one place to another by three major types of transportation: *individual transit* (private automobile, taxi, motorcycle, moped, bicycle, walking); *mass transit* (railroad, subway, trolley, bus), which moves large groups of people; and *para transit* (carpools, vanpools, and dial-a-ride systems), which moves small groups of people. Each type has certain advantages and disadvantages, as summarized in Table 5-1.

Effects of Automobiles on Cities By providing almost unlimited mobility, the automobile has been a major factor in the decentralization of American cities. Most suburbanites and many people living in nonmetropolitan areas now depend almost completely on the private automobile to get to work, schools, and shopping centers, which are sprawled over vast areas of land. In the United States the car is used for about 97.5 percent of all travel in urban areas (Altshuler 1977), and the average American family now spends more on transportation than on food (National Wildlife Federation 1978). In spite of warnings about future oil shortages, in 1977 two out of three U.S. workers drove to work, one out of six used a carpool, and only one out of eight used

---

[1]For more details on energy conservation, see the following: Adkins 1974, American Physical Society 1975, Berg 1973a, 1974a, 1974b, Berry & Makino 1974, Boretsky 1977, Bormann 1976, Carr 1976, Center for Science in the Public Interest 1977, Citizens Advisory Committee on Environmental Quality 1973, Clegg 1975, Committee on Interior and Insular Affairs 1972, Cook 1976b, *Consumer Guide* editors 1977, Darmstadter 1975, Energy Policy Project 1974, Federal Energy Administration 1974a, 1976, 1977a, Fowler 1975a, 1975b, Freeman 1974, Fritsch 1974, Georgia Conservancy 1976, Hammond 1972, 1974a, Hannon 1974, 1975, 1977a, 1977b, Hayes 1976a, 1977, Healy & Hertzfeld 1976, Hirst 1973b, 1976a, 1976b, Hirst & Carney 1978, Hirst & Moyers 1973, Hyman 1973, Kleeberg 1977, Large 1976, League of Women Voters Education Fund 1977a, 1977b, Lincoln 1973, Lovins 1977c, Metz 1975, Meyer & Todd 1973, *Mother Earth News* 1974, Murphy 1976a, Novick 1973a, Office of Emergency Preparedness 1972, ORNL-NSF Environment Program 1974, Price & Price 1976, Rice 1974, Ross & Williams 1976, 1977a, 1977b, Rothchild & Tenny 1978, Rubin 1974, Schipper 1976b, Schipper & Darmstadter 1978, Schipper & Lichtenberg 1976, Socolow 1977, Udall et al. 1974, Widmer & Gyftopoulos 1977, Williams 1975.

Table 5–1 Major Forms of Urban Transportation

Type	Advantages	Disadvantages
Individual Transit		
Automobile and taxi	Freedom of movement (door-to-door service) Convenient Usually not crowded Can carry one or several people	Requires much land (highways, parking areas, etc.) Wastes energy and matter resources Pollutes air Promotes urban sprawl Increasingly expensive to buy and operate or to hire
Motorcycle and moped	Freedom of movement Convenient Less expensive to buy and operate than car Uses and wastes less matter and energy resources than car Requires relatively little land Less pollution than car	Rider not sheltered from weather, noise, and air pollution Carries only 1 or 2 persons Less protection from injury
Bicycle	Freedom of movement Convenient Just as fast as car in urban trips less than 8 km (5 mi) Very inexpensive to buy and operate Provides exercise Conserves energy and matter resources Requires little land Nonpolluting	Rider not sheltered from weather, noise, and air pollution Carries only 1 or 2 persons Less protection from injury Slow for trips greater than 8 km (5 mi)
Walking or running	Freedom of movement Convenient for short trips Free Provides exercise Conserves energy and matter resources Requires very little land Nonpolluting	Slow and difficult for long trips No protection from weather, noise, and air pollution
Mass Transit		
Railroad and subway (heavy rail systems)	Handles large number of passengers Rapid once boarded and if on time Safer than car Fairly inexpensive for rider Uses fewer matter and energy resources than car Requires much less land than car Less pollution than car	Very expensive to build and operate Economically feasible only along heavily populated routes Lacks door-to-door service Fixed routes Can be crowded and noisy
Trolley and streetcar (light rail systems)	Handles large number of passengers Fairly rapid once boarded and if on time Safer than car Fairly inexpensive for rider Uses fewer energy and matter resources than car Requires less land than car Relatively little pollution if electric Cheaper to build and operate than railroad and subway	Expensive to build and operate Economically feasible only along heavily populated routes Lacks door-to-door service Fixed routes Can be crowded and noisy
Bus	Handles large number of passengers More flexible routes than railroad and trolley Safer than car Fairly inexpensive for rider Uses fewer energy and matter resources than car Requires less land than car Normally cheaper to build and operate than railroads	Fairly expensive to build and operate Lacks door-to-door service Fairly restricted freedom of movement Often not on time Can be crowded and noisy Pollutes air

Table 5-1 Major Forms of Urban Transportation (continued)

Type	Advantages	Disadvantages
Para Transit		
Carpools and vanpools	Carries small group of people Saves money Wastes fewer energy and matter resources than car Provides social interaction	Fairly inconvenient Promotes urban sprawl Restricts freedom of movement Requires much land Pollutes air Wastes matter and energy resources
Dial-a-ride (minibuses, vans, and shared taxicab systems)	Handles small to moderate number of passengers Safer than car Moderately inexpensive for rider Usually provides door-to-door service Uses fewer energy and matter resources than car Requires less land than car Cheaper to build and operate than railroad Very useful for the poor, young, elderly, and handicapped	Fairly expensive to operate Can require long waits Can be crowded and noisy Pollutes air

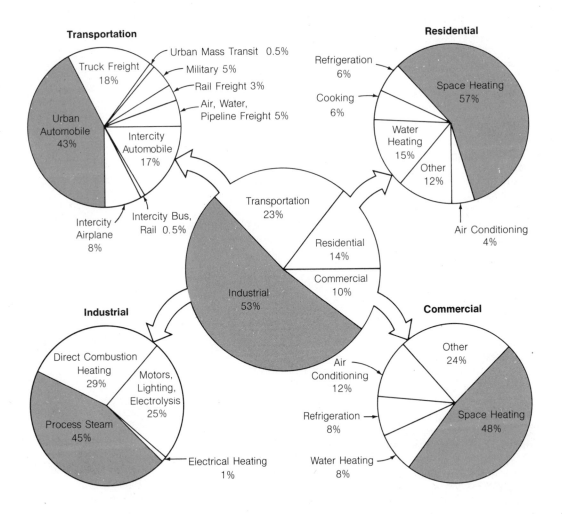

Figure 5-1 Uses of energy in the United States in 1976. (Data from Brookhaven National Laboratory 1977, Darmstadter et al. 1978, Hayes 1976a, Large 1976, Yegge et al. 1974)

public transportation. In 1977 there were 134 million motor vehicles in the United States—half of all the cars in the world—which means there was one vehicle for every two Americans (National Wildlife Federation 1978).

The automobile provides many advantages, as shown in Table 5–1. In addition, the U.S. economy is built around the car. One out of every five dollars spent in the United States is related directly or indirectly to the automobile industry or related industries (oil, steel, rubber, plastics, highway construction). This giant industrial complex accounts for about 20 percent of the annual gross national product (GNP), provides about 18 percent of all federal taxes, and employs over 15 percent of the total U.S. work force. It is no wonder that British author J. B. Priestly remarked, "In America, the cars have become the people."

In spite of its advantages, the automobile has a number of harmful effects on human lives and on air, water, and land (Conservation Foundation 1972, Jerome 1972, Leavitt 1970, Marston 1975, Moskin 1973, Mumford 1963, Owen 1972, Rosenthal 1977, Schneider 1971, Shinnar 1972, Traffe & Gauthier 1973). By allowing urban sprawl, the automobile has been a key factor in the decline of mass transit systems in the central cities, where up to 60 percent of the population does not own a car (Havlick 1974). Without cars and adequate public transportation, almost 100 million poor, young, elderly, and handicapped Americans do not enjoy the freedom of travel for work and pleasure that other Americans have. To make matters worse, each year about 51,000 mostly poor Americans are displaced from their homes to make way for highways that most of them don't use because they don't have cars (U.S. Department of Transportation 1973). Motor vehicles also kill about 60,000 Americans and injure about 2 million each year. Since the automobile was introduced almost 2 million Americans have been killed on the highways—about twice the number killed in all U.S. wars. Throughout the world automobile accidents kill 170,000 people, permanently maim 500,000, and injure 7 million each year (van Dam 1978).

Motor vehicles also use vast amounts of mineral and energy resources, including 56 percent of the petroleum, 72 percent of the rubber, 30 percent of the zinc, and almost 20 percent of the aluminum used each year in the United States. But cars are so inefficient (Section 2–3) that they waste 80 percent of the energy available in gasoline. Automobiles also produce about 85 percent (by weight) of the air pollution in many cities and about 85 percent of all urban noise. Furthermore, over 6 million junked cars litter the countryside.

Motor vehicles also have a horrendous appetite for land. Roads and parking spaces take up over half the land in Dallas and Los Angeles and over a third of New York City and Washington, D.C. (Ward 1976). Each 1.6 kilometers (1 mile) of freeway typically consume at least 0.10 square kilometer (24 acres) of land (Sullivan & Montgomery 1972). Highways cover about 9 million square kilometers (3.5 million square miles) of land in the United States (Laycock 1970, Leavitt 1970, U.S. Department of Transportation 1973). This is equivalent to paving over Vermont, New Hampshire, Connecticut, Massachusetts, and Rhode Island.

Building more highways and freeways encourages more automobiles and travel, and the resulting congestion decreases the average automobile speed in many urban areas. According to former New York Transportation Director Arthur E. Palmer, "In 1907, the average speed of horse drawn vehicles through New York City's streets was 18.5 kilometers per hour [11.5 miles per hour]. In 1966 the average speed of motor vehicles (with the power of 200 to 300 horses) through the central business district was 13.7 kilometers per hour [8.5 miles per hour]—and during the midday crushes slower still."

There are three basic methods for reducing the problems created by the automobile: (1) Encourage the use of bicycles and develop urban mass and para transit systems; (2) discourage automobile use; and (3) reduce pollution and energy and matter waste in automobiles. Let's look more closely at these options.

The Bicycle The bicycle won't replace cars in urban areas, but its use could be greatly increased. It uses no fossil fuels and only small amounts of resources, and is very useful for trips under 8 kilometers (5 miles), which make up about 43 percent of all urban trips (Environmental Protection Agency 1974a). In traffic, cars and bicycles both travel at about the same average speed, 21 kilometers per hour (13 miles per hour). To increase the use of bicycles, city governments should build bicycle paths. A survey in Philadelphia showed that 38 percent of all bicycle owners would commute to work by bicycle if safe bikeways and secure parking were available (Environmental Protection Agency 1974a). Davis, California, setting an example for the rest of the United States, has 28,000 bicycles, wide bicycle lanes, and some streets closed to automobiles for its population of 35,000.

Mass Transit Because of the switch to cars since 1950, the number of riders on all forms of mass transit has declined sharply (Figure 5–2). In many cities mass transit systems have either gone out of business or cut back their services. A vicious circle sets in. As the number of riders decreases, operating costs and fares rise. Service deteriorates, causing the number of riders to decline even further.

Urban mass transportation is a complex and controversial problem (Altshuler 1977, Bell 1978, Brand 1976, Bruce-Briggs 1976, Creighton 1970, Hamilton & Nance 1969, Kemp & Cheslow 1976, Mervine 1974, Owen 1976, Reisch 1970). Some see *fixed-rail rapid transit systems* as the key to urban transportation problems (Owen 1972, Stone

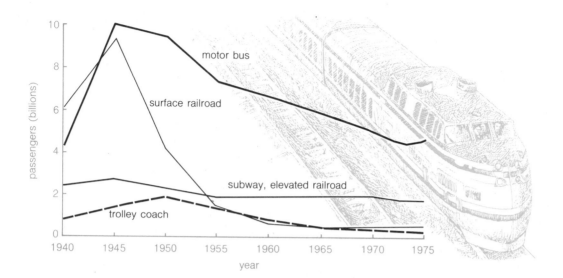

Figure 5–2 The decline in mass transit use in the United States. (Data from American Public Transit Association, *74–75 Transit Fact Book*, 1976)

1971). Others argue that such technological solutions are extremely expensive and do not serve many people in today's decentralized cities (Altshuler 1977, Rae 1972). They are primarily useful where many people live along a narrow corridor, and even then their high construction and operating costs may outweigh their benefits.

Problems with the new Bay Area Rapid Transit system, or BART, in San Francisco and the METRO system in Washington, D.C., support the latter argument. With its sleek, air conditioned, 129-kilometer-per-hour (80-mile-per-hour) cars, the $1.6 billion BART system was supposed to be a model for future rapid mass transit systems. However, since its opening in 1974, BART has been plagued with breakdowns, massive financial losses, and worst of all, far too few riders (Webber 1976). Paradoxically, part of the problem may be that BART is too rapid. Its stations are widely spaced so that the trains can run at high speeds. Since many passengers have to take a bus or car to the nearest BART station, they don't bother to use BART at all. In addition, this expensive, tax-supported system primarily benefits affluent suburban commuters and does little to help the poor (Bruce-Briggs 1976). A whole fleet of new buses that would carry all of BART's passengers would have cost only 2.5 percent of BART's original cost. Washington, D.C., appears to be having problems with its METRO system, which so far has cost $5.5 billion—more than twice the original cost estimate. In 1976 it was losing about $75,000 a day. Atlanta is also building an expensive rapid mass transit system and may be falling into the "moonshot mentality" trap.

These problems have caused mass transit planners in other cities to "think small," and they are switching back to the use of trolleys (also called streetcars or light rail systems) and buses (Figure 5–2) (Hollyer 1977). Fixed rails limit the flexibility of trolleys, but trolleys have several important advantages: (1) By moving on a median strip between traffic lanes, trolleys can move much faster than buses; (2) linking several cars together, one operator can carry a large number of passengers during rush hours; (3) electric-powered cars cause relatively little direct pollution; and (4) construction costs are relatively low—from $2.5 million to $5 million per 1.6 kilometers (1 mile) compared with $15 to $20 million for urban highways and $30 to $45 million for underground subways.

Buses are cheaper and much more flexible than trolleys. They can be routed to almost any area in today's widely dispersed cities. About three-fourths of all people using public transportation in 1976 took the bus (Dole 1977). To attract more riders and to help buses avoid traffic congestion, more than 50 urban areas in the United States and 30 European cities have set aside bus express lanes. However, when Los Angeles tried bus express lanes, outraged car commuters, restricted to lanes that were more jammed than ever, protested loudly. For political reasons the experiment had to be abandoned, even though it tripled bus ridership and increased carpool riders by 65 percent.

Bus systems require less capital and have lower operating costs than most light and heavy rail mass transit systems. But by offering low fares they usually lose money. To be successful and effective, most bus systems must be subsidized by government funds. With new federal and local subsidies, some cities such as Atlanta, St. Louis, Portland, and Los Angeles have reduced bus fares. Free fares to the downtown zone in Seattle tripled the number of daily bus riders, reduced downtown automobile traffic by 7 percent, and increased downtown business—although it did not reduce air pollution. Raising fares considerably, however, penalizes the poor, who already have the least access to urban mass transit. Other experiments indicate that ridership of buses and other forms of mass transit increases most when service is improved and when vehicles are well-engineered, quiet, and comfortable (Domencick & Kraft 1970).

The argument that rail and bus systems use less energy than cars is being challenged (Hannon & Puelo 1974, Hirst 1975b, Lave 1977b, Orski 1977, Rosenthal 1977). With low average daily loads (typically only 25 percent of their seats are occupied), trains, trolleys, and buses use about the same amount of energy per passenger as the private automobile.

Para Transit   Para transit, which includes carpools, vanpools, and dial-a-ride systems, attempts to combine the advantages of the private automobile and mass transit (Chasan 1973, *Consumer Reports* 1975, Newman 1974, Roos 1974, Saltzman 1973, Transportation Research Board 1976). Carpools and vanpools can be very useful during a gasoline shortage. But as soon as the crunch is over, most riders return to their private automobiles. Pooling has been most successful when large employers have made intense efforts to establish and support it (Altshuler 1977).

Dial-a-ride systems are in operation in about 40 American cities in 22 states. Users call a central exchange, and small buses, vans, or tax-subsidized taxis are routed to pick them up at their doorsteps, usually about 20 to 50 minutes after they call. These systems are fairly expensive to operate, but compared with most large-scale mass transit systems, they are a bargain. They are one of the best ways to provide transportation for the poor, the young, the elderly, and the handicapped.

In 1975, San Jose, California, began the largest dial-a-ride system. It failed after a few months' operation because of poor management and too much success (Walworth 1975). So many people tried to use the system that the central switchboard was usually overloaded; many had to wait hours to reach the dispatcher. Many users were frustrated even more because the drivers were prohibited from picking up any riders on the street who had not called in. The ludicrous result was empty buses despite many would-be passengers. City officials were not willing to put up the money that would have doubled the number of buses and expanded the central switchboard.

One cheaper and simpler approach to dial-a-ride systems is to use tax dollars to subsidize taxi fares. In El Cajon and La Mesa, California, the local taxicab company offers citywide dial-a-ride services for 50¢ a ride, with city taxes paying the company a subsidy of about $1 a trip. Some cities can offset this subsidy by reducing or eliminating little-used bus routes.

Discouraging Automobile Use   Proposals for reducing automobile use in cities include: (1) refusing to build new highways into and out of the city, (2) setting aside express lanes for buses and carpools, (3) charging higher road and bridge tolls during peak hours, (4) eliminating or reducing road and bridge tolls for cars with three or more passengers, (5) raising parking rates by taxing parking lots, (6) eliminating some downtown parking lots, (7) charging automobile commuters high taxes or fees, (8) staggering work hours to reduce rush hour traffic, and (9) prohibiting cars on some streets or in entire areas. A combination of these approaches can greatly reduce car use. In Singapore, the number of automobiles entering the business district has decreased 75 percent since 1975 as a result of a commuter fee of $50 to $90 per month and an increased parking rate of $6 a day. In the United States, elected officials are usually unwilling to risk the wrath of commuters and voters by imposing such coercive approaches (Altshuler 1977).

Improving the Automobile   In spite of attempts to increase the use of mass and para transit systems, the private automobile will likely remain the primary means of transportation in dispersed urban areas. Americans are not about to give up their love affair with the car. Even if a rapid shift away from automobiles was possible, the resulting economic decline of the giant automobile industry and its supporting industries could upset the entire economy and lead to unemployment and economic hardship for millions.

Since we can't get most Americans out of their cars, the next best goal is to reduce energy and matter wastes and pollution caused by automobiles. Methods include: (1) modifying existing internal combustion engines to burn less fuel and produce less pollution, (2) shifting to more energy efficient and less polluting kinds of engines, (3) reducing car weight by using more plastics and lightweight metals, and (4) discouraging the use or improving the efficiency of gas-guzzling options such as air conditioning and automatic transmissions.

Principles of an Urban Transportation Plan   The four major goals of any urban transportation plan should be (1) to provide cheap and efficient transportation within an urban area for the poor, the elderly, the young, and the handicapped; (2) to allow suburban commuters to move efficiently into and out of the central city; (3) to conserve matter, energy, and land resources; and (4) to reduce pollution. The best way to accomplish the first goal is to increase para transit and express lane bus services with tax dollars. The second goal can be accomplished by improving highways and mass transit services. The third and fourth goals require more energy efficient and less polluting cars, improved traffic flow, less automobile use, more bicycle use, and compact cities rather than urban sprawl.

Any successful urban transportation plan will require an integrated mix of individual, mass transit, and para transit methods that is designed to fit the needs of the particular urban area. We need greatly increased federal, state, and local aid and coordination to develop such integrated plans. Most of the funds for improving urban transportation will have to come from the federal government. Ironically, the Public Highway Act of 1956 was a major factor in causing our present transportation mess. It established the Highway Trust Fund, which by 1976 was receiving about $6.7 billion a year from taxes on gasoline, trucks, buses, tires, and parts. Since 1956 these funds have been used to finance 90 percent of the costs of the interstate highways and freeways, which have encouraged urban sprawl. After a long battle by environmentalists, the Federal-Aid Highway Acts of 1973 and 1976 allowed more money from this fund to be used for other purposes. States can use funds approved for interstate highways for mass transit, para transit, and other transportation programs. But this alternate use is discouraged because the federal government puts up 90 percent of the cost of highway projects and only 80 percent of substitute projects. Thus, states and cities must put up twice as much money for mass and para transit as for highways.

There has been pressure to set up a separate trust fund for mass transit, but such an approach could be disastrous. It would separate planning for highways from planning for mass transit and emphasize expensive, highly technological mass transit projects that don't solve many urban transportation problems. The United States needs to eliminate the Highway Trust Fund and create a Transportation Fund. Revenues from this new fund would be used to plan and finance balanced, integrated transportation programs rather than programs that overemphasize highway or mass transit schemes that waste money, energy, and matter resources.

Summary of Methods for Transportation Savings   As we have seen, transportation accounts for about 40 percent of the energy used each year in the United States (Figure 5–1), with about 23 percent used to move people and materials from one place to another (Figure 5–1) and another 17 percent used to build and maintain vehicles, highways, parking lots, and other vehicle support services (Hayes 1977). Ways to save energy in transportation include the following:[2]

1. Build smaller, lighter cars, averaging 1,135 kilograms (2,500 pounds) by 1985 and 909 kilograms (2,000 pounds) by 1990 using smaller engines, more plastic,

aluminum, and glass and less steel. Cutting a car's weight in half typically halves fuel consumption (Hayes 1976a, Rubin 1974).

2. Enforce fuel economy standards (Environmental Policy and Conservation Act of 1976) which require automobiles sold in the United States to average 8.5 kilometers per liter (20 mpg) by 1980 and 11.7 kilometers per liter (27.5 mpg) by 1985. Raise these standards to 14.5 kilometers per liter (34 mpg) by 1990 and 17 kilometers per liter (40 mpg) by 1995.

3. Raise the gasoline tax to discourage excessive automobile use (Boshier 1978, Hirst 1976b) as a short-term method while mandatory fuel standards are being phased in.

4. Cut fuel consumption by 46 to 57 percent by making easier rolling radial tires standard equipment (up to 10 percent savings), making cars sleeker and smoother to reduce wind resistance (up to 10 percent savings), using standard transmissions (up to 10 percent savings), omitting air conditioning (9 to 20 percent savings), and using better ignition systems (about 7.5 percent savings) (Hayes 1976a).

5. Increase present federal funding for the development of new and more efficient automobile and truck engines (Figure 4–2). Give tax credits for businesses using more efficient engines and require that at least 50 percent of all government cars use more efficient engines.

6. Double average car life from 5 to 10 years by 1985 and recycle all cars at the end of their useful life (Berry & Fels 1973).

7. Buy a small, energy-efficient car and maintain it to save energy. Obey the 88-kilometer-per-hour (55 mph) speed limit, drive smoothly, cut idling time, don't race the engine, keep tires properly inflated, clean the air filter, and keep the engine tuned.

8. Organize and use carpools or vanpools. Reduced tolls, free parking, and income tax deductions should be provided for those using carpools.

9. Walk or ride a bicycle, especially for trips less than 8 kilometers (5 miles). Use Highway Trust Funds to build bike paths on all major streets and highways in urban areas.

10. Shift most freight from trucks and airplanes to less wasteful rail, water, and pipeline transport.

11. Use existing mass transit systems as much as possible. Building new, high technology mass transit systems in urban areas may save too little energy and attract too few drivers from their cars to justify the cost (Hirst 1976b, Hirst & Stuntz 1976, Lave 1977).

---

[2]For more details on energy savings in transportation, see the following: Bendixson 1975, Berry & Fels 1973, Citizens Advisory Committee on Environmental Quality 1973, Dark 1975, Hayes 1976a, 1977, Hirst 1976b, Hirst & Stuntz 1976, Large 1976, Lave 1977a, Rechel 1976, Rice 1974, Wildhorn 1975.

5-3 Energy Savings in Residential and Commercial Sectors

Over half of the 24 percent of energy used in these two sectors is for space heating (primarily of stores, office buildings, and hotels), followed by water heating, air-conditioning, refrigeration, and cooking (Figure 5-1). American buildings consume about 40 percent more energy each year than they would if they were oriented, designed, insulated, and lighted to use energy more efficiently (Freeman 1974, Stein 1977). Eliminating this waste could save energy equivalent to 1.9 billion liters (12.5 million barrels) of oil *per day* by 1990 (Freeman 1974, Hayes 1977).

A monument to energy waste is the 110-story World Trade Center in lower Manhattan, which uses as much electricity each year as the entire city of Schenectady, New York, with 100,000 persons (Carr 1976). Not a single window in its four towering walls of glass can be opened to take advantage of nature's warming and cooling, and its heating and cooling system works around the clock even when the building is empty.

Major ways to save energy in the residential and commercial sectors include the following:[3]

1. Insulate roofs, walls, and sub-floors; use double- or triple-glazed windows, storm doors, and weather stripping around doors and windows. Enforce the insulation standards established for all new housing by the Energy Conservation and Production Act of 1976 to save 50 percent of the energy requirements for a typical home (Hayes 1976a, Hirst 1976a). Raising mandatory insulation standards to superinsulation standards of 30 centimeters (12 inches) in ceiling, 15 centimeters (6 inches) in walls, and 25 centimeters (11 inches) under floors can save homeowners so much energy (60 to 80 percent) that their initial investment would be paid back within a few years (Hayes 1976a, Hirst, private communication).

2. Require all new buildings to take advantage of the heating and cooling provided free by the environment (Hayes 1976a, Stein 1972, 1977). All homes and commercial buildings should be oriented to take advantage of sunlight and prevailing winds and should have windows that can be opened to take advantage of natural heating and cooling.

3. Use solar heating where possible and design all new heating, cooling, and hot water systems for eventual solar conversion. If solar heating is not economically feasible at present, use efficient electric heat pumps, solar-assisted heat pumps, or natural gas furnaces for home heating instead of resistance electric heating or oil-burning furnaces and be sure to insulate all heating system ducts (Hayes 1976a, Hirst & Carney 1978). Prohibit the use of natural gas as a fuel to generate electricity in power and industrial plants, and ban decorative outdoor natural gas lights. Gas pilot lights for furnaces, stoves, clothes dryers, and other appliances should also be banned (as is done in California) and replaced with electric igniters.

4. Reduce heating requirements during cold weather by planting trees (conifers) on the north side of houses (Niering & Goodwin 1975), lowering the thermostat to 18°C (65°F), cutting off or drastically lowering the heat in bedrooms coupled with use of sleeping bags or more blankets (nonelectric), using humidifiers to provide comfort at lower thermostat settings, wearing heavier clothing, closing off unused rooms, opening draperies by day and closing them by night, closing fireplace dampers, cleaning and adjusting the furnace at least once a year, vacuum-cleaning furnace air filters at least every 2 weeks, and installing new filters every 4 to 6 months depending on their condition.

5. Reduce cooling requirements during hot weather by planting deciduous trees on the south side of a house (Niering & Goodwin 1975), adding awnings, raising air conditioner thermostat settings to 26°C (78°F), using dehumidifiers to provide comfort at higher thermostat settings, wearing lighter clothing, closing draperies by day and opening them by night, installing an attic fan, not cooling unused rooms, using natural breezes as much as possible, using white or light-colored roofing and outside paint to reflect incoming solar energy, and turning off lights and machines as much as possible to reduce the heat load.

6. Require utility companies to provide a total energy systems analysis for any home or building. Give owners long-term loans added to existing mortgages for reducing energy waste in existing homes. Continue and increase the tax credits provided in the National Energy Plan of 1978 for homeowners who add solar energy devices and energy-conserving devices and materials.

7. Consider building an earth-covered or partly earth-covered (underground) house or commercial building as a way to reduce cooling and heating requirements, eliminate exterior maintenance, and provide more

---

[3]For more details on energy savings in the residential and commercial sectors, see the following: Adams 1975, Adkins 1974, Alves & Milligan 1978, Appel & Mackenzie 1974, Berg 1973a, Caudill et al. 1974, Citizens Advisory Committee on Environmental Quality 1973, City of Davis Community Development Department 1977, Clarke 1977, Dubin 1972, Eccli 1976, Gibson 1977, Hammond 1974a, Hand 1977, Hannon et al. 1978, Hart 1978, Hayes 1976a, 1977, Hirst 1976a, Hirst & Carney 1978, Kern 1975, Knowles 1975a, Large 1976, Leckle et al. 1975, Love 1975, Mason 1976, *Mother Earth News* 1974, Niering & Goodwin 1975, Rafalik 1974, Schoen et al. 1975, Skurka & Noor 1976, Snell et al. 1976, Steadman 1975, Stein 1977, Stoner 1975, Todd 1977, Vale & Vale 1977, Wade & Ewenstein 1977, Wells 1973, 1976, 1977b.

privacy, quietness, and security than conventional buildings (Mason 1976, Moreland 1975, Scalise 1975, Smay 1977, Wells 1973, 1976, 1977b).[4]

8. Reduce the energy used to construct buildings 20 percent by using less energy-intensive building materials (for example, steel instead of aluminum), using as little glass as possible (especially on the south and west sides), designing buildings to minimize total lifetime energy cost, and saving energy in industries that supply building materials (Hannon et al. 1978, Hayes 1976a, Stein 1977).

9. Develop district heating systems that use local conditions (such as the sun, wind, geothermal energy, and industrial waste heat). In many areas these local sources could eliminate the need for new, large, centralized power plants (Lovins 1977c).

10. Switch from inefficient electric hot water heaters to either solar water heaters (first choice) or natural gas water heaters (with electric igniters instead of pilot lights). At least half of all conventional water heaters could be replaced with solar water heaters, saving 2 percent of all energy used in the United States each year (Berg 1973a). Heat water no higher than 49° to 60°C (120° to 140°F). Require all new hot water heaters to meet minimum efficiency and insulation standards, and give tax credits for upgrading heater insulation and insulating hot water pipes.[5] Reduce hot water use and overall water use decisively: by installing low-flow shower heads, repairing all leaky hot water faucets, doing only full loads in washers and dishwashers, washing clothes and dishes in warm or even cold water, taking 3- to 5-minute showers rather than baths, and not letting hot water run while washing, shaving, or washing dishes. Recover heat from exhaust gases on hot

water heaters and from used hot water, and use it to help heat living areas. Use excess or waste steam from power plants and industrial plants to heat water for distribution to nearby homes and buildings.

11. Reduce lighting levels and number of lights, and improve lighting efficiency. Recommended lighting levels in buildings have risen 300 percent in the past 15 years with no concrete evidence that the new levels are necessary or desirable (Hayes 1976a, Stein 1972, 1977). Reducing lighting levels by 50 percent, providing strong lighting only for small work areas (as with the small reading lights in an airplane), switching from incandescent to screw-in Litek fluorescent light bulbs (which last 10 years and use 70 percent less electricity), reducing wattage in lights, turning off lights and appliances when not needed, and making better use of natural daylight could reduce total annual electricity use in the United States by 4 to 5 percent (Stein 1972, 1977). In large commercial buildings, collect and reuse waste heat from lights, computers, office machines, and machinery. Individual light switches should be required for all rooms in commercial buildings so that a janitor or late worker doesn't have to light up an entire floor to work.

12. Make appliances more efficient. Enact progressively stricter efficiency standards for all major energy-consuming appliances and continue to show energy efficiency or lifetime energy operating costs on all appliances. Run dishwashers or clothes dryers at night after peak load periods if possible. Let dishes dry by room air rather than in drying cycles in automatic dishwashers. Better yet, don't use automatic dishwashers. Don't buy or use gadget appliances (electric can openers, hot dog cookers, etc.), self-defrosting refrigerators (which require about 50 percent more energy), instant-on TVs,[6] and self-cleaning ovens. Substitute a crock pot for an oven whenever possible.

13. Always use the lifetime energy cost, not the initial cost, to determine what type of house, building, or appliance you should buy.

5–4 Energy Savings in Industry

Industry uses more energy—53 percent—than any other sector of the American economy (Figure 5–1). About 99 percent of that energy goes for three purposes (Hayes 1976a; Figure 5–1): (1) producing process steam (45 percent), (2) providing heat for manufacturing processes and buildings (29 percent), and (3) running motors, lights, and

---

[4]Architect Malcolm Wells has pioneered in designing ecologically sound earth-covered homes. Anyone wishing further information should read his superb book *Underground Designs* (1977b), obtainable for $6.00 from Wells, Box 1149, Brewster, Maine 02631. Contrary to popular belief, living in an earth-covered building is not like living in a cave. The interior can look like that of any ordinary home, and atriums, small windows, or skylights can provide more lighting than in most conventional homes. Building an earth-covered home is an excellent way to prepare for the oil and financial crunch that will probably hit the United States between 1985 and 1995 (Sections 1–1 and 1–2) (Center for Science in the Public Interest 1977, Clarke 1977, Eccli 1976, Hammond 1974a, Leckle et al. 1975, Love 1975, *Mother Earth News* 1974, Skurka & Noor 1976, Stein 1977, Stoner 1975, Todd 1977, Vale & Vale 1977, Wade & Ewenstein 1977).

[5]For existing electric water heaters, replace the typical jacket of 5 centimeters (2 inches) of fiberglass with 10 centimeters (4 inches) of urethane foam. For natural gas water heaters, replace the typical insulation of 2.5 centimeters (1 inch) of fiberglass with 5 centimeters (2 inches) of urethane foam (Hirst & Carney 1978). These insulation jacket thicknesses should become minimum standards on all new hot water heaters. All hot water pipes should be wrapped with 2.5 centimeters (1 inch) of fiberglass insulation (Hirst & Carney 1978).

[6]If you have any instant-on appliances, turn them on and off using the plug or deactivate this feature with the switch often found on the back.

electrolytic processes (bringing about chemical changes by passing electricity through solutions of chemicals) (25 percent). Most of the steam used is produced by the plants themselves, whereas most electricity is purchased from utilities. Over 52 percent of the energy consumed by industry is in three sectors: primary metals (especially iron, steel, and aluminum), chemicals (including synthetic fibers and plastics), and petroleum refining.

Although U.S. industry uses and wastes more energy than other sectors, it has also made the greatest efforts to cut waste since 1973 (Whiting 1978). Even more energy can be saved by using the following methods:[7]

1. Save 10 percent by putting automatic shutoff timers on all electrical devices, insulating, maintaining boilers, turning off lights, and reducing or eliminating unnecessary lighting, heating, and cooling.

2. Save 20 to 30 percent within existing industrial processes by collecting and reusing waste heat, using computerized monitors and controls, and using industrial waste heat to co-generate electricity for use at the plant instead of buying it from utilities. Co-generation will probably be the major way to save energy after 1985 and could provide as much new electricity as the U.S. economy will need by 2000 (Williams 1978).

3. Develop and convert to more efficient equipment and processes. Here the savings will vary from industry to industry. Steel, for example, has the biggest energy appetite of any United States industry (Reese 1977). Half of all American steel is still being made in open-hearth furnaces using four times as much energy as the basic-oxygen process. In aluminum production, which accounts for about 5 percent of all the electricity used in the United States each year, phasing in a recently developed new process could save about 45 percent of that energy (Reese 1977, Rubin 1974).

4. Step up extensive recycling. For example, steel made from scrap in an electric furnace uses only about one-fourth the energy of steel made from virgin ore. Recycling aluminum cans uses far less energy than producing new aluminum, but banning aluminum cans altogether and using returnable bottles saves much more energy. Provide economic incentives and favorable transportation rates for secondary (recycled) materials industries and users, require that all materials bought by government agencies use an average of 50 percent recycled material, and impose a manufacturing tax on all energy-intensive products. Virgin materials may have to

be taxed to slow down their use and favor recycled materials.

5. At least double the useful life of all products and add a disposal or resource recovery tax to all products that last less than a specified number of years.

6. Reverse the electricity rate structure by giving smaller users the lowest rates.

7. Increase electrical rates during peak load times to shift some of the electrical load and to reduce waste. The size and number of electrical power plants are determined by peak loads, not by average daily or annual use.

8. Encourage industrial energy conservation by buying only the most energy-efficient products and appliances, buying goods made of recycled materials, avoiding products packaged in throwaway containers or excessive packaging, and buying products that are designed to last.

Putting into practice the energy-saving steps discussed in this section is crucial for making the transition to a new earthmanship era.

A country that runs on energy cannot afford to waste it.

Bruce Hannon

Discussion Topics

1. Explain why energy conservation should form the basis of any individual, corporate, or national energy plan. Does it form a significant portion of your personal energy plan or life-style? Why or why not? Is it a significant factor in our national energy policy? Why?

2. List 20 ways in which you unnecessarily waste energy each day, and try to order them according to the amount of energy wasted. Draw up a plan showing how you could eliminate or reduce each type of waste. Which ones are the most difficult to reduce? Why?

3. Make an energy use study of your campus or school, and use the findings to develop an energy conservation program.

Further Readings

See also the references for Chapter 4.

---

[7]For more details on methods for saving energy in industry, see the following: Berg 1975, 1976, Large 1976, Reese 1977, Rimberg 1974, Rubin 1974, Schipper 1976b, Whiting 1978, Williams 1978.

Center for Science in the Public Interest. 1977. *99 Ways to a Simple Lifestyle.* New York: Doubleday. Superb summary of how you can conserve matter and energy. Try to read this book.

Clarke, Robin. 1977. *Building for Self-Sufficiency.* New York: Universe Books. Superb summary. Use this to see how you might prepare for the energy and economic crunch that may come between 1985 and 1995. See also Hammond 1974a, Todd 1977.

Hyman, Barry I. 1973. *Initiatives in Energy Conservation.* Staff report prepared for the Committee on Commerce, U.S. Senate. Washington, D.C.: Government Printing Office. Stock no. 5270–01960. One of the best summaries available. Highly recommended.

Office of Emergency Preparedness. 1972. *The Potential for Energy Conservation.* Washington, D.C.: Government Printing Office. Stock no. 4102–00009. Superb evaluation. Highly recommended. Extensive bibliography.

Ross, Marc H., and Robert H. Williams. 1977. "The Potential for Fuel Conservation." *Technology Review,* February, pp. 49–56. Excellent overview of opportunities for conservation. See also Williams 1975.

Stein, Richard G. 1977. *Architecture and Energy.* Garden City, N.Y.: Anchor Books. Outstanding analysis of energy conservation in buildings.

Wells, Malcolm, and Irwin Spetgang. 1978. *How To Buy Solar Heating and Cooling . . . Without Getting Burnt.* Emmaus, Pa.: Rodale. Before you install solar energy, be sure to read this important book.

6

Nonrenewable Energy Resources: Fossil Fuels

We seem to believe we can get everything we need from the supermarket and corner drugstore. We don't understand that everything has a source in the land or sea, and that we must respect these sources.

Thor Heyerdahl

6–1   Formation and Recovery of Fossil Fuels

We are near the end of the so-called *fossil fuel era,* in which natural gas, petroleum, and coal are the major sources of energy for industrial societies. The original source of the chemical energy stored in fossil fuels is the sun. Over eons, green plants have used photosynthesis (Section 3–3) to change solar energy to chemical energy stored in glucose and other chemicals. As plants and animals died and decayed, they were converted over millions of years to rich deposits of natural gas, petroleum, and coal.

Natural gas consists of 50 to 90 percent methane (a hydrocarbon compound made of hydrogen and carbon, CH_4) and small amounts of more complex hydrocarbon compounds such as propane (C_3H_8) and butane (C_4H_{10}). **Petroleum,** or **crude oil,** is a dark greenish brown, foul-smelling liquid containing a complex mixture of hydrocarbon compounds plus small amounts of oxygen, sulfur, and nitrogen compounds. Low-sulfur petroleum is the most valuable, because one of the most dangerous air pollutants —sulfur dioxide—forms when sulfur impurities in petroleum combine with oxygen as oil burns.

Typically, deposits of natural gas and petroleum accumulate together under a dome-shaped layer of rock several thousand meters under the earth's surface (Figure 6–1). If a hole is drilled through the rock layer, the pressure under the dome forces the gas and oil to the surface. Once this pressure is gone, oil must be pumped to the surface, and eventually extracted by pumping water or gas in to repressurize the reservoir (secondary recovery). At today's prices drillers usually recover about 35 percent of the oil. But as oil prices rise, they may go after the remaining oil. One common tertiary-recovery method is to pump steam into the well. But since it takes useful fossil-fuel energy to produce the steam, this is a poor energy investment (Section 4–2; Odum & Odum 1976).

When a natural gas deposit is tapped, the propane and butane are liquefied and taken off as LPG (liquefied petroleum gas) before the remaining gas (mostly methane) is pumped into pipelines for distribution. The liquid propane and butane are stored in pressurized containers for use in areas (often rural) not served by natural gas pipelines. Of all the fossil fuels, natural gas is the easiest to process and transport in pipelines, and it burns the hottest with the least pollution—which explains why it is so widely used. Natural gas heats roughly half of all U.S. homes, and it fuels about 40 percent of all industry.

In many oil- and natural-gas-producing countries, the natural gas released when an oil well is tapped is simply burned off (flared) because there is no local market. Only 1 percent of gas produced in the United States is flared, but elsewhere the figure is over 20 percent (Brown 1978b). One way to reduce this gross waste is to liquefy the gas at −161°C, transport it to markets, and regasify the liquid at receiving terminals. Unfortunately, there are three problems with this approach: (1) it is expensive; (2) about 25 percent of the gas's original energy content is lost in the process; and (3) an LNG (liquefied natural gas) explosion or accident in a port could create a massive and deadly fireball.

Once out of the ground, crude oil goes to a refinery. There its various components, such as gasoline, kerosene, heating oil, diesel fuel, lubricating oils, and greases, are separated from one another by means of their different boiling points (temperatures at which they change to gas). All of the separated components are used commercially, but the greatest demand is for *gasoline,* which makes up 25 to 45 percent of refined petroleum. The gasoline that originally boils off is not good enough for today's high-compression car engines, so refineries upgrade it and also convert other petroleum components into high-quality gasoline. Of course, some of the useful chemical energy in the petroleum is lost in this processing.

Petroleum and natural gas are valuable not only as sources of high-quality energy, but also as raw materials in manufacturing most of the industrial chemicals, fertilizers, pesticides, plastics, synthetic fibers, medicines, and other products used in modern society (Figure 6-2). About 6 percent (Figure 4-3) of all fossil fuels used in the United States each year go to produce these petrochemicals. From Figure 6-2 we can see why most prices go up when oil and natural gas prices go up. Some of these chemicals can be produced from coal and from the fermentation of biomass (plants, trees, and organic waste materials) (Wishart 1978). But such a major transformation of the entire chemical industry in an industrialized nation would take decades and huge amounts of capital.

Thus, natural gas and petroleum can be considered almost too valuable to burn up as a fuel and perhaps we should set aside a third of the world's known petroleum and natural gas reserves as raw materials for producing petrochemicals in the future. However, Barry Commoner (1971) has argued that we should use fewer harmful petrochemical products and more natural products.

Coal, the other major fossil fuel, is a solid containing from 55 to 90 percent carbon and small amounts of hydrogen, oxygen, nitrogen, and sulfur compounds. As with petroleum, the low-sulfur type is the more desirable because it produces less sulfur dioxide when burned. Coal is formed over millions of years in several stages, each representing an increase in carbon content and fuel quality (Figure 6-3). Depending on its location, coal is mined from deep underground deposits or by strip mining (Section 6-6) shallow deposits near the earth's surface.

About 70 percent of the coal mined each year in the world is burned to provide heat, to supply steam for industry and transportation, and to produce electricity at power plants. Most of the remaining 30 percent is converted to coke, liquid coal tar, or a mixture of gases known as coal gas. Coke is used in making iron and steel. Coal tar, which contains from 65 to 90 different chemicals, is used in dyes, plastics, explosives, drugs, medicines, and many other products.

6-2 Petroleum, Natural Gas, Oil Shale, and Tar Sands

Estimates of Petroleum and Natural Gas How much longer can nonrenewable fossil fuels last if the world's ap-

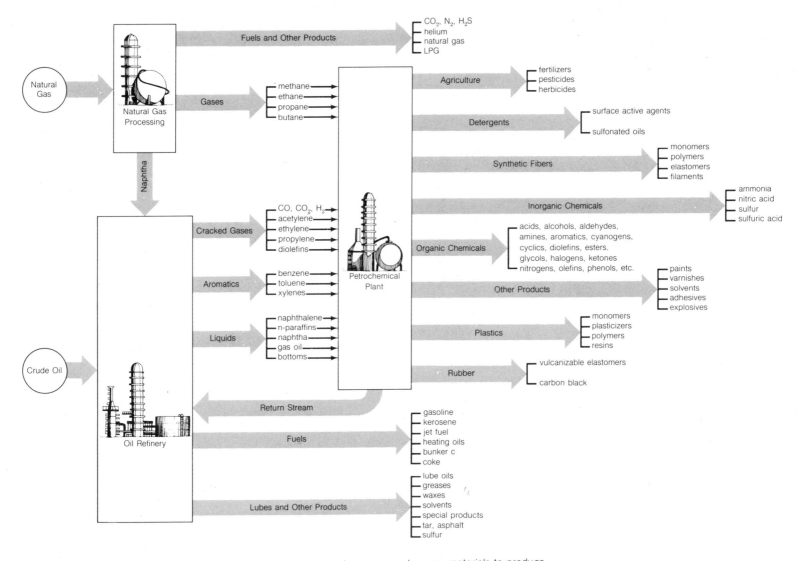

Figure 6–2 The petrochemical industries. Crude oil and natural gas are used as raw materials to produce most of the products in modern society.

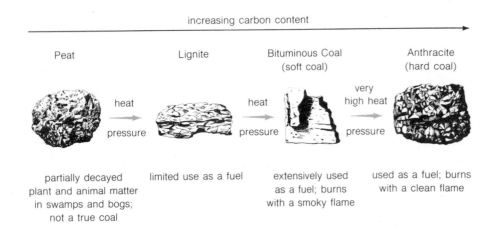

increasing carbon content →

| Peat | Lignite | Bituminous Coal (soft coal) | Anthracite (hard coal) |

heat / pressure → heat / pressure → very high heat / pressure →

partially decayed plant and animal matter in swamps and bogs; not a true coal

limited use as a fuel

extensively used as a fuel; burns with a smoky flame

used as a fuel; burns with a clean flame

Figure 6–3 Stages in coal formation over many millions of years.

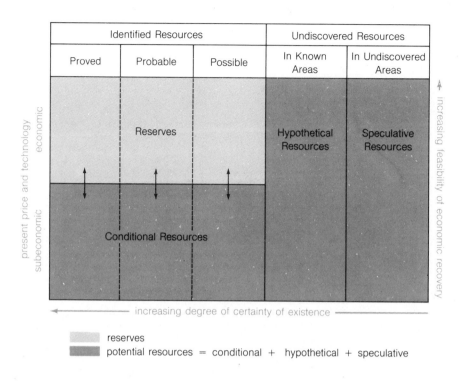

Identified Resources			Undiscovered Resources	
Proved	Probable	Possible	In Known Areas	In Undiscovered Areas
Reserves			Hypothetical Resources	Speculative Resources
Conditional Resources				

← ——— increasing degree of certainty of existence ——— →

present price and technology · economic / subeconomic

increasing feasibility of economic recovery

reserves

potential resources = conditional + hypothetical + speculative

Figure 6–4 U.S. Geological Survey classification of nonfuel and fuel mineral resources. (Brobst & Pratt 1973)

petite for energy continues to grow (Figure 1–4)? Since deposits of natural gas, petroleum, and coal are hidden under the ground, no one really knows how extensive they are. As with nonrenewable metal and mineral resources, estimates of recoverable amounts of fossil fuels depend on how well geologists can determine identified, undiscovered, and speculative supplies (Figure 6–4) and on the rate of use.[1] However, there is an important difference. The supplies of some metals and minerals can be extended by recycling and reuse, but the useful energy from fossil fuels (or any energy source) cannot. Once burned they are gone forever.

The U.S. Geological Survey classifies resources in several categories according to the relative certainty of their existence and economic feasibility of mining and

processing them (Brobst & Pratt 1973), as summarized in Figure 6–4. Resources are broadly classified as either identified or undiscovered. **Identified resources** are specific bodies of mineral-bearing rock whose existence and location are known. This category is subdivided into **reserves** (or *economic resources*), identified resources that can be recovered profitably with present prices and technology, and **conditional resources** (or *subeconomic resources*), identified resources that cannot be recovered profitably with present prices and technology. Estimates of reserves and conditional reserves are based on analyses of rock samples and on geological projections. Since the certainty of these measurements and projections varies, these two categories are further subdivided into proven, probable (or indicated), and possible (or inferred) (Figure 6–4).

Undiscovered resources are those that are believed to exist. They are described as either hypothetical resources or speculative resources. **Hypothetical resources** are deposits that can be reasonably expected to exist in areas where deposits have been found in the past. **Speculative resources** are deposits that are thought to be in areas that have not been examined and tested for resources. If actual discoveries are made, hypothetical and speculative resources can then be reclassified as reserves (economic resources) or conditional resources (subeconomic resources).

From this classification scheme we can see why there are so many conflicting estimates of the potential supply of a resource. Often estimates found in newspapers and articles do not specify which category is being used.

---

[1]For estimates of supplies of natural gas, oil, oil shale, tar sands, and coal, see the following: Berg et al. 1974, Brown 1978b, Central Intelligence Agency 1977, Cheney 1974, Committee on Interior and Insular Affairs 1973, Cook 1972, 1976b, Darmstadter 1971, 1977, Exxon Company 1976, Federal Energy Administration 1974a, 1976, Fisher 1974, Flower 1978, Grenon 1977, Griffith & Clarke 1979, Häfele 1974, Hubbert 1962, 1969a, 1971, 1973, 1974, Joint Committee on Atomic Energy 1973, Knowles 1975b, Maugh 1976c, McLean 1972, Miller et al. 1975, Moody & Geiger 1975, National Academy of Sciences 1975b, National Petroleum Council 1972, Office of Science and Technology 1972, Organization for Economic Cooperation and Development 1977, Peach 1973, Schanz 1978, Schmidt & Hill 1976, Singer 1975b, Theobald et al. 1972, United Nations 1976, U.S. Bureau of Mines 1976b, U.S. Department of the Interior 1975, Whittemore 1973, Wilson 1977, Woodwell 1974.

Geophysicist M. King Hubbert (1962, 1969a, 1971, 1973, 1974) has projected depletion curves for world and U.S. supplies of petroleum (Figure 6–5). Some observers are more optimistic (Exxon Company 1976, Fisher 1974, Peach 1973, Theobald et al. 1972), but recent estimates generally agree with Hubbert's (Brown 1978b, Central Intelligence Agency 1977, Federal Energy Administration 1976, Flower 1978, Grenon 1977, Miller et al. 1975, Moody & Geiger 1975, National Academy of Sciences 1975b, Organization for Economic Cooperation and Development 1977, United Nations 1976, U.S. Bureau of Mines 1976b, Wilson 1977).

If current trends in exploration and usage continue, world supplies of oil could exceed the demand somewhere between 1985 and 2000 and become 80 percent depleted between 2015 to 2030 (Figure 6–5). Figure 6–5 also shows that petroleum production in the United States peaked in

Figure 6–5 Estimated depletion curves for world and U.S. supplies of petroleum. Estimate 1 is based on what most experts believe to be the ultimately recoverable supplies if usage increases at 5 percent annually. Estimate 2 assumes either twice the petroleum supply of Estimate 1 or an annual rate of use increase of 2.5 percent. (Modified from Berg et al. 1974, Hubbert 1969a, 1974)

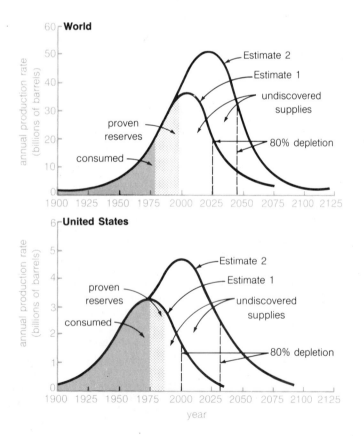

1970 (just as Hubbert predicted many years ago), with 80 percent depletion predicted for 1990 to 2015. Estimate 2 in Figure 6–5 assumes either that we will find twice as much oil as the experts expect or that conservation and high prices will cut usage rates in half. Even if Estimate 2 proves to be correct, 80 percent depletion would only be postponed a few decades.

Supplies of natural gas are harder to predict, but at best they are expected to last only several decades longer than those of petroleum (Hubbert 1969a, 1973, Wilson 1977). Thus, world supplies of natural gas could be 80 percent depleted somewhere between 2025 and 2060 (in the United States between 2015 to 2040) (Hubbert 1974, Miller et al. 1975, U.S. Bureau of Mines 1976b).

Even the estimates in Figure 6–5 may be too optimistic because they are based on total energy resource supplies, not net useful energy supplies. For example, between 1870 and 1970 the average depth of an oil well in the United States increased 20-fold (Cook 1976b). Most of the undiscovered and potential natural gas reserves in the United States are believed to lie at deeper than 7,000 meters (20,000 feet), and most of the remaining oil reserves are either in remote areas (such as Alaska) or in deep offshore deposits (Cook 1976b). These deeper and more remote oil fields require a larger energy input than that required by Middle Eastern and other more accessible oil deposits.

The world still has lots of natural gas and oil, and before peak production is reached, companies may in some years produce more oil and natural gas than the world can consume. Such short-term gluts should in no way be interpreted as indications that a long-term energy crisis is a hoax. The message of Figure 6–5, even Estimate 2, is very clear. Don't waste oil and natural gas, but use them only for essential purposes; look for more oil and natural gas to buy a little time; and start a crash program to shift to other forms of energy over the next 50 years.

Oil Shale Recent reports have raised the possibility of getting oil from oil shale.[2] Actually, **oil shale** is not shale rock, and contains no oil. Instead, it is an underground formation of marlstone sedimentary rock containing varying amounts of a rubbery solid mixture of hydrocarbons known as **kerogen.** The conventional way to extract the kerogen is to strip mine or deep mine the oil shale rock (much like coal). The rock is then sent to a nearby processing plant, where it is crushed and then heated to about 462°C (900°F) in a large vessel called a *retort*. This process vaporizes the

---

[2]For more details on oil shale, see the following: Bishop 1974, Carr 1976, Dinneen & Cook 1974, Environmental Protection Agency 1974d, Gannon 1974, Grenon 1977, Hammond et al. 1973, Hubbert 1973, Maugh 1977c, Peach 1973, Perrini 1975, Rattien 1976, Staff report 1974b, Wilson 1977.

solid kerogen; the vapor is then condensed to yield an extremely viscous (slow-flowing) dark brown fluid called **shale oil.** Part of the decomposed kerogen stays a gas and can be burned to furnish power at the processing plant or upgraded to pipeline-quality synthetic natural gas. After its viscosity is reduced, the shale oil is upgraded and then sent through a pipeline to a refinery, where it can be converted to petroleum products (see Figure 6–2). Shale oil is fairly low in sulfur but it is high in nitrogen (about 10 times the amount in petroleum) and paraffinic waxes (Maugh 1977c). Since nitrogen compounds make car engines knock and the waxes foul engines, these substances must be removed before refining—adding to its cost and cutting the net useful energy yield.

The world's largest known deposits of oil shale lie in the United States, with significant amounts in Canada, China, and the U.S.S.R. and smaller deposits in Zaire, Italy, Sweden, and Brazil (Grenon 1977). The richest United States deposit underlies about 44,500 square kilometers (11 million acres) of federally owned land where Colorado, Utah, and Wyoming meet (Figure 8–8). The total amount of shale oil locked in this deposit may equal the entire world's proven and estimated petroleum deposits (Rattien 1976). Even the 0.004 to 0.03 percent of it that seems economically feasible to extract and upgrade could equal the world's proven reserves of crude oil, and could supply all U.S. oil needs at 1977 levels for 90 years (Hubbert 1973, Rattien 1976, Staff report 1979b).

Before painting a rosy future rich in shale oil, however, let us face the problems involved. The main one is economics. At 1979 prices shale oil could cost $18 to $25 per barrel (159 liters) compared to $14.50 per barrel for OPEC crude oil (Staff report 1979b). OPEC oil prices may rise to $30 or more per barrel by 1990 (or sooner), but the economically feasible price per barrel for shale oil would probably also rise because of inflation and environmental controls. Moreover, the 40 large-scale shale-oil plants needed to produce even 10 percent of U.S. needs by the year 2000 (Staff report 1976c) would cost $40 billion, a heavy investment for private capital. Thus shale may never provide much oil unless heavily subsidized by government funds (Maugh 1977c, Rattien 1976, Staff report 1976c).

In addition, shale oil may have a low net useful energy yield. Because the kerogen is widely dispersed in the rock, low-grade deposits will almost certainly take more energy to mine, heat, refine, and ship than they will provide (Odum & Odum 1976). Even high-grade deposits extracted by the conventional method may yield relatively little net useful energy (Odum & Odum 1976).

Producing shale oil also creates serious environmental problems (Environmental Protection Agency 1974d, Pfeffer 1974, Rattien 1976). The basic problems are (1) land disruption from surface mining (Section 6–6) and disposal of the waste or spent shale rock, (2) air and water pollution from the mining and retorting operations, and (3) the possible impact of shale oil boom towns on fragile semi-arid ecosystems (Gilmore 1976).

The amount of solid waste that processing shale rock produces is staggering. The 40 shale-oil processing plants mentioned above would produce 86 billion kilograms (950 million tons) of waste rock per year—almost eight times the total solid waste produced by all homes and businesses in the United States during 1975. Because the rock breaks up and expands when heated, the waste takes about 12 percent more space than the original—so it can't just be stuffed back into the ground. If dumped into canyons and ravines, the rock could scar the land, upset drainage patterns, and threaten surface and groundwater supplies as sediment, soluble salts, and toxic metal compounds leach or erode out of it (Environmental Protection Agency 1974d).

Air pollution from emissions of sulfur oxides, nitrogen oxides, hydrocarbons, and particulates would also be a serious problem without a large investment in air pollution control equipment (Council on Environmental Quality, *Environmental Quality*, 1975, Environmental Protection Agency 1974d). The uncontrolled sulfur dioxide emissions from 40 shale-oil plants would equal those from nine uncontrolled 1,000-megawatt power plants burning low-sulfur coal (Council on Environmental Quality, *Environment Quality*, 1975).

Even if all the other problems could somehow be solved, the production of shale oil may be limited by a lack of water (Environmental Protection Agency 1974d, Harte & El-Gasseir 1978, Rattien 1976). The 40 projected oil-shale-processing plants would use as much water each year as all the households in New York City (Environmental Protection Agency 1974d). Already short of water, the oil-shale region has competing plans to irrigate crops, supply cities, strip-mine coal, and develop geothermal energy deposits (Section 8–4). In addition, water used to process shale could return to the Colorado River basin so full of dissolved minerals that downstream users in the rich agricultural valleys of Arizona, California, and Mexico could not use it for irrigation.

One possible solution to many of these problems is to retort the kerogen out of the rock in place—under ground (Figure 6–6; Environmental Protection Agency 1974d, Rattien 1976). After conventional explosives loosen the rock, natural gas can be pumped in and ignited in controlled fire at the top of the formation. As steam and air force the flames downward, the kerogen flows out through pipes at the bottom. A by-product gas, recovered separately, powers electric generators and sustains the flame front. Other exhaust gases pass through a scrubber to remove air pollutants. This approach is in the pilot-plant stage, far too early to determine its financial, net-energy, and environmental feasibility.

Scientists have also suggested detonating small atomic bombs underground to break up the shale rock and retort the kerogen (Rattien 1976). But this approach could con-

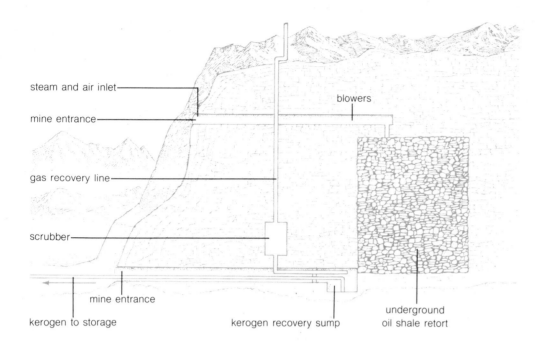

Figure 6-6 In situ processing of oil shale may reduce costs, water requirements, and environmental impact compared with the above-ground approach. Oil-shale rock is blasted to bits and heated, and the kerogen is extracted—all in an underground retort.

steam and air inlet

mine entrance

blowers

gas recovery line

scrubber

mine entrance

kerogen to storage

kerogen recovery sump

underground oil shale retort

taminate both groundwater and kerogen with radioactivity and trigger small earthquakes. Just to supply 18 percent of projected U.S. oil by 1985 would require about six underground nuclear blasts a day.[3] Such an approach in Colorado needs approval by voters.

Tar Sands   **Tar sands** (or oil sands) are enormous swamps of fine clay and sand mixed with water and variable amounts of a black, molasses-thick high-sulfur tar known as bitumen, or heavy oil, which is about 83 percent carbon.[4] Shallow deposits can be dug up by strip mining and then heated with steam to make the viscous tar flow and float to the top. The extracted heavy oil, which can contain large amounts of sulfur, must then be upgraded to synthetic crude oil and purified by removing the sulfur impurities. Deeper underground deposits must be processed in place by a process yet to be developed.

Canada has the world's largest known deposits located in a cold, desolate, area of north central Alberta. The 29 to 32 trillion liters (200 to 300 billion barrels) from these deposits that could be recovered economically (Cook 1976b, Hubbert 1973, Paehlke 1976) almost equal the Middle East's remaining known oil reserves (Paehlke 1976). Only

about 10 percent of the extractable Canadian deposits can be processed by strip mining. The remaining 90 percent is too deeply buried and must somehow be processed in place (Cook 1976b, Paehlke 1976, Wilson 1977).

Venezuela's tar sands may be almost as rich as Canada's (Wilson 1977). The U.S.S.R. probably has another large deposit with smaller ones in Albania, Rumania, Colombia, and Utah (Cook 1976b, Maugh 1978). Estimates of total worldwide deposits vary from 1 to 4 times the world's known oil reserves (Maugh 1978, Staff report 1979b).

But large-scale production of synthetic crude oil from tar sands is beset with problems (Carr 1976, Paehlke 1976, Pratt 1975). Tar sands are more difficult to handle than any other substance ever mined on a large scale (Maugh 1978). They are so abrasive that they wear out the teeth of gigantic bucket scrapers every 4 to 8 hours (Carr 1976, Maugh 1978). In addition, they stick to everything, clog up extraction equipment and vehicles, and slowly dissolve natural rubber in tires, conveyor belts, and machinery parts (Carr 1976, Maugh 1978).

No wonder then that mining and upgrading the bitumen is such a costly and risky proposition (Maugh 1978). World oil prices of $16 to $19 per barrel (158 liters), which were exceeded in 1979, may make extraction and processing economically feasible (Maugh 1978, Staff report 1979b).

Since large amounts of steam and electricity must be used to mine and process the tar sand, the estimated net useful energy yield will probably be low (Odum & Odum 1976. Paehlke 1976, Staff report 1979b). There are also potentially serious environmental problems (Carr 1976,

---

[3]This is based on Cohen's estimate (1967) that one 50-kiloton atomic bomb could pulverize about 1 million tons of rock and yield at best about 0.5 million barrels of oil.

[4]For more details on tar sands, see the following: Allen 1975, Carr 1976, Grenon 1977, Maugh 1978, Maurer 1977, Paehlke 1976, Pratt 1975.

Paehlke 1976). Strip mining tar sands produces more waste per unit of heavy oil than is produced in mining oil shale (Carr 1976). In addition, the steam extraction and processing of the heavy oil requires large quantities of water (Paehlke 1976). Thus, as with oil shale, long-range production may be limited by the available water supplies (Paehlke 1976). Researchers are trying to find ways for reusing the processing water (Maugh 1978). Now, though, much of the water ends up as an oily mess in ever growing ponds, which mar the landscape and could contaminate nearby rivers with organic chemicals and metal compounds. Underground water supplies could also be polluted if an in situ process is eventually developed (Paehlke 1976). Also, the refining process spews sulfur dioxide, hydrogen sulfide, hydrocarbons, and nitrogen oxides into the air (Paehlke 1976) unless they are removed, at considerable expense, from stack emissions (Maugh 1978).

In 1964 Great Canadian Oil Sands, Ltd., which is 96 percent owned by Sun Oil Company of Philadelphia, began building a small-scale extraction and processing plant at the Athabasca tar sands site in Alberta. By 1978 the plant was producing a modest 7.9 million liters (50,000 barrels) of synthetic crude oil per day (Maugh 1978). Despite a profit of $25 million during 1976 and 1977, the company still had a net loss of $54 million.

This project is dwarfed by the new $2.5 billion Syncrude project being developed by a consortium of three oil companies (Exxon, Gulf, and Cities Service) and the governments of Canada, Alberta, and Ontario. When in full operation (1983) the Syncrude project should produce about 20 million liters (127,000 barrels) of synthetic crude oil per day—about 6 percent of the total Canadian demand (Maugh 1978). This immense project staggers the imagination. An enormous power plant will produce enough electricity to light a city of 300,000 people (Maugh 1978). Four mammoth electric dragline scoops, each with a bucket the size of a two-car garage attached to a boom that is longer than a football field will mine the sands. Two electric conveyor belts, each 4.8 kilometers (3 miles) long and 1.8 meters (6 feet) wide, will take the scooped-up sand to what must be the world's largest washing machine. The extracted heavy oil will then go to a massive processing plant before being piped throughout Canada.

Once the surface deposits are gone, the company will need an underground process only now being developed. It will take at least 20 years and billions of dollars to determine whether such processes are technologically and economically feasible (Staff report 1979b).

Even if the projects succeed, little or none of the synthetic crude oil produced in Canada will reach the United States. The experience gained, however, will be useful in determining the feasibility of developing large tar sand deposits in Venezuela and the U.S.S.R. and perhaps the small deposit in Utah (Maugh 1978).

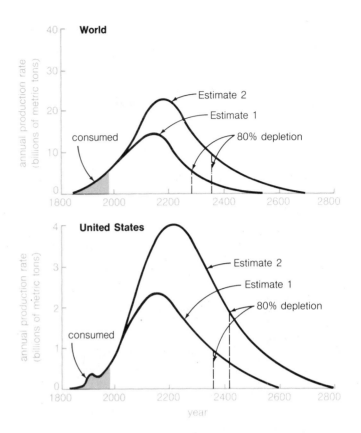

Figure 6–7 Estimated depletion curves for world and U.S. supplies of coal with the use of coal increasing by 3.56 percent annually. Estimate 2 assumes that the ultimately recoverable supplies of coal are roughly twice as large as those assumed in Estimate 1. (Modified from Hubbert 1969a, 1974)

6–3 Coal: A Possible Transition Fuel

Based on known reserves, coal is the most abundant fossil fuel in the world and in the United States, making up 90 percent of America's and 93 percent of the world's remaining fossil fuel resources, as shown in Figure 6–7 (Griffith & Clarke 1979, Hubbert 1969a, 1973, Sheridan 1977, Wilson 1977).[5] Known and potentially recoverable coal reserves in

[5]For more details on coal supplies and related problems, see the following: Boulding 1976, Carter 1978b, 1978e, Cook 1976b, Dials & Moore 1974, Doyes 1976, Dunham 1974, Energy Research and Development Administration 1976b, Executive Office of the President 1977, Federal Energy Administration 1976, Fowler 1975a, 1975b, Gordon 1978, Grenon 1977, Griffith & Clarke 1979, Hayes 1979, Hubbert 1969a, 1973, 1974, McBride et al. 1978, Naill et al. 1975, National Academy of Sciences 1975b, 1977c, 1977d, Nephew 1973, Neyman 1977, Noyes 1978, Osborn 1974, Schmidt & Hill 1976, Sheridan 1977, Staff report 1977f, 1977g, 1978d, U.S. Bureau of Mines 1976b, Walsh 1974, Whipple 1976, Wilson 1977.

the United States could contain more energy than all the remaining domestic supplies of petroleum, natural gas, oil shale, and tar sands combined. Known economically recoverable world reserves of coal are estimated to contain energy equivalent to 5 times as much as in the world's proven reserves of oil—6 times as much if we add the potentially recoverable coal (Griffith & Clarke 1979, Wilson 1977). Recoverable coal resources could support the world's current level of coal use for about 1,000 years and current world levels of all fossil fuel use for at least 200 years (Hayes 1977). But supplies would only last about 81 years if world demand for coal increased by 5 percent each year (Hayes 1977).

Known world coal reserves, however, are very unevenly distributed. The United States, the U.S.S.R., and China account for nearly 60 percent of present world production with Poland, Great Britain, and West Germany producing another 15 percent (Wilson 1977). Among the developing nations, only India is a fairly large coal producer (Griffith & Clarke 1979). The U.S.S.R. has an estimated 56 percent of the world's coal resources—a higher percentage of the world's coal than the Middle East has of the world's oil (Hayes 1977). The United States has about 19 percent of the world's estimated coal resources, and China has about 8 percent (Hayes 1977).

Known coal resources in the United States could support American coal needs at present levels for about 300 years (Staff report 1977h, U.S. Bureau of Mines 1976b). If coal became America's sole source of fossil fuel energy, however, proven reserves would last only about 47 years, and proven plus estimated reserves would only last about 80 years, assuming a 5 percent rise in energy demand each year (Perry 1974).

Regardless of the supply estimates and usage rates, the world and the United States have enough coal to use as a transition fuel until a mix of solar, wind, and renewable energy sources can be phased in over the next 50 years (Clarke & Griffith 1979, Dunham 1974, Executive Office of the President 1977, Hayes 1977, 1979, Naill et al. 1975, Nephew 1973, Osborn 1974). Coal is not only more plentiful, but at present cheaper than oil, natural gas, and nuclear energy (Griffith & Clarke 1979). Although coal prices will undoubtedly rise as stricter environmental controls are added, coal is expected to remain competitive with and probably cheaper than other energy alternatives for the remainder of this century and well into the next (Griffith & Clarke 1979, Staff report 1977h).

Coal also has a high net useful energy yield that is decreasing at a slower rate than the yields of oil and natural gas. The net useful energy yield for coal is much higher than the low to moderate net useful energy yield for conventional nuclear fission energy (Table 4–4).

Why, then, has coal dropped sharply in use since 1900, supplying only 27 percent of the world's energy in 1975 (Figure 1–2) and only 19 percent of the energy used in the United States in 1976 (Figure 1–3)? Compared with oil and natural gas, coal is dirty to mine and burn and awkward to distribute and use. However, coal could become a major fuel once more as oil and natural gas supplies decline and become more expensive, and as the once bright promise of nuclear energy rapidly fades because of safety problems, long-term nuclear waste disposal, plutonium theft for bombs, and drastically rising costs (Chapter 7).

President Carter's proposed national energy plan for the United States projected a doubling of U.S. coal output between 1976 and 1985 to provide 29 percent of all energy by 1985. This plan includes a stringent energy conservation program and price rises in domestic oil in order to reduce a dollar drain because of oil imports as discussed later (Section 10–3; Executive Office of the President 1977). The National Energy Act of 1978 (Section 10–3) was so weak that none of the proposed goals for 1985 will be met, although coal production should increase by at least 36 and perhaps as much as 70 percent between 1976 and 1985 (Hayes 1979, Staff report 1978d).

Before the United States (and other coal-producing nations) can use coal as a major transition fuel, they must solve many formidable environmental, logistic, water supply, and social problems (Dials & Moore 1974, Griffith & Clarke 1979, Hayes 1977, McBride et al. 1978, Naill et al. 1975, Sheridan 1977, Staff report 1977g, 1977h). Coal is the most polluting fossil fuel, emitting dangerous toxic metal compounds, cancer-causing organic radioactive substances (McBride et al. 1978), and sulfur oxides and particulates when it burns (Section 6–4). These air pollutants, especially particulates and sulfur oxides, have been shown to contribute to illness and premature death from respiratory ailments such as asthma, bronchitis, emphysema, and lung cancer. The sulfur dioxide in coal smoke can attack plants directly and also create an acid rain that can leach nutrients from the soil, stunt trees and food crops, and kill fish in lakes and ponds.

In addition, the burning of coal spews more carbon dioxide into the air per unit of heat released than any other fossil fuel (Griffith & Clarke 1979). There is growing concern that increasing carbon dioxide concentrations in the atmosphere could change global climate (Section 9–2). This threat rather than the supply may be the factor that limits the use of coal—and all fossil fuels—in the long run (National Academy of Sciences 1977a). Coal-burning plants also produce large amounts of fly ash and solid waste that must be disposed of safely.

Underground mines can cause surface lands to cave in, and their drainage has seriously polluted about 18,000 kilometers (11,000 miles) of American streams (Council on Environmental Quality 1973). The strip mining of coal can disrupt land, water supplies, wildlife, and humans (Section 6–6). In addition, since 1900 more than 100,000 miners have been killed and more than a million permanently disabled in mine accidents (Sheridan 1977). About 75 percent of all retired miners suffer from black lung disease and spend their last few years gasping for breath. Each year the federal government pays black lung victims $1 billion, and this figure could rise to $8 billion by 1982 (Sheridan 1977). Stricter laws have improved mine safety since 1969, but coal mining is still the nation's most dangerous industrial occupation, and the United States still has the worst mine safety record among Western industrial nations (Lanovette 1977, Naill et al. 1975).

The harmful environmental impact of mining and burning coal can be minimized by strictly enforcing or even strengthening current air pollution, water pollution, strip mining, and mine safety laws. But this plan will reduce the net useful energy yield somewhat, require large capital investments, and thus raise the price of coal—although coal should still be competitive with other alternatives. Meeting environmental standards also slows things down. A company may need 100 permits before it can start on a new mine. As a result, the time needed to open a large coal mine has increased from 5 to 10 years or more (Abelson 1978). For the same reason, the time to bring a coal-fired power plant on line has increased by several years and is approaching the 10 to 12 years required for a nuclear power plant (Abelson 1978).

Another problem is that many of the richest low-sulfur coal deposits are in the western states (Figure 8-8). Even if water shortages don't limit production (Section 8-6), shipping most of the coal to the East where it is needed will raise its price and decrease its net useful energy yield. Western coal also has no air pollution advantage. It has a lower sulfur content by weight, but most of it also has a lower heat value per unit of weight than eastern coal (Boulding 1976). As a result, western coal will actually produce more sulfur dioxide pollution per unit of *heat* (which is the measure that really counts) than eastern coal (Boulding 1976).

Other factors that could slow increased use of coal include the threat of strikes and shortages of capital, miners, geologists, mining engineers, housing near mining areas, and railroad coal cars (Naill et al. 1975, Schmidt & Hill 1976, Sheridan 1977, Staff report 1977h). For example, the U.S. Bureau of Mines says that to increase U.S. coal production by 50 percent between 1978 and 1985, the industry will have to open 254 new large mines (an average of 41 per year), recruit and train 157,000 new miners for the nation's most hazardous occupation, and raise $15.7 billion in capital (more than twice the capital raised between 1965 and 1974). By 1985 railroads will also have to spend $8 billion to upgrade and build new tracks and to buy 140,000 new hopper cars and 900 new engines.

Electric utilities plan to build 229 new coal-fired power plants by 1985 at enormous costs and spend $71 billion to convert existing oil- and gas-burning plants to coal. All of this means that the use of coal will increase in the United States—but not as fast as projected in the National Energy Act of 1978.

Burning Coal More Cleanly and Efficiently   Two promising ways to burn coal more efficiently, use less water, and reduce harmful sulfur dioxide emissions without expensive scrubbers are the *fluidized-bed combustion* (Lovins 1977b, 1978a, Yaverbaum 1977) and *magnetohydrodynamic* (MHD) *generation* (Somers et al. 1976, Staff report 1978e).

In **fluidized-bed combustion,** a stream of hot air flows up through the boiler and suspends a mixture of powdered coal and limestone. The better heat transfer thus provided lets the coal burn more efficiently. Efficiency should be 40 to 50 percent, compared with 35 percent for conventional coal-burning power plants and 25 to 30 percent for a conventional nuclear power plant (Freeman 1974). The lower heat output of fluidized combustion plants will also reduce the threat of thermal water pollution (Section 9-5). In addition, the limestone removes 90 to 95 percent of the sulfur in the coal. However, the resulting solid calcium sulfate must be disposed of safely, and particulates and nitrogen oxides emissions will have to be controlled as with conventional coal-burning plants.

Fluidized-bed combustion should also be cheaper than conventional coal-burning boilers and could easily be used in both large-scale and smaller district power plants (Lovins 1977a, 1978a). Successful pilot plants have been built, and commercial-scale boilers should be available by the mid-1980s.

In a **magnetohydrodynamic** or MHD **generator,** crushed coal (or any fossil fuel) is treated with potassium; it then flows into a combustion chamber and burns at about 2,760°C (5,000°F). The chemicals in the rapidly expanding hot gas produced during combustion are converted to ions (charged chemical species) by the potassium. This hot stream of ionized gases (or plasma) is then forced at the speed of a bullet down a pipe and through a magnetic field, producing electricity. This is a much simpler and more efficient method for producing electricity than the conventional power plant that burns coal, produces heat to turn water into steam, and then uses the steam to spin a turbine to produce electricity. A plant with an MHD generator should operate at about 55 percent efficiency—almost two-thirds higher than conventional coal-burning plants and almost twice the efficiency of conventional nuclear power plants. In addition, the potassium used to produce ionized gases removes 95 percent or more of the sulfur. Particulate emissions are about the same as in conventional coal-fired plants, but nitrogen oxide emissions are higher because of the higher combustion temperatures.

Unfortunately, many technical difficulties remain. After over 20 years of research in the United States, the

U.S.S.R., and Japan, only a few pilot plants are operating. With expanded research, however, MHD might be available for commercial use as early as 1985 in the U.S.S.R. and by 1995 in the United States (Staff report 1978e).

Coal Gasification and Coal Liquefaction Two ways to avoid serious air pollution with coal burning are **coal gasification** and **liquefaction** to convert the solid coal to synthetic natural gas or synthetic crude oil.[6]

Coal has more carbon and less hydrogen than oil or natural gas. Thus, in simplest terms, converting coal to synthetic oil or synthetic natural gas is a hydrogenation process—getting some of the carbon atoms to react with hydrogen atoms in gas produced from steam. Once high pressures and temperatures convert solid coal to gases, these gases are then fed into a second unit, where they react at high temperatures with hydrogen gas to produce organic hydrocarbons with the right carbon-to-hydrogen ratio. The resulting gases or liquids are then purified to remove sulfur and other impurities. Thus a bulky, inconvenient, dirty solid fuel becomes a clean gaseous or liquid fuel that can be easily transported in existing pipelines.

Processes for producing low-energy fuel gas, called industrial gas, have been used for hundreds of years. This gas can be burned in industrial boilers and electric power plants, but it has too little heat content per unit of fuel to use in home heating. In recent years a number of different methods for producing high-grade or pipeline-quality synthetic natural gas have been developed (Cochran 1976, Linden et al. 1976). Several of the processes have been carried through small pilot plant development in the United States, the U.S.S.R., and some European nations. Several liquefaction processes have also been developed (Cochran 1976, Swabb 1978). Full-scale, commercial coal gasification plants could be built in the United States by the late 1980s. By 2000 some 20 coal gasification and liquefaction plants could supply energy equal to 6 percent of all energy used in the United States in 1976 (Cochran 1976).

There are some problems, however. A major problem is cost. These synthetic fuels, if made by existing processes, would cost $25 to $33 (in 1978 dollars) per barrel (159 liters)—more than the 1979 prices of crude oil and natural gas (Staff report 1979b). In addition, the capital cost of building a coal gasification of liquefaction plant is very high—$1.3 to $1.5 billion (Staff report 1979b). This is much higher than the cost of an equivalent coal-fired power plant equipped with stack gas scrubbers. Without large government subsidies and a sharp rise in the price of coal and oil, private industry will not take the financial risks associated with synthetic-fuel production plants (Cochran 1976, Griffith & Clarke 1979).

A second problem is water (Section 8–6). Coal gasification and liquefaction plants would be built near coal-mining sites to cut shipping costs. Water may be short in some of these areas. In the Rocky Mountain states, for example, synthetic-fuel plants could seriously deplete water supplies (Figure 8–8). Thus, water availability may be the limiting factor in the production of synthetic fuels in the United States.

A third difficulty is the lower net useful energy yield compared with the direct burning of coal. When coal is converted to synthetic natural gas or synthetic crude oil, about 30 to 40 percent of its energy content escapes as waste heat (Cook 1976b, Linden et al. 1976, Tillman 1976). Synthetic-fuel production also requires much more coal, which means much more strip mining (Section 6–6) and more water for both cooling and processing (Griffith & Clarke 1979). Air pollution from coal gasification is estimated to be about one-tenth that of scrubber-equipped, coal-burning electric power plants (Council on Environmental Quality, *Environmental Quality*, 1975). On the other hand, toxic metal and organic compounds may be released during the conversion process (Council on Environmental Quality, *Environmental Quality*, 1975, Koppenaal & Manahan 1976).

At present, the best way to avoid some of these problems is the underground gasification of coal (Maugh 1977b). In this process superheated air and steam or air and lighted charcoal are forced into an underground coal seam already loosened by explosives. As the coal burns, it is converted to industrial gas (carbon monoxide and hydrogen), which can either be burned in power plants and industrial boilers or possibly upgraded to synthetic natural gas or alcohol. The U.S.S.R. has used this process for more than 50 years and has several underground gasification plants that fuel electric power plants (Maugh 1977b). Underground gasification is the cheapest way to produce industrial gas. Widespread use of this process could triple or even quadruple the usable coal supplies in the United States, since it allows gasification of deep underground coal deposits that are too expensive to mine by conventional methods. Underground gasification might contaminate underground water supplies, but choosing sites carefully could minimize this problem (Maugh 1977b).

6–4 Fossil Fuels and Air Pollution

Our Polluted Air Take a deep breath. If the air you just took in was not polluted, you are in a small and fast-

---

[6]For more details on coal gasification and coal liquefaction, see the following: Chase 1977, Cochran 1976, Council on Environmental Quality, *Environmental Quality*, 1975, Federal Energy Administration 1974b, Hammond 1976a, Hammond & Baron 1976, Hammond & Zimmerman 1975, Hammond et al. 1973, Koppenaal & Manahan 1976, Linden et al. 1976, Maugh 1972c, 1977b, Mills 1971, Perry 1974, Richardson 1975, Squires 1974, 1976, Staff report 1979b, Swabb 1978, Tillman 1976.

shrinking minority. It makes little difference whether you are in Los Angeles, Denver, Washington, D.C., Tokyo, or Mexico City, inside a home, or in a rural area. Most Americans breathe air that is considered harmful to their health despite the fact that between 1970 and 1977 air pollution control efforts improved the overall air quality (Council on Environmental Quality, *Environmental Quality*, 1977).

To escape the smog you might rush home, close the doors and windows, and breathe in clean air. But two University of California scientists found that the air inside homes is often more polluted and dangerous than outdoor air on a smoggy day (Environmental Protection Agency 1975b, Staff report 1977b). The indoor pollutants come from gas stoves and furnaces, cigarettes, aerosol spray cans, and cleaning products. Energy conservation efforts (Chapter 5) to make houses even more airtight could lead to even higher indoor pollution levels.

Air pollution from human activities, of course, is not new. Our ancestors had it in their smoke-filled caves and later in their cities. Over 2,000 years ago Seneca complained of bad air in Rome. In 1273 King Edward I of England passed the first known air quality laws, which forbade the use of a particular type of coal. One man was even hanged for burning coal (Griggin 1965). In 1300 King Richard III put a heavy tax on coal to discourage its use. In the early 1800s Shelley wrote, "Hell is a city much like London, a populous and smoky city." In 1911, 1,150 Londoners died from the effects of coal smoke. In his report on the disaster, Dr. Harold Antoine Des Voeux coined the word *smog* for the mixture of smoke and fog that often hung over London. An even more deadly London air pollution incident killed 4,000 people in 1952. This triggered a massive air pollution control effort that has made London's air today cleaner than it has been in over 100 years.

In America the industrial revolution brought air pollution as coal-burning industries and homes filled the air with soot and fumes. In the 1940s the air in industrial centers, such as Pittsburgh, became so thick with dust that automobile drivers sometimes had to use their headlights at midday. The rapid rise in the use of the automobile, especially since 1940, brought new forms of pollution. The first known air pollution disaster occurred in 1948 when fumes and dust from steel mills and zinc smelters became trapped in a stagnated air mass over Donora, Pennsylvania. Twenty people died and over 6,000 became ill (Schrenk et al. 1949). In the 1950s and 1960s recurrent air pollution disasters in New York, Los Angeles, and other large cities eventually led to efforts to reduce U.S. air pollution levels.

Our Finite Air Supply The J curves of increasing urbanization, population growth, industrialization, and automobile use have forced us to realize that we can no longer take for granted the 14 kilograms (30 pounds) of relatively pure air that every person must breathe each day. We can control

or reject contaminated water and food, but we cannot stop breathing. Thus there is a significant difference between the problems of air and water pollution. Unlike water, we can't get our supply of clean air through pipes. We normally use an output approach for water, cleaning up polluted water by passing it through water treatment plants. This is not physically or economically feasible for polluted air. Air pollution control must rely primarily on input approaches, as discussed in more detail in Kenneth E. F. Watt's Guest Editorial at the end of this chapter.

Contrary to popular belief, we do not live at the bottom of an infinite sea of air. The *atmosphere* is the gaseous envelope that surrounds the earth. It consists of several distinct layers. About 95 percent of the air is found in the **troposphere**, which extends only 8 to 12 kilometers (5 to 7 miles) above the earth's surface. In fact, if we were to compare the earth with a waxed apple, our vital air supply would be no thicker than the layer of wax.

Most air pollutants are added to the troposphere, where they mix vertically and horizontally and often react chemically with each other or with the natural components of the atmosphere. Eventually, most of these pollutants and the chemicals that they form are returned to the land or water by precipitation or fallout. For example, in 1975 the troposphere received about 498 million kilograms (548,000 tons) of air pollutants *each day* from the United States (Council on Environmental Quality, *Environmental Quality*, 1976)—an average of about 2.3 kilograms (5 pounds) per day for each American.

Major Air Pollutants Table 6–1 summarizes the major sources and effects of the major pollutants and possible methods for controlling them.[7]

Sources of Air Pollution If we look at the total amount of each major pollutant emitted each year in the United States, carbon monoxide is the number one air pollutant and the automobile is by far the major source of air pollution, as shown in Table 6–2. But we should not judge either the importance of an air pollutant or its source solely on the basis of the total amount emitted each year. We must also consider how harmful a pollutant is—especially to human health (Babcock 1970, Council on Environmental Quality, *Environmental Quality*, 1972, 1975, Lynn 1976).

---

[7]For more details on air pollutants, see the following: American Chemical Society 1978, Bach 1972, Berry 1970, Berry et al. 1974, Brodine 1972b, 1973, Council on Environmental Quality, *Environmental Quality* (published annually), Davies & Davies 1975, Elipper 1970, Hesketh 1974, Hodges 1977, Lave & Seskin 1977, League of Women Voters 1970, Lynn 1975, 1976, Moore & Moore 1976, National Academy of Sciences 1969, 1975a, Newell 1971, Perkins 1974, Pryde 1973, Quarles 1976, Robinson & Robbins 1971, Stern 1968, Stern et al. 1973, Stoker & Seager 1976, Waldbott 1978, Williamson 1973.

Table 6–1 Major Air Pollutants

Pollutant	Sources	Effects	Control Methods
Carbon oxides Carbon monoxide	Forest fires and decaying organic matter; incomplete combustion of fossil fuels and other organic matter in cars and furnaces; cigarette smoke	Reduces oxygen-carrying capacity of blood; impairs judgment; aggravates heart and respiratory diseases; can cause headaches and fatigue at moderate concentrations (50 to 100 ppm); can cause death at prolonged high concentrations (750 ppm or more)	Modify furnaces and automobile engines for more complete combustion; remove from automobile, home, and factory exhaust gases; stop smoking
Carbon dioxide	Natural aerobic respiration of living organisms; burning of fossil fuels	Could affect world climate through the "greenhouse effect" at excessive concentrations (see Section 9–2)	Switch away from use of fossil fuels; remove from automobile, home, and factory exhaust gases
Sulfur oxides	Combustion of sulfur-containing coal and oil in homes, industries, and power plants; smelting of sulfur-containing ores; volcanic eruptions	Aggravates respiratory diseases; impairs breathing; irritates eyes and respiratory tract; increases mortality; damages plants and reduces growth; causes acid rain; corrodes metals; deteriorates building stone, paper, nylon, and leather	Use low-sulfur fossil fuels; coal gasification; remove from fuels before use; remove from smokestack exhaust gases; shift to non-fossil fuel energy sources
Nitrogen oxides	High-temperature fuel combustion in motor vehicles and industrial and fossil fuel power plants; lightning	Aggravates respiratory and heart diseases; irritates lungs; causes acid rain; inhibits plant growth; decreases atmospheric visibility; fades paints and dyes; takes part in formation of photochemical smog; injures respiratory system	Discourage automobile use; shift to mass transit, electric cars, and fuel cells; modify automobiles to reduce combustion temperature; remove automobile and smokestack exhausts
Hydrocarbons	Incomplete combustion of fossil fuels in automobiles and furnaces; evaporation of industrial solvents and oil spills; forest fires; plant decay	Injures respiratory system; some cause cancer; takes part in formation of photochemical smog	Modify furnaces and automobile engines for more complete combustion and less evaporation; remove from automobile exhaust; improve handling of solvents and petroleum to reduce spills (Section 6–5) and loss by evaporation
Photochemical oxidants	Sunlight acting on hydrocarbons and nitrogen oxides	Aggravates respiratory and heart diseases; irritates eyes, throat, and respiratory tract; injures leaves and inhibits plant growth; decreases atmospheric visibility; deteriorates rubber, textiles, and paints	Reduce emissions of nitrogen oxides and hydrocarbons
Particulates Dust, soot, and oil	Forest fires, wind erosion, and volcanic eruptions; coal burning; farming, mining, construction, road building, and other land-clearing activities; chemical reactions in the atmosphere; dust stirred up by automobiles; automobile exhaust	Can cause cancer; aggravates respiratory and heart diseases; is toxic at high levels; causes coughing, irritates throat, and causes chest discomfort; interferes with plant photosynthesis; harms animals; reduces atmospheric visibility; soils and deteriorates buildings and painted surfaces; may affect weather and climate (Chapter 9)	Decrease use of coal; improve land use and soil erosion control; remove from smokestack exhausts
Asbestos	Asbestos mining; spraying of fireproofing insulation in buildings; deterioration of brake linings	Can cause cancer; hinders breathing; aggravates respiratory and heart diseases; causes fibrosis of lungs	Reduce use; prevent escape into the atmosphere; protect construction workers and miners from inhaling dust

Table 6-1 Major Air Pollutants (continued)

Pollutant	Sources	Effects	Control Methods
Metals and metal compounds	Mining; industrial processes; coal burning; automobile exhaust	Can cause respiratory diseases, cancer, nervous disorders, and death; is toxic to some animals; damages plants	Remove from exhaust gases; ban highly toxic chemicals
Other inorganic compounds			
Hydrogen fluoride	Petroleum refining; glass etching; aluminum and fertilizer production	Burns skin and eyes; irritates mucous membranes; damages plants and animals	Control industrial processes more carefully; remove from smokestack exhausts
Hydrogen sulfide	Chemical industry; petroleum refining	Has unpleasant odor; causes nausea; irritates eyes and throat; is toxic at high levels	Control industrial processes more carefully; remove from smokestack exhausts
Ammonia	Chemical industry; fertilizers	Irritates upper respiratory passages; forms particulates in atmosphere; corrodes metals	Control industrial processes more carefully; remove from smokestack exhausts
Sulfuric acid	Reaction of sulfur trioxide and water vapor in atmosphere; chemical industry	(Same as sulfur oxides.)	(Same as sulfur oxides.)
Nitric Acid	Reaction of nitrogen dioxide and water vapor in atmosphere; chemical industry	(Same as nitrogen oxides.)	(Same as nitrogen oxides.)
Other organic compounds			
Pesticides and herbicides	Agriculture; forestry; mosquito control	Is toxic or harmful to some fish, shellfish, predatory birds, and mammals; concentrates in human fat; may cause birth and genetic defects and cancer	Reduce use; switch to biological and ecological control of insects
Radioactive substances	Natural sources (rocks, soils, cosmic rays); uranium mining; nuclear processing; power generation; nuclear weapons testing; coal burning	Causes cancer and genetic defects; injures leaves; reduces plant growth	Ban or reduce use of nuclear power plants and weapons testing; strictly control processing, shipping, and use of nuclear fuels and wastes; remove from exhausts; reduce burning of coal; coal gasification
Heat	Use of fossil and nuclear fuels	May affect world climate (see Chapter 9)	Reduce population; reduce energy use
Noise	Automobiles, airplanes and trains; industry; construction	Causes annoyance; disrupts activities; causes nervous disorders; impairs hearing	Reduce noise levels of automobiles, airplanes, trains, machines, and factories; protect workers and residents from noise by ear cover and better building construction

Source: Council on Environmental Quality, *Environmental Quality*, 1975.

When considering harmful health effects, we get a very different picture of the relative importance of various air pollutants and their sources, as shown in Table 6-2. On this basis sulfur oxides and particulates rank as the top two pollutants, and carbon monoxide drops to last place among the pollutants listed. In terms of air pollution sources, stationary fuel combustion (primarily at fossil fuel power plants) emerges as the most dangerous, with industry (especially pulp and paper mills, iron and steel mills, smelters, petroleum refineries, and chemical plants) and transportation in second and third places, respectively.

The health rankings of air pollutants provide a more realistic basis for designing programs to reduce air pollution. Of course, controlling automobile emissions is very important, but controlling emissions from fossil-fuel-burning electric power plants is even more so. This is particularly important in the United States, which is increasing its reliance on coal-burning electric power plants as part of its national energy strategy (Section 10–3).

Effects of Air Pollution   Air pollution can affect humans in a number of ways. After decades of research there is overwhelming statistical evidence that air pollution can kill, induce and aggravate a number of diseases, and increase human suffering. Air pollution is particularly harmful to the very young (Kane 1976, Shy et al. 1972), the old, the poor (who are usually forced to live in highly polluted areas, and those already weakened by heart and lung diseases.[8] In spite of the evidence, proving that a particular pollutant causes a particular disease or death is extremely difficult. Officially almost no one dies of air pollution. Instead the death certificate reads chronic bronchitis, emphysema, lung cancer, stomach cancer, or heart disease, even though air pollution may have been a major contributing factor.

Correlating air pollution and health is difficult because of (1) the number and variety of air pollutants, (2) the difficulty of detecting pollutants that cause harm at extremely low concentrations, (3) the interaction of pollutants, (4) the difficulty in isolating single harmful factors when people are exposed to so many potentially harmful chemicals over many years, (5) the unreliability of records of disease and death, (6) the multiple causes and lengthy incubation times of diseases such as emphysema, chronic bronchitis, cancer, and heart disease, and (7) the problem of extrapolating test data on laboratory animals to humans (Ehrlich et al. 1977). Because of these difficulties and public misunderstanding of the nature of science, many people are misled when they hear such statements as "science has not proven absolutely that air pollution or smoking has killed anyone." Like the statement "cats are not elephants," such a statement is true but meaningless. Science never has proven anything absolutely and never will. Science does not establish absolute truths but only a degree of probability or confidence in the validity of an idea.

Air pollution has been connected with suffering and death from heart disease, chronic respiratory diseases (such as bronchial asthma, chronic bronchitis, and pulmonary emphysema), and lung cancer. Diseases of the heart and blood vessels caused only 20 percent of U.S. deaths in the

---

[8]For more details and documentation, see the following: Brodine 1972a, Connolly 1972, Eckholm 1977, Epstein & Hattis 1975, Higgins 1974, Holland 1972, Kagawa & Toyama 1975, Lave & Seskin 1970, 1977, Lave & Silverman 1976, Lynn 1976, National Academy of Sciences 1975a, National Tuberculosis and Respiratory Disease Association 1969, Purdom 1971, Resources for the Future 1974, Shy & Finklea 1973, Stokinger 1971, Waldbott 1978.

Table 6–2 Relative Importance of Major Pollutants and Their Sources in the United States in 1975

	Annual Emissions		Relative Health Effect	
	Percentage of Total	Rank	Percentage of Total	Rank
Pollutant				
Sulfur oxides	12.9	3	34.6	1
Particulates	9.7	4	27.9	2
Nitrogen oxides	8.6	5	18.6	3
Hydrocarbons	13.1	2	17.7	4
Carbon monoxide	55.7	1	1.2	5
Total	100.0		100.0	
Source				
Stationary fuel combustion	16.9	2	43.0	1
Industry	15.3	3	25.7	2
Transportation	54.5	1	22.2	3
Agricultural burning	7.3	4	4.4	4
Solid waste disposal	4.2	5	3.0	5
Miscellaneous	1.8	6	1.7	6
Total	100.0		100.0	

Source: Council on Environmental Quality, *Environmental Quality*, 1975; Lynn 1976.

early 1900s but now account for more than half. Heart disease has many causes but has been linked to carbon monoxide, even at low levels (Anderson et al. 1973, Bodkin 1974, Goldsmith & Landaw 1968, Hexter & Goldsmith 1975, Kuller et al. 1975, Wright et al. 1975), and inhaled sulfate particles (Lave & Seskin 1977).

As you might expect, there are strong correlations between air pollution and chronic respiratory diseases (Higgins 1974, Holland 1972, Lave & Seskin 1977). Although cigarette smoking almost certainly ranks as the major cause of chronic respiratory disease, sulfur oxides, sulfuric acid, particulates, and nitrogen dioxide have been shown to cause and aggravate bronchial asthma, chronic bronchitis, and pulmonary emphysema (Eckholm 1977, Environmental Protection Agency 1976a, Fennelly 1976, French et al. 1973, Holland & Reid 1965, Ishikawa et al. 1969, Lambert & Reid 1970, Lave & Seskin 1977, Lynn 1976, National Academy of Sciences 1975a, Rall 1974, Shy et al. 1972, Winkelstein & Gay 1971). *Chronic bronchitis* now affects one out of five American men between 40 and 60 and has been related to smoking and to living in polluted urban areas.

Figure 6–8 The lung of a normal person (above) and the lung of a person with pulmonary emphysema (below).

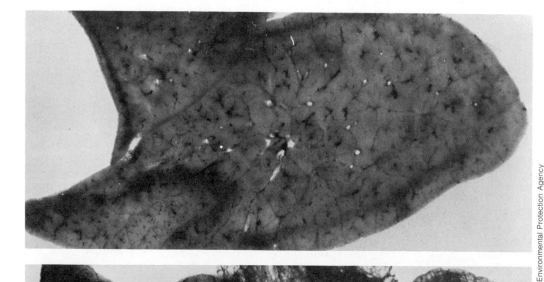

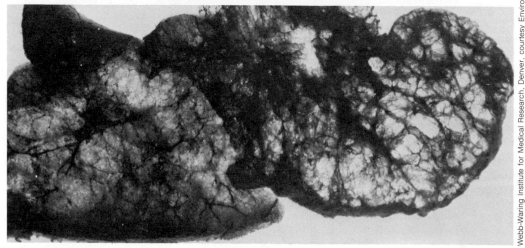

Emphysema is the fastest-growing cause of death in the United States, killing almost more Americans each year than lung cancer and tuberculosis put together. In addition, an estimated 1.5 million emphysema sufferers in the United States (over half of them under 65) cannot work or live normal lives because even the slightest exertion causes them to gasp for breath (Figure 6–8). Emphysema is caused by a number of factors, including smoking, air pollution, and heredity (Lynn 1976). About 25 percent of emphysema cases seem due to a hereditary condition in which a protein is lacking that is vital in keeping the lungs elastic. Such persons have a very good chance of getting emphysema, especially if they smoke or if they live or work in a polluted area. Recently a test has been devised to detect this genetic defect. Anyone who smokes or lives in a polluted atmosphere should have this test made.

Lung cancer is caused by a number of factors. Smoking is considered the number one cause, but lung cancer has also been linked to air pollution (Blot & Fraumeni 1975,

Buell & Dunn 1967, Davidson et al. 1974, Epstein & Hattis 1975, Fennelly 1976, Lave & Seskin 1977, Menck et al. 1974, National Academy of Sciences 1975a, Pierce & Katz 1975, Shettigrra & Morgan 1975, Winkelstein & Gay 1971). Urban nonsmokers are 3 to 4 times more likely than rural nonsmokers to develop lung cancer (Buell & Dunn 1967).

Most air pollution damage to materials and property is caused by photochemical oxidants (such as ozone), particulates, and sulfur oxides. Much of this damage occurs when sulfur oxides are converted to highly destructive droplets of sulfuric acid. For example, marble statues and building materials such as limestone, marble, mortar, and slate are discolored and attacked by sulfuric acid (and nitric acid formed from nitrogen oxides). As a result, some of the world's finest historical monuments—cathedrals, sculptures, and public buildings—have deteriorated rapidly in recent years. Famous Greek ruins in Athens have deteriorated more during the past 40 years than during the previous 2,000 years. Atmospheric fallout of soot and grit also soils statues, buildings, cars, and clothing—causing greatly increased costs for cleaning.

Sulfuric acid and ozone also attack and fade rubber, leather, paper, some fabrics (such as cotton, rayon, and nylon), and paint (U.S. Department of Health, Education and Welfare 1968b). Women walking down the street have had their nylon stockings and blouses disintegrate. Extra lighting needed because of skies darkened by particulates costs Americans at least $16 million a year and uses large amounts of energy that produce more pollution—thus creating a vicious circle (U.S. Department of Health, Education and Welfare 1969a, 1969b).

Air pollution can also stunt plant growth and damage food crops (Benedict et al. 1973, Knabe 1976, Marx 1975, Mudd & Kozlowski 1975, National Academy of Sciences 1975f, Smith 1974a, U.S. Department of Health, Education and Welfare 1968b, 1970a). Many plants are sensitive to high and very low concentrations of sulfur dioxide, ozone, and PAN. Fruits and vegetables grown near big cities are particularly vulnerable (especially in Connecticut, New Jersey, Long Island, eastern Pennsylvania, and Delaware, and in southern California) (Benedict et al. 1973, U.S. Department of Health, Education and Welfare 1970a). In southern California citrus crops are damaged mainly by ozone and PAN in photochemical smog. In the Middle Atlantic states potatoes, tomatoes, green peas, corn, apples, peaches, and leafy vegetables are damaged primarily by sulfur dioxide and sulfuric acid, which discolor leaves and sometimes stunt growth.

Types of Smog Serious air pollution occurs mostly in cities, with each city facing unique problems (Figure 6–9). However, big cities generally fall into one of two basic classes—the *"gray air" cities* and the *"brown air" cities* (Berry 1970). These correspond to two major types of smog, *industrial smog* and *photochemical smog*, respectively. The characteristics of these two types of smog are summarized in Table 6–3.

Formation and Control of Industrial Smog Gray air, or industrial smog, cities[9] usually have cold, wet, winter climates; such cities include London, Chicago, Baltimore, Philadelphia, and Pittsburgh. These cities also depend on the burning of coal and oil for heat, manufacturing, and electric power. These fuels release two major classes of pollutants—**particulates** (solid particles or liquid droplets suspended in the air), which give the air over such cities its gray cast, and

[9]A well-matured photochemical smog can also look gray. Southern California often has a gray haze caused by the particulates produced in photochemical smog, because the nitrogen dioxide level has been diluted until its brownish color can't be seen.

sulfur oxides (SO_2 and SO_3) that are the major ingredients of **industrial smog.**

Coal and oil contain small amounts (0.5 to 5 percent by mass) of sulfur as an impurity. When the fuel is burned, the sulfur impurities react with oxygen to produce sulfur dioxide (SO_2). This gas spews out of chimneys and smokestacks and enters the atmosphere. Within several days most of the sulfur dioxide in the atmosphere is converted to sulfur trioxide (SO_3), which reacts almost at once with water in the air to form droplets of sulfuric acid (H_2SO_4). This atmospheric mist of sulfuric acid eats away metals and other materials and can irritate and damage the lungs.

Some of the sulfuric acid droplets can react with ammonia (NH_3) in the atmosphere to form solid particles of ammonium sulfate. Droplets of sulfuric acid and other chemicals that are inhaled can then become attached to these particles once they are also inhaled. The combined effect of sulfuric acid droplets and ammonium sulfate particles is considered the most serious air pollution threat to human health (Lave & Seskin 1977).

Fortunately, in many areas this mist of sulfuric acid droplets and ammonium sulfate particles is washed out of the atmosphere by rain within a few days or weeks. However, if it does not rain and if winds do not disperse them, these pollutants can build up to deadly levels. Such events are associated with the air pollution disasters in London in 1952 (3,500 to 4,000 deaths) and 1956 (900 deaths), in Donora, Pennsylvania, in 1948 (20 deaths, 6,000 sick), and in New York City in 1965 (400 deaths).

Control of sulfur oxides and particulates is closely related to the energy crisis because the burning of fossil fuels (especially coal) in electric power plants and industrial plants is the major source of these pollutants. Emissions of

Figure 6–9 The types of air pollution in three cities. (The percentage values are crude estimates.)

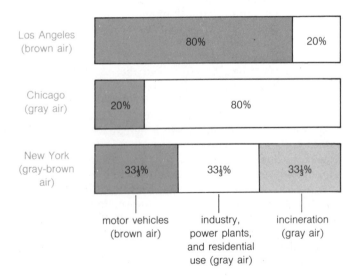

Table 6–3 Basic Types of Smog

Characteristic	Industrial Smog	Photochemical Smog
Typical city	London, Chicago	Mexico City, Los Angeles
Climate	Cool, humid air	Warm, dry air
Chief pollutants	Sulfur oxides, particulates	Ozone, PAN, aldehydes, nitrogen oxides, carbon monoxide
Main sources	Industrial and household burning of oil and coal	Motor vehicle gasoline combustion
Time of worst episodes	Winter months (especially in the early morning)	Summer months (especially around noontime)

sulfur oxides and particulates can be controlled by (1) reducing wasteful uses of energy, (2) shifting from fossil fuels to other energy sources such as nuclear, solar, wind, biomass, and geothermal energy, (3) burning gasified or liquefied coal instead of solid coal, (4) shifting to low-sulfur fossil fuels (less than 1 percent sulfur), (5) removing sulfur impurities from coal before burning, (6) removing sulfur oxides and particulates during combustion or from smokestack exhaust gases, (7) discharging emissions from very tall smokestacks (a short-term method that reduces local pollution levels but increases levels in more distant areas), (8) using emission control devices on automobiles to reduce or remove particles from exhausts, (9) shifting to less polluting automobile engines and fuels, and (10) discouraging automobile use and shifting to mass and para transit.

Formation and Control of Photochemical Smog Brown air cities, like Los Angeles, Denver, Salt Lake City, Sydney, Mexico City, and Buenos Aires, usually have warm, dry climates, and their main source of air pollution is the internal combustion engine. At normal temperatures the nitrogen gas (N_2) and oxygen gas (O_2) that make up most of the atmosphere do not react with each other, but at the high temperatures inside an internal combustion engine, they react to produce nitric oxide (NO), which then passes out of the exhaust and into the atmosphere. Once in the atmosphere, nitric oxide reacts with the oxygen to form nitrogen dioxide (NO_2), a yellowish-brown gas with a pungent, choking odor that is mostly responsible for the brownish haze over brown air cities.

Typically nitrogen dioxide remains in the atmosphere for about 3 days. Just as sulfur dioxide can be converted into sulfuric acid, small amounts of nitrogen dioxide can react in the atmosphere to form nitric acid (HNO_3), which can then be precipitated out of the atmosphere (another contribution to acid rainfall). Atmospheric nitric acid can also react with ammonia in the air to form particles of ammonium nitrate, which eventually fall to the earth's surface or are washed out of the atmosphere by rainfall.

Most of the air pollution problems with nitric oxide and nitrogen dioxide arise when ultraviolet radiation from sunlight causes them to react with gaseous hydrocarbons, which mostly come from spilled or partially burned gasoline. This reaction forms a complex mixture of new pollutants called *photochemical oxidants*. These oxidants and other compounds form what is called **photochemical smog**. This mixture includes ozone and a number of compounds similar to tear gas, which are known collectively as PANs (for *peroxyacylnitrates*). Mere traces of these compounds in the air can cause the eyes to smart and can damage crops.

Although the distinction between photochemical smog cities and industrial smog cities is convenient, most cities suffer from both types of air pollution (Figure 6–9).

Photochemical smog can be controlled[10] by (1) reducing automobile use, (2) shifting to mass and para transit systems (Table 5–1), (3) developing less polluting and more energy-efficient automobile engines (Figure 6–10), (4) using cleaner burning fuels (such as natural gas or hydrogen) for car engines, (5) improving fuel efficiency by reducing the size, weight, wind resistance, and power of cars, (6) modifying the internal combustion engine to lower emissions and improve gas mileage, (7) removing pollutants from automobile exhaust by the use of afterburners and catalytic converters, and (8) treating urban air with chemicals to reduce formation of photochemical smog (Maugh 1976a).

Misplaced Priorities With all the advantages of alternate fuels and improved types of engines (Figure 6–10), why

---

[10]For more details, see the following: Bockris 1971, 1972, Cohn 1975, Cole 1972, Environmental Protection Agency 1974b, Gouse 1970, Grad et al. 1975, Hackelman 1977, Harvey & Menchen 1974, Jamison 1970, Jet Propulsion Laboratory 1975, Jones 1971, Maugh 1976a, National Academy of Sciences 1973, Netscheat 1970, Pierce 1975, Reitze 1977a, 1977b, Schurr 1971, Staff report 1973a, U.S. Department of Health, Education and Welfare 1970b, Waler 1973, Wilson 1978, Wouk 1971.

Now to 1985

electronic fuel injection
three-way catalytic converters
stratified-charge engines (Honda CVCC)
conventional diesel engines
turbocharged diesel engines

1986 to 2000

gas turbine engines
Stirling engines
Rankine engines
electric cars (limited use in urban areas)

After 2000

fuel-cell-powered cars
hydrogen-fueled cars
solar electric cars (?)

Figure 6-10 Possible automobile engines and fuels of the future. (Harvey & Menchen 1974, Jet Propulsion Laboratory 1975)

don't we have these technological improvements now? For the most part the reasons are political rather than technological (Davies & Davies 1975, Elipper 1970, Esposito & Nader 1970, Lynn 1976, MacDonald 1972, Morgan et al. 1970, Quarles 1976). The problem is one of misplaced corporate and individual priorities.

At the *corporate level*, priorities are grossly out of balance. Large corporations with capital and outstanding research staffs often refuse to do serious research and development on new, cleaner engines and must be forced step by step to meet safety and emission standards. General Motors proudly announced a $40 million annual budget for pollution control, but this figure represented only about *16 hours* of its gross revenue ($2.5 million an hour), 0.17 percent of its gross annual sales of $23 billion, and only one-sixth of its annual advertising budget of $240 million.

At the *individual level* many of us also have upside-down priorities. We insist on large cars with hundreds of horsepower on streets so crowded that we can only drive 19 kilometers per hour (12 miles per hour). We fail to ride on or support the development of mass and para transit systems. We are duped by misleading corporate advertising, or we fail to become politically involved to change outrageous practices and to correct misplaced priorities

that degrade the quality of our lives. We continue to consume the earth's finite resources of fossil fuels as if they were infinite.

6–5 Oceans and Oil Spills

The Ultimate Sink The oceans are truly the ultimate sink for both natural and human wastes. Everything flushed from the land, whether by humans or by natural erosion, eventually reaches the sea. Water used and contaminated in homes, factories, and farms flows into rivers, which eventually empty into the ocean.

Fortunately, the vastness of ocean waters and their constant mixing dilute many of these wastes to harmless levels. Other wastes are broken down and recycled by natural chemical cycles (Section 3–3) in ocean ecosystems (Cushing & Walsh 1976). Some believe that the oceans will continue to absorb all the wastes we pump into them and still help feed a protein-starved population and burst forth with oil, minerals, and other riches to sustain our J-curve age. But the vastness of the oceans as a resource can be deceiving. Although the oceans can purify and recycle large amounts of some pollutants, their capacity to do so has limits. The sheer magnitude of discharges, especially near the coasts, can overload these natural purifying systems. In addition, these natural processes cannot readily degrade many of the plastics, pesticides, and other synthetic chemicals created by human ingenuity.

Ocean Oil Pollution Each year about 6.11 billion kilograms (6.73 million tons) of oil and petroleum are added to the oceans (National Academy of Sciences 1975d). This oil comes from a number of sources, as shown in Figure 6–11. About 10 percent of the annual international input is due to natural seepage of crude petroleum from deposits below the ocean bottom (Wilson et al. 1974). Human activities account for the remaining 90 percent, which is added in the forms of *crude petroleum* (oil as it comes out of the ground) and *refined petroleum* (obtained by distillation and chemical processing of crude petroleum). Despite widespread publicity, spills from oil tanker accidents, such as the *Torrey Canyon*, which broke up off the coast of England in 1967, account for only about 4.9 percent of the annual input. The accidental rupture of offshore oil wells, such as the Santa Barbara, California, oil blowout in 1969, make up only about 1.0 percent of the annual input (National Academy of Sciences 1975d). About 61 percent of the annual input comes from two sources: (1) river and urban runoff, mostly from the disposal of lubricating oil from machines and automobile crankcases (31.1 percent), and (2) intentional discharges from tankers during routine shipping operations, including loading, unloading, cleaning oil tanks,

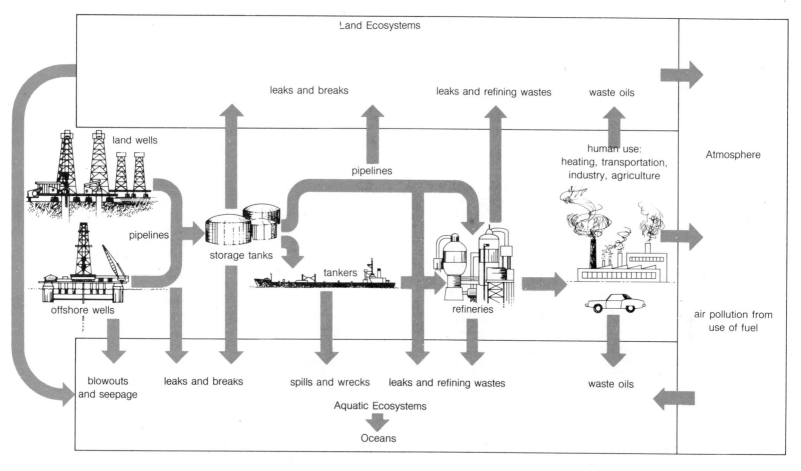

Figure 6–11 Major sources of oil pollution of the hydrosphere, lithosphere, and atmosphere.

and discharging oil-contaminated ballast water (30.0 percent). The discharge of ballast and cleaning water is the major problem. After a tanker unloads its oil cargo, it takes on seawater to help stabilize the large and unwieldy craft and also to clean the emptied oil tanks. Then at sea or just before the tanker reaches its home port, this water-oil mixture is discharged into the ocean.

Tanker accidents and blowouts, however, could become a more important source of ocean oil pollution in the future (Council on Environmental Quality, *Environmental Quality*, 1975, Grundlach 1977, National Academy of Sciences 1975d, Potter 1973, Ramseir 1974, *Technology Review* 1976). Tanker transportation and offshore oil well exploration are increasing rapidly in order to meet the world's mushrooming energy demands (Chapter 1). Even with the more stringent safety regulations that have been introduced, the sheer increase in the number of wells and tankers could lead to more spills. On any given day in 1977, there were about 5.3 million cubic meters (1.4 billion gallons) of oil on the high seas—with an average of 1.3 million

cubic meters (349 million gallons) of imported oil arriving at U.S. ports each day (Federal Energy Administration 1977b). Routine discharges of oil by widely dispersed ships at sea are diluted, but tanker accidents and blowouts can have serious effects on nearby ocean and estuarine ecosystems. Also, because supertankers are still increasing in size, just one serious tanker accident could release vast quantities of oil (Environmental Protection Agency 1975a, Grundlach 1977, Mostert 1974). This occurred in 1978 when the Amoco Cadiz supertanker broke up off the coast of France and released more than 254 million liters (67 million gallons) of oil that polluted 322 kilometers (200 miles) of coastline.

There is considerable dispute, uncertainty, and conflicting evidence concerning the short-term and long-term effects of oil on ocean ecosystems (Blumer 1971, Boesche et al. 1974, Coan 1971, Cowell 1976, Holcomb 1969, Johnston 1976, Kerr 1977b, Krebs & Burns 1977, Loftas 1971, Marx 1971, Moore 1976, National Academy of Sciences 1975d, *Oceanus* 1977, Potter 1973, Radcliffe & Murphy 1969, Steinhart & Steinhart 1972, Vernberg & Vernberg 1974). The effects of oil spills are very difficult to predict because they depend on a number of complex factors, including the type of oil spilled (crude or refined), the amount spilled, how close the spill is to the shore, the time of year, weather, tidal currents, and wave action (Atlas 1978, Grundlach 1977, Kerr 1977b, Moore 1976).

Crude and refined oil are not single chemicals but collections of hundreds of substances with widely different properties. The primary cause of immediate kills of a number of aquatic organisms, especially in their larval forms, are low-boiling, aromatic hydrocarbons. Fortunately, most of these highly toxic chemicals evaporate into the atmosphere within a day or two. Some other chemicals remain on the water surface and form floating tarlike globs, which can be as big as tennis balls, while other chemicals sink to the ocean bottom. A number of these chemicals are degraded by marine microorganisms (Atlas 1978), but this natural process is slow (especially in cold Arctic and Antarctic waters) (Martin & Campbell 1974, Ramseir 1974), requires a large amount of dissolved oxygen, and tends to be least effective on some of the most toxic petroleum chemicals (Atlas 1978, Horne 1978).

Some marine birds, especially diving birds, die when oil interferes with their normal body processes or destroys the natural insulating properties of their feathers. Some oil components find their way into the fatty tissues of some fish and shellfish, making the fish unfit for human consumption because of their oily taste. Among these compounds may be such well-known carcinogenic (cancer-causing) chemicals as 3,4-benzopyrene (Blumer 1971, Carruthers et al. 1967, Environmental Protection Agency 1975a, Graef & Winter 1968). Some petroleum chemicals can also cause subtle changes in the behavioral patterns of aquatic organisms (Council on Environmental Quality, *Environmental Quality,* 1975, Environmental Protection Agency 1975a, Krebs & Burns 1977). For example, lobsters and some fish may lose their ability to locate food, avoid injury, escape enemies, find a habitat, communicate, migrate, and reproduce. Floating oil slicks can also concentrate other hazardous compounds, such as DDT and other pesticides, that are soluble in oil.

Most of the publicity and outcry against oil pollution has resulted from its economic, recreational, and aesthetic damage, such as oil-coated beaches and pleasure boats and thousands of killed seabirds. Although these are important concerns, there may also be hidden long-term ecological effects that could upset and damage aquatic communities (Boesche et al. 1974, Environmental Protection Agency 1975a, Farrington 1977, Loftas 1971).

In general, crude oil spills cause less damage than those of refined oil. In addition, if spills are far enough offshore, many of the toxic compounds may evaporate or be de-

graded or dispersed before they reach the vulnerable shore zone (Moore 1976, National Academy of Sciences 1975d). For example, the large spills of crude oil from the *Torrey Canyon* tanker accident and the Santa Barbara blowout have apparently had less serious effects on marine life than was initially predicted (National Academy of Sciences 1975d). Indeed, the deaths of most of the birds and other organisms killed after the *Torrey Canyon* disaster have been blamed not on the oil but on the detergent used to disperse it (Linden 1975). In contrast, spills of oil (especially refined oil) near shore or in estuarine zones, where sea life is most abundant, have much more damaging and long-lasting effects (Blumer 1971, *Oceanus* 1977). For example, damage to estuarine zone species from the spill of refined oil at West Falmouth, Massachusetts, in 1969 was still being detected 7 years later (Krebs & Burns 1977, Sanders 1977).

Oil spills damage the environment. They are also a waste of valuable energy resources and are expensive to clean up—at least $25,000 for each 3.8 cubic meters (1,000 gallons) of oil spilled. Since the *Torrey Canyon* and Santa Barbara incidents, a great deal of effort has gone into trying to reduce the amount of oil reaching the ocean (input approaches) and to remove or minimize its effects once it does (output approaches) (Boesche et al. 1974, Council on Environmental Quality, *Environmental Quality,* 1975, Lehr 1973). The major input and output methods for controlling oil pollution are summarized in Table 6–4. Emphasis should be placed on input approaches to reduce environmental effects, oil wastes, and costs.

6–6 Strip Mining: A Land-Energy Trade-Off

Types and Extent of Surface Mining Imagine a shovel 32 stories high, with a boom as long as a football field, that is capable of gouging out 152 cubic meters (200 cubic yards) of land every 55 seconds and dropping this 295,000 kilogram (325-ton) load a block away. This is a description of Big Muskie, a $25 million power shovel now used for surface mining coal in the United States.

Surface mining (of which strip mining is one form) is the process of removing the overburden of topsoil, subsoil, rock, and other strata so that underlying mineral deposits can be removed. There are several types of surface mining employed (Figure 6–12): (1) **open pit mining** (used primarily for stone, sand and gravel, and copper); (2) **area strip mining,** in which trenches are cut out of flat or rolling terrain (used primarily for coal and phosphate); (3) **contour strip mining,** in which a series of contour bands are cut out of the side of a hill or mountain (used primarily for coal); and (4) **dredging** of sea beds (used primarily for sand and

Table 6–4 Approaches to Oil Pollution Control

Input Approaches	Output Approaches
Use and waste less oil and reduce population growth	Use mechanical barriers to prevent oil from reaching the shore. Then vacuum oil up or soak it up with straw. This works well only on calm seas and is like trying to get smoke back into a smokestack (the second energy law again)
Collect used oils and greases from service stations and other sources (possibly by a payment-incentive plan) and reprocess them for reuse (Maugh 1976b)	
Strictly regulate the building of supertankers and superports (Lehr 1973, Marcus 1973, Mostert 1974)	Treat spilled oil chemically (usually with detergents) so that it will disperse, dissolve, or sink. Since this method can kill more marine life than does the oil, it is not favored by ecologists (Blumer 1971)
Use load-on-top (LOT) procedures for loading and emptying all oil tankers (already done on 80 percent of all tankers)	
Build supertankers with double bottoms, or hulls, to reduce chances of a spill and to separate oil cargo from ballast water	Ship oil in a solid state, much like a gel, so that it can be picked up quickly and easily if an accident occurs
Reduce the potential for tanker accidents by better training for tanker crews and better navigation aids	Develop bacterial strains (by genetic recombination) that can degrade compounds in oil faster and more efficiently than natural bacterial strains (Atlas 1978). Possible ecological side effects of these "superbugs" should be investigated before widespread use
Strictly enforce safety and disposal regulations for offshore wells and international agreements prohibiting discharge of oily ballast and cleaning water from tanks	
Strictly enforce safety and disposal regulations for refineries and industrial plants	Add oil-soluble ferrofluids (iron-containing material) to the spill, which will enable electro-magnets to remove the oil
Strengthen existing international agreements on oil spills and establish a strong international control authority for the oceans	

gravel). Of these types, contour strip mining is usually the most destructive.

An estimated 52,000 square kilometers (13 million acres) of land in the United States have been disrupted by surface mining (Environmental Protection Agency 1973), and only about half of this land has been reclaimed (Council on Environmental Quality, *Environmental Quality,* 1976). By the year 2000 an estimated 60,000 additional square kilometers (15 million acres) of land will be torn up by surface mining (Karsch 1970, Weisz 1970). If these disrupted lands are not reclaimed, the resulting 86,000 square kilometers (21.5 million acres) of wasteland will equal the combined land area of Connecticut, Delaware, New Hampshire, Rhode Island, New Jersey, Vermont, and Washington, D.C.

Strip Mining of Coal About 45 percent of all surface mining in the United States is for coal. Strip mining has rapidly replaced the underground mining of coal, because coal companies find it much faster, cheaper, safer, and more efficient. The percentage of coal obtained from strip mines has been rising steadily, increasing from about 9 percent to over 60 percent between 1940 and 1976.

Many people associate strip mining with West Virginia, Kentucky, and Pennsylvania, but it already affects about half of the states. The newest and largest battleground over strip mining is in the Great Plains—primarily the coal-rich states of Montana, South Dakota, North Dakota, Wyoming, Colorado, and New Mexico. Under these vast grasslands and high plateaus lie more than 40 percent of the nation's coal supply and 77 percent of the coal that can be strip mined at reasonable cost. Much of this western coal is on federally owned land.

Strip mining can have a severe impact on land, water supplies, wildlife, and humans (Caudill 1971, Dials & Moore 1974, Environmental Protection Agency 1974c, Greenburg 1973, Stacks 1972, Surface Mining Research Library 1972). These effects have been graphically described by Representative Ken Hechler (Democrat, West Virginia) in testimony before Congress in 1973:

a

b

c

Figure 6-12 (a) Open pit mining of copper in Butte, Montana. (b) Area strip mining of coal in Colstrip, Montana. (c) Contour strip mining of coal in Kemmerer, Wyoming.

Photos from U.S. Department of Reclamation and Soil Conservation Service, U.S. Department of Agriculture

Strip mining has ripped, torn, and scarred our land. It has polluted our streams with acid, silt, and sediment. It has destroyed valuable topsoil and seriously disturbed or destroyed wildlife habitats. It has created miles of ugly high walls. Strip mining has left a trail of utter fear and despair for thousands of honest and hard-working people whose only fault is that they have their homes near the strip mines.

The major problems of strip mining and land reclamation vary throughout the United States (Doyes 1976, National Academy of Sciences 1974c). In the East, especially Appalachia, contour surface mining (Figure 6–12) on steep slopes causes massive land disruption and acid runoff into nearby streams. Much of this coal contains sulfur compounds, which when exposed to air are converted into sulfuric acid. Rainfall washes this acid down the slopes, contaminating streams and rivers. Almost 18,000 kilometers (11,000 miles) of U.S. waterways have been polluted from acid runoff and silting caused by strip and underground coal mining (Council on Environmental Quality, *Environmental Quality*, 1973).

In the Midwest, especially in Illinois, strip mining destroys prime farm land. In the West, strip mining destroys valuable rangeland and depletes underground water supplies in the arid regions where most of the coal is located (Atwood 1975). Much of this western land can probably never be fully reclaimed (National Academy of Sciences 1974c).

The arguments for and against strip mining are summarized in Table 6–5.

Some Solutions The argument over strip mining is not whether it should be banned, but to what degree and under what control it should be allowed. Many states have attempted to control surface mining, especially the strip mining of coal, by passing laws. But it has been a difficult political battle (Landy 1976), and enforcement of the laws has varied widely from state to state. In the early 1970s environmentalists began campaigning for strict federal regulations on the strip mining of coal. In 1977, after years of work and debate and two presidential vetoes, such a federal law, the Surface Mining Control and Reclamation Act of 1977, was enacted.

Table 6–5 The Strip Mining Controversy

Arguments for	Arguments against
Strip mining results in short-term environmental damage that can be repaired with available technology. Surface mining and reclamation often improve the land.	Surface mining destroys land, forests, soil, and water. It scars the landscape, disrupts wildlife habitats and recreational areas, can cause landslides and soil erosion, and may pollute nearby rivers and streams with silt and acid runoff. Some land can be reclaimed, but without strictly enforced regulations, the coal companies do not restore the land.
Strip mining is the cheapest and best way to produce coal and meet growing energy demands. A ban on or severe restriction of strip mining would disrupt energy supplies and damage the economy by raising the price of coal.	The nation's energy needs could be met by greater development of underground coal reserves, which are 8 times more plentiful than surface coal reserves. The only reason strip mining is cheaper than underground mining is that coal companies are not paying the environmental and social costs of their ecological disruption of land and water resources.
Coal companies cannot convert to deep mining quickly enough to replace the surface coal that is now used for electric power generation.	More than 1,500 deep mines have been closed since 1969. Many of these mines still contain coal that could replace the supplies lost due to a restriction of strip mining.
It takes 5 years to bring an underground mine to full production.	New underground mines could start production within 18 months with more efficient technology and management.
Surface mining recovers nearly 100 percent of the coal, compared with 55 percent for underground mining. New technology that permits a higher recovery of underground coal cannot be used in all mines.	Recovery in most deep mines could be increased significantly by using new mining technology.
Underground miners who have been laid off are too old to return to the mines, and their skills are outdated because of new technology.	Underground mining requires 20 times more workers than strip mining and thus reduces unemployment and improves the economy. Enough miners can be trained to greatly increase the amount of underground mining.
Surface mining is safer than underground mining by a ratio of 2 to 1.	Underground mining can be made as safe as surface mining by enacting and enforcing more stringent safety standards. The injury rate in the safest mines is lower than those for real estate, higher education, and wholesale and retail trade (Energy Policy Project 1974), and black lung disease could be almost eliminated if existing dust-level regulations were enforced (National Academy of Sciences 1975b).

Some major features of this law are: (1) In order to get a mining permit, mine operators are required to prove beforehand that they can reclaim the land. (2) Land must be restored so that it can be used for the same purposes as it was used before mining. Such restoration includes filling in holes, contouring the land to its original shape, preserving all soil, removing all wastes, and replanting the land with grass and trees. (3) Strip mining is banned on some prime agricultural lands in the West, and farmers and ranchers have the right to veto mining under their lands, even though they do not own the mineral rights. (4) Mining companies must minimize the effects of their activities on local watersheds and water quality, using the best available technology, and they must prevent acid from entering local streams and groundwater. (5) A $4.1 billion fund is provided for restoring strip-mined land that has never been reclaimed. The fund is financed by a fee of 35 cents per ton of strip-mined coal and 15 cents per ton of underground-mined coal; the fees will be collected until 1993. Responsibility for enforcement of this law is delegated to states, with enforcement by the Department of Interior where the states fail to act.

If interpreted and enforced strictly and adequately funded, this law should go a long way to protect valuable ecosystems from the effects of the strip mining of coal. The next step should be the enactment of similar laws governing the surface mining of all other materials.

What is the use of a house if you don't have a decent planet to put it on?

Henry David Thoreau

Guest Editorial: Pollution Control: An Input or an Output Approach?

Kenneth E. F. Watt

Kenneth E. F. Watt is a professor of zoology at the University of California at Davis and one of the foremost scholars applying systems analysis to ecological problems. He is the principal investigator in a 30-person team engaged in building computer simulation models of human society. He has done research in 24 countries and has been awarded the Fisheries Ecology and Management Award of the Wildlife Society and the Gold Medal of the Entomological Society of Canada. He combines research talents with the ability to communicate complex ideas to others. He has lectured at 80 institutions and among his 75 publications are five important books: Mathematical Models for Use in Insect Pest Control, Environmental Realities and Economic Revolution, Ecology and Resource Management, Principles of Environmental Science, *and* The Titanic Effect.

There are two possible approaches to solving the pollution problem, an input approach and an output approach. Remarkably, almost all the attention has been focused on the latter, though it is far less useful and effective. We can think of all industrial and transportation activity as the systems analyst's black box, into which useful energy and matter flow and out of which pollutant solid, liquid, and gaseous end products emerge. The current philosophy of pollution control is to ask, "Given the amount of matter and energy flowing into the black box, what can we do to get rid of the output?" Even recycling is an output approach to this problem, albeit a sophisticated one.

A more useful approach is to question why so much matter and energy flow into the system in the first place. If, for example, all the goods, services, and transportation now available in our society could be available with 5 percent of the present expenditure of matter and energy, then we would have 5 percent of the present pollution without even trying to control it.

When we inspect the relevant figures, it appears that the central reason we use so much matter and energy is not our demand for goods, services, and transportation but rather the fantastically inefficient way in which we now use matter and energy. For example, consider transportation. Cars, with the typical load of 1.3 passengers, deliver only 7.8 passenger-kilometers of transportation per liter of fuel (18.3 passenger-miles per gallon). Jet aircraft average 54 passengers (most flights are not full) and deliver only 5.5 passenger-kilometers of transportation per liter of fuel (13 passenger-miles per gallon). These form the backbone of the current U.S. transportation system. Buses, amazingly, can deliver about 115 passenger-kilometers of transportation per liter of fuel (270 miles per gallon), and electric trains can deliver about 481 passenger-kilometers per liter (1,130 miles per gallon) in terms of fuel equivalents. Thus, we have drifted into a social system that makes shockingly wasteful use of matter and energy and develops a totally unnecessary amount of pollution per passenger-kilometer.

But this is only the beginning. Cars and aircraft also make fantastically inefficient use of the space around cities. Trains and buses use a small fraction of the right-of-way to move a given number of passengers per hour: A train can move about 100 times the number of people per meter-width of right-of-way per hour as a car-freeway system.

Some readers will argue that the reason for traveling by car and aircraft is to save time. An analysis of the portal-to-portal times on a series of sample trips between various pairs of points will show how faulty this argument is. On some short jet trips, mean velocity, portal to portal, can be as little as 30 kilometers per hour (24 miles per hour). We in North America forget about the Tokkaido High Speed Express train in Japan, which runs at 282 kilometers per hour (175 miles per hour), and much faster trains are already in use.

Personal experience makes these numbers very real. I grew up in Toronto and remember vividly the unimaginable traffic jams before the advent of the rail subway system. The Toronto rail system has made travel so much more rapid and pleasant that masses of people now return downtown at night for entertainment. The result has been a rebirth of the urban core. Recently, I was traveling by rail in Switzerland. I noticed that between Geneva and Lausanne, where the highway parallels the railway, the train passed every car I could see on the highway, even though European drivers are known for their high speeds. The North American traveler is always amazed at the ease with which one can move around in much of Europe because of the integrated transportation system.

This same type of analysis can be applied to most areas of our lives. We have unwittingly drifted into a life-style in which we pay a tremendous price in matter, energy, pollution, and pollution-related sickness for goods, services, and transportation that are less useful or of poorer quality than those we could buy with less pollution and resource depletion if we reconsidered the aims of our society. If the true purpose of society is to provide a high-quality existence for people, we somehow seem to have lost sight of this. We should now use our best scientific and engineering know-how to get back on a rational track.

Guest Editorial Discussion

1. Why has the input approach to pollution control been so neglected in the United States?

2. Why are output approaches used more often for water pollution control and input approaches more frequently for air pollution control? Relate this to the second law of energy (Section 2–3).

3. What are the economic, political, and ecological consequences of shifting to an input approach for pollution control? How would it affect your life-style?

Discussion Topics

1. Criticize the following statements:

   a. Since shale oil deposits in the United States equal the entire world's proven and estimated petroleum deposits, shale oil is the key to America's energy future.

   b. Coal gasification and liquefaction can solve America's energy problems.

   c. New discoveries of oil and natural gas will solve the energy crises for the United States and the world.

   d. Recycling energy will reduce the waste of energy.

   e. Tar sand deposits can solve America's energy problems.

2. Debate the following resolution: The United States uses far too many of the world's energy resources relative to its population size and should deliberately cut back on consumption.

3. Trace your own direct and indirect contribution to air pollution for 1 day. Try to list pollutants and relative amounts. Don't forget electricity (from all kinds of devices, including hall lights), heating, and air conditioning, and don't forget to trace the air pollution produced back to the power plant, fuel transportation to the power plant, and the strip mine or oil well.

4. Distinguish between photochemical smog and industrial smog in terms of major pollutants and sources, major human health effects, time when worst episodes occur, and methods of control.

5. Evaluate the pros and cons of the statement "Since we have not proven absolutely that anyone has died or suffered serious disease from nitrogen oxides, automobile manufacturers should not be required to meet the federal air pollution standards."

6. Rising oil and natural gas prices and environmental concerns over nuclear power plants could force the United States to depend more on coal, its most plentiful fossil fuel, for electric power. Comment on this in terms of air pollution. Would you favor a return to coal instead of increased use of nuclear power?

7. Discuss the favorable and unfavorable effects of the automobile on the ecosphere, the social environment, and your personal life-style. Consider the following: (a) building of roads and superhighways, (b) access to national parks and other areas hitherto rarely visited, (c) billboard advertising, (d) solid wastes, (e) the spread of suburbs, (f) the use of petroleum, (g) the use of iron ore and rubber, (h) international tension related to petroleum supplies, (i) air pollution, and (j) mass transit systems.

8. Simulate an air pollution hearing at which the automobile manufacturers request a delay in meeting the 1981 air pollution standards until 1985. Assign three members of the class as members of a decision-making board and other members as the president of an automobile manufacturing company, two lawyers for that company, two government attorneys representing the Environmental Protection Agency, the chief engineer for an automobile manufacturer, a public health official, and two citizens (with one opposing and one favoring the proposal). Have a class discussion of the final ruling of the board.

9. Explain why aesthetic and economic damage to recreational areas and the killing of seabirds are not necessarily the most serious consequences of oil pollution.

10. Should the United States ban all offshore oil wells? Why or why not? What might be the consequences of this restriction for the nation? For foreign policy? For security? For your town? For you? What might be the consequences of not doing this?

11. Should regulations for the strip mining of coal be relaxed so that the United States can mine more coal to relieve its dependence on nuclear power and imported oil? Why?

Further Readings

Grundlach, Erich R. 1977. "Oil Tanker Disasters." *Environment*, vol. 19, no. 9, 16–28. Superb summary.

Lave, Lester B., and Eugene B. Seskin. 1977. *Air Pollution and Human Health*. Baltimore: Johns Hopkins University Press. The most comprehensive analysis available.

Lynn, David A. 1976. *Air Pollution—Threat and Response*. Reading, Mass.: Addison-Wesley. One of the best available treatments at a slightly higher level. Highly recommended.

National Academy of Sciences. 1969. *Resources and Man*. San Francisco: Freeman. One of the most authoritative references on our resources. See especially chapter 8 on energy resources.

National Academy of Sciences. 1975. *Air Quality and Stationary-Source Emission Control*. Washington, D.C.: National Academy of Sciences. Authoritative summary of control of sulfur oxides and particulate emissions.

National Academy of Sciences. 1975. *Petroleum in the Marine Environment*. Washington, D.C.: National Academy of Sciences. Authoritative summary of this problem and possible solutions.

Steinhart, Carol E., and John S. Steinhart. 1972. *Blowout: A Case Study of the Santa Barbara Oil Spill*. North Scituate, Mass.: Duxbury. Superb case study.

Stoker, H. S., and Spencer L. Seager. 1976. *Environmental Chemistry: Air and Water Pollution*. 2nd ed. Glenview, Ill.: Scott, Foresman. Probably the best summary of air and water pollution at a slightly higher level than that found in this book.

Surface Mining Research Library. 1972. *Energy and the Environment: What's the Strip Mining Controversy All About?* Charleston, W. Va.: Surface Mining Research Library. Balanced analysis and pictures showing both sides of the strip mining controversy.

Williamson, Samuel J. 1973. *Fundamentals of Air Pollution*. Reading, Mass.: Addison-Wesley. Magnificent discussion at a slightly higher level. Highly recommended.

7

Nonrenewable Energy Resources: Nuclear Fission and Fusion

*We nuclear people have made a Faustian
compact with society; we offer . . . an
inexhaustible energy source . . . tainted with
political side effects that if not controlled could
spell disaster.*

Alvin M. Weinberg

7–1   Energy from Nuclear Fission

A Fading Dream   One of the most important, complex, and hotly debated decisions facing the developed nations is whether to use the energy from nuclear fission as a major source of electrical power in coming decades.[1] Nuclear

---

[1] For more details on the pros and cons of nuclear energy, see the following: Abrahamson 1972, Ackerman 1972, Alfvén 1974, American Assembly 1976, American Nuclear Society 1976, Barber Associates 1975, Beckmann 1976, Berg et al. 1976, Berger 1977, Bethe 1976, 1977, Brodine 1975, Bryerton 1970, Bupp & Derian 1978, Bupp et al. 1975, Carr 1976, Chapman 1974, Clark 1974c, Cohen 1974a, 1974b, 1976c, Commoner 1970b, Dahlberg 1978, Douglas 1976a, Ehrlich et al. 1977, Farmer 1977, Feiveson et al. 1979, Feld 1974, Flowers 1976, 1978, Ford 1977, Ford et al. 1974, Foreman 1971, Fowler 1975a, 1975b, Fowler et al. 1978, Francis & Abrecht 1976, Fuller 1975, Geesaman & Abrahamson 1974, Gillinsky 1977, Gofman & Tamplin 1971, Greenwood et al. 1977, Gwynne et al. 1976, Hammond 1977a, Hardin 1976a, 1976b, Hayes 1976c, 1977, 1979, Hendrie 1976, Hohenemser & Goble 1978, Hohenemser et al. 1977, Holdren 1974, Hoyle 1977, Iklé 1976, Inglis 1973, Institute for Energy Analysis 1976, 1977, Jacoby 1977, Keeny 1977, Kendall 1975, 1977, Kneese 1973, Knelman 1976, Komanoff 1976, 1977, Lapp 1973b, 1974, League of Women Voters Education Fund 1977a, Lewis 1972, Lovins 1975, 1977b, 1977c, 1978b, Lovins & Price 1975, Margen & Lindhe 1975, McBride et al. 1978, McIntyre 1975, McPhee 1974, Metzger 1972, Miller & Severance 1976, Morgan 1977, Murphy 1976b, Nader & Abbotts 1977, Nelkin & Fallows 1978, Novick 1973b, 1974b, 1976b, Nuclear Energy Policy Study Group 1977, Nye 1979, Patterson 1976, Pigford 1974, Rabinowitch 1973, Rickard & Dahlberg 1978, Robertson 1978, Rose 1974b, Rose et al. 1976, Rose & Lester 1978, Rossini & Rieck 1978, Rotblat 1977, Sagan 1973, Sagan & Eliassen 1974, Schmidt & Bodarsky 1977, Scientists' Institute for Public Information 1976b, Seaborg & Corliss 1971, Selbin 1977, Speth 1978, Speth et al. 1974a, 1974b, Spinrad 1973, Sweet 1977, Tamplin & Gofman 1970, Union of Concerned Scientists 1977, von Hippel & Williams 1976, Webb 1976, Weinberg 1973, 1976, 1977, 1978, Weinberg & Hammond 1972, Wilson 1977, Zebroski & Levenson 1976.

power has been heralded as a clean, cheap, and already developed source of energy that could replace fossil fuels (Table 4–3), with as many as 1,800 plants providing as much as 21 percent of the world's energy by the year 2000 (Wilson 1977).

The Atomic Energy Commission's 1973 predictions showed 1,500 of these 1,800 plants located in the United States alone, producing more than half of the electricity and a quarter of all the nation's energy (U.S. Department of Energy 1978). By 1979, however, though 72 large (1,000 megawatt) plants produced 13 percent of the electricity and about 3 percent of all U.S. energy (Hayes 1979), the once bright hope of United States nuclear power was fading fast. Between 1975 and 1978, only 7 new nuclear power plants were ordered, while 16 previous orders were cancelled, and 66 others delayed. In 1978 the turn-of-the-century projections were slashed from 1,500 to 200–300 (U.S. Department of Energy 1978, Hayes 1979, Speth 1978). In addition, the partial meltdown and release of some radiation in 1979 from the Three Mile Island nuclear plant in Pennsylvania raised serious questions about the safety of nuclear power and greatly increased public distrust of reassuring statements by proponents of nuclear power. Instead of being a major energy source in 2000, nuclear power may provide only about as much of all U.S. energy as it did in 1979—3 percent (Lovins 1977d).

Thus, in effect, there is already a moratorium on the expansion of nuclear power in the United States. To reverse this situation, the United States government (the taxpayers) would have to bail out the nuclear industry with a $100 billion subsidy—money that is needed to develop other energy alternatives (Lovins 1977d). Nuclear power is also in economic and political trouble in Japan, Sweden, Great Britain, France, Austria, and West Germany (Hayes 1977, Sweet 1977). In the words of energy expert Amory B. Lovins (1977d), "It is my considered judgment that nuclear power is dead—in the sense of a brontosaurus that has had its spinal cord cut, but because it's so big, and has all those ganglia near the tail someplace, can keep thrashing around for years not knowing it is dead yet."

There are seven obstacles hindering the development of nuclear power as a major energy source: (1) controversy over whether there are sufficient supplies of uranium fuel,

(2) concern over the possibility of a serious nuclear plant accident (meltdown) or plant sabotage that could expose humans to deadly, long-lived radioactive materials, (3) possible hijacking of nuclear fuel shipments, (4) the waste-storage problem, (5) possible proliferation of nuclear weapons, (6) soaring costs, and (7) controversy over the net useful energy yield for the entire system (Section 4–2). Before examining the major obstacles to the development of nuclear power, let's look briefly at how a nuclear power plant works.

How a Nuclear Power Plant Works In a nuclear power plant (Figure 7–1), a nuclear fission reactor is substituted for the firebox in a fossil fuel power plant. Inside the reactor, energy is released by the process of **nuclear fission** in which the nucleus of a heavy atom such as uranium-235 is split apart by a slow-moving neutron into lighter fission fragments plus two or three neutrons (see Figure 7–2).[2] Slowed by passing through a *moderator* (Figure 7–1), such as graphite or water, these neutrons can split other uranium-235 nuclei, releasing more energy and more neutrons. If controlled, the result is a *self-sustaining nuclear chain reaction* that steadily releases enormous amounts of energy. The fission rate is controlled by moving neutron-absorbing *control rods* (usually made of cadmium) in or out of the fuel core. A coolant—water, heavy water (where the hydrogen is hydrogen-2, or deuterium), gas, or a liquid metal such as sodium—is then passed through the reactor to absorb heat. The heat is used directly or indirectly to convert water into superheated steam. This steam drives the blades of a turbine, which in turn runs an electrical generator, as with fossil fuel plants.

In contrast to the continuous refueling of fossil fuel plants, a nuclear fission reactor is loaded only with about 100,000 kilograms (110 tons) of thimble-sized uranium oxide pellets[3]—with about one-third of the fuel being replaced each year (Figure 7–3). About 10 million of these tiny pellets are inserted in a series of long tubes, or *fuel rods.* Precisely arranged bundles of these rods are then lowered into the huge steel pressure vessel with walls 15 centimeters (6 inches) thick. The pressure vessel is surrounded by a massive shield, and the entire system is then surrounded by a containment shell for added safety should the reactor core vessel rupture (Figure 7–1).

Normally operating nuclear plants emit no air pollutants and less radiation than coal-burning plants (McBride et al. 1978). In addition, the mining of the much smaller amounts of uranium disturbs land and water systems less than either coal mining or the production and refining of oil and natural gas. Nuclear plants, however, produce considerable amounts of high- and low-level radioactive materials as wastes and as spent fuel. These wastes must not escape to the environment, and so they must be taken periodically to reprocessing or waste disposal sites. Because they are only about 25 to 30 percent efficient, present light-water reactor nuclear power plants emit more heat to the surrounding air or body of water per unit of electricity generated than fossil fuel plants, thus increasing the potential for thermal water pollution (Section 9–5).

The Nuclear Fuel Cycle Of course when we evaluate the nuclear alternative, we must look at the whole nuclear fuel cycle (Figure 7–4), of which the nuclear plant is only one part (Energy Research and Development Administration 1975c, Ford et al. 1974, Zebroski & Levenson 1976). This cycle involves the mining, transportation, processing, use, reprocessing, and storage of various nuclear materials. Unlike natural chemical cycles, this cycle has been designed totally by humans. Because of the deadly chemicals involved (especially plutonium-239), this cycle must operate in essentially absolute safety with no leaks or disruptions at

---

[2]As a crude model, the nucleus of an atom contains *neutrons* (uncharged particles) and *protons* (positively charged particles), each with a relative mass of 1. The number of protons plus the number of neutrons in a nucleus gives the **mass number,** which is a measure of the atom's mass. Atoms of the same element can have different numbers of neutrons in their nucleus, and these different forms are called **isotopes.** For example, there are three isotopes of hydrogen and three of uranium.

Isotope	Mass Number	No. of Protons	No. of Neutrons
Hydrogen-1	1	1	0
Hydrogen-2 (deuterium)	2	1	1
Hydrogen-3 (tritium)	3	1	2
Uranium-233	233	92	141
Uranium-235	235	92	143
Uranium-238	238	92	146

A sample of uranium ore contains only about 0.7 percent of fissionable uranium-235. The remaining 99.3 percent is nonfissionable uranium-238, which has three more neutrons in its nucleus. Some isotopes of an element are stable, while others are unstable (radioactive) and emit radiation in the form of **alpha particles** (a helium nucleus with two protons and two neutrons), **beta particles** (an electron), or **gamma rays** (high-energy electromagnetic radiation).

[3]Following are the three major types of fission reactors: (1) The *boiling-water reactor,* in which water is used as both the coolant and moderator and is converted directly to steam inside the reactor core. (2) The *pressurized-water reactor* (Figure 7–1), where water is used as both the coolant and moderator but is kept under pressure to keep it from changing directly to steam. Water in a second circuit and under less pressure is then converted to steam to drive the turbine. Finally, (3) the *high-temperature-gas-cooled reactor* uses a gas, such as helium, as a coolant. The superheated gas is passed through a heat exchanger and used to convert water to steam in a second heat-transfer loop. Most reactors in the United States are either boiling-water or pressurized-water reactors and are known collectively as *light-water reactors.*

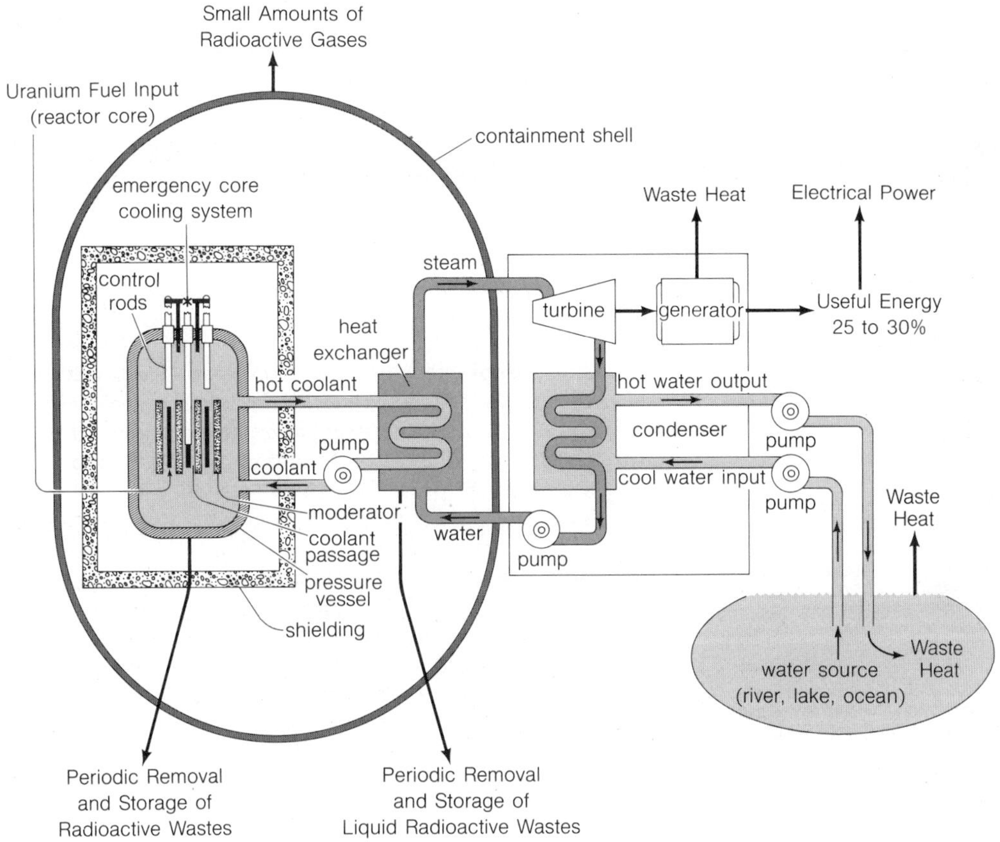

Small Amounts of
Radioactive Gases

Uranium Fuel Input
(reactor core)

containment shell

emergency core
cooling system

control
rods

heat
exchanger

hot coolant

pump

coolant

moderator

coolant
passage

pressure
vessel

shielding

steam

turbine

Waste Heat

generator

Electrical Power

Useful Energy
25 to 30%

hot water output

condenser

pump

cool water input

pump

water

pump

Waste
Heat

water source
(river, lake, ocean)

Waste
Heat

Periodic Removal
and Storage of
Radioactive Wastes

Periodic Removal
and Storage of
Liquid Radioactive Wastes

Figure 7–1 A pressurized-water reactor (PWR) nuclear power plant.

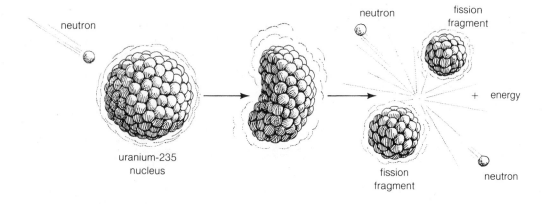

neutron

neutron

fission
fragment

uranium-235
nucleus

fission
fragment

+ energy

neutron

Figure 7–2 Nuclear fission of a uranium-235 nucleus.

any point. As the rate and volume of materials moving through it increase, the difficulty increases significantly.

The fuel cycle for a light-water reactor begins with uranium ore, which is mined and processed to form a concentrate of uranium oxide (U_3O_8) containing a mixture of uranium-238 and a little uranium-235. The oxide is then converted to a gas (uranium hexafluoride, UF_6), which goes to an enrichment plant. There the concentration of uranium-235 is increased from the naturally occurring 0.7

percent to about 3 percent for light-water reactor fuel. At a fuel preparation plant, the UF_6 is converted to uranium dioxide (UO_2), encapsulated into pellets (Figure 7–3), and then placed in fuel tubes for shipping to the power plants.

About one-third of the radioactive fuel elements in a reactor are replaced each year. These spent elements and other contaminated radioactive reactor materials are removed and allowed to cool for several months. Sealed in heavily shielded casks, they are then transported to repro-

Figure 7-3 Fuel pellets of enriched uranium oxide. Each pellet weighs less than 1 gram (1/30 of an ounce) but has the energy equivalent of 234 kilograms (366 pounds) of coal.

cessing plants, where they are cut open, their contents dissolved in acid, and the uranium and plutonium recovered and shipped to fuel preparation plants for reuse (Figure 7-4).[4] Large volumes of gaseous and liquid radioactive wastes from reprocessing plants must be stored permanently or released to the environment after temporary storage.

Until 1974, fuel processing in the United States was done in government-operated plants built for military purposes. In 1974 this arrangement was cancelled for new power plants because the government facilities had reached capacity. A private fuel-reprocessing plant near Buffalo, New York, was built but was then shut down because of engineering difficulties. The future of a second commercial reprocessing plant being built in South Carolina is uncertain. In 1977 President Carter proposed that the development of commercial fuel-reprocessing plants in the United States be deliberately slowed down and perhaps delayed indefinitely to reduce the chance of the worldwide proliferation of nuclear weapons.

In 1978, no commercial reprocessing facility for light-water reactor fuel was operating anywhere in the world.

---

[4]For more details on fuel reprocessing, see the following: Bebbington 1976, Berg 1973b, Cook 1972, Metz 1977b, 1977e, Resnikoff 1974, U.S. Atomic Energy Commission 1969a.

Only the United States can reprocess fairly large volumes of nuclear wastes—although other nations may soon build such facilities to reduce dependence on the United States (Jacoby 1977).

Now let us return to the seven obstacles to nuclear development listed above.

7-2 Uranium Supplies and Breeder Fission Reactors

Uranium Supplies Estimates of how long our uranium-235 will last vary amazingly from less than a decade (Boyd & Silver 1977, Energy Research and Development Administration 1975c, Hayes 1979, Lieberman 1976, Selbin 1977) to 1,500 years (Bupp & Derian 1974, Cohen 1977a).[5] This very long estimate assumes that since price rises in uranium fuel add relatively little to the overall cost of nuclear-generated electricity, even a price of $440 per kilogram ($200 per pound) will not price the fuel out of the market, but will stimulate the discovery and mining of low-grade deposits. Another way to extend uranium supplies is to switch from light-water reactors to the more efficient heavy-water or CANDU-type reactors used successfully in Canada since 1972 (McIntyre 1975, Robertson 1978). These plants use natural uranium as fuel (thus eliminating the expensive and energy-consuming enrichment step) and heavy water (D_2O) rather than light water (H_2O) as the moderator.

Breeder Fission Reactors Proponents of nuclear power argue that if uranium becomes scarce by 2000 to 2020, the problem could be solved for the foreseeable future by a crash program to develop the **nuclear fission breeder reactor**.[6] The liquid-metal fast breeder reactor (LMFBR), for example, uses a mixture of uranium-238 and plutonium-239 as a fuel and liquid sodium as a coolant. U-238 is rela-

---

[5]For more details on future uranium supplies, see the following: Bethe 1977, Boyd & Silver 1977, Bupp & Derian 1974, 1978, Cohen 1977a, Day 1975, Energy Research and Development Administration 1975c, Grenon 1977, Hammond 1976b, Hayes 1979, Holdren 1975b, Lieberman 1976, Nye 1979, Rose et al. 1976, Selbin 1975, 1977, von Hippel & Williams 1976, U.S. Atomic Energy Commission 1973c.

[6]For more details on breeder reactors, see the following: Alfvén 1974, Boffey 1976, Bupp & Derian 1974, Chow 1975, 1977, Cochran 1974a, 1974b, Cochran et al. 1975, Dahlberg 1978, Douglas 1976b, Energy Research and Development Administration 1975a, Feld 1974, Ford et al. 1974, Fuller 1975, Gofman & Tamplin 1971, Greenwood et al. 1977, Häfele et al. 1977, Holdren 1974, Inglis 1973, Jacoby 1977, Kneese 1973, Lapp 1973a, Lovins 1973, Lovins & Price 1975, McPhee 1974, Montefiore & Gosling 1977, Novick 1974a, 1975, Nye 1979, Rotblat 1977, Seaborg & Bloom 1970, Speth et al. 1974a, 1974b, 1975, Spinrad 1978, U.S. Atomic Energy Commission 1974a, Vitti & Staker 1972, Webb 1976, Weinberg 1976, 1977, 1978, Willrich & Taylor 1974b.

Figure 7-4 The nuclear fuel cycle; the relative radioactivity level of the nuclear materials at each step is shown.

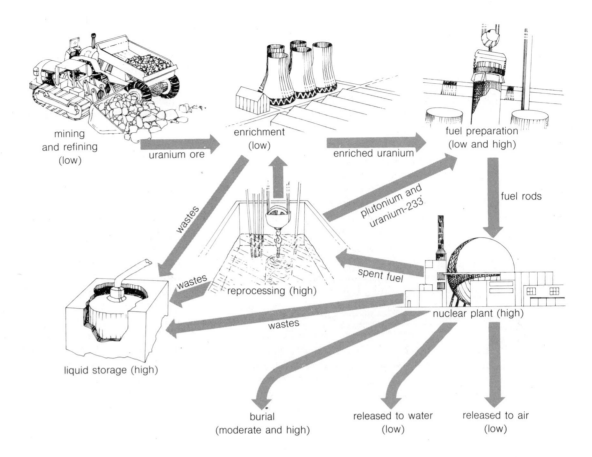

mining and refining (low)

uranium ore

enrichment (low)

enriched uranium

fuel preparation (low and high)

fuel rods

plutonium and uranium-233

wastes

wastes

reprocessing (high)

spent fuel

nuclear plant (high)

wastes

liquid storage (high)

burial (moderate and high)

released to water (low)

released to air (low)

tively abundant, and plutonium-239 can be purified from conventional reactor wastes. In the LMFBR, fast neutrons fission plutonium-239 and at the same time convert non-fissionable uranium-238 into fissionable plutonium-239, thus "breeding" its own fuel. If successful, LMFBR's would extend U.S. uranium supplies at least 50-fold (Cohen 1977a), running on $66-per-kilogram ($30-per-pound) uranium for at least 1,500 years and on $440-per-kilogram ($200-per-pound) uranium for 100,000 years.

However, in recent years a growing number of experts favor delaying breeder reactors or scrapping them altogether (Alfven 1974, Chow 1975, 1977, Cochran 1974a, 1974b, Cochran et al. 1975, Gofman & Tamplin 1971, Holdren 1974, Hohenemser et al. 1977, Inglis 1973, Kneese 1973, Lapp 1973a, Lovins 1973, Novick 1974a, 1975, Nuclear Energy Policy Study Group 1977, Rotblat 1977, Speth et al. 1974a, 1974b, 1975). The major arguments against the development of breeder reactors are as follows: (1) They are unnecessary either because uranium supplies will not run out or because a mix of safer energy alternatives can be developed faster (Lovins 1973, Speth et al. 1974a); (2) the costs would be prohibitive (Chow 1975, 1977, Cochran 1974a, 1974b, Cochran et al. 1975, Energy and Environment

Subcommittee of the U.S. House of Representatives Government Operations Committee 1978); (3) if a cooling system failed and the breeder's plutonium fuel fused together in a critical configuration (Webb 1976), the resulting explosion (equivalent to that from about 9,090 kilograms [20,000 pounds] of TNT) could shatter the reactor containment building and release large quantities of highly radioactive materials (Lovins 1973, Novick 1973b, 1974a, Rose 1974a, Webb 1976); (4) the hijacking nightmare (Ford et al. 1974, Gillinsky 1971, Kreiger 1975, McPhee 1974, Speth et al. 1974a, 1974b, 1975, Stencel 1974, Willrich & Taylor 1974b); and (5) nuclear weapons could proliferate because of the spread of breeder technology, fuel reprocessing, and plutonium fuel elements to other countries (Gillinsky 1977, Nye 1979, Rotblat 1977).

Despite these problems, prototype LMFBR reactors have been built in the U.S.S.R., Great Britain, and France; West Germany and Japan have active development programs (Metz 1976d, O'Sullivan 1978). British and Russian reactors have had engineering difficulties, but the French Phoenix reactor has performed very well so far (Metz 1976d). But even if technical and economic problems are overcome, the large-scale development of commercial breeder reactors in Europe and Japan still depends on the development of the presently delayed fuel-reprocessing facilities in the United States.

Arguments against the breeder gain force when we look at its performance record. In the United States, one of the three experimental government LMFBR reactors suffered a core meltdown in Idaho in 1961, killing three workers. In 1966 the experimental Enrico Fermi breeder near Detroit was shut down after part of its core melted down after its cooling system became blocked (Fuller 1975). A quarter-size prototype reactor, scheduled for completion in Clinch River, Tennessee, by 1985, was delayed indefinitely in 1978 because of engineering design problems, an astronomical rise in cost estimates from $700 million to $2.7 billion, and especially concern about proliferation of nuclear weapons. Suggestions for avoiding the dangers of nuclear proliferation (and hijacking) include the following: (1) greatly increasing security measures (Nye 1979, Rose & Lester 1978), (2) doctoring the fuel elements to make it difficult and dangerous to hijack and convert to bombs (Feiveson 1978, Feiveson et al. 1979, Leachman & Seaborg 1977, Nye 1979), and (3) shifting to proliferation-resistant breeder reactors—called "advanced converters" or "thermal breeders"—that use a mixture of thorium-232 and fissionable uranium-233 instead of uranium-238 and plutonium-239 (Dahlberg 1978, Feiveson 1978, Feiveson et al. 1979, Hafemeister 1979, Rickard & Dahlberg 1978, Spinrad 1978). In these reactors, nonfissionable thorium-232, which is abundant and cheap compared with uranium, is converted by slow neutrons to fissionable uranium-233 (Spinrad 1978). But as Amory Lovins (1979) has pointed out, uranium-233 is similar and in some respects superior to plutonium-239 as a material for making atomic bombs (Lovins 1979). At present there is pressure to provide massive funding to build a large prototype breeder in the United States that would be capable of using either uranium-238 and plutonium-239 or thorium-232 and uranium-233 as fuels.

7-3 How Safe Are Nuclear Fission Power Plants?

Radiation Effects and Levels When people shudder about nuclear accidents, what they fear, of course, is radiation. Radiation damage to humans varies with the type of radioactivity and the parts of the body exposed. In general, however, exposure to radiation has two major effects: genetic damage (mutations that can be passed on to future generations) and damage to nonreproductive tissues, which can cause leukemia, various forms of cancer, miscarriages, cataracts, and death.

Most experts agree that *any* exposure to radiation can have genetic effects. But experts don't agree on whether exposure to very low radiation levels causes nongenetic

damage, such as cancer. Some say that any dose of radiation is harmful; others hold that doses are not necessarily harmful if they are below a certain *threshold level* (Figure 7-5). Unfortunately, the evidence is not clear,[7] although nuclear workers exposed to very low levels of radiation may be getting cancer at higher than average rates (Morgan 1978a, Najarian 1978, Raloff 1978b, 1979, Rotblat 1978). Until this controversy is resolved, human radiation-exposure standards must be set as low as possible and still allow for some beneficial exposures (such as medical X rays) and for the natural or **background radiation** from naturally radioactive materials and from cosmic rays entering the atmosphere (between 38 and 150 millirems[8] per year in the United States) (Environmental Protection Agency 1971). In addition, human activities expose each person to an additional radiation dose of about 80 to 125 millirems per year (Environmental Protection Agency 1976c). This brings the total annual average exposure for U.S. residents to between 210 and 255 millirems.

Present federal and international standards set the maximum allowable occupational exposure to radiation at 5,000 millirems per year (Najarian 1978). Standards for the maximum allowable exposure of the general population to artificial sources of radiation (except X rays) have been set at a much lower figure of 170 millirems per year (Oakley

---

[7]For more details on radiation levels and effects, see the following: Brown 1976b, Comar & Sagan 1976, Ehrlich et al. 1977, Environment Staff Report 1973, Environmental Protection Agency 1971, 1976c, Gofman & Tamplin 1970a, 1970b, Hodges 1977, Holcomb 1970, Inglis 1973, Lindop & Rotblat 1971, Morgan 1971, 1978a, Najarian 1978, National Academy of Sciences 1972, National Council on Radiation Protection and Measurements 1975, Oakley 1972, Pauling 1970, Raloff 1978b, 1979, Rotblat 1978, Schurr 1971, Sternglass 1973, U.S. Atomic Energy Commission 1966.

[8]A millirem is equivalent to the radiation dose that delivers 10^{-10} joule of energy to 1 gram of matter.

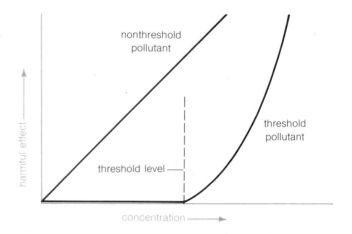

Figure 7-5 Effects of nonthreshold and threshold pollutants.

1972). There is growing pressure to lower both of these standards by a factor of 10 because of the increasing evidence that low levels of radiation cause cancer (Gofman & Tamplin 1970a, 1970b, Morgan 1978a, Najarian 1978, Pauling 1970, Raloff 1978b, 1979, Rotblat 1978).

The major sources of artificial radiation in the United States are X rays (72 millirems per person per year); nuclear weapons fallout (4 millirems); TV, consumer products, and air travel (2.7 millirems); radioactive isotopes used to diagnose and treat disease (2 millirems); job exposure (0.8 millirem); and nuclear power plants, fuel-processing plants, and nuclear research facilities (0.06 millirem) (Environmental Protection Agency 1971, Oakley 1972).

From this information we see that the largest average exposure to artificial radiation each year is from X rays and our smallest exposure is from nuclear power plants and related facilities (assuming, of course, that they are operating normally). Such comparisons, however, don't tell the whole story. X-ray radiation comes from brief exposure to an energy source that does not stay in the environment and requires no long-term protection. In contrast, radioactive wastes from nuclear plants must be isolated from the environment, for hundreds of thousands of years. Because of its half-life of 24,000 years, for example, plutonium-239 can remain active for up to 250,000 years (based on the rule of thumb that an isotope decays to a safe level after about 10 times its half-life).

Plutonium-239 is not the most toxic substance on earth, as is often claimed.[9] Moreover, the alpha particles it emits cannot penetrate the skin. But it is highly toxic and it can cause cancer (especially lung cancer) in humans. In fact, according to the controversial hot-particle hypothesis, a single tiny particle of plutonium-239 (as plutonium oxide or PuO_2) inhaled into the lungs can cause lung cancer 15 to 45 years later. A breeder reactor that suffered a meltdown and small nuclear explosion could release up to 3,000 kilograms (3.3 tons) into the environment. Plutonium could also be released if crude atomic bombs made from hijacked plutonium fuel were set off in populated areas by terrorist groups.

Nuclear Reactor Safety   Almost everyone agrees that nuclear fission is *potentially* the most hazardous of all known energy alternatives, not so because of nuclear explosions, but because a serious accident could contaminate large areas for hundreds of thousands of years. The most feared such accident would begin with a break in one of the heavy pipes that conduct cooling water and steam to and from the reactor core (Figure 7–1). The first result would be a

"blowdown," in which a mixture of steam and water would be expelled from the reactor core. In the presence of the core's intense radioactivity, steam could be converted into hydrogen and oxygen, which could then explode violently and rupture the reactor core. Radioactive materials and gases would be released, but if the strong containment shell did not rupture they would be prevented from entering the atmosphere. Meanwhile the residual heat from the radioactive materials in the core would be enough to melt the fuel rods within an hour or less and cause a complete meltdown of the reactor core. Within another hour the molten core would drop to the bottom of the reactor containment vessel, melt through its thick concrete slab, and melt itself into the earth. Depending on the geological characteristics of the underlying strata it might sink to a depth of 6 to 30 meters (20 to 100 feet) and gradually dissipate its heat (Hammond 1974b) or it might burn itself deeply into the earth's crust. A melt-through accident is sometimes called "China syndrome" because the molten reactor core would melt itself into the earth, presumably heading in the general direction of China.

A melt-through is a nightmare for reactor engineers, but the most serious hazard would be the release of highly radioactive gases and particulates to the atmosphere that could occur from blowholes in the ground or failure of the containment shell during the first hour or two. This cloud of radioactive materials would be at the mercy of the winds and weather.

Such a meltdown and radioactive spill would demand the simultaneous failure of multiple safeguards. First, fuel pellets are clad in metal to confine most of the fission products. Next, the primary reactor pressure vessel (Figure 7–1) provides very strong containment for the radioactive materials in the reactor core. Third, a sophisticated backup system automatically inserts control rods into the core to stop fission if certain emergencies occur. Finally, if the coolant water pipeline breaks, the system has an emergency core cooling system (ECCS) that should flood the reactor core with emergency cooling water within one minute. But intense steam pressure or a large hydrogen bubble could keep the emergency cooling water out. The intense debate over nuclear reactor safety is over the relative probability of a meltdown and the resulting risks compared to those from other energy alternatives.[10]

---

[9]For more details on plutonium hazards, see the following: American Nuclear Society 1976, Bair & Thompson 1974, Cohen 1976a, 1976b, Cuddihy et al. 1977, Edsall 1976, Gillette 1974a, 1974b, Gofman 1975a, 1975b, Gofman & Tamplin 1971, Healy 1976, Lovins 1973, Morgan 1975, Novick 1973b, Rose 1974b, Tamplin & Cochran 1974, Tardiff 1975.

[10]For more details on nuclear reactor safety, see the following: American Nuclear Society 1976, Berger 1977, Bethe 1976, 1977, Carter 1974, 1978c, Cohen 1974a, 1976c, Ehrlich et al. 1977, Environmental Protection Agency 1976b, Farmer 1977, Forbes et al. 1972, Ford 1977, Ford & Kendall 1972, 1975, Hammond 1974b, 1977a, Hendrie 1976, Hohenemser 1975, Hohenemser et al. 1977, Inglis 1973, Institute for Energy Analysis 1977, Kendall 1975, Lapp 1974, Lewis et al. 1978, McBride et al. 1978, Novick 1974b, Nuclear Regulatory Commission 1975, Patterson 1976, Pigford 1974, Pollard 1976a, Primack 1975, Primack & von Hippel 1974, Rose et al. 1976, Sagan 1973, Shapley 1977, Shea 1976, Union of Concerned Scientists 1977, 1978, U.S. Atomic Energy Commission 1974c, von Hippel 1974, Webb 1976, Weinberg 1976, 1977.

Since the 1950s, the Atomic Energy Commission (AEC) has commissioned several studies to assess the probability of a serious nuclear accident and to project the resulting deaths, injuries, and property losses. The first of these studies, published in 1957 (and known by its document number, WASH-740), projected that a "maximum credible accident," releasing 50 percent of all fission products 48 kilometers (30 miles) from a city of 1 million people with no evacuation, might kill 3,400 persons, injure 43,000, and cause property damage valued between $500,000 and $7 billion (Brookhaven National Laboratory 1957). In the early 1960s a second, updated version of the 1957 safety study was commissioned by the AEC but was not made available to the public. Documents obtained under the Freedom of Information Act revealed that between 1955 and 1975, the AEC suppressed this study and a number of other documents and studies concerning the risks of nuclear power (Mulvihill et al. 1965, Nader & Abbotts 1977). This is not surprising, since the AEC had the dual and often conflicting roles of promoting and regulating nuclear power. In 1975 the AEC was dissolved and its two roles were split, with its research role assigned to the Energy Research and Development Administration (ERDA) (now a part of the Department of Energy) and its regulatory role assigned to the Nuclear Regulatory Commission (NRC).

The most recent and extensive reactor safety study (known by various names, including WASH-1400, the Rasmussen report, and RSS) was published in 1975 (Nuclear Regulatory Commission 1975). This $83 million, 3-year study was carried out by members of the Atomic Energy Commission and outside experts under the direction of Dr. Norman Rasmussen, professor of nuclear engineering at Massachusetts Institute of Technology. This report attempted to evaluate the probability and consequences of serious nuclear accidents involving 100 light-water reactor power plants either in operation or planned, but it did not cover hijacking and dangers associated with other parts of the nuclear fuel cycle. According to this study, the most likely core meltdown would occur on an average of once every 17,000 years per plant and cause no more than one death, one injury, and property damage of $100,000 (excluding damage to the plant). The chance of an accident causing 1,000 or more deaths was estimated at 1 in 100 million per plant per year. For 100 plants, such an accident might occur once in a million years—about the same likelihood that a meteor would strike a major population center and cause 1,000 fatalities. Under the worst-case accident, there might be 825 to 13,200 immediate deaths, 7,500 to 180,000 deaths from cancer a number of years later, 12,375 to 198,000 illnesses, 4,750 to 171,000 delayed genetic effects, and property damage ranging from $2.8 billion to $28 billion (Nuclear Regulatory Commission 1975). But according to the study, the probability of this

happening with 100 plants in operation is about 1 in 1 billion per plant per year.

The Rasmussen report, however, has been criticized by a number of prominent scientists and nuclear safety experts for (1) underestimating the chances and consequences of serious reactor accidents, (2) covering only part of the risks from the entire nuclear fuel cycle, (3) covering only 100 plants rather than the 1,000 or more projected for the future, and (4) using some questionable assumptions and statistical procedures that make many of its fatality and risk projections almost meaningless (Carter 1978c, Environmental Protection Agency 1976b, Hohenemser et al. 1977, Institute for Energy Analysis 1977, Kendall 1975, Lewis et al. 1978, Primack 1975, Shapley 1977, Union of Concerned Scientists 1977, 1978, von Hippel 1974). In January 1979, after reviewing these criticisms, the Nuclear Regulatory Commission repudiated the Rasmussen report because of its deficiencies. Since the report evaluated the probability of mechanical failure, we still don't know the more likely effects of accidents from human errors or deliberate malice or sabotage. We can do a lot to make mechanical systems safer, but what can we do to reduce human error? In evaluating something as risky and complex as nuclear power, perhaps we should assume that both Murphy's law—if anything can go wrong, it will—and its corollary—Murphy was an optimist—will control events (Hardin 1976a). This became evident in 1979 when a highly improbable series of mechanical failures and human operator errors caused a partial core meltdown and the release of some radiation from the Three Mile Island nuclear plant in Pennsylvania. In this accident, described as the worst in the history of commercial nuclear power, no lives were lost. But it will take 15 to 40 years to learn whether cases of cancer will show up in the nearby residents (especially unborn and young children) exposed to radiation that leaked from the plant. In addition, confusing and conflicting statements about the seriousness of the accident by power plant officials and Nuclear Regulatory Commission officials eroded public confidence in the safety of nuclear power and in the ability of nuclear officials to provide the public with accurate and truthful information about the potential or actual dangers of nuclear power.

Thus, after over 25 years of studies on nuclear reactor safety, we are back at square one. By mid-1979 no identifiable loss of life has resulted from radiation releases in any commercial reactors in the United States or in other nations (no statistics are available for the U.S.S.R.). This enviable record, although reassuring, does not really tell us much about the probability of future accidents, when there might be 500 to 1,000 nuclear power plants in the United States and thousands of shipments of nuclear materials around the country each year. Nor does it tell us about the long-term effects of low levels of radiation released accidentally from nuclear plants and other parts of the nuclear fuel cycle. We still have no authoritative evaluation of nuclear reactor safety and no study at all evaluating the safety of the entire nuclear fuel cycle. Nuclear power could be as safe—or even safer—than the Rasmussen report. But it could also be much less safe. We don't know!

It seems significant, however, that insurance companies have refused since the 1950s to insure a nuclear reactor for even $500 million. Because this would have prevented the fledgling nuclear industry from ever getting off the ground, Congress in 1957 passed the Price-Anderson Act, which makes the public primarily responsible for nuclear liability payments. The government liability for any single nuclear accident will not exceed $560 million, and of this amount at most only $140 million would be paid out by private insurance companies, with the government (you and me) accounting for the remaining $420 million. Nuclear proponent Alvin M. Weinberg has called for utilities to show that they really believe in the low-risk figures they keep quoting to the public by insuring each reactor for damage up to $1 billion with their own funds, with the government assuming responsibility for losses greater than $1 billion, as it now does in the case of floods and natural disasters (Weinberg 1977).

Nuclear energy expert Alvin M. Weinberg (see his Guest Editorial at the end of this chapter) believes that nuclear power can be safe. But he has also been one of the few strong proponents of nuclear power who emphasize that the widespread use of nuclear power is the greatest single long-term risk ever taken by humankind, one that should be accepted only after intensive public education and debate. In his words, "We nuclear people have made a Faustian compact [a compact with the devil] with society; we offer . . . an inexhaustible energy source . . . tainted with potential side effects that if not controlled, could spell disaster" (Weinberg 1972). Weinberg envisions a permanent nuclear priesthood of responsible technologists who will guard and protect all nuclear plants, shipments, and waste deposits for hundreds of thousands of years.

But an increasing number of prominent nuclear physicists, including David R. Inglis (see his Guest Editorial at the end of this chapter), other scientists, economists, some industrialists, and a number of environmentalists are expressing serious doubts about the commitment of the United States to nuclear fission power (especially the breeder reactor) as a major source of electrical energy for the intermediate- and long-term future.

Despite a strict licensing procedure, supervising and monitoring all present and projected nuclear power plants in the United States over their 30- to 40-year lifetime with essentially a zero tolerance for error is a formidable, if not impossible, task. Critics of nuclear power were not encouraged when one of the first responses to the 1973 energy crisis was an AEC proposal (later proposed again by the Nuclear Regulatory Commission) to speed up licensing procedures for nuclear plants, especially in light of the Three Mile Island accident in 1979.

7–4 Transportation and Storage of Radioactive Materials

Terrorism and Hijacking of Nuclear Fuel Shipments
Like any industrial facility, a nuclear power plant could be sabotaged by a team of trained people (American Nuclear Society 1976, DeNike 1974, Flood 1976, Kreiger 1975, Willrich & Taylor 1974b). The team would have to overpower the guards, disable or destroy all of the plant's safety systems, and then blow up or threaten to blow up the reactor containment vessel to release radioactive materials into the environment. By 1978 no nuclear plant had been severely sabotaged. But between 1969 and 1975, there were 11 bombs set off, hundreds of threats and hoaxes, 15 acts of vandalism and sabotage, and 15 breaches of security in or near nuclear test laboratories and nuclear plants throughout the world but mostly in the United States (Flood 1976). A nuclear plant is a centralized facility that can be made very secure, and since 1975 the often lax security around nuclear plants has been tightened. But absolute protection cannot be guaranteed (American Nuclear Society 1976).

A much more dangerous problem is the hijacking of nuclear fuel shipments.[11] Protecting hundreds to thousands of nuclear material shipments is much harder than protecting a few centralized nuclear power plants. The hijacking of spent fuel being sent to reprocessing plants (Figure 7-4) is not a serious problem, since the materials are intensely radioactive and must be shipped in radiation-shielding casks weighing up to 91,000 kilograms (100 tons). But shipments of uranium from enrichment plants to fuel preparation plants and of uranium fuel elements from fuel preparation plants to light-water nuclear power plants (Figure 7-4) are much more vulnerable. Even so, upgrading the 3 percent uranium-235 fuel material to the bomb-grade 90 to 93 percent uranium-235 requires very sophisticated

---

[11]For more details on the hijacking of nuclear fuel shipments, see the following: American Nuclear Society 1976, Chester 1976, Cohen 1976c, 1977d, Comey 1976, DeNike 1974, Energy Research and Development Administration 1975c, 1977a, Feiveson 1978, Feld 1975, Ford et al. 1974, Gillette 1973a, Holdren 1974, Inglis 1973, Kreiger 1975, Lapp 1973b, 1974, Leachman & Althoff 1971, Leachman & Seaborg 1977, Lovins 1979, McPhee 1974, Novick 1973b, Phillips & Michaelis 1978, Rose 1974b, Salisbury 1976, Schurr 1971, Stencel 1974, Taylor 1975, Willrich & Taylor 1974b, Willrich 1975b.

and expensive facilities (American Nuclear Society 1976, Rose 1974b).[12]

If commercial breeder reactors are ever developed, the prime target of hijackers would be shipments of plutonium-239 from fuel preparation plants to breeder power plants (Figure 7–4). Plutonium-239 can be used directly to make crude nuclear bombs (Gillinsky 1977) that could easily blow up a large building or a city block and contaminate much larger areas with deadly radioactive materials (Cohen 1977d). Only about 4.5 kilograms (10 pounds) of plutonium-239 metal or about 10 kilograms (22 pounds) of plutonium oxide are needed to make an atomic bomb (American Nuclear Society 1976, Gillinsky 1971). To get this amount of plutonium would require from 227 to 682 kilograms (500 to 1,500 pounds) of plutonium reactor fuel (American Nuclear Society 1976). The projected future use of breeder reactors, which will require annual inventories of 30,000 to 200,000 kilograms (66,000 to 444,000 pounds) of plutonium, makes the diversion of a few hundred kilograms of plutonium quite possible (Hohenemser et al. 1977). Plutonium-239 is deadly, but only when inhaled. Thus, in its solid form it poses little danger to the thieves.

How easy would it be to convert stolen plutonium to a "blockbuster" atomic bomb? Experts disagree (Cohen 1976a, 1977b, McPhee 1974, Willrich & Taylor 1974b). But since an average Princeton undergraduate and several other college students have used library resources to develop a credible plan for building a nuclear bomb from plutonium (Phillips & Michaelis 1978), a small group of trained people could probably make a crude atomic bomb.

But the hijackers need not bother to make atomic bombs. They could simply use a conventional explosive charge to blow the stolen plutonium into the atmosphere from atop any tall building. Dispersed in this manner, only 2.2 kilograms (1 pound) of plutonium could theoretically contaminate 7.7 square kilometers (3 square miles) with lethal radioactivity for 250,000 years (DeNike 1974).

In 1973, John O'Leary, then AEC director of nuclear plant licensing, asked a group of outside consultants to evaluate the danger of nuclear theft. Their report, released to the public by Sen. Abraham Ribicoff (D-Conn.) over the objections of the AEC, stated that U.S. security safeguards against possible nuclear theft or blackmail were "entirely inadequate to meet the threat" and "that the potential harm to the public from the explosion of an illicitly made nuclear weapon is greater than that from any plausible power plant accident."[13]

This evaluation, plus the report by Willrich and Taylor (1974b), has prompted the Nuclear Regulatory Commission to tighten security measures for nuclear plants and fuel shipments. Plutonium fuel is carried in armored trucks

with expert marksmen as guards, who have orders to shoot to kill. Elaborate communications facilities should bring help rapidly. A new $100,000 shipment vehicle is being considered that permanently locks its wheels on a signal. Its sides are made of a material that resists attack, but in case of attack, a rapidly hardening plastic foam is automatically injected into the interior to cover the nuclear fuel (American Nuclear Society 1976). With such security measures, it is estimated that a nuclear security force of a few thousand persons could guard plutonium in the United States—less than the number of guards used to guard and transport money in the U.S. banking system (Cohen 1977d). If adequate security measures are established and rigidly monitored and enforced, it would be much harder—but still by no means impossible—for a shipment of plutonium fuel to be stolen.

Even Alvin M. Weinberg, one of the strongest and most optimistic advocates of nuclear energy (see his Guest Editorial at the end of this chapter), believes that the problem of shipping dangerous breeder fuel will be "difficult" and suggests that we develop nuclear parks to minimize this risk (Weinberg & Hammond 1972). A cluster of 8 to perhaps 40 nuclear plants, along with fuel preparation, fuel-reprocessing, and waste storage plants, would be grouped in one complex to reduce the need for shipping. But such large complexes would be very expensive to build and might affect local climate, and opposition from nearby residents would be strong. Another suggestion for reducing hijacking risks is to deliberately contaminate the plutonium fuel with hot radioactive wastes, which would make the fuel very dangerous to steal and hard to purify. But so far there is no acceptable spiking agent. Some possible isotopes would require a major overhaul of the fuel cycle processing steps, and others are too scarce (Salisbury 1976).

Nuclear Wastes If 1,000 grams of uranium-235 undergo fission, some 999 grams of radioactive waste products are left over—a mixture of solids, liquids, and gases that must be stored until their radioactivity is no longer harmful.[14] Table 7–1 shows some of the isotopes produced in nuclear fission reactors. Iodine-131 and cesium-137 are particularly dangerous because, unlike most radioisotopes, they can become concentrated in food chains.

---

[12]This would not be true if we switched to high-temperature-gas-cooled reactors, which use bomb-grade fuel.

[13]See *Congressional Record*, April 30, 1974, S. 6623.

[14]For more details on nuclear wastes, see the following: Alfvén 1974, American Nuclear Society 1976, Angino 1977, Blomeke et al. 1974, Breckhoeft et al. 1978, Bull 1975, Carter 1978d, Cohen 1977c, de Marsily et al. 1977, Dreschhoff et al. 1974, Ehrlich et al. 1977, Energy Research and Development Administration 1976a, Farney 1974, Fisher 1978, Gillette 1973b, Gilmore 1977, Gwynne 1976, Hambleton 1972, Hammond 1977a, Jakimo & Bupp 1978, Kubo & Rose 1973, LaPorte 1978, Lapp 1974, Lepkowski 1979, MacLeish et al. 1977, Metz 1978d, Micklin 1974, National Academy of Sciences 1978b, Nuclear Regulatory Commission 1976a, 1976b, Rochlin 1977, Salisbury 1976, Starr & Hammond 1972, Stencel 1976, Swann 1977, U.S. Atomic Energy Commission 1969b, 1973c, 1974b, Zinberg 1979.

Table 7-1 Some Dangerous Isotopes Produced in Nuclear Fission Reactors

Isotope	Half-Life*	Organ Affected
Iodine-129	17,000,000 years	Thyroid
Plutonium-239	24,000 years	Entire body, but especially lungs
Cesium-137	27 years	Entire body
Hydrogen-3 (tritium)	12 years	Entire body
Krypton-85	11 years	Lungs, skin
Iodine-131	8 days	Thyroid

*Isotopes must be stored for periods of 10 to 20 times their half-life before they decay to safe levels. For a more complete listing of isotopes, see U.S. Atomic Energy Commission 1969b (pp. 40–42).

Three methods are used to dispose of radioactive wastes: (1) dilute and disperse, (2) delay and decay, and (3) concentrate and contain. In *dilution and dispersion,* low-level wastes are released into the air, water, or ground to be diluted to presumably safe levels. As wastes proliferate, this already dangerous practice will begin to add significantly to artificial radiation levels in the environment, particularly from hydrogen-3 (tritium) and krypton-85, which are difficult and fairly expensive to contain and remove. *Delay and decay* can be used for radioactive wastes with relatively short half-lives. They are stored as liquids or slurries in tanks. After 10 to 20 times their half-lives, they decay to harmless levels, at which time they can be diluted and dispersed to the environment.

The third method, *concentration and containment,* is used for highly radioactive wastes with long half-lives. These wastes must be stored for tens, hundreds, or thousands of years, depending on their composition. They are not only extremely radioactive but also thermally hot (primarily from cesium-137 and strontium-90). Official assurances from nuclear scientists (American Nuclear Society 1976, Cohen 1976c, 1977b, 1977c, Kubo & Rose 1973, Starr & Hammond 1972), the NRC, and the Department of Energy that the problem of long-term waste storage can be solved has not satisfied environmentalists and scientists who think that the widespread use of nuclear power should not proceed until the waste storage problem has been solved (Alfvén 1974, Angino 1977, Carter 1978d, de Marsily et al. 1977, Ehrlich et al. 1977, Kneese 1973, Micklin 1974, Rabinowitch 1973, Stencel 1976). To such critics, this proceeding with nuclear power without an acceptable solution to the waste problem is like jumping out of an airplane without a parachute while the pilot reassures you, "Don't worry, we'll find a way to save you before you hit the ground." By 1978 California, Iowa, Maine, and Wisconsin had banned the construction of new nuclear power plants until the government demonstrated a risk-free method for long-term nuclear waste disposal (Fisher 1978).

In 1978 about 4.7 million kilograms (5,200 tons) of spent fuel from U.S. nuclear power plants were being stored temporarily underwater in huge, specially constructed pools at nuclear plants until a method for long-term disposal was found. By 1990 the amount of stockpiled spent fuel is expected to reach 34 million kilograms (37,900 tons). Experts doubt that such a large quantity of spent fuel can continue to be stored safely at nuclear plants. Thus, unless one or more permanent storage sites are developed by 1990, some nuclear plants may be forced to close and new plant construction may be halted. Large volumes of liquid wastes from nuclear weapons production are also awaiting some form of permanent storage and are being temporarily stored in underground tanks in government facilities in Idaho Falls, Idaho, Savannah River, South Carolina, and Hanford, Washington. These tanks must be carefully guarded against sabotage and continuously maintained and checked to prevent corrosion and leaks. More than 1.7 million liters (450,000 gallons) of highly radioactive wastes have already leaked from 20 underground tanks at the Hanford, Washington, site. However, a study by the National Research Council concluded that because of the isolation of the site, the leaks have not caused any significant radiation hazard to public health (Fisher 1978).

Table 7-2 summarizes the methods proposed for long-term storage or disposal of nuclear wastes. For over 20 years most scientists have considered disposal in underground salt or granite deposits the best sites for long-term disposal of dangerous nuclear wastes. West Germany has been storing its nuclear wastes in a deep underground salt mine for several years. The U.S. Department of Energy tentatively plans to build a $450 million waste isolation pilot plant (WIPP) by 1988 in rooms dug out of a geologically stable, dry salt dome, located 792 meters (2,600 feet) below the surface of the desert area near Carlsbad, New Mexico (Figure 8–8). But several reports by geologists have raised doubts about the long-term stability of salt deposits exposed to high-temperature nuclear wastes (Angino 1977, Breckhoeft et al. 1978, de Marsily et al. 1977). In addition, environmental groups and some citizens oppose locating a national nuclear depository in New Mexico, and such opposition is growing in other states (Lepkowski 1979, Metz 1978c, Zinberg 1979). By 1978, some 11 states declared they would not accept a nuclear waste depository, and 15 more were thinking of following suit (Fisher 1978).

Conceivably, salt deposits or one of the other disposal schemes (Table 7-2) may work. But any failure in this Faustian bargain will be visited upon 7,000 future generations.

7-5 Economics of Nuclear Fission Energy

Soaring Costs Concern over the safety, hijacking, long-term storage, and nuclear proliferation are important issues. But the present major depression in the U.S. nuclear industry has occurred primarily for economic reasons and because the use of electricity has not risen as rapidly as originally projected since the 1973 oil embargo—thus decreasing the need for new power plants (Bupp & Derian 1978, Bupp et al. 1975). Utilities are finding it harder and harder to get stockholders' approval for borrowing and tying up billions of dollars for the 10 to 12 years required to bring a nuclear plant into operation. Coal-fired power plants can be on-line in half the time, saving as much as $100 million a year on interest payments alone. The time needed to bring coal-fired plants on-line, however, is increasing, so this time difference may decrease significantly in the future.

As with most aspects of nuclear power, there is a heated and complex debate over the economics of nuclear power compared with that of its chief competitor, coal-fired power plants.[15] Nuclear plants completed in the United States between 1974 and 1977 were, on average, 73 percent more expensive than comparable coal plants completed during the same period (Staff report 1979e). To make matters worse, construction costs have soared faster for nuclear than for coal-fired plants (Bupp & Derian 1978). Nuclear

plants, however, have lower operating costs than coal-fired plants. Originally they were also projected to have an 80 percent *capacity performance*—the percentage of time during which a plant actually operates. But because of frequent breakdowns, lengthy maintenance operations, and federally required safety precautions, commercial nuclear power plants have operated well below the 80 percent capacity figure, the larger plants having the poorest performance (Fowler et al. 1978). The exact capacity figures vary with plant size and age and are a subject of heated controversy (Comey 1975, Fowler et al. 1978, Hohenemser & Goble 1978, Margen & Lindhe 1975). Coal-fired plants performed only slightly better (Fowler et al. 1978), but with their lower

---

[15]For more details on the economics of nuclear power, see the following: Berg et al. 1976, Bupp & Derian 1974, 1978, Bupp et al. 1975, Chow 1975, 1977, Cochran 1974a, 1974b, Cochran et al. 1975, Comey 1975, Energy and Environment Subcommittee of the U.S. House of Representatives Government Operations Committee 1978, Fowler et al. 1978, Hohenemser & Goble 1978, Komanoff 1976, 1977, Margen & Lindhe 1975, Miller & Severance 1976, Morgan 1977, Saunders 1976, Scientists' Institute for Public Information 1976b, Speth 1978, Staff report 1979e, Stauffer et al. 1975.

Table 7-2 Proposed Methods for Long-Term Storage or Disposal of Nuclear Wastes

Proposal	Possible Problems
Surround wastes with concrete and store in surface warehouses until a better solution is found.	Concrete might deteriorate; warehouses may be difficult to guard against sabotage.
Solidify wastes, encapsulate them in glass or ceramic, place in metal containers, and bury the containers deep underground in earthquake- and flood-free geological formations, such as dug-out salt or granite deposits.	Long-term occurrence of natural disasters cannot be predicted; heat from radioactive decay might crack glass containers, fracture salt or granite formations so that groundwater could enter the depository, or release water from water-containing minerals that could leach radioactive materials into groundwater supplies; transportation of deadly radioactive wastes to depository sites could be dangerous; wastes might be difficult to retrieve if project fails.
Use rockets to shoot the wastes into the sun or into space.	A launch accident could disperse deadly radioactive wastes over a wide area.
Bury wastes in an underground hole created by a nuclear bomb so that the wastes eventually melt and fuse with surrounding rock into a glassy ball.	Effects unknown and unpredictable; if project fails, wastes cannot be retrieved and could contaminate groundwater supplies.
Bury wastes under Antarctic ice sheets.	Long-term stability of ice sheets is unknown; knowledge about thermal, chemical, and physical properties of large ice sheets is lacking; retrieval could be difficult or impossible if project fails.
Encase wastes in well-designed containers and drop them into the ocean.	No one knows how to design a container that will last long enough; oceans and marine life could become seriously contaminated if containers leak.
Enclose wastes in well-designed containers and drop them into deep ocean bottom sediments that are descending toward the center of the earth.	Long-term stability and motion of these sediments are unknown; containers might leak and contaminate the ocean before they are carried downward; containers might migrate back to the ocean or be spewed out somewhere else by volcanic activity; wastes probably cannot be retrieved if project fails.
Change harmful isotopes into harmless ones by using high-level neutron bombardment, lasers, or nuclear fusion.	Technological feasibility has not been established; this process could create new toxic materials also needing disposal.

Sources: Angino 1977, Breckhoeft et al. 1978, de Marsily et al. 1977, Fisher 1978, Jakimo & Bupp 1978.

construction costs today they can produce electricity more cheaply where coal is available.

This controversy is also clouded by the use of figures from older plants. The real question is whether nuclear power will be cheaper than coal power in the future. With the total cost of generating nuclear power rising rapidly, any advantage it presently holds over coal may soon disappear. In addition, the projected costs of electricity from nuclear power do not include either the costs of waste disposal or the expensive decommissioning and the subsequent almost perpetual guarding of the abandoned plant.

Because of the economic risks involved, utility companies in the United States have become quite cautious about investing in new nuclear power plants. Indeed, some utilities have begun to sell some of their nuclear power plants to cooperative groups of small communities. Unfortunately, these communities may not realize that in the long term they will probably have to face safety shutdowns, expensive maintenance and waste disposal costs, decommissioning costs, and improvements to meet stricter safety standards. Such communities could eventually find themselves both bankrupt and blacked out. Perhaps such communities should think more about why the utilities are willing to sell them nuclear power plants.

A Complex Decision   From the discussion in this chapter we have seen that major reliance on nuclear energy as a major source of energy is by no means a simple issue. Proponents of nuclear power argue that it is safe and economical, and that it is the only energy technology sufficiently developed to reduce dependence on fossil fuels over the next 30 to 50 years. In sharp contrast, opponents argue that nuclear power is unsafe, uneconomical, unethical (since it commits future generations to storing our radioactive wastes in absolute safety), and unnecessary since a mix of coal-burning power plants (with adequate pollution control) and other energy sources (such as the sun, wind, and biomass) can reduce dependence on fossil fuels over the next 30 years.

7–6   Nuclear Fusion

Nuclear Fusion Reactions   In laboratories in the United States, the U.S.S.R., Japan, and western Europe, scientists are competing to harness nuclear fusion as a source of energy.[16] The potential energy locked in atomic nuclei can be released by two processes, *nuclear fission* and *nuclear fusion*. In nuclear fission (Section 7–1), a slow neutron splits the nucleus of a heavy atom, such as uranium-235, into two lighter fragments, releasing more neutrons, and energy (see Figure 7–2). In **nuclear fusion**—as in the sun and hydrogen

bombs—two nuclei of light, nonradioactive atoms (such as hydrogen) are forced together at ultrahigh temperatures to form a heavier nucleus (such as helium), releasing energy in the form of fast neutrons. Fusion releases 4 times as much energy per gram as fission (uranium) and about 10 million times as much as the combustion of fossil fuel (Post 1976). At present, the two most attractive fusion reactions are the D-D reaction, in which two deuterium (or hydrogen-2) nuclei fuse to form a helium-3 nucleus, and the D-T reaction, in which a deuterium nucleus and a tritium (hydrogen-3) nucleus fuse to form helium-4 (Figure 7–6).

Since atomic nuclei have positive electric charges, they repel one another and stubbornly resist fusing. Forcing the nuclei together requires an enormous input of energy. The D-D reaction, for example, requires an ignition temperature of about 1 billion °C. Because of its much lower ignition temperature (100 million °C) the deuterium-tritium reaction is the only one being studied seriously at this time.

Even though deuterium is a rare form of hydrogen, seawater provides an almost inexhaustible supply. If nuclear fusion is ever developed, the deuterium in the ocean could supply humankind with energy at many times present consumption rates for 100 billion years—about 10 times the estimated age of the universe (Post 1976). But such rosy projections are based on the deuterium-deuterium fusion reaction, which will not be even remotely considered as a possible energy source for at least 100 years, if ever. The long-term supply for the deuterium-tritium fusion reaction is not so optimistic, since there is no significant natural source of tritium. As a result, the tritium supply must be continuously bred in a nuclear fusion reactor by bombarding the rather rare element lithium with neutrons. Thus, the supply of lithium—an element not much more abundant than uranium—may limit the life of D-T fusion (Fowler 1975b, Holdren 1971a, 1978, Metz 1976a, Stein 1976).

Problems To Overcome   Controlled nuclear fusion has important advantages (see Table 4–3), but it also has many incredibly difficult and complex problems. After 25 years and almost $2 billion spent in research, no sustained fusion reaction yielding any net useful energy has yet (1979) even been achieved in the laboratory.

There are three difficult requirements for a sustained nuclear fusion reaction, and they must all be met simultaneously. Scientists must (1) heat a small quantity of fusion fuel to about 100 million °C, (2) contain and push the re-

---

[16]For more details on nuclear fusion, see Coppi & Rem 1972, Cowen 1977, Edelson 1974, Emmett et al. 1974, Fowler 1975b, Fowler & Post 1976, Gough & Eastlund 1971, Hammond et al. 1973, Holdren 1978, Holzman 1978b, Kulcinski 1974, Kulcinski et al. 1979, Landis 1973, Leonard 1973, Lidsky 1972, Lubin & Fraas 1971, Metz 1976a, 1976b, 1976c, 1978e, Parkins 1978, Post 1976, Post & Ribe 1974, Rose 1971, 1976, Steiner 1971, Steiner & Clarke 1978, Wood & Nuckolls 1972, Yonas 1978.

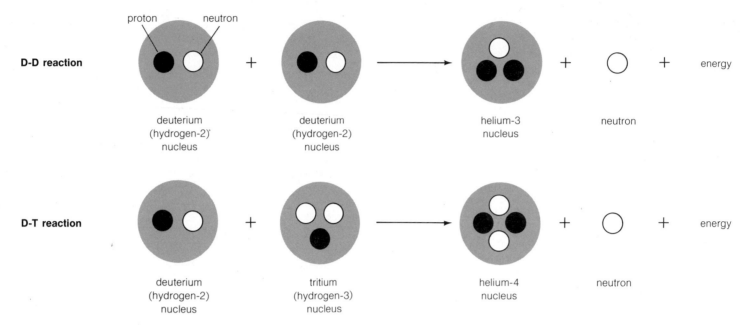

D-D reaction

proton   neutron

deuterium   deuterium   helium-3   neutron
(hydrogen-2)   (hydrogen-2)   nucleus
nucleus   nucleus

+   +   +   energy

D-T reaction

deuterium   tritium   helium-4   neutron
(hydrogen-2)   (hydrogen-3)   nucleus
nucleus   nucleus

+   +   +   energy

Figure 7–6   Two potentially useful nuclear fusion reactions.

sulting plasma[17] together long enough and at a high enough density for the fuel atoms to fuse, and (3) recover enough net useful energy to make fusion profitable. Each of these requirements has been met separately, but by 1979 no single experiment had achieved all three at once.

Most of the past research has sought a nonmaterial means or "magic bottle" that could confine the plasma safely and press it together long enough for self-sustaining fusion to occur. The two major approaches are *magnetic confinement* and *inertial containment* (Figure 7–7). Since the particles of a plasma are charged, they can be guided—attracted or repelled—by magnetic fields. The most promising magnetic approach is the Russian *tokamak*, in which the plasma is confined in a doughnut shape by two magnetic fields (Figure 7–7). The giant tokamak fusion test reactor (TFTR) under construction in 1978 at the Princeton University Plasma Physics Laboratory may be the first to reach the break-even point (producing as much power as it uses). But some researchers still consider the tokamak noncommercial because of engineering problems and costs—probably 2 to 4 times as much as for breeder fission (Metz 1976b).

A second approach to nuclear fusion is *inertial containment*. High-powered laser beams, electrons, or atoms bombard and implode a tiny pellet crammed with deuterium and tritium fuel (Figure 7–7). The impact should drive the contents of the pellet inward, creating an intensely hot, dense core where fusion can take place. In effect, the beams set off miniature hydrogen bombs whose released energy produces electricity. Major problems are developing lasers with enough power and containing and preventing a sudden shock wave of energy from destroying the containment vessel.

Unlike breeder fission, the tokamak approach poses no threat of nuclear weapons proliferation. The inertial containment approach, however, could give other nations access to technological insights leading to hydrogen or nuclear fusion bombs (Holdren 1978, Holzman 1978b). As a result, much of the research on inertial containment is highly classified. Another fear is that in the rush to show the feasibility of nuclear fusion, scientists might be tempted to use a hybrid fusion-fission reactor, in which a breeder fission reactor would be used to provide the ignition temperature for fusion. Such an approach would combine the worst and most potentially dangerous aspects of fusion and breeder fission (Section 7–2; Cowen 1977, Holdren 1978, Leonard 1973, Metz 1976c).

Even if the ignition and confinement problems are solved, scientists still face formidable problems in developing a workable nuclear fusion reactor and plant (Holdren 1978, Holzman 1978b, Kulcinski et al. 1979, Metz 1976a, 1976b, Parkins 1978, Rose 1976). One proposed scheme is shown in Figure 7–8.

One such problem is a little like trying to preserve an ice cube next to a blazing fire—only harder. At the center of

---

[17]At ultrahigh temperatures, the nuclei are stripped of their surrounding negatively charged electrons, leaving an intensely hot mixture of positively charged nuclei and negatively charged electrons known as *plasma.*

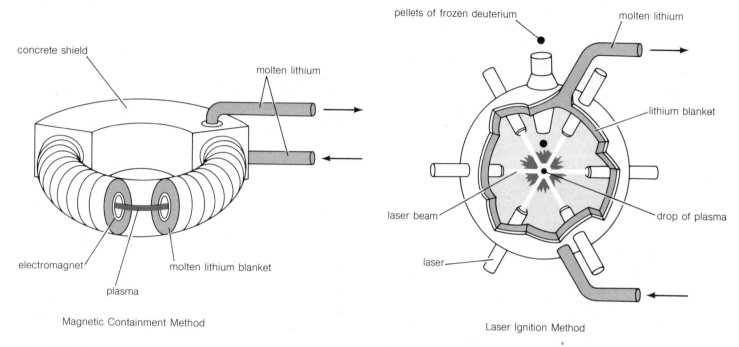

Figure 7-7 Comparison of magnetic containment and laser ignition methods for initiating a nuclear fusion reaction.

the reactor the plasma may be 100 million °C, but only 2 meters away, around the magnets, the temperature must be near absolute zero (−273°C) to be achieved by using liquid helium—a substance that may soon be scarce (National Academy of Sciences 1978a). The entire massive chamber must also be maintained at a near perfect vacuum. More mind-boggling still, the inner wall of the reactor must resist constant baths of highly reactive liquid lithium

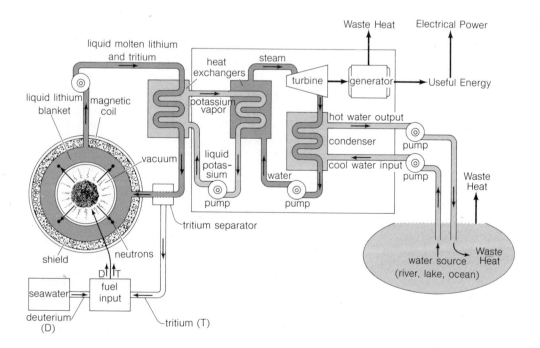

Figure 7-8 A proposed nuclear fusion power plant using deuterium (D) and tritium (T) as fuel.

(at 1,000°C) and steady bombardment by neutrons (which destroy most known materials) for 10 to 20 years. A wall of any known metal would have to be replaced every 2 to 10 years at such an enormous cost that fusion may never be economically feasible (Kulcinski et al. 1979, Metz 1976b, Parkins 1978). Many of these wall materials might also be scarce (Kulcinski et al. 1979). In addition, repairs would have to be made by automatic devices since no human worker could withstand the radiation (Holzman 1978b, Kulcinski et al. 1979).

Fusion reactors, though much less dangerous than conventional or breeder reactors (Holdren 1978, Kulcinski et al. 1979, Post 1976, Steiner 1971) do have some potential radioactivity hazards. Worst would be the release of radioactive tritium (hydrogen-3), either as a gas or as tritiated water, which in turn could enter the human body through the skin, mouth, or nostrils (Holdren 1978, Holzman 1978b, Kulcinski et al. 1979, Metz 1976b). Tritium is extremely difficult to contain, because at high temperatures and high neutron densities it can diffuse through metals (Holzman 1978b). It is also produced in fission reactors, and scientists are already testing methods for controlling it (Holdren 1978). The long-term disposal of worn-out radioactive metal parts from fusion reactors could also create a problem. Worn-out lithium blankets from fusion reactors would create ten times the volume of wastes created by fission plants (Holzman 1978b, Metz 1976a, 1976b).

Future Prospects The scientific, engineering, and economic problems associated with nuclear fusion stagger the imagination. However, many fusion scientists feel that these difficulties can eventually be overcome with enough government funding (Holdren 1978, Kulcinski et al. 1979, Post & Ribe 1974, Rose 1976, Steiner & Clarke 1978). If everything goes right—which may be one of the biggest ifs in scientific and engineering history—laboratory feasibility might be established by 1985, and commercial feasibility sometime between 2000 and 2020. Then, between 2050 and 3000, nuclear fusion might produce as much as 18 percent of U.S. annual energy needs (Holdren 1978, Kulcinski et al. 1979). At best, nuclear fusion is a very long-term energy possibility.

Nuclear fission energy is safe only if a number of critical devices work as they should, if a number of people in key positions follow all their instructions, if there is no sabotage, no highjacking of the transports, if no reactor fuel processing plant or reprocessing plant or repository anywhere in the world is situated in a region of riots or guerrilla activity, and no revolution or war—even a "conventional one"—takes place in these regions. . . . No acts of God can be permitted.

Hannes Alfvén

Guest Editorial: A Faustian Bargain We Should Accept

Alvin M. Weinberg

Alvin M. Weinberg is former director of the Oak Ridge National Laboratory and former director of energy research and development for the Federal Energy Administration. He now serves as director of the Institute for Energy Analysis at Oak Ridge, Tennessee. He has been one of the leading advocates of nuclear energy and has written extensively on some of the difficult public policy problems posed by modern science. In 1960 he received both the Atoms for Peace Award and the Atomic Energy Commission's E. O. Lawrence Memorial Award for his contributions to the theory and development of nuclear fission reactors for electric power plants.

There are two basically different views of the world's future. The one most popular these days is attributed to Malthus and holds that the resources of Spaceship Earth are limited. Nothing except drastic reduction in population, affluence, or technology can avoid the ultimate disaster predicted by Thomas Malthus in 1803 and more recently by a team of scientists (Meadows et al. 1972, 1974). The other view, attributed sometimes to the economist David Ricardo, holds that as scarce materials are exhausted there will always be new, more expensive ones to take their place: Spaceship Earth has practically infinite supplies of resources, but it will cost more and more to stay where we are as we use up those that are readily available.

The Ricardian view seems to me to be the more reasonable, especially since all of our past experience has shown that as one resource becomes scarce, another takes its place. We do not use whale oil any longer, yet we have far better artificial lighting than did our lamp-lighting ancestors. And, in the very long run, humankind will have to depend on the most common and almost infinitely abundant elements: iron, sodium, carbon, nitrogen, aluminum, oxygen, silicon, and a few others. Glass, cement, and plastics will perform many more functions than they now do. Our standard of living will be diminished, but I cannot see this reduction as being by a factor of 10: More likely it would be, say, a factor of 2.

Thus, in contrast to what seems to be the prevailing mood, I retain a certain basic optimism about the future. My optimism, however, is predicated on certain assumptions.

1. Technology can indeed deal with the effluents of this future society. Here I think I am on firm ground, for, on the whole, where technology has been given the task and given the time, it has come through with very important improvements. For example, many experts believe that the stringent emission standards imposed on cars by the Clean Air Act will indeed be met by 1985, if not before.

2. Phosphorus, though essentially infinite in supply (1,000 ppm in the earth's crust), has no substitute. Will we be able to so revolutionize agriculture that we can eventually use this "infinite" supply of residual phosphorus, at acceptable cost, for growing our food? This technological question is presently unresolved, though I cannot believe it to be unresolvable.

3. All of this presupposes that we have at our disposal an inexhaustible, relatively cheap source of energy. As we now see the technological possibilities, there is only one that we can count on—and this is nuclear fission, based on fission breeder reactors. This is not to say that nuclear fusion or geothermal or solar energy will never be economically available. We simply do not know now that any of these will ever be successful, whereas we know that fission reactors are feasible.

In opting for nuclear fission breeders—and we hardly have a choice in the matter—we assume a moral and technological burden of serious proportion. A properly operating nuclear reactor and its subsystems are environmentally a very benign energy source. The issue hangs around the words "properly operating." Can we ensure that henceforth we shall be able to maintain the degree of intellectual responsibility, social commitment, and stability necessary to manage this energy form so as not to cause serious harm? This is basically a moral and social question, though it does have strong technological components.

It is a Faustian bargain that we strike: In return for this inexhaustible energy source, which we must have if we are to maintain ourselves at anything like our present numbers and our present state of affluence, we must commit ourselves—essentially forever—to exercise the vigilance and discipline necessary to keep our nuclear fires well behaved. As a nuclear technologist who has devoted his career to this quest for an infinite energy source, I believe the bargain is a good one, and that it may even be an inevitable one. It is well that the full dimension and implication of the Faustian bargain be recognized, especially by the young people who will have to live with the choices that are being made on this vital issue.

Guest Editorial Discussion

1. Do you agree that the resources of Spaceship Earth are practically infinite?

2. The author bases his optimism on three assumptions. What evidence can you provide to support or question the reasonableness of these assumptions? Are there any other assumptions that should be added?

3. Who was Faust and what is a Faustian bargain?

4. Do you agree that we should accept the Faustian bargain of nuclear fission with either conventional or breeder reactors? Why or why not? What are the consequences of not having this service and depleting our fossil fuels over the next few decades? How will your life be affected?

Guest Editorial: The Energy Frontier

David Rittenhouse Inglis

David Rittenhouse Inglis is a prominent nuclear physicist and professor emeritus of physics at the University of Massachusetts. He is on the editorial board of the Bulletin of the Atomic Scientists *and on the board of directors of the National Committee for Nuclear Responsibility. Inglis has written many articles and books on atomic and nuclear physics. His book* Nuclear Energy: Its Physics and Social Challenge *(1973) is considered one of the best descriptions and evaluations of nuclear power for students and educated citizens, and his most recent book,* Windpower and Other Energy Options *(1978), is a superb evaluation of energy alternatives.*

Among all possible future energy sources, nuclear fission energy from reactors has been the darling of government funding because it is a spin-off from the military nuclear adventure. The development of the first atomic bomb during World War II was an intense and dedicated exploration into the unknown in a spirit of national urgency. In spite of all the uncertainty and enormous obstacles, President Franklin D. Roosevelt made a brave decision. Two billion 1945 dollars were poured into the gamble and it paid off.

After the war, reactors were developed almost to the point of commercial practicability with government funding in the new national laboratories. Then in the mid-1950s the decision was made to throw to industry the main task and opportunity of engineering the development and construction of commercial nuclear reactors, with the national laboratories playing a backup role in research. Both government and industry have since poured billions of dollars into the project, and because of this there is strong vested interest and an inclination to scorn other energy alternatives.

The proponents of an enormous expansion of nuclear reactor deployment rightly point out that such a program can probably be kept reasonably safe if eternal vigilance and the meticulous care appropriate to so dangerous an enterprise can be maintained. But there are already abundant signs that with pressures to build a large number of reactors, this safety cannot be assured. For example, a welding inspector was fired at a nuclear power plant at Virginia Beach, Virginia, for being too faithful in reporting faults in the welds, which are vital to the safety of any nuclear plant. Anyone who guesses that the probability of a catastrophic accident in a large nuclear power plant is only 1 in 10,000 per year is guessing about the performance of vessels with inadequately inspected welds and of much more intricate apparatus. In 1979, a partial meltdown and release of radiation from the Three Mile Island nuclear plant raised serious questions about the safety of nuclear power.

It would be much easier and less disruptive of our way of life to seek safe alternatives to nuclear power and even to fall far short of doubling U.S. per capita electricity consumption every decade. Of all the reasons to seek alternate energy sources, the most important is avoiding the proliferation of nuclear materials that adds to the likelihood of nuclear war and blackmail.

What we need again today is a brave decision by national leaders to explore with vigor and dedication the unknown but real potential of new energy sources. True, some effort and some public funds are being devoted to developing exotic new energy sources, but these funds are miserably small compared with the need. With the exception of nuclear fusion, exotic energy sources are receiving perhaps half as much development funding as they could use (see Table 10–2). Fusion is a noble gamble, a bit more than a gleam in the scientist's eye. It may work. It may not. If it does, it will be several decades hence and it will have its troubles, including radioactive troubles less severe than those of fission reactors. It has the blessing of the vested interests because it could serve as a later-generation nuclear energy source.

Of the meager funds going into some of the other possibilities, it seems that more is going into paper studies and committee reports than into enthusiastic developmental work. Yet there are enthusiasts with ideas who cannot get money for research.

Of the solar energy possibilities, the Meinels' worthy steam-turbine-in-the-desert scheme (Meinel & Meinel 1971, 1972) and the biological production of fuels are receiving some funding, but still far below what is needed.

As another example of inadequate effort, no one is building a giant windmill. One prototype, built on a limited experimental basis during World War II, fed 1,000 kilowatts into the electricity grid in Vermont. That experiment came just at the dawn of the atomic age and was not followed up, probably because of early rosy hopes for infinite, cheap, and trouble-free nuclear power. Now that those early dreams have faded, it is high time to follow up on wind power development. The potential is enormous—almost limitless. Modern engineering stands ready, without awaiting further research and development, to build large numbers of giant windmills either in the sparsely settled parts of the Great Plains or offshore near the edge of the continental shelf, where they will bother almost no one. They can generate hydrogen to be stored and provide a steady source of power. The immediate need is for a few million dollars to build the first full-scale prototypes to convince decision makers that thousands of windmills would provide as much power as the nuclear plants that are being proposed.

New legislation is providing sharply increased funds for energy research and development (Table 10–2). But for 1979 only about 10 percent of the total federal energy budget was designated for development of solar and wind energy. Money alone will not do the job, but money in abundance and properly administered could foster the surfacing and development of all sorts of brave new ideas. A wide gamut of such ideas should be explored so that we may have available the best options 10 and 20 years from now and, even more importantly, for the next century, when the more serious crunch will come. Anything less is shunning the challenge of the energy frontier.

Guest Editorial Discussion

1. Compare the viewpoint in this editorial with that of the previous editorial. Which position do you support? Why?

2. Should a massive commitment to the evaluation and development of solar, wind, geothermal, biomass, and other types of energy be undertaken simultaneously with the continuing development of nuclear power, or should the latter be slowed down or stopped for a period? Defend your answer.

3. Why do these alternate energy sources continue to receive so little money compared with conventional and breeder reactors and nuclear fusion (see Table 10–2)?

Discussion Topics

1. Criticize the following statements:

   a. A nuclear fusion plant can blow up like a hydrogen bomb.

   b. A nuclear fission plant can blow up like an atomic bomb.

   c. Nuclear fusion plants could release large amounts of radioactive materials.

2. Compare the major parts and major environmental impacts of fossil fuel, normal fission, and breeder electric power plants. How does a breeder "breed" new fuel? Which type of plant do you prefer? Why?

3. Debate the issue now before Congress: We should declare a moratorium on the licensing of all nuclear power plants until we can be more assured of their safety and of the feasibility of safe transportation and storage of nuclear wastes.

4. Explain why the "atomic bomb syndrome" frequently associated with nuclear power plants is not a valid fear or criticism. What is a "grand excursion"? Why is it sometimes called the "Chinese syndrome"? List the series of multiple safeguards in a nuclear reactor that make such an excursion extremely improbable.

5. Explain the fallacy in the statement that nuclear power plants are safer than driving your car, flying in an airplane, or engaging in most everyday activities. It is estimated by different sources that the chances of a serious nuclear accident are 1 in 10,000 to 1 in 1,000,000,000. Is this an acceptable risk for you? Explain.

6. In May of 2020, the director of the National Nuclear Security Guard announces that one of the several thousand heavily guarded shipments of deadly plutonium made each year to nuclear breeder reactors has been hijacked by a small but well-organized terrorist group calling itself the Nuclear Liberation Army (NLA). About 23 kilograms (50 pounds) of plutonium was taken. Because plutonium is a weak emitter of alpha radiation, its presence is almost impossible to detect. The hijackers could break up the material into smaller pieces and carry it in their pockets, briefcases, or suitcases with only newspaper, aluminum foil, or any thin covering to protect themselves from the radiation. The primary danger is lung cancer if plutonium dust particles are inhaled. One week after the hijacking, the president of the United States receives an ultimatum from the NLA that within 6 weeks he must shut down and dismantle all nuclear power plants and have the U.S. Treasury send checks for $15,000 to every person below the poverty level. Otherwise the NLA threatens to use conventional plastic explosives to blow up the plutonium, injecting particles into the air above 10 major U.S. cities,

and pour dissolved plutonium compounds into the water systems of these cities. If this occurs, thousands and probably millions could contract lung or other cancers within 15 to 45 years, and large urban areas of the United States would be uninhabitable for centuries. As president of the United States, how would you respond? Check the feasibility of this scenario with a chemist, a physicist, and a security expert and see if you can conceive of a way to prevent such a possibility. Do you favor a U.S. energy plan based on the widespread phasing in of breeder reactors between 2000 and 2040? Why or why not? What are the alternatives?

7. Debate the issue of whether we should accept the Faustian bargain of nuclear fission with conventional reactors. With breeder reactors. Either way, how might your life be affected? Your children's lives?

Further Readings

See also the references for Chapter 5.

Alfvén, Hannes. 1974. "Fission Energy and Other Sources of Energy." *Bulletin of the Atomic Scientists*, January, pp. 4–8. Superb analysis of the dangers of nuclear energy that includes a proposed alternative plan. Highly recommended.

American Nuclear Society. 1976. *Nuclear Power and the Environment.* Hinsdale, Ill.: American Nuclear Society. Excellent defense of nuclear power. Highly recommended. See also Beckmann 1976, Hammond 1974b, Rose 1974b, Rose et al. 1976, Seaborg & Corliss 1971.

Berger, John J. 1977. *Nuclear Power: The Unviable Option.* New York: Dell. Superb discussion of the case against nuclear power. Highly recommended.

Bupp, Irvin C., and Jean-Claude Derian. 1978. *Light Water: How the Nuclear Dream Dissolved.* New York: Basic Books. Outstanding discussion of why nuclear power is an economic disaster.

Cohen, Bernard L. 1974. *Nuclear Science and Society.* New York: Anchor Books. Excellent defense of nuclear power. Highly recommended. See also Cohen 1976c, 1977b.

Gofman, John W., and Arthur R. Tamplin. 1971. *Poisoned Power: The Case against Nuclear Power.* Emmaus, Pa.: Rodale. Hard-hitting popularized attack on nuclear power plants by two prominent nuclear scientists.

Hayes, Dennis. 1976. *Nuclear Power: The Fifth Horseman.* Washington, D.C.: Worldwatch Institute. Superb presentation of the case against nuclear power. Highly recommended. See also Hayes 1977.

Inglis, David R. 1973. *Nuclear Energy: Its Physics and Social Challenge.* Reading, Mass.: Addison-Wesley. Probably the best introduction to nuclear energy available. See also Nuclear Energy Policy Study Group 1977.

Jakimo, Alan, and Irvin C. Bupp. 1978. "Nuclear Waste Disposal: Not in My Backyard." *Technology Review,* March–April, pp. 64–72. Excellent summary. See also Farney 1974, Starr & Hammond 1972.

Kendall, H. W., ed. 1977. *The Risks of Nuclear Power Reactors.* Washington, D.C.: Union of Concerned Scientists. Excellent discussion of problems with nuclear power.

Kulcinski, G. L., et al. 1979. "Energy for the Long Run: Fission or Fusion." *American Scientist,* vol. 67, 78–89. Superb evaluation of nuclear fusion. See also Lidsky 1972, Post 1976, Rose 1976.

Lapp, Ralph E. 1974. *The Nuclear Controversy.* Greenwich, Conn.: Fact Systems. One of the best presentations of the case for nuclear power. Highly recommended.

Lovins, Amory B. 1973. "The Case against the Fast Breeder Reactor." *Bulletin of the Atomic Scientists,* March, pp. 29–35. A physicist presents a strong case against the breeder.

Najarian, Thomas. 1978. "The Controversy over the Health Effects of Radiation." *Technology Review,* November, pp. 78–82. Excellent summary.

Weinberg, A. M. 1972. "Social Institutions and Nuclear Energy." *Science,* vol. 177, 27–34. Highly optimistic view based on widespread and safe use of nuclear energy. See also Weinberg 1977.

8

Renewable Energy Resources

The Great Spirit made fresh air, sunshine, and good water to work for us. The white man does not obey the Great Spirit.

Chief Flying Hawk
The Sioux Tribe

8-1 Energy from Rivers and Oceans

Hydroelectric Power Humans have used falling water as a source of renewable energy for centuries (Stoker et al. 1975). As water flows downward from high to low land its gravitational potential energy is converted into the kinetic energy of streams and rivers. This kinetic energy can turn waterwheels to do useful work (such as milling or driving machinery) or to spin turbines to produce electricity. Dams have stored water in reservoirs where it can be released to produce electricity at any time. Although water power is theoretically a renewable resource (Table 1–1), all hydroelectric power dams have finite lives, ranging from 50 to 300 years, because their reservoirs eventually fill up with silt (Cook 1976b, Nisbet 1974).

Hydroelectric power plants have several important advantages: high efficiency, high net useful energy yield (Figure 4–1), low to moderate environmental impact on the air and water, a long life, and relatively low operating costs (Table 4–3). In addition, they are run by a free source of energy (falling water). The large-scale development of hydroelectric power, however, is limited by the availability of suitable sites. A good site has a high head (height of the water fall), a high rate of flow, a large storage capacity (reservoir), and nearness to a large population center (Cook 1976b). As a result, the best hydroelectric sites are in areas that have heavy rainfall and large variations in elevation. In the United States, most hydroelectric projects are concentrated in two areas, the Southeast and the Northwest, as shown in Figure 8–1. Not only are good sites limited, but they are also unevenly distributed throughout the world and are often far from major population centers.

Most of the best hydroelectric sites in the United States (except Alaska) and other industrial nations have already been developed. Canada, Africa, South America, Southeastern Asia, and Siberia, however, have major sites that can still be developed (Carr 1976). In the 1920s water power provided about one-third of all electricity used in the United States (Broad 1978). Between 1950 and 1978 hydroelectric capacity in the United States more than doubled, but it provided only about 13 percent of the electricity and only about 3 percent of the total energy used in 1978 (Broad 1978, Stoker et al. 1975) (Figure 1–3). Even if it doubles again between 1975 and 2000 (Stoker et al. 1975), its growth rate is expected to lag so far behind the growth in total energy use that water power may provide no more than 1 to 2 percent of the total energy used by 2000 (Stoker et al. 1975).

And this second doubling may not happen. Although operating costs are low for a hydroelectric plant, construction costs can be very high, depending on size, land costs, and the expense of relocating people and facilities flooded out by the reservoir. Large-scale hydroelectric installations also harm the surrounding land, lowering water levels below the dam and submerging farmland, wildlife habitats, mineral deposits, timber areas, and historical and archaeological sites above it (Stoker et al. 1975). As a result, the Wild and Scenic Rivers Act and pressure from environmentalists will kill some remaining major dam proposals in the United States.

One possibility is to revitalize some of our abandoned or underused small hydroelectric sites (Broad 1978, Lovins 1977c, 1978a, McGuigan 1979). Throughout the United States nearly 50,000 small dams might be put back to work, providing as much electricity as 85 nuclear or coal-burning power plants (Broad 1978). As always, there are some problems: (1) Silting may have cut their reservoir capacity; (2) about 60 percent are on streams that dry up for part of most years; (3) American industries are geared to produce only large-scale hydroelectric machinery; and (4) the owners may block their use (Broad 1978).

Despite the problems, developing these sources would be much simpler, cheaper, and more environmentally favorable than developing other major energy alternatives (Table 4–3).

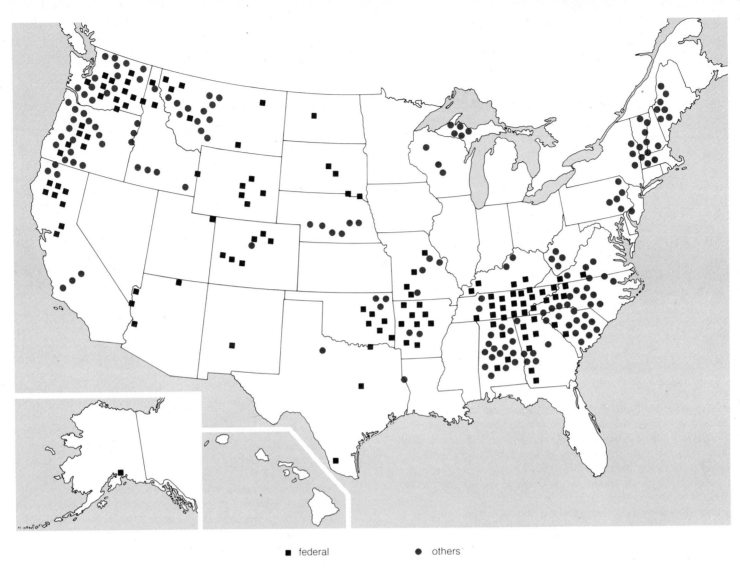

■ federal   ● others

Figure 8–1   Locations of major U.S. hydroelectric projects in 1976. (U.S. Department of the Interior)

Tidal and Wave Power   Two potential sources of energy from the sea are *tidal power* (Hubbert 1969b, Merriam 1978, Stoker et al. 1975) and *wave power* (Merriam 1978, Stoker et al. 1975). As the tide rises and falls, water flows into and out of bays and estuaries. If the bay or estuary can be closed by a dam, the energy in the tidal flow can be extracted 4 times a day and used to spin a turbine to produce electricity. But only about two dozen places in the world have enough change in water height between tides to provide economically feasible energy (Hubbert 1969b, Merriam 1978). Other problems are intermittent delivery of power, seawater corrosion, and damage from severe storms. Today there are only two commercial tidal electric installations in use, one in France and one in the U.S.S.R. (Stoker et al. 1975). The only two feasible locations in the United States are the Cook Inlet in Alaska and Passamaquoddy Bay in Maine. Canada has the largest tidal fluctuation in the world—17 meters (55 feet)—in the areas along the Bay of Fundy. If this area and all other well-suited locations in the world were developed, they would produce electricity equivalent to only 13 nuclear or coal-burning power plants (Udall et al. 1974).

Wave energy is derived from wind energy, which in turn is derived from solar energy. Capturing this energy has been a dream since at least 1799, when two Frenchmen patented a wave-power device, and serious research is under way, especially in Japan and Great Britain, to develop devices for harnessing it (Fisher 1975a, Merriam 1978). Despite such serious problems as high cost, seawater corrosion, storm damage, variability in wave height, transmission of the energy to shore, and low net useful energy yields, some scientists believe that wave-power machines could supply all of Great Britain's electricity needs cleanly, safely, and eternally (Fisher 1975a).

8–2 Solar Energy

Types of Solar Energy Breeder reactors, nuclear fusion, and solar energy are the only energy alternatives that could support a high-energy civilization indefinitely. But breeders have potentially serious environmental and economic problems (Section 7–2) and nuclear fusion is so complex it may never be economically feasible (Section 7–6). In contrast, solar energy is an abundant, clean, safe, and virtually inexhaustible, free fuel (Table 4–3). Thus, it is not surprising that more and more energy specialists see solar energy as an important energy alternative.[1]

Broadly defined, **solar energy** includes not only direct radiation from the sun but also energy resulting from the interaction of solar energy with the earth—notably wind power (Section 8–3), water power (Section 8–1), ocean power (as stored in thermal gradients, and biomass power (stored in plants) (Section 8–5). With a $113 billion crash program, the Department of Energy and the Council on Environmental Quality estimate that these direct and indirect sources could supply 20 to 25 percent of all U.S. energy needs by 2000 and more than half by 2020 (Carter 1978a, 1979, Council on Environmental Quality 1978, Energy Research and Development Administration 1975b, Riesenberg 1978, Staff report 1977i). One observer goes even further: 40 percent of the world's energy by 2000 and 75 percent by 2025 (Hayes 1977). In this section we will look at *direct* solar energy.

Direct Solar Energy The direct sunlight falling on the earth in only 3 days, if concentrated and converted to usable forms of energy, would equal all of the energy in the earth's known reserves of coal, oil, and natural gas (Staff

report 1977i) and is 15,000 times the energy consumed by the world each day (Riesenberg 1978). The solar energy falling on the roof of a typical American house each day is nearly 10 times the energy needed to heat the house for a year (Large 1976).

Along with its many advantages (Table 4–3), direct solar energy has some serious problems. First, the solar energy reaching the earth's surface is so diffuse that collecting and concentrating it present serious difficulties. Concentrating it slightly to heat water and buildings makes sense, but concentrating it to high-temperature heat will probably yield a negative net useful energy yield (Odum 1973, Odum & Odum 1976). Second, some locations and seasons are far sunnier than others. In some areas of the United States, for example, solar energy can provide essentially all space heating needs, in other areas, only part of these needs (Figure 8–2). The fuel (sunlight) is free, but the collecting and backup equipment can be quite costly initially. In terms of lifetime cost, however, solar energy is economically attractive in most areas of the United States, with backup heat pumps in some areas (Hayes 1977). This long-term economic advantage will increase as fossil fuel and nuclear power prices rise.

Besides photosynthesis in plants, there are two basic and well-tested ways of using direct solar energy. One is to collect and concentrate the energy and use it for space heating, air conditioning, and hot water heating. The other is to convert it to electricity using solar, or photovoltaic, cells.

Low-Temperature Solar Heating The simplest task is heating water. More than 2 million solar water heaters are used in Japan, thousands are being used in Israel, and solar heaters are required by law on all new buildings in northern Australia, where conventional fuels are expensive (Hayes 1977). In 1978 commercial solar water heating systems cost between $1,200 and $2,800 to buy and install in the United States, and they were already cheaper than electric systems in most parts of the country. As energy prices rise, small rooftop solar collectors for heating water will be a common sight throughout the world.

Direct solar heating can be either passive or active. *Passive solar heating systems* use solar heat directly. They rely upon natural energy flows and upon a building's design and composition to capture and store the sun's energy rather than upon an array of fans, pumps, and special collectors (Anderson & Michael 1978, Bliss 1976). A typical passively heated house is tightly built and well insulated, with double- or triple-glazed windows (two or three panes with air between) on the south side, and few (if any) windows on the north. All but the south wall may even be covered with earth. The south-facing windows also have an overhang to allow sun to enter in the winter but not in the summer. Easily movable insulating panels cover the windows at night to retard loss of the heat stored in the build-

---

[1]For more details on solar energy, see the following: American Physical Society 1979, Anderson & Michael 1978, Anderson & Riordon 1976, Antal 1976, Behrman 1976, Bliss 1976, Bossong 1978, Bregman 1978, Brinkworth 1974, Caputo 1977, Carter 1978a, 1979, Cassiday 1977, Cheremisinoff & Regino 1978, Commoner 1978, Council on Environmental Quality 1978, Daniels 1964, 1976, Duffie & Beckman 1976, Duguay 1977, Energy Research and Development Administration 1975b, 1977b, Environmental Protection Agency 1974d, Federal Energy Administration 1974c, Foster 1976, Fowler 1975a, Franta & Olson 1978, Goodenough 1976, Halacy 1973, Hamer 1976, Hammond 1973c, 1975, 1977d, Hammond et al. 1973, Hayes 1977, 1978b, Hildebrant & Vant-Hull 1977, Kalhammer & Schneider 1976, Keyes 1975, Lyons 1978, Makhijani 1976, McDaniels 1979, McCaull 1976b, McVeigh 1977, Meinel & Meinel 1971, 1972, 1976, Metz 1977c, 1978b, 1978c, Metz & Hammond 1978, Morrow 1973, Morse & Simmons 1976, National Academy of Sciences 1976b, NSF/NASA Solar Energy Panel 1973, Office of Technology Assessment 1977, O'Neill 1975, Oregon Office of Energy Research Planning 1975, Palz 1977, Pollard 1976c, Public Interest Group 1975, Raloff 1978a, Riesenberg 1978, Schultz 1978, Scientists' Institute for Public Information 1976a, Shurcliff 1976, 1978, Sørenson 1975, Stoker et al. 1975, Sunset Books editors 1978, Tamplin 1973, von Hippel 1977, von Hippel & Williams 1975, Watson 1977, Wells & Spetgang 1978, Williams 1974.

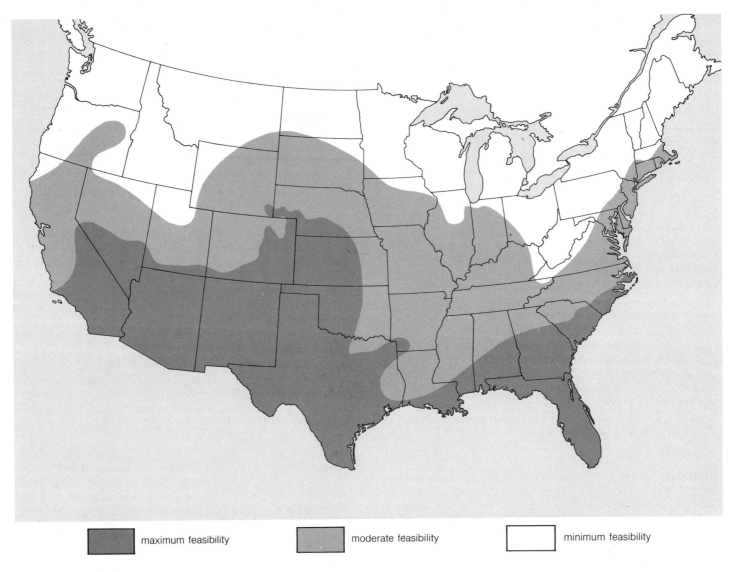

Figure 8–2 Solar space heating feasibility in the United States. In the darker areas, homes can be heated entirely by solar energy; in the light gray areas, solar energy can provide a large portion of the heat; in the white areas, only a small part of the space heating can be provided by solar energy. (Data from Fowler 1975b)

maximum feasibility   moderate feasibility   minimum feasibility

ing's walls and floors during the day. During hot weather the panels are closed during the day and opened at night.

Other approaches include the following: (1) attaching a greenhouse to the building to serve as a solar collector as well as to grow food, (2) reducing temperature variations by storing the solar energy in special south-facing, heat-storage walls (Trombe walls) or water-filled oil drums, and (3) storing the heat in a roof pond that is exposed to the sun during the day and covered with an insulated panel at night, (and vice versa during the summer) (Anderson & Michael 1978, Metz & Hammond 1978). A well-designed passive solar heating system can typically cut annual heat-

ing bills in half and provide all of the heat needed in Los Angeles homes, 60 percent in New York City, 57 percent in Boston, 52 percent in Seattle, and 42 percent in Madison, Wisconsin (Staff report 1978j). The only problem anyone sees so far is that people living in tightly sealed, passively heated solar houses may face high concentrations of indoor air pollutants, the accumulation of molds, high humidity, and stuffiness (Bossong 1978).

In a typical *active solar heating system*, either flat-plate solar collectors or evacuated tubes are mounted in the roof facing south, angled to capture the sun's rays (Figure 8–3). Flat-plate collectors are coated with a black heat-

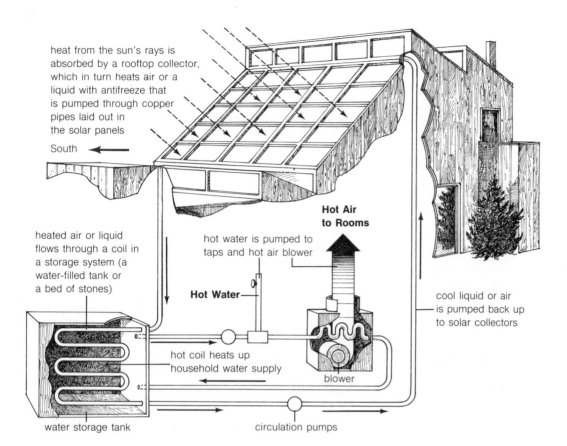

heat from the sun's rays is absorbed by a rooftop collector, which in turn heats air or a liquid with antifreeze that is pumped through copper pipes laid out in the solar panels

South

heated air or liquid flows through a coil in a storage system (a water-filled tank or a bed of stones)

hot water is pumped to taps and hot air blower

Hot Air to Rooms

Hot Water

cool liquid or air is pumped back up to solar collectors

hot coil heats up household water supply

blower

water storage tank

circulation pumps

Figure 8–3 An active home solar energy system for space and hot water heating.

absorbing substance covered by one or more glass or plastic transparent covers that trap the absorbed heat. Transferred to air or a water and antifreeze solution circulating in pipes behind the collector, this heat can then be pumped or blown into the heating system's radiators and ducts or stored in a large bed of rocks or an insulated hot water tank for release at night or in bad weather (Figure 8–3). Evacuated tube collectors can be twice as efficient and half as costly as flat-plate collectors (Metz & Hammond 1978). In 1978, a typical active solar heating system for a moderate-sized American home cost $5,000 to $12,000. Even with this high initial cost, active solar heating systems are already economically feasible in much of the United States when both lifetime costs and tax credits for installation are considered (Hayes 1977). With better and cheaper designs and mass production, costs should drop and make solar energy even more attractive (Hayes 1977, Metz & Hammond 1978).

By 1977, some 2 million buildings in Japan and 220,000 (one-fifth of all homes) in Israel were equipped with solar devices (Hayes 1977). By late 1978, over 80,000 American homes had solar devices for water or space heating, and by 1985 at least 1 million and perhaps 2.5 million homes are expected to be equipped with solar heating devices—

saving from 4.6 to 12 billion liters (29 to 73 million barrels) of oil a year.

Solar energy can also cool buildings by evaporation and by driving absorption air conditioners. But at present such devices are still too expensive for widespread use (Hayes 1977). Before solar energy is used widely, people will have to establish solar rights to prevent a neighbor from putting up trees or buildings that block out the sun. In addition, homeowners should get adequate warranties for solar devices, and they must become aware of solar energy con artists (Wells & Spetgang 1978).

High-Temperature Solar Heating and Conversion to Electricity Active research is seeking technologies for concentrating solar energy to high-temperature heat and converting solar energy directly to electricity with photovoltaic cells.

In the solar-thermal approach, large desert solar "farms" situated in Arizona and California might well serve as combined solar-electric power and water desalination plants (Meinel & Meinel 1972, 1976). Large parabolic lenses would concentrate sunlight to 500°C (932°F) on plastic, heat-absorbing pipes laid out in large fields. A gas or molten solid (such as sodium) flowing through the pipes could transfer the heat to steam boilers, which would eventually produce electricity. Excess heat might be stored in chemicals or rock formations and either be released on cloudy days or used to produce hydrogen gas. By the year 2000, solar farm plants constructed over a 39,000-square-kilometer (15,000-square-mile) desert area could produce about half of the estimated U.S. electricity needs for that year (Meinel & Meinel 1972, 1976).

Such solar farms would, of course, require a large area of land and might disturb fragile desert ecosystems. However, they would require much less land and have much less impact than the strip mining of coal. To minimize the land impact, several smaller farms might be built over an eight-state area. Getting such systems to produce enough net useful energy cheaply enough will require significant breakthroughs in collector and concentration efficiencies and an even more spectacular breakthrough in electrical transmission (Carr 1976, Odum 1973, Odum & Odum 1976).

Another solar-thermal method is the power tower, or solar furnace, approach (Antal 1976, Caputo 1977, Hildebrant & Vant-Hull 1977, Metz 1977c, Metz & Hammond 1978, Schultz 1978). A 10- to 20-story-high tower containing a boiler is located near the center of a field containing hundreds of computer-controlled mirrors. These mirrors track the sun and focus its rays on the boiler to produce steam, which can be used to produce electricity. A prototype (1-megawatt) power plant in southern France has been producing electricity since 1977. In the United States a $100 million 10-megawatt pilot power tower near Barstow, California, should be completed by 1981. It could produce enough electricity for a community of 6,000 to 8,000 people. If it works, the next step will be a 100-megawatt plant. Electricity from the Barstow plant, however, will cost about 20 times as much as in an equivalent coal-burning plant and 10 times as much as from a conventional nuclear plant. Obviously, a number of engineering breakthroughs will be needed to make this approach competitive for widespread use.

Another promising—but distant—approach is to use photovoltaic cells to transform sunlight directly into electricity (American Physical Society 1979, Council on Environmental Quality 1978, Hammond 1977d). The cell consists mainly of two layers of material, one a semiconductor (such as silicon, germanium, or cadmium sulfide) and the other a metal (such as aluminum or silver). When light strikes the cell, it causes electrons to flow between the two layers—the so-called voltaic effect—and generates electricity.

Solar cells have many advantages. Panels of them can be installed virtually anywhere—thus eliminating the need for long transmission lines. The cells are also safe, since they don't get hot. Photovoltaic cells are already used to power all U.S. space satellites, and some people envision the day when solar cells will be delivered to houses like rolls of roofing paper, tacked on, and plugged in to provide the home's electrical needs (Hamer 1976). But today's solar cells have such low energy conversion efficiencies (10 to 15 percent) that at today's costs the cells needed to provide all of the electricity for an average home would cost more than $100,000 (Hamer 1976). Researchers are trying to bring down the costs, ideally making solar cells competitive by 1985. Nevertheless, some scientists doubt that solar cells will ever make a significant contribution (Pollard 1976c). In addition to high costs, their use could eventually be limited by scarce supplies of arsenic, gallium, and cadmium (Bossong 1978, Environmental Protection Agency 1974d).

An even more futuristic—and extremely expensive—proposal is to use space shuttles to orbit billions of photovoltaic cells in space to capture solar energy on a 24-hour basis. Each such satellite station, which could theoretically power the city of New York, would convert solar energy to microwaves and beam them down to earth to vast farms of microwave antennas for conversion to electricity.

Even if the technical problems could be solved and the raw materials were always available, the costs would be phenomenal—at least $800 billion for a 100-satellite system (Staff report 1978k). The hydrochloric acid dumped into the stratosphere by the large number of space shuttle flights needed for this project could deplete the vital ozone layer (von Hippel & Williams 1975). In addition, the microwaves beamed to earth might have adverse effects on humans, such as causing cataracts, genetic damage, and injury to the central nervous system (Staff report 1978k).

Energy from Ocean Thermal Gradients Another potential indirect source of solar energy in deep tropical oceans is **ocean thermal gradients**—the temperature differences between warm surface waters and cold deep-lying waters (Environmental Protection Agency 1974d, Fisher 1975b, Hagen 1976, Karnaky 1977, Kohl 1976, Metz 1973, 1977a, Othmer & Roels 1973, Stoker et al. 1975, Swann 1976, Tamplin 1973, Walters 1971, Whitmore 1978, Zener 1973, 1976). The sea collects and stores this solar energy for us free of charge. But getting it out and transmitting it long distances to shore in a useful form is quite expensive.

To produce electric power, a floating ocean thermal energy conversion (OTEC) plant would have to be built in the Gulf Stream or in other deep warm-water areas where the temperature difference between surface and bottom waters is about 17° to 22°C (30° to 40°F). This gigantic floating platform with 15-meter- (50-foot-) wide pipes projecting down 305 meters (1,000 feet) would use warm surface water to vaporize ammonia liquid at high pressure. The vapor would power a turbine and generate electricity. Cold water drawn up from the ocean bottom could then cool and reliquefy the vapor for reuse. The nutrients brought up at the same time might nourish schools of fish and shellfish. Moreover, an ocean gradient plant could also desalinate ocean water. The technology for such plants is already available, but the economics and a satisfactory method for transmitting the electricity to land have yet to be worked out. An alternative would be to use the electricity at the site to electrolyze water and produce hydrogen gas, which could be piped or transported in tankers to shore (Tamplin 1973). Advocates of this approach project that with enough research funding, large-scale OTEC plants could be built within 5 to 10 years and could meet 1 to 5 percent of all U.S. energy needs by 2000 (Swann 1976, Whitmore 1978, Zener 1976).

But these rosy projections are clouded by problems (Environmental Protection Agency 1974d, Hayes 1977, Metz 1977a, Stoker et al. 1975): (1) seawater corrosion, (2) damage from severe storms, (3) few good sites—usually they are far offshore in tropical oceans and often far from population centers, (4) transmission of the electricity (or hydrogen gas produced by the electricity) long distances to shore, (5) unknown and potentially harmful changes in the ecology of large ocean areas, and (6) an energy conversion efficiency of only 2 to 3 percent.

Because of this low energy efficiency, the net useful energy yield will probably be low (Metz 1977a, Stoker et al. 1975). Moreover, a third of the energy produced would have to be used to pump the enormous amounts of water through the plant, with a moderate-sized (100-megawatt) plant having to pump as much water *each second* as flows through Boulder Dam (Metz 1977a). Withdrawing very large amounts of heat from such warm currents as the Gulf Stream, might affect the climate of western Europe (von Hippel & Williams 1975). Nutrients brought up from the ocean depths by OTEC plants could increase fish catches, but more carbon dioxide might be released from the ocean to the atmosphere, possibly affecting global climate (Chapter 9; von Hippel & Williams 1975). Despite the enthusiasm of OTEC advocates, this energy source may never compete economically with other alternatives (Metz 1977a).

Summary of Solar Energy Development   Because of fairly low net useful energy yields and high costs, the concentration of solar energy to provide high-temperature heat and electricity may never meet a significant fraction of the world's energy needs. But clearly the low-temperature concentration of solar energy—primarily for heating buildings and water—is one of the world's safest and most important energy alternatives. Nevertheless, direct and indirect solar energy will not meet the goals of providing 20 to 25 percent of all U.S. energy needs by 2000 and at least 50 percent by 2020 without a massive, federally supported crash program (Carter 1979). Such a program should include the following: (1) giving large tax credits to builders who use passive solar design features, (2) requiring that all new federal,

state, and privately owned buildings incorporate passive solar design features by 1985, (3) increasing tax credits to homeowners and businesses who use active solar devices beyond the credits provided by the National Energy Act of 1978, and (4) greatly increasing federal support for the development of solar energy as a major energy alternative (Carter 1979).

The federal budget for research and development of direct solar energy increased more than fourfold between 1975 and 1979. But in 1979 the government spent only about 6 percent of its total energy budget for this purpose (Table 10–2)—a trifling amount compared with its importance. Nobel Laureate Sir George Porter put it very well: "I have no doubt we will be successful in harnessing the sun's energy . . . . If sunbeams were weapons of war, we would have had solar energy centuries ago."

8–3   Wind Energy

Wind power is actually an indirect form of solar energy that can be used to produce electricity.[2] The first windmills appeared in the seventh century A.D. and have been used ever since to pump water, grind grain, and—in this century—to produce small amounts of electricity. In the early 1900s more than 6 million windmills pumped water and generated electricity in rural areas throughout the United States (Hayes 1977). By the 1940s cheap hydropower, fossil fuels, and rural electrification replaced most of these windmills; by 1976, only about 150,000 were still in use (Hayes 1977). In 1941 the world's largest wind turbine was built on a mountaintop in central Vermont, but one of its massive rotors broke off during a storm. Because of a wartime shortage of materials and a lack of funds by the investor, the project was abandoned. The still unfulfilled promise of cheap nuclear power caused the United States to abandon the development of large-scale wind turbines to produce electricity—a trend that hopefully will be reversed in the next few decades (Inglis 1978).

Wind is an almost unlimited, free, renewable, clean, and safe source of energy that has a moderate net useful energy yield and is based on a fairly well-developed technology (Table 4–3). Unlike solar energy, wind energy in a windy area can be tapped 24 hours a day. The World Meteorological Organization estimates that tapping the choicest

---

[2]For more details on wind power, see the following: Burke & Meroney 1977, Chase 1978, Cheremisinoff 1978, Clark 1973, Dennis 1976, Eldridge 1976, Hayes 1977, Heronemus 1972a, 1972b, 1975, Inglis 1975, 1978, Lockheed-California 1978, McCaull 1973, McGuigan 1978, Merriam 1977, 1978, Metz 1977d, Reynolds 1970, Simmons 1975, Sørenson 1976, Technology Information Center 1975, von Hippel & Williams 1975, Wade 1974, Zelby 1976.

wind sites around the world (not even including large clusters of wind turbines at sea) could produce about 13 times the electricity now produced in the world each year (Hayes 1977). Perhaps a more realistic estimate is that, with a crash program, wind energy could provide 7 to 19 percent of all electricity used in the United States by 2000 (Chase 1978, Clark 1973, Hamer 1976, Lockheed-California 1978)—still a major contribution.

As a result of such estimates, there has been a modest—but totally inadequate—attempt to develop the vast potential of wind power (Inglis 1975, 1978). Emphasis has been on the development of 5- to 10-story-high wind turbines with 30-meter- (100-foot-) diameter (or longer) rotors that would tap the wind flow 20 to 30 meters (66 to 98 feet) above the ground in windy areas (Chase 1978, Metz 1977d). Since electric power production increases with the square of the rotor diameter, large wind turbines are more efficient than small ones (Hayes 1977). Thus, a wind turbine with a 30-meter rotor puts out 4 times as much power as one with a 15-meter rotor. In addition, wind power increases as the cube of wind velocity, so that a 16-kilometer-per-hour (10 mph) wind produces 8 times as much power as an 8-kilometer-per-hour wind (Chase 1978). Since the wind doesn't always blow at optimum speeds, the electrical output of a wind turbine over a year's time might be 15 to 30 percent of the energy in the wind—or less, depending on the site and design characteristics of the machine (Merriam 1978)—still about twice the efficiency of solar systems (Metz 1̇

Wind power expert William E. Heronemus (1972a) calculates that 957 specially designed 260-meter- (850-foot-) high wind turbines could supply more than twice the additional electrical power needed by the state of Vermont between 1975 and 1990. He also suggests that a band of about 300,000 to 1 million of these giant wind turbines in the high-wind belt from Texas to the Dakotas could provide half of the annual electrical needs of the United States. For the heavily populated eastern seaboard, wind turbines could be floated on offshore platforms. In this case the wind energy would probably be used to produce hydrogen gas from the electrolysis of water, which could be piped or shipped to land as fuel.

There is no doubt that wind turbines work. The real problem is whether they can produce enough power cheaply enough (Chase 1978). Today's large wind turbines produce electricity at a cost 3 to 4 times that from coal-burning and nuclear power plants (Chase 1978), and home windmills cost between $5,000 and $25,000. For this reason some observers think developing sophisticated, moderate-sized wind turbines makes more economic sense (Hayes 1977, Lovins 1978a). Smaller windmills are easier to mass-produce, and their small rotors are less vulnerable to the stress and metal fatigue that make large wind turbines so expensive to maintain (Hayes 1977). In addition, small windmills can produce more power in winds than large

ones and can thus operate a greater percentage of the time. They are also easier to locate close to the ultimate users (thus reducing electricity transmission costs). Finally, small-scale turbines allow greater decentralization of ownership and control and reduce the impact from equipment failure (Hayes 1977).

Wind energy does have its problems, however. Its use will be limited to areas having steady and moderate winds—neither too weak nor too strong (which could damage the rotors). As Figure 8-4 shows, most of the areas with the greatest wind energy potential lie mainly in the west central Great Plains and the coastal regions of the Northeast and Northwest.

Another problem is how to store the energy for use during calms. Today, wind energy can be stored for homes and small buildings by charging batteries, by producing hydrogen gas to be used as a fuel, or by using a flywheel. While spinning, the flywheel stores energy, which can be tapped as it runs down after the wind stops. A good home flywheel system can provide electrical power for a week of windless days (Clark 1973). If the electricity was fed into the lines of an electric utility, energy from the wind could be stored by using it to pump water into a huge reservoir or to compress air in an underground deposit. Released on windless days, the water or air could operate an electric generator.

Other proposals bypass the need for storage. For example, a series of windmills (probably on top of existing electric transmission towers) could be coupled directly to the regional utility power grid to provide a base of power with no fuel costs. On windless days the system could be boosted by other fuel sources. In addition, homeowners or small communities with wind generators could sell excess electricity to utilities when the wind was blowing and then buy electricity from the utilities when the wind died down. This approach is technologically and probably economically feasible today and could be developed within a short time. Predictably, power companies have not been thrilled about buying indefinite, intermittent amounts of power from small producers, providing expensive backup facilities for calms, and developing complex, expensive metering and bookkeeping systems to keep accounts straight. In the few areas of the United States where utilities have gone along with this idea, they have imposed substantial surcharges on wind turbine operators for the privilege of hooking into utility electricity grids (Chase 1978). Ultimately, however, when power shortages become more severe, utilities may be glad to buy this source of electricity.

One environmental objection to wind power is the visual pollution of large turbines dotting the landscape, especially in areas of high prevailing winds, where turbines would be concentrated. We also need to determine whether several wind turbines in one area could affect the weather or migratory-bird flight patterns. Although their environmental impact will be small compared with that of most

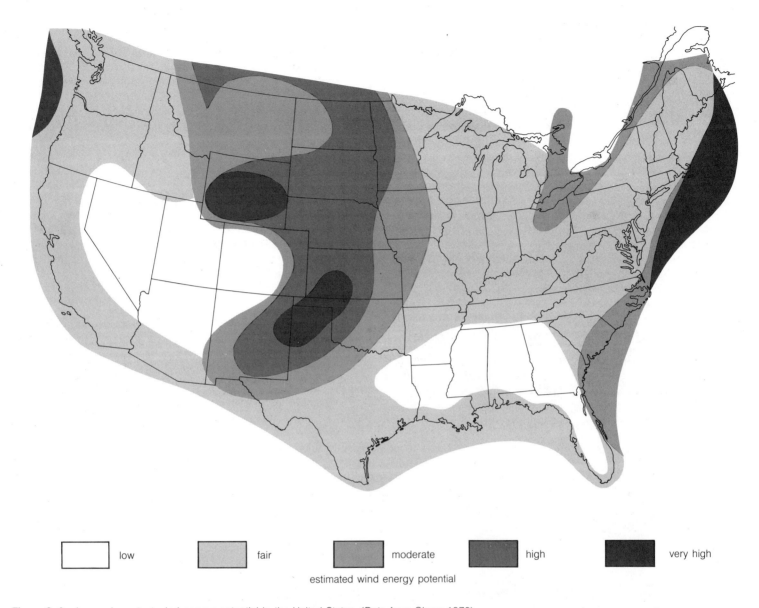

low   fair   moderate   high   very high

estimated wind energy potential

Figure 8–4 Areas of greatest wind energy potential in the United States. (Data from Chase 1978)

other energy alternatives (Table 4–5), wind systems will require large amounts of materials whose mining, manufacturing, processing, and waste disposal will affect the environment. Large wind turbines might also interfere with TV signals depending on the site (Metz 1977d). However, the use of fiberglass blades (also much cheaper than metal blades) would cut TV interference in half (Metz 1977d).

Although the potential for wind power is great in many areas and its technology well developed, industry and the federal government have shown very little interest in it. In 1979 the amount approved for windpower research and development in the federal energy budget was only 1 percent of the total energy budget (Table 10–2).

8–4   Geothermal Energy

Geothermal energy is produced when rocks lying deep below the earth's surface are heated to high temperatures by energy from the decay of radioactive elements in the earth and from magma (a mixture of rock and gases). When magma penetrates through to the earth's surface, it erupts as a volcano. But when it does not reach the surface, the trapped magma heats rocks near the surface to form geothermal reservoirs—analogous to concentrations of minerals in ore deposits or petroleum in underground reservoirs. The resulting heat energy may remain trapped in hot rocks

Renewable Energy Resources   **123**

or be transferred to underground water and form hot water or steam. Natural crevices, such as hot springs or geysers, or drilled geothermal wells can then bring this steam or hot water to the surface.

Geothermal reservoirs must be used in the region where they are found, which is usually the site of volcanic and mountain-building activity. Outside these zones geothermal energy is not a renewable resource and so geothermal reservoirs could be depleted. Geothermal energy can be considered a renewable energy source if deep underground continuous heat flows can be tapped. At least 80 nations have geological conditions favorable for geothermal energy. Because geothermal energy is cheap, almost inexhaustible, and fairly clean (Table 4–3), it is already being developed in some 25 countries.[3]

There are five basic types of geothermal wells: (1) dry steam wells, which contain superheated dry steam, (2) hot water or wet steam wells that contain superheated dry steam, (3) hot water or wet steam wells that contain steam mixed with either superheated water or brine (mineral-laden water), (4) hot rock wells in which water is pumped into deliberately fractured layers of deep underground hot rocks, converted to steam, and then brought to the surface by another well nearby, and (5) geopressurized water fields or zones that trap hot water mixed with large quantities of dissolved natural gas and are found far beneath ocean beds.

Only natural dry steam wells can be tapped easily and economically at present. This is done by drilling a well into the reservoir and piping the superheated and pressurized steam into a nearby turbine (Figure 8–5). A typical dry steam well has a moderate net useful energy output of 13 calories of useful energy for each calorie of useful energy input (Gilliland 1975). A large natural dry steam well near Larderello, Italy, has been producing electricity since 1904 and is a major source of power for Italy's electric railroads. Three other major dry steam sites are Japan (Matsukawa), New Zealand (Wairakei), and the Geysers steam field, located about 145 kilometers (90 miles) north of San Francisco. The Geysers field has been producing electricity since 1960 more cheaply than comparable fossil fuel and nuclear plants (Stoker et al. 1975). By 1980 it should be producing more than enough electricity to supply all of the

[3]For more details on geothermal energy, see the following: Armstead 1973, Armstead & Christopher 1973, Axtmann 1975, Barnea 1972, Berman 1975, Britton 1979, Collie 1978, Cummings et al. 1979, Ellis 1975, Environmental Protection Agency 1974d, Fenner & Klarman 1971, Futures Group 1977, Garnish 1978, Geothermal Project et al. 1976, Hammond et al. 1973, Henahan 1974, Hess 1976, Hickel et al. 1972, Keller 1976, Kiefer 1974, Kruger 1976, Kruger & Otte 1972, Malin 1973, Muffler 1973, Panel on Geothermal Energy Resources 1972, Rex 1971, Robson 1974, Stoker et al. 1975, White & Williams 1975.

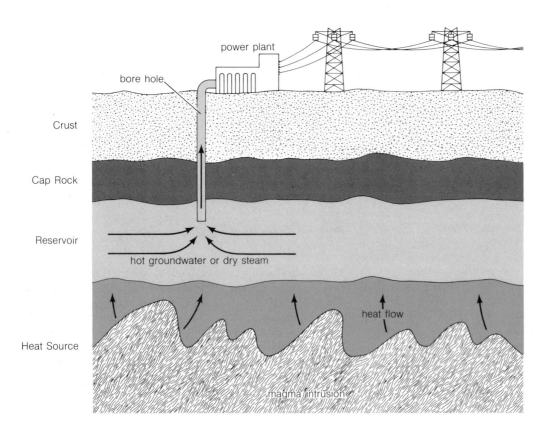

Figure 8–5 Dry (steam) or wet (hot water or brine plus steam) geothermal well and power plant.

electricity needs for a city the size of San Francisco (Malin 1973). A dry steam plant costs less to build and is cheaper to operate than either fossil fuel or nuclear plants (Stoker et al. 1975). A typical dry geothermal plant can also be put into operation in about 3 years—compared with about 5 to 10 years for a fossil fuel plant and 7 to 12 for a nuclear plant—and should have a useful life of 30 to 50 years before the geothermal deposit is depleted.

Although little serious worldwide exploration has been undertaken, it appears that dry steam deposits are relatively rare. *Wet* (hot water or brine) *geothermal fields*, with a net useful energy ratio of 11 calories output per calorie input (Gilliland 1975), are much more common, and are already generating electricity in New Zealand (Wairakei), Mexico, Japan, the Soviet Union, and Iceland. Reykjavik, the capital of Iceland, has been 99 percent heated by geothermal energy for years. In the United States, most accessible and fairly hot geothermal sites lie in the West (Figure 8–6). Geothermal energy heats hundreds of homes in Klamath Falls, Oregon, and Boise, Idaho. One expert (Rex 1971) estimates that just the hot water geothermal resources below southern California's Imperial Valley could produce enough electrical energy to meet the needs of the entire American Southwest for at least 200 years. As energy prices rise, there is also increasing interest in exploiting low-temperature wet geothermal deposits found in other parts

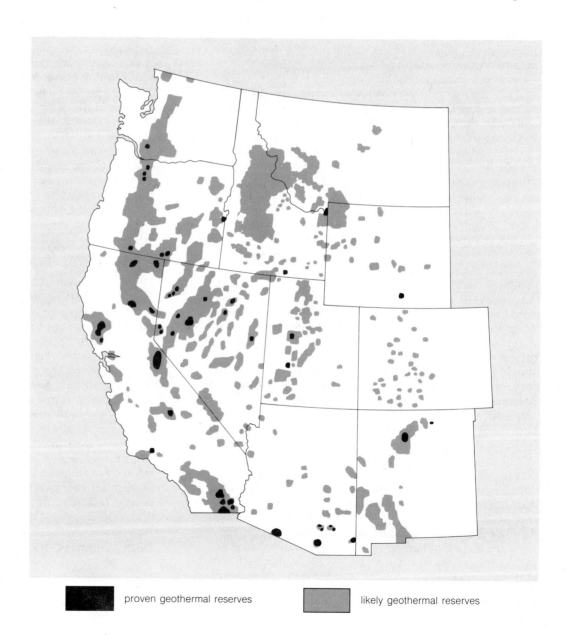

Figure 8–6 Most of the proven and potential geothermal fields in the United States are located in the West. (Data from Muffler 1973)

proven geothermal reserves likely geothermal reserves

of the United States, especially along the East Coast between New Jersey and Florida, where exploratory wells are being drilled (Britton 1979). These deposits are too cool for generating electricity, but if they can be tapped at an acceptable cost, they could be used to heat buildings and for other low-temperature applications.

In wet fields, the steam is mixed with hot water or mineral-laden brine. Such fields can provide energy in three ways: the existing steam separated from the hot water, hot water converted to steam, or hot water used to vaporize another low-boiling-point liquid that can then be used to drive a turbine. The main problem is brine, which is highly corrosive to metal parts and could pollute nearby water sources.

Another method now being tested avoids these problems completely. A heat exchanger containing a low-boiling-point liquid (such as isobutane or Freon) is immersed in the underground well. The heat from the hot water is used to vaporize the liquid, which is then brought to the surface to spin the turbine. Not only does this avoid corrosion and wastewater problems, but it leaves the water and steam in the well for continual reheating rather than depleting the resource.

Hot dry rock deposits lying deep underground might be tapped by drilling two wells. Either cold water could be pumped in under pressure to crack the rock, or artificial cavities could be formed by conventional or nuclear explosives. Water would then be circulated down through the hot rock and up the second well. After the heat was extracted, the cooled water could be sent down the first well again—thus reducing water use and pollution. This approach also eliminates most air pollution. Several experimental projects are already operating in the United States (Cummings et al. 1979). Among the many questions that need to be answered are: Will the water dissolve large quantities of minerals and have to be purified? How much water will leak out underground? Since wells must be drilled so deep, will costs be too high? If this approach should become economically feasible, the world's potential for geothermal energy could be greatly expanded. Although potential natural geothermal well sites in the United States are mostly confined to the West (Figure 8–6), hot rock formations less than 20,000 feet below the earth's surface probably occur in many regions.

So far little is known about the *geopressurized zones* that lie far beneath ocean beds in the Gulf of Mexico (Carr 1976). These mysterious deposits contain not only large quantities of hot rock but also large amounts of natural gas that would significantly expand U.S. reserves. But these deeply buried zones must be approached with great caution, since they apparently contain hot water under so much pressure that the natural gas is dissolved in it. If one of these zones blew up, it might wipe out entire cities along the Gulf Coast (Carr 1976).

There are some potentially harmful environmental effects from geothermal energy, but most experts consider them to be less than or at worst about equal to those from fossil fuel and nuclear power plants (Table 4–5) (Axtmann 1975, Ellis 1975, Environmental Protection Agency 1974d, Kruger 1976). Mineral-laden water wastes are produced, but they can be reinjected into the deep wells or desalinated to produce fresh water and saleable minerals. Large-scale withdrawal of geothermal fluids could also lead to sinking land and earthquakes, but reinjecting the fluids into the wells could minimize this danger. Air pollution occurs in most wells from the traces of highly toxic hydrogen sulfide (which smells like rotten eggs) and boron particles that escape in the steam. This could be controlled by emission devices or eliminated by using the underground heat-transfer system. There is also concern over emissions of radioactive radium-226 and radon-222 (Kruger 1976) and toxic mercury compounds comparable to those emitted by coal-burning power plants (Axtmann 1975, Robertson et al. 1977, Siegel & Siegel 1975). Noise pollution also occurs because of the earsplitting hiss of escaping steam, but presumably most geothermal wells would not be located near populated areas. As with most energy sources, waste heat injected into the atmosphere or bodies of cooling water is a problem and could affect local weather patterns (Section 9–5), but no more so for geothermal than for fossil fuel and nuclear plants.

At present, the potential of geothermal energy in the United States remains largely unknown. Estimates vary widely from about 0.5 percent to 100 percent of the nation's projected electrical energy needs (Berman 1975, Hickel et al. 1972, Kruger 1976, Muffler 1973, Panel on Geothermal Energy Resources 1972, Robson 1974, Theobald et al. 1972, White & Williams 1975).

So far, most geothermal deposits in the United States remain undeveloped for several reasons. First, most of the rich ones are on government-owned lands in the Rocky Mountain states (Figure 8–8). The government has been slow in leasing these lands to private companies for exploratory drilling and development primarily because of concern over water rights and resources (Section 8–6). Second, there are legal problems in that geothermal deposits are classified as mineral resources in some states, water resources in others, and as a vague third category in still others. Finally, despite its potential, and despite increased funding as a result of the Geothermal Act of 1974, geothermal energy received only about 4 percent of total energy research and development expenditures in 1979 (Table 10–2).

8–5 Biomass, Biofuels, and Hydrogen Gas

Plant Power: Energy from Biomass Another indirect source of solar energy is plant biomass—the earth's plant life produced by photosynthesis.[4] Biomass is a catchall category that includes wood and wood wastes, agricultural products and wastes, and aquatic plants such as algae and kelp. It can also include animal wastes and municipal sewage and wastes that are derived from plants.

Biomass energy has several appealing advantages (Table 4–3). Like other types of solar energy, it is renewable; unlike direct solar energy, it has no storage problem. The solar energy is naturally stored in the leaves, stems, and trunks of plants and trees, and can be tapped as needed either by direct burning or by conversion to biofuels (fuels derived from biomass), such as synthetic natural gas (methane) and alcohols. When collected and burned directly near its source, biomass has a moderate net useful energy yield, but yields are low when the biomass must be collected in areas of sparse growth and then transported long distances for use (Pimentel et al. 1978). Because biomass and biofuels are low in sulfur, they cause less air pollution from sulfur dioxide than the burning of coal and oil. They also yield smaller amounts of both large particulates, which are easier to filter out, and nitrogen oxides (Holzman 1978c). Furthermore, as long as trees and plants are not cut faster than they grow back, burning biomass and biofuels will not add to the net amount of carbon dioxide in the atmosphere (since plants use carbon dioxide in photosynthesis).

Wood and wood wastes are the most commonly used forms of biomass. In developing nations, as in 19th century America, wood is a major source of energy (Hayes 1977). As energy prices have risen, Americans have rediscovered the wood-burning stove (Gay 1974, Holzman 1978c, Shelton & Shapiro 1977). Unlike fireplaces; which at 10 percent efficiency may remove more heat from a home than they add (Holzman 1978c), good wood stoves, costing about $400 to $500, are about 30 to 55 percent efficient and throw their heat into the room instead of up the chimney (Shelton & Shapiro 1977). Between 1970 and 1978, the use of wood as a source of energy in New England grew sixfold. In Maine, New Hampshire, and Vermont, 18 percent of all households relied on wood as their primary heating source in 1978 (Holzman 1978c). Wood burning is also increasing in the heavily forested Pacific Coast states. Nevertheless, in 1978 only about 1.5 percent of the energy used in the United States came from biomass—with wood wastes burned for fuel by the pulp, paper, and forest industries accounting for most of this use (Pimentel et al. 1978).

Wood and wood wastes can be an important source of energy in some areas. But using it on a large scale has problems (Burwell 1978, Pimentel et al. 1978). Supplying all the world's energy needs from forests would take only 5 percent of the earth's surface (F.A.S. 1978), but this is twice as much land as now is forested—clearly an impossibility (F.A.S. 1978).

Burning all of the wood and wood waste biomass that is readily available in the United States would provide only 1.9 percent as much energy as now derived from fossil fuel (Pimentel et al. 1978). Wood has a much lower energy content per unit of weight than coal, oil, or natural gas, and it also contains a lot of water (Cook 1976b). Thus, large quantities of wood must be cut to get the amount of energy provided by a much smaller quantity of fossil fuel. Intensive wood farming could also cause extensive erosion, siltation, and flooding; deplete soil nutrients; and pollute water with erosion and runoff of fertilizers and pesticides (Environmental Protection Agency 1974d, Holzman 1978c). Wood-burning stoves also greatly increase the chances of home fires and indoor air pollution in well-insulated, tightly sealed, energy-efficient homes (Holzman 1978c).

In agricultural areas, crop residues (the inedible, unharvested portions of food crops) and animal manure can be collected and burned or converted to biofuels. But most plant residues are widely dispersed and require large amounts of energy to collect, dry, and transport (Pimentel et al. 1978). In addition, it makes more sense ecologically to use these valuable nutrients to feed livestock, retard erosion, and fertilize the soil. There is also greatly increased interest in burning urban wastes as a source of energy (Galveke & McGavhey 1976, Kasper 1974, Wilson & Freeman 1976). But it may be sounder ecologically to compost or recycle these organic wastes instead of burning them.

Another approach is to establish large *energy plantations,* where specific trees, grasses, or other crops would be grown for biomass. This biomass would be directly burned, converted to biofuels, or converted to plastics, rubber, and other products produced from petroleum and natural gas (Figure 6–2) (Calvin 1974, 1976, 1978, Hayes 1977, Sarkanen 1976). Ideal energy crops would be fast-growing, high-yield perennials that reproduce themselves from cuttings (since seed requires costly collection and sowing). Possible crops include warm-season grasses (such as Sudan grass, Bermuda grass, sugarcane, sorghum, and cassava) and certain deciduous trees (such as alder, poplar, eucalyptus, cottonwood, and sycamore). Grasses would be harvested every few weeks. Trees, planted close together like crops, would be harvested by clear-cutting every 3 to 4 years on a rotating schedule. This approach, however, could compete with food crops for land.

An intriguing suggestion is to plant "petroleum plantations" of plants (such as *Euphorbia lathyrus* and *Euphorbia tirucalli*) that store energy in hydrocarbons rather than car-

---

[4]For more details on energy from biomass, see the following: Burwell 1978, Calef 1976, Calvin 1974, 1976, 1978, Cheremisinoff & Morres 1977, Galveke & McGavhey 1976, Gay 1974, Hammond 1977c, Hayes 1977, Holzman 1978a, 1978c, Mitsui et al. 1977, Navickis 1978, Pimentel et al. 1978, Pollard 1976b, Poole 1976, Shelton & Shapiro 1977, Staff report 1979c, Tillman 1978, Vivian 1976, von Hippel & Williams 1975, Washington Center for Metropolitan Studies 1976, Wilson & Freeman 1976.

bohydrates and thus could be used to produce gasoline directly (Calvin 1974, 1976, 1978). Such plants could be grown on semiarid, currently unproductive land and possibly produce petroleum at a cost of about $10 to $20 a barrel (158 liters) (Calvin 1976, 1978). If successful, planting a land area the size of Arizona could produce all of the gasoline needed by the United States (Calvin 1976). The economic feasibility and net useful energy yield of this approach, however, have not yet been determined, and such plantations may not be applicable on a large scale because of a lack of sufficient water.

Another category of potential biomass resources is the large-scale growth and harvesting of aquatic plants such as algae, water hyacinths, and kelp seaweed (Hammond 1977c, Hayes 1977, Navickis 1978). Collecting and processing these plants, however, might require so much energy (and money) that net useful energy yields would be too low and costs would be too high. In addition, large-scale harvesting could disrupt ocean and freshwater ecosystems.

Biofuels There is increasing interest in converting biomass into biofuels such as biogas or methane (the major component of natural gas), methanol (methyl alcohol or wood alcohol), and ethanol (ethyl alcohol or grain alcohol) and into raw material chemicals that would replace petrochemicals.[5] The processes for such bioconversions have been known and used for centuries, but their products have been too expensive compared to fossil fuels. As gasoline, natural gas, and coal prices continue to rise, however, this picture could change.

All biomass except wood can be converted to a mixture of methane and carbon dioxide, or biogas, by *anaerobic digestion*—fermentation by microorganisms in the absence of oxygen. Many developing and some developed nations are returning to this ancient technology. When they work, such anaerobic digesters are highly efficient, but they are somewhat slow and unpredictable, and vulnerable to low temperatures, acidity imbalances, and contamination by heavy metals, synthetic detergents, and other industrial effluents (Hayes 1977). These same contaminants can cause serious problems if the digested residues are used to fertilize food crops (Hayes 1977). As a result, few developed nations use anaerobic digestion on a large scale. The economics of biogas production varies widely depending on the type of biomass fuel and the predictability of the process, with prices ranging from 1 to 7 times the price of natural gas (Holzman 1978a).

Anaerobic digestion occurs spontaneously, of course, in the estimated 20,000 landfill sites around the United

States. Los Angeles has tapped into this source to heat some 3,500 homes (Holzman 1978a). In 1976, an Oklahoma company, Calorific Recovery Anaerobic Process, Inc.—CRAP for short—began providing Chicagoans with methane made from cattle manure collected from animal feedlots (Hayes 1977, Navickis 1978). Converting all the manure that U.S. livestock produce each year to methane could provide nearly 5 percent of the nation's total natural gas consumption at 1977 levels. But collecting and transporting this manure would require a large energy input. Recycling this manure to the land to replace artificial fertilizer, which requires large quantities of natural gas to produce, would probably save more natural gas.

A second promising source of biofuels is the conversion of biomass to alcohols. Wood, wood residues, sewage sludge, garbage, and coal can be gasified and converted to methanol or wood alcohol, a premium fuel that has long been used to power racing cars. Almost any form of biomass that contains starch and cellulose—anything from urban wastes to corn stalks and manure—can be converted by fermentation and distillation to ethanol or grain alcohol.

In the long run, some methanol or ethanol might be used to fuel cars when petroleum supplies are depleted. But at present these fuels are much more expensive than gasoline. In addition, because of their lower energy content, it takes about two tankfuls of methanol or ethanol to go the same distance as one tankful of gasoline (Carr 1976). At present, the main interest is in *gasohol*—gasoline with 10 to 20 percent methanol or ethanol (Anderson 1978, Bernton 1978, Carr 1976, Hammond 1977b, Wigg 1974). Today's cars can run on gasohol with only minor carburetor adjustments as long as the alcohol content does not get too high (Hammond 1977b). A gasohol mixture containing 10 to 20 percent alcohol should improve fuel economy and reduce emissions on older cars (pre-1973) but perform about the same as gasoline in newer, lower-compression cars with emission controls (Carr 1976, Wigg 1974). Gasohol can also help solve the problems of waste disposal in large cities and grain surpluses in farms, with each city or area using its most plentiful type of biomass to produce either methanol or ethanol.

But there are problems. Methanol can cause vapor lock (summer) and engine failure (a few drops of water can cause the methanol to separate out from the gasoline) (Carr 1976). Engine corrosion is another possible problem.

Oil companies that have large coal holdings are particularly interested in using methanol for gasohol, since methanol can be produced from coal as well as biomass—thus giving these companies an added share of the market (Bernton 1978).

So far, however, most of the emphasis has been on ethanol since ethanol can be made so easily from so many forms of biomass, has a higher heat content per unit of volume than methanol, and is much less likely to cause vapor lock and engine shutdown (Carr 1976). Brazil is

---

[5]For more details on biofuels, see the following: Anderson 1978, Bernton 1978, Carr 1976, DeRenzo 1978, Eskridge 1978, Hammond 1977b, Hayes 1977, Holzman 1978a, Jewell et al. 1978, Lovins 1978a, Pollard 1976b, Sarkanen 1976, Tamplin 1973, U.S. Department of Agriculture 1978, Wigg 1974.

leading the way with an ambitious program to convert surplus sugarcane and cassava (manioc) into ethanol and have 20 percent gasohol blends in all gas pumps in the country by 1980 to 1985 (Bernton 1978, Hammond 1977b). Hawaii hopes to make ethanol gasohol from sugarcane, distilled in now-idle rum plants (Holzman 1978a). In Nebraska, surplus corn is being converted to ethanol and used to produce a 10 percent blend of gasohol. By early 1979, at least 250 gas stations in the United States, mostly in midwestern farm states, were selling gasohol.

But can gasohol ever become a major fuel source? Some observers suggest that biomass would be more valuable as feed stocks for the petrochemical industry (Figure 6-2) than for direct use as a fuel (Goldstein 1975, Pimentel et al. 1978, Sarkanen 1976). At best the net useful energy yield is low, and it may be negative (Anderson 1978, Bernton 1978, Eskridge 1978, U.S. Department of Agriculture 1978). Gasohol proponents, however, dispute these estimates (Anderson 1978, Eskridge 1978), pointing out that replacing all gasoline with gasohol would cut annual U.S. consumption of gasoline by 10 percent and reduce dependence on foreign oil by 20 percent (Eskridge 1978).

Hydrogen Gas as a Fuel   How will cars and other vehicles be powered when petroleum gets too expensive? Solar energy, nuclear fission, and most of the alternatives discussed in this chapter are schemes for producing electricity at power plants. They do not apply to automobiles and other forms of everyday transportation. Electric cars are extremely wasteful of energy (Figure 4-2), and a number of technological problems must be solved to develop batteries with sufficient life and power output.

Hydrogen (H_2) gas has been suggested as the transportation fuel of the future (Figure 8-7). Lightweight, easily transportable, colorless, odorless, and rapidly renewed in the water cycle, it can be burned cleanly in a fuel cell (a device that can convert the energy in chemical

fuels directly into low-voltage, direct-current electricity), a power plant, or an automobile to produce water. By producing water or fog—not smog—it eliminates most of the serious air pollution problems associated with the gasoline-burning internal combustion engine. If air is used as the source of oxygen for combustion, however, small amounts of nitrogen oxides will be formed as by-products. In addition, present water electrolysis cells used to produce hydrogen can release small cancer-causing asbestos particles into the air (Environmental Protection Agency 1974d).[6]

Because seawater could be used as the basic resource for H_2, we have a cheap, readily available, and almost infinite energy supply, in sharp contrast to fossil fuels. The H_2 could be stored in tanks (like compressed air) and shipped or transported by pipeline to households, industries, or fueling stations (once gas stations). It could also be reacted with metals such as magnesium or nickel and stored, transported, and used in cars as metal hydrides, which would release hydrogen gas when heated. Large-scale use of this approach, however, might be limited by available supplies of nickel and magnesium (Environmental Protection Agency 1974d). Also, hydrogen is highly explosive and dangerous. Gasoline is also dangerous, but hydrogen is stored as a gas under high pressure and would explode even more readily if it came in contact with a spark.

Besides being used for vehicle fuel hydrogen can be used, as mentioned above, to store energy from other sources. For example, the electrical energy from a wind turbine or from a solar, hydroelectric, nuclear, or geothermal power plant could be stored by using it to produce H_2 by the electrolysis or high-temperature decomposition of

---

[6]For more details on hydrogen as an energy source, see the following: Bamberger & Braunstein 1975, Bockris 1972, 1975, Carr 1976, Dickson 1977, Dickson et al. 1976, Environmental Protection Agency 1974d, Fowler 1975a, Gregory & Pangborn 1976, Kelley & Laumann 1975, Lindsley 1975, Mathias 1976, Stanford Research Institute 1976, Stoker et al. 1975.

Figure 8-7 The hydrogen energy cycle has a number of advantages over the present fossil fuel energy system. But its widespread use requires the availability of an almost infinite and economically feasible energy source for decomposing water to produce hydrogen gas.

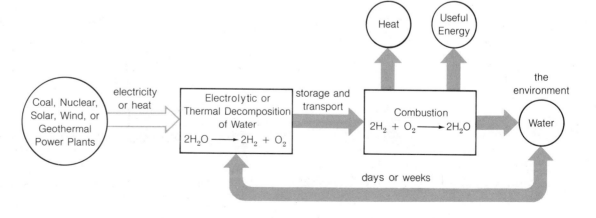

Uranium

Geothermal

■ proven reserves

▨ likely reserves

Electric Power Plants (greater than 300 megawatts)

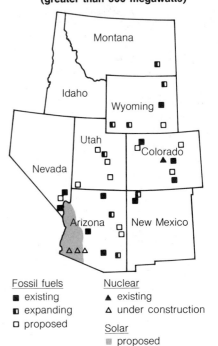

Fossil fuels
■ existing
▨ expanding
□ proposed

Nuclear
▲ existing
△ under construction

Solar
▨ proposed

Potential Nuclear Waste Storage

▨ major underground salt deposits

● proposed site for first national nuclear waste repository

National Parks and National Forests

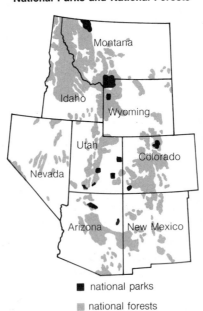

■ national parks

▨ national forests

Water Shortages

▨ shortages today

□ shortages by 2000

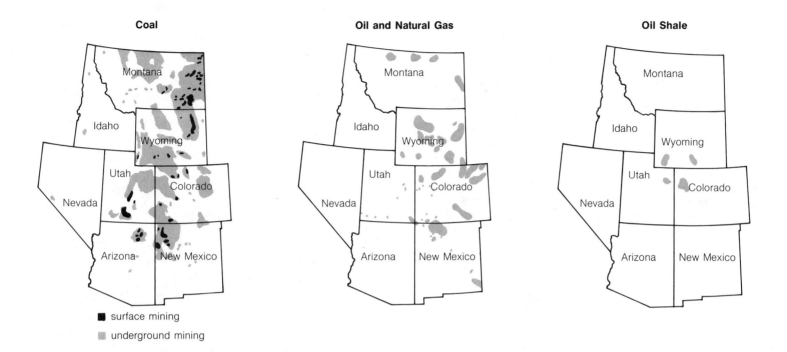

Coal

Montana
Idaho
Wyoming
Utah
Nevada
Colorado
Arizona
New Mexico

■ surface mining
▨ underground mining

Oil and Natural Gas

Montana
Idaho
Wyoming
Utah
Nevada
Colorado
Arizona
New Mexico

Oil Shale

Montana
Idaho
Wyoming
Utah
Nevada
Colorado
Arizona
New Mexico

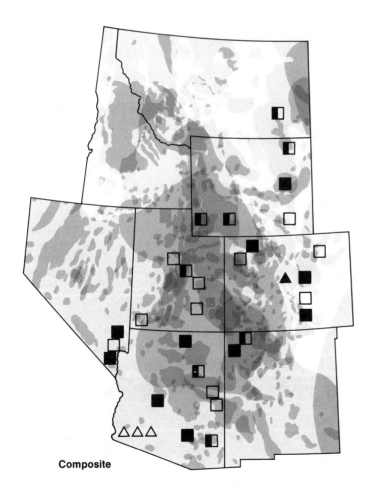

Composite

Figure 8–8 Conflicts between land use, energy resources, and water resources in the eight Rocky Mountain States. Composite map shows areas of most intense overlap and conflict (darkest regions). (Data from Anthrop 1978, Atwood 1975, Cook 1976b, Micklin 1974, Morgan 1978b, Muffler 1973, Murray & Reeves 1977)

water or by the high-temperature decomposition of solid hydrogen-containing compounds.

But there are some major catches to this glowing hydrogen energy future. The basic problem is that hydrogen gas is not found in nature. It is a secondary fuel that must be produced by using electricity or high temperatures to decompose water or other hydrogen-containing compounds. It takes so much energy (and money) to produce, that its net useful energy yield is low and could even be negative, depending on the other basic energy resource used to generate the hydrogen. Thus, an affordable large-scale hydrogen fuel system is feasible only if an essentially limitless and cheap energy source, such as nuclear fission (from breeder reactors), nuclear fusion, solar energy, geothermal energy, or wind energy can be used to produce the hydrogen fuel.

8–6   Land, Energy, and Water Resources in the Rocky Mountain Region: A Case Study

The major storehouse of undeveloped energy resources in the United States is found in the eight Rocky Mountain states—Arizona, Colorado, Idaho, Montana, Nevada, New Mexico, Utah, and Wyoming. As a result, this region has become a major battleground for conflicts over how its land, energy, and water resources should be used.

The diverse land of the Rocky Mountain region consists of rolling plains, irrigated farmland, ranchlands, Indian-owned lands, arid deserts, national forests, and some of the nation's most scenic national parks. Almost half of the land in this region is owned by the federal government —or, more accurately, the citizens of the United States. According to a U.S. Senate (1976) study, the region also contains (1) about 42 percent of this nation's bituminous and lignite coal, (2) 60 percent of the low-sulfur coal that can be strip mined economically, (3) almost all of the richest oil shale deposits, (4) 95 percent of U.S. uranium, (5) vast potential supplies of geothermal energy, (6) potential sources of natural gas and petroleum, (7) a large, sunny desert area that might be the site of a giant electric power plant complex run by solar energy, which could desalinate water for this water-starved region and provide about half of all the electricity needed in the United States in the year 2000 (Meinel & Meinel 1971, 1972), and (8) underground salt deposits that might be useful for storing the nation's deadly radioactive wastes. If fully utilized, the energy resources in these eight states could supply U.S. energy needs for the next 100 years (Staff report 1975, U.S. Senate 1976).

As Figure 8–8 shows, the deposits of many of these energy resources either overlap or are located near one another; some also overlap with national forests and parks.

In addition, some of these energy resources lie under land now used for farming and ranching, and 50 percent of the uranium and about 20 percent of the coal reserves lie on Indian lands.

The result is an extremely complex conflict over how the land should be used.[7] Farmers want to have enough irrigation water, and along with ranchers they don't want their land torn up and their water supplies polluted. Environmentalists want to preserve the sparsely populated land from severe ecological disruption due to mining and rapid population growth. Energy companies want to develop the area's rich energy resources to make a profit, supply the nation's energy needs, and reduce dependence on foreign oil. Some residents of these states welcome the money and jobs that energy development and boom towns would bring, but other residents do not want their nonurban way of life disrupted by the doubling and tripling of populations of isolated rural hamlets, which could occur in a matter of months (Gilmore 1976). These citizens and landowners, along with environmentalists, hope to slow or at least control the rate and manner in which the nonrenewable energy resources are developed, so that once they are removed, the land can still be used for agriculture, tourism, recreation, and wildlife as it is today.

The federal government, which owns much of the land, is caught in this crossfire of conflicting interests and is trying to decide which of the resources should be developed and in what order or mix (U.S. Senate 1976). State governments are torn between preserving the environment, encouraging economic growth, and ensuring that the federal government allows energy development in a manner that would not harm nearby nonfederal lands.

The conflict over the use of land and energy resources is made even more intense by a lack of water. Much of this arid region already has serious water shortage problems, and these are expected to get worse by 2000 (Figure 8–8). To extract and subsequently process almost any one of the region's energy resources will require enormous amounts of water (Environmental Protection Agency 1974d, Federal Energy Administration 1974a, Harte & El-Gasseir 1978, McCaull 1974, Staff report 1976d, U.S. Senate 1976). Large quantities of water are required for cooling power plants, washing mined coal, coal gasification and liquefaction, mixing coal with water to form a slurry that can be transported by pipeline, converting oil shale to liquid fuel, and reclaiming mined arid lands. For example, a single 1,000-megawatt coal-burning power plant uses enough water each year to supply a city of 12,000; a coal gasification plant,

---

[7]For more details on this conflict over resource use, see the following: Anthrop 1978, Arrandale 1978, Christiansen & Clark 1976, Gilmore 1976, Harte & El-Gasseir 1978, Lang & Fisher 1975, McCaull 1974, Staff report 1975, U.S. Senate 1976.

enough for 7,000 people; a pipeline to pump coal in slurry form, enough for 10,000 people; and an oil shale processing plant, enough for 11,000 people (Environmental Protection Agency 1974d, Federal Energy Administration 1974a, Harte & El-Gasseir 1978).

At present, the major emphasis is on increased coal production to reduce U.S. dependence on oil imports by 1990. Since most of the energy produced in this region will be exported to other heavily populated areas of the United States, there is a conflict over whether the coal should be mined and shipped out by rail or slurry pipeline, burned in projected new power plants near mining sites (Figure 8–8) and exported as electricity, or converted to synthetic natural gas in coal gasification plants near mining sites and then distributed by pipeline (U.S. Senate 1976). Shipping coal by rail wastes the least amount of energy and does not require water but would produce some air pollution. Mixing the coal with water to form a slurry for pipelines is also fairly energy efficient but requires large quantities of water. Producing electricity in power plants at the mine mouth would waste 4 to 5 times as much energy as rail or slurry transport, would subject the region to potentially serious air pollution (Table 4–5), and would require large amounts of cooling water. Coal gasification would produce only about 10 percent as much air pollution as direct burning in power plants but requires large amounts of water. Committing the area to a particular approach could preclude the future development of another energy resource because of a lack of sufficient water (Harte & El-Gasseir 1978). In addition, if air pollution levels should rise as a result of new coal-burning power plants, dust from mining, and population growth, the sky could become hazy enough to decrease the possibility of developing a national solar energy power plant complex (Figure 8–8), if such a scheme should ever prove to be economically and ecologically feasible.

Water, then, may be the limiting factor that determines which, if any, of the energy resources in the Rocky Mountain region will ever be developed on a large scale (Harte & El-Gasseir 1978). With careful planning and circumspect management there may be enough water for considerable energy development, but only at the expense of agriculture. At present, agriculture uses 90 percent of the region's annual water supply, much of it allegedly "inefficiently applied and producing low-value crops" (U.S. Senate 1976). Some additional water could be supplied by tapping underground water aquifers (permeable layers of rock or sand formations that serve as conduits for the underground flow of water). But this would amount to mining precious water that is needed during drought years, since it takes hundreds to thousands of years to replenish underground aquifers. Depleting this precious supply merely for short-term purposes could set up an irreversible conversion of western grasslands to desert if a drought should last more than a year (Carr 1976). There is already concern that coal mining could upset the region's underground water system, since many coal seams serve as aquifers for groundwater (Carr 1976, Staff report 1976d).

Thus, the people of the United States, especially people in the Rocky Mountain region, face some difficult and important questions in this conflict between the use of land, energy, and water resources. Should the United States develop the rich energy resources in the Rocky Mountain region to reduce dependence on oil imports at the risk of seriously degrading the area's precious water and land?

In this chapter we have seen that each energy alternative has a mixture of advantages and disadvantages. With the exception of energy conservation—which must form the backbone of any energy plan—our energy supplies in the future must be based on a mix of energy sources. Deciding upon and developing the appropriate mix is the most urgent task facing the world today.

Not to decide is to decide.

Harvey Cox

Discussion Topics

1. Contrast fossil fuel, conventional fission, breeder fusion, geothermal, and solar power plants in terms of (a) how they work, (b) their environmental impact, and (c) their technological and economic problems.

2. Criticize the following statements:

   a. Solar power plants shouldn't be developed because they will take up 10 percent of the desert area in the United States.

   b. Development of solar and wind energy should be left up to private enterprise rather than the federal government.

   c. Wind power is not feasible at present.

   d. Natural dry geothermal fields offer a clean and abundant source of energy.

   e. Hydroelectric power can solve America's energy problems.

   f. Tidal energy is a clean, untapped source that can solve our problems.

   g. Using hydrogen as a fuel will save us.

   h. We can solve the energy crisis by converting agricultural, forest, animal, and urban wastes to biofuels.

   i. Large-scale solar electric power plants can solve our energy problems.

3. In what respects does tidal power differ from hydroelectric power?

4. Solar, geothermal, wind, and biomass energy and conservation are all proposed as significant and less harmful energy sources than fossil fuel and nuclear fission energy. Assuming this is valid, explain in each case why they haven't been developed. Outline a plan for their development.

5. Outline the major advantages and disadvantages of the following types of energy: nuclear fusion, solar, wind, biomass, hydroelectric, tidal, and geothermal. In each case explain how they are limited by the first and second laws of thermodynamics. How do these limitations compare with those on fossil fuel and nuclear fission energy?

6. Distinguish between direct use of solar energy as heat, its conversion into electricity, and solar power from ocean thermal gradients. Which is the most promising and has the least environmental impact?

7. How is the sun's energy responsible for (a) wind energy, (b) biomass energy, (c) hydroelectric energy, and (d) tidal energy?

8. Which, if any, of the major energy resources in the Rocky Mountain region of the United States should be developed first and under what restrictions? Defend your choice. Which resource, if any, should be developed second? If none of these resources were developed, what effects might this have on the United States and on your own life and life-style in 1990?

Further Readings

See also the references for Chapter 4.

Bockris, J. O. 1975. *Energy: The Solar Hydrogen Alternative.* New York: Halsted. Authoritative discussion of the potential of hydrogen as an energy alternative.

Calvin, Melvin. 1976. "Photosynthesis as a Resource for Energy and Materials." *American Scientist,* vol. 64, no. 3, 270–278. Details of proposal to provide biomass energy by growing "energy plantations" of specific plants.

Cummings, Ronald G., et al. 1979. "Mining Earth's Heat: Hot Dry Rock Geothermal Energy." *Technology Review,* February, pp. 58–78. See also Malin 1973, Robson 1974.

Inglis, David R. 1978. *Windpower and Other Energy Options.* Ann Arbor: University of Michigan Press. Outstanding evaluation of potential for wind, solar, biomass, and other energy alternatives. Highly recommended.

Metz, William D., and Allen M. Hammond. 1978. *Solar Energy in America.* Washington, D.C.: American Association for the Advancement of Science. Superb summary of the solar energy alternative. Highly recommended. See also Hayes 1977, Meinel & Meinel 1976.

Pimentel, David, et al. 1978. "Biological Solar Energy Conversion and U.S. Energy Policy." *BioScience,* vol. 28, no. 6, 376–381. Excellent evaluation of potential of biomass energy.

Wells, Malcolm, and Irwin Spetgang. 1978. *How To Buy Solar Heating and Cooling . . . Without Getting Burnt.* Emmaus, Pa.: Rodale. Before you install solar energy, be sure to read this important book.

9

Energy Use, Heat, and Climate: The Ultimate Problem

Our knowledge about global climate can be summed up in one word—ignorance.

Anonymous

When it comes to global climate, the question is not "Will it change?" but "How will it change and over what length of time?" Natural changes in global, regional, and local climate have taken place throughout the earth's history. In recent years, however, concern has mounted that human activities may be influencing climate at the local and regional levels and perhaps even at the global level.[1] In this chapter we will examine this important issue.

9-1 Natural and Human-Related Climate Change

Past Climate Changes One way to predict how climate might change in the future is to see how it has changed in the past. Although official climate records have only been kept for the past 100 years, scientists have attempted to reconstruct climatic history for the past several hundred years by using tree rings, burial sites, records of grape harvests, sea ice, and other historical data (Ladurie 1973, Lamb 1972, 1977). Scientists have also attempted to trace climate change even further back by examining the fossil evidence of climate-sensitive forms of life, such as pollens, beetles, and ocean plankton found in rock strata, cores

from ice sheets, and sediments on the ocean bottom (Gribbin 1976, 1977, Kellogg 1977, National Academy of Sciences 1975g).

This detective work—which is, of course, crude and speculative—indicates that eight great ice ages, or glacial periods, have occurred over the past 700,000 years, during which thick ice sheets spread southward over much of North America, Europe, and parts of Asia. Each glacial period lasted about 100,000 years and was followed by a warmer interglacial period lasting about 10,000 to 12,500 years (Figure 9-1). The last great ice age ended about 10,000 years ago and at its coldest point the mean temperature of the atmosphere near the earth was only about 5°C (9°F) cooler than the atmosphere today (Dansgaard et al. 1971). A new ice age could be triggered if the mean temperature of the atmosphere dropped only 2.0° to 3.5°C (3.6° to 6.3°F) and remained at that level for several years (Rasool & Schneider 1971, SCEP 1970).

For the past 10,000 years we have been enjoying the warmer temperatures (compared with those in the last ice age) of the latest interglacial period (Dansgaard et al. 1971). During this period of favorable climate, agriculture began and spread rapidly throughout the world to support the increase in the world's population that the warmer weather allowed. If climatic history does in fact repeat itself and is not altered by human activities, we are due for a new ice age sometime within the next 2,500 years (Calder 1974, Halacy 1978, Hays et al. 1976). Until recently it was assumed that the transition from an interglacial period to an ice age took place gradually over several thousand years. But analysis of pollen in cores of ice drilled from glaciers indicates that about 90,000 years ago the earth shifted from an interglacial period like that of today into a full ice age in less than 100 years (Bryson 1974, Bryson & Murray 1977, Calder 1974, 1975, Dansgaard et al. 1971, Gribbin 1976, 1977, Kennett & Huddleston 1972, Lamb 1972, 1977). According to a more recent theory, we could move from a warm period to a full ice age within 10 to 20 years as a result of a *snowblitz* (Calder 1974, 1975, Central Intelligence Agency 1974a, Gribbin 1976, 1977, Lamb 1972, 1977). Massive amounts of snow and ice could blanket many parts of the world during one winter and then not melt in the

---

[1]For general overviews and more details on natural and human-induced climate changes, see the following: Bolin 1977b, Brown 1971, Bryson 1974, Bryson & Murray 1977, Budyko 1974, Calder 1974, 1975, Central Intelligence Agency 1974a, 1974b, Clairborne 1970, Fletcher 1969, Gribbin 1976, 1977, Halacy 1978, Hess 1974, Hobbs et al. 1974, Impact Team 1977, Kellogg 1977, 1978, Kellogg & Robinson 1971, Kellogg & Schneider 1974, Ladurie 1973, Lamb 1972, 1977, Landsberg 1970b, MacDonald 1975, Mitchell 1972, National Academy of Sciences 1975g, 1977a, Norwine 1977, Ponte 1976, SCEP 1970, Schneider 1975, 1976a, 1976b, Schneider & Bennett 1975, Singer 1970, 1975a, SMIC 1971, Wilcox 1976, Woodwell 1978, Woodwell & Pecan 1973.

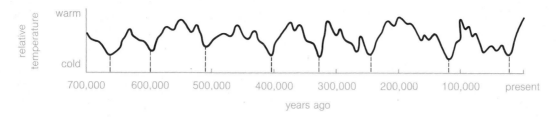

Figure 9–1 Estimated average atmospheric temperature through geological time. During the past 700,000 years eight great ice ages have occurred (dotted lines), each lasting around 100,000 years and followed by a warmer interglacial period lasting about 10,000 to 12,500 years. If natural climatic history repeats itself, we are due for another great ice age within the next 2,500 years. (Data from SMIC 1971)

spring and summer because of a drop in mean global temperature. This increased snow and ice cover would reflect more sunlight, causing a further drop in mean air temperature and leading to more snow and ice each succeeding year. Within a decade or so much of North America, Europe, and eastern Asia could be covered with ice. Thus, by looking at the earth's long-term natural climate change, we can speculate that much of the world could be covered with ice sometime within the next 10 to 2,500 years.

To make more accurate predictions of how climate might change during the next 10 to 200 years, we need to look at what has happened during the present interglacial period—particularly during the past 100 years. Any recurring trends during these shorter time periods might give us clues about what might happen over the next few decades. Climate fluctuates between hot and cold during an interglacial period, but the swings are not enough to set off a 100,000-year great ice age. Instead we get a series of cooling periods called *little ice ages*, when glaciers spread southward for up to several hundred years before retreating. During the past 10,000 years, six to eight little ice ages —the last one occurring between 1550 and 1870—have occurred (Lamb 1972, 1977). The cooler atmospheric temperatures during a little ice age also alter global precipitation patterns, and these two factors change the parts of the world where certain foods can be grown. During the last little ice age, cereal cultivation ended in Iceland, vineyards were abandoned in England, and in 1816 New England had snow in June and fall frost starting in August—the "year without a summer" (Lamb 1972).

Following the end of the last little ice age, the mean global temperature of the atmosphere rose by about 0.4° to 0.6°C between 1880 and 1940 and then dropped slightly between 1940 and 1965 (SMIC 1971) (Figure 9–2). Between 1965 and 1975, however, the Southern Hemisphere warmed 0.2°C, while temperature in the Northern Hemisphere changed very little (Damon & Kunen 1976).

Predicting Future Climate Changes How can we explain these trends and use them to predict what might happen

over the next few decades? Scientists are sharply divided on this issue (Calder 1974, Central Intelligence Agency 1974b, Gribbin 1976, 1977, Impact Team 1977, Norwine 1977). There are three major views: (1) We don't have enough knowledge and evidence either to explain these short-term (and perhaps random) swings or to use them as clues about future short-term changes (Landsberg 1970b, Smagorinsky 1974); (2) it will get colder as we move into a new great ice age (or into a new little ice age) because of long-term natural trends (Figure 9–1) (Calder 1974, 1975, Willett & Prohaska 1977) or a combination of natural trends and human activities (Bryson 1974, Bryson & Murray 1977, Impact Team 1977, Ponte 1976); and (3) it will get warmer primarily because of human activities that counteract the natural and human-caused cooling trends (Bolin 1977b, Broecker 1975, Damon & Kunen 1976, Elliot & Machta 1977, Kellogg 1977, 1978, Kellogg & Schneider 1974, Manabe & Wetherald 1975, Mitchell 1972, Schneider 1975, 1976a, Schneider & Bennett 1975, Siegenthaler & Oeschger 1978, Stuiver 1978, Wilcox 1976, Woodwell 1978).

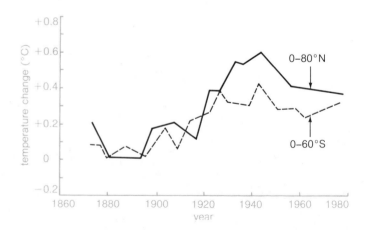

Figure 9–2 Changes in mean surface temperatures of the atmosphere in the Northern Hemisphere (solid line) and Southern Hemisphere (dotted line) between 1870 and 1975. (Data from Damon & Kunen 1976, Mitchell 1972, SMIC 1971)

In other words, experts are making three predictions about climate change in the next few decades: We can't tell what will happen, it will get colder, and it will get hotter. The experts also have three views on the effects of human activities on global climate: no effect, a small effect, and a major effect.

You might be thinking that experts aren't necessary to come to these conclusions, which cover all possibilities. The problem is that climate change is an incredibly complex process, which is influenced by many factors interacting over short and long periods of time. The major factors determining the earth's overall climate are (1) the input of solar energy (Section 3–3), (2) the earth's rotation rate, (3) the chemical composition of the earth's atmosphere, which controls how much sunlight gets through and how rapidly heat is radiated back into space (Figure 3–7, Section 3–3), (4) the properties of the oceans (which are vast heat reservoirs) and their interactions with the atmosphere, and (5) the reflectivity (albedo), vegetation, and other surface characteristics of the land and sea (Budyko 1974, Global Atmospheric Research Program 1975, Kellogg 1978, Kellogg & Schneider 1974). The difficulty is in learning how these factors interact with one another.

Climatologists have developed a number of dynamic mathematical models to predict the effects of changing one climatic factor (such as increased atmospheric dust from volcanic eruptions or human land-clearing and industrial activities) on other climatic factors (Global Atmospheric Research Program 1975, Gribbin 1977, Kellogg 1977, 1978, Schneider & Dickinson 1974, Smagorinsky 1974). Despite these important advances, these models are still too crude to make accurate short- and long-term predictions (Kellogg 1977). Thus, the vigorous debate over conflicting theories is a natural and healthy characteristic of science—especially when there is insufficient knowledge.

Why Worry about Climate Change?   If the experts can't agree, then why should we worry about this issue? Why not wait until the smoke clears and we have a better understanding of climate change? Unfortunately, we can't afford this tempting luxury. Climate change is too important in human affairs to postpone action until it is thoroughly understood from a scientific viewpoint—if that ever occurs.

Although climatologists disagree on how climate will change and on what the major causes of change are, they generally agree that we are probably in for some rather far-reaching changes in climate over the next century. Just a slight rise or fall in the mean global temperature of the atmosphere can trigger effects that could be with us for thousands of years.

If seasonal temperature and precipitation changes should come a few weeks earlier or later on a regular basis in various parts of the world, food production could be thrown into chaos (Bryson & Murray 1977, Gribbin 1976,

1977, National Academy of Sciences 1976a, Newman & Pickett 1974, Schneider 1976a, Thomson 1975). This in turn could lead to political and social disruption. With over 4 billion people to support and perhaps 8 billion within a few decades, there is not really much margin for error in knowing where the climate might be most favorable for food production in the future. Thus, climate change is not merely a scientific problem—it is also a political, economic, and ethical problem that demands our attention regardless of how little we know.

Climate and Human Activities   A major thrust of this concern must be to determine the potential effect of human activities on climate. Until recently it was assumed that we had very little effect on global and regional climate compared with volcanic eruptions, sunspots, and other natural phenomena. Now we have evidence that human activities are already affecting local climates, especially in and near urban areas (Landsberg 1970a), and that we may have major effects on regional and even global climate in the future (Bryson & Murray 1977, Fletcher 1969, Hobbs et al. 1974, Kellogg 1977, 1978, Kellogg & Robinson 1971, Kellogg & Schneider 1974, MacDonald 1975, Mitchell 1972, National Academy of Sciences 1975g, 1977a, SCEP 1970, Schneider 1976a, Schneider & Bennett 1975, Singer 1970, SMIC 1971, Wilcox, 1976).

From Table 9–1 we see that most human activities tend to warm the lower atmosphere. This is in contrast to the natural trends, which according to climatic history may lead to cooling (Figure 9–1). Thus, the interaction of human activities with natural climate trends could determine whether we descend into a new little ice age or a great ice age, have a much warmer climate, or maintain the relatively good weather we have had during the past several thousand years.

In the remainder of this chapter we will look more closely at the possible effects of increasing the amounts of carbon dioxide, particles, and heat in the atmosphere from human activities.

9–2   Carbon Dioxide and the Greenhouse Effect: Is the Atmosphere Warming?

The Greenhouse Effect   Approximately 30 percent of the solar radiation reaching the earth is reflected back into space (Figure 3–7). Most of the remaining 70 percent is absorbed by the land, sea, and clouds. When the land and water bodies cool, the absorbed energy is radiated into the atmosphere as long-wavelength infrared (IR) radiation, or heat energy (Figures 3–7, 9–3). Instead of immediately escaping back into space, some of this infrared radiation is absorbed by carbon dioxide (CO_2) gas and water vapor

Table 9–1 Climate and Human Activities

Human Activity	Probable Climatic Effect	Present Area of Impact	Estimated Years before Global Impact	Potential for Controlling
Release of carbon dioxide from burning fossil fuels	Warming of lower atmosphere (greenhouse effect) and cooling of upper atmosphere	Local, regional, possibly global	10 to 50 years	Poor until fossil fuels used up
Diffusion of chlorofluorohydrocarbons (freons) and nitrous oxide into the stratosphere and injection of nitrogen dioxide into stratosphere by SSTs	Warming of lower atmosphere and cooling of upper atmosphere; reduction of stratospheric ozone, allowing more harmful ultraviolet radiation to reach the earth	Possibly minor global effect	Major impact within 20 to 30 years	Fair (freons) to poor (nitrous oxide)
Land clearing (deforestation, agriculture, overgrazing, irrigation)	Warming or cooling of lower atmosphere because of changes in surface albedo (reflectivity) and warming because of carbon dioxide released from land clearing	Local, regional	Speculative, 20 to 200 years	Fair to poor
Release of particles (aerosols) from industry, burning of fossil fuels, and land clearing	May cool lower atmosphere by reflecting sunlight over water or heat lower atmosphere by absorbing sunlight over land	Local, regional	Unknown, but may have little global effect since most particles remain in atmosphere for only a few days	Fair (large particles) to poor (fine particles)
Release of heat from urbanization and burning of fossil and nuclear fuels faster than the heat can be radiated back into space	Direct warming of lower atmosphere	Local, regional	100 to 200 years	Poor

Source: Modified from Kellogg 1977, 1978.

(H_2O) in the atmosphere. These chemical gatekeepers radiate part of the absorbed heat into space and part back to the earth; thus, some of the heat that would normally be lost to space fairly rapidly is reradiated to warm the lower atmosphere (Manabe & Wetherald 1975, Plass 1959, Schneider 1975, 1976a) (Figure 9–3). This warming effect is sometimes called the **greenhouse effect,** because the atmosphere acts similarly to the glass in a greenhouse or a car window, which allows visible light to enter but hinders the escape of long-wavelength IR, or heat radiation.[2] The mean global atmospheric temperature today is about 10°C (18°F) higher than it would be without any CO_2, or H_2O in the atmosphere (National Academy of Sciences 1977a).

Thus, the mean temperature of the earth's lower atmosphere is strongly affected by changes in the average amount of carbon dioxide and water vapor present. The oceans, as part of the carbon cycle, dissolve an estimated one-third to one-half of all carbon dioxide injected into the atmosphere within a few years (Berger & Libby 1969, Keeling 1973b, Machta 1973, Manabe & Bryan 1969). Without

this major sink, the average global concentration of CO_2 would probably be twice its present value.

Because of the large amount of water vapor and its relatively rapid rate of cycling, humans can do little to upset the average water concentration in the atmosphere. However, the relatively small average concentration of carbon dioxide (about 0.03 percent) can be increased significantly as the earth's fossil fuels are burned up and as forests are cleared. When coal, oil, natural gas, wood, or any carbon-containing fuel is burned, CO_2, H_2O, and heat are released into the atmosphere. For example, burning 909 kilograms (1 ton) of coal releases about 2,700 kilograms (3 tons) of CO_2. Green plants and trees also remove some of the carbon dioxide from the atmosphere through photosynthesis. However, when plants and trees are cut down and either burned as fuel or allowed to decay, CO_2 is added to the atmosphere. If plants are being removed from the earth faster than they are being replanted or faster than they regrow naturally, the amount of CO_2 released is greater than that removed by photosynthesis. Additional carbon dioxide can be released from decay in soil humus that has been exposed to the sunlight when a forest or field is cleared of vegetation (Bolin 1977a, Woodwell et al. 1978). Assuming that the sun sends off energy at a constant rate and that the earth's reflectivity and emissivity (Section 3–3)

[2]Strictly speaking, the term *greenhouse effect* is misleading. A greenhouse, or a closed car on a sunny day, not only traps heat energy but also reduces heat exchange with the wind. Even though technically incorrect, the use of this term is widespread.

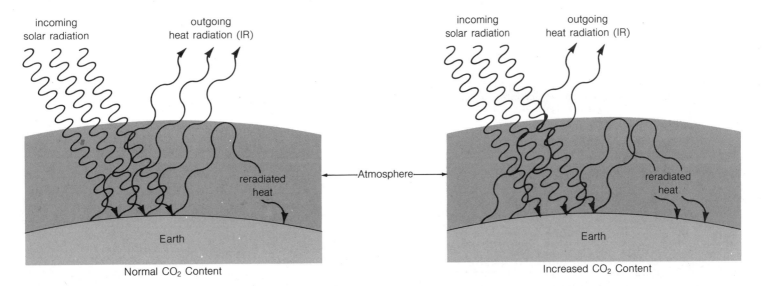

Figure 9–3 The greenhouse effect. Short-wavelength solar radiation strikes the earth and is transformed into long-wavelength IR, or heat radiation, some of which is absorbed and reradiated back to the earth by the CO_2 and water vapor in the atmosphere. Compared with CO_2, the average amount of water vapor in the air is so large that human activities do not significantly change its average global concentration. The average CO_2 content, however, can be significantly increased by burning wood and fossil fuels and clearing forests; this could lead to a warming of the earth's atmosphere.

are constant, then as the level of CO_2 increases, the mean global temperature of the atmosphere should rise. Of course, neither of these assumptions is necessarily true; some factors may tend to cool and others may tend to warm the atmosphere. No one really knows how these factors may have affected the changes in global climate since 1880 (Schneider & Mass 1975).

Carbon Dioxide Levels Are Increasing Measurements since 1958 and estimates of past values show that average global concentrations of CO_2 have been increasing since the beginning of the industrial revolution in the 1880s, with a sharp increase since 1940 and an even sharper rise since 1958 (Figure 9–4) (Callendar 1958, Keeling 1977, Keeling et al. 1976, Lepkowski 1977, Machta 1973, Mitchell 1975). Between 1880 and 1950, an estimated one-third of the CO_2 added to the atmosphere came from the burning of fossil fuels, with the remaining two-thirds from forest clearing and wood burning (Stuiver 1978). Since 1950 fossil fuel combustion is believed to have been the dominant source of CO_2 (Stuiver 1978). Because of a lack of information, there is considerable debate over (Kellogg 1978, Kerr 1977a) how much CO_2 deforestation has added in recent years; estimates range from 10 to 35 percent (Bolin 1977a) to as high as 50 percent (Woodwell 1978, Woodwell et al. 1978) of the CO_2 added from burning fossil fuels.

According to the greenhouse model, the increase in CO_2 between 1880 and 1975 should have increased the

mean global atmospheric temperature by about 0.3°C (0.5°F) (Manabe 1971, Schneider 1975). Assuming that the use of fossil fuels continues to grow at 3 to 4 percent a year, that the oceans and plant life remove 50 percent of the total CO_2 added to the atmosphere, and that all other factors remain constant, then between 1975 and 2000 the average atmospheric CO_2 concentration should rise from 330 parts per million by volume (ppmv) to between 365 and 400 ppmv, causing an additional atmospheric temperature rise of 0.3° to 0.6°C (0.5°to 1.0°F) (Bacastrow & Keeling 1973, Broecker 1975, Machta 1973, Manabe 1971, Manabe & Wetherald 1967, 1975, Mitchell 1975, National Academy of Sciences 1977a, Schneider 1975). A doubling of the 1880 CO_2 levels, which with increasing fossil fuel use could occur by 2150, could raise the mean global temperature by 2° to 3°C (4° to 5°F) (Bacastrow & Keeling 1973, Broecker 1975, Manabe & Wetherald 1975, Mitchell 1975, National Academy of Sciences 1977a, Schneider 1975, Siegenthaler & Oeschger 1978). Perhaps even more significant, the temperature rise in the polar regions is expected to be 3 to 5 times larger than the average global increase (Manabe & Wetherald 1975, Schneider 1975, Sellers 1974, Van Loon & Williams 1976).

The increase in atmospheric CO_2 and the resulting temperature change could occur more rapidly or more slowly than these models predict. For example, as the lower atmosphere warms, some of the CO_2 now dissolved in the oceans could be released—like the dissolved CO_2 released when soda pop or beer warms up. This positive feedback loop could accelerate the warming and release even more dissolved CO_2, so that the warming effect could be intensified (McLean 1978, Siegenthaler & Oeschger 1978). In addition, increased deforestation (Woodwell 1978, Woodwell et al. 1978) and the heat automatically released by the use of any form of energy could add to the warming effect as population and energy use continue to rise (see Section 9–4). There is also some evidence that if CO_2 levels rise rapidly, the ocean becomes less effective in removing CO_2 (Bacastrow & Keeling 1973).

Conversely, the warming of the atmosphere could evaporate more water from the ocean, producing more clouds, which could shield and cool the ocean surface. But whether clouds tend to warm or cool the earth depends on their altitude; low-level clouds tend to cool the atmosphere, and high-level clouds tend to warm the earth since water vapor is an infrared absorbant like CO_2 (Bryson 1974, Manabe & Wetherald 1967, SMIC 1971). Higher CO_2 levels could also increase the rate of photosynthesis so that plants grow faster and thus remove more CO_2 from the atmosphere (Bacastrow & Keeling 1973). This assumption, however, has been questioned; even if it is valid, such a phenomenon could be overcome by increased cloudiness and deforestation (Woodwell et al. 1978).

The greenhouse model may have caused much of the 0.4° to 0.6°C (0.7° to 1.0°F) rise in mean atmospheric tem-

perature between 1880 and 1940, but how can this model explain the approximately 0.3°C (0.4°F) drop in temperature in the Northern Hemisphere between 1940 and 1970 (Figure 9–2)? This slight decline could be due to a natural cooling trend (Broecker 1975) or a combination of natural and human factors (such as more dust in the air) that could counteract the CO_2 warming effect. The sharpest rise in CO_2 is expected between 1975 and 2000 (Figure 9–4); by 2000, if not sooner, many scientists expect that the CO_2 warming effect will overwhelm any natural or human-caused cooling effects (Bacastrow & Keeling 1973, Baes et al. 1977, Broecker 1975, Elliot & Machta 1977, Keeling 1977, Kellogg 1977, 1978, Mitchell 1972, 1975, National Academy of Sciences 1977a, Rotty & Weinberg 1977, Schneider & Bennett 1975, Siegenthaler & Oeschger 1978, Wilcox 1976, Woodwell et al. 1978). The apparent leveling off of the temperature in the Northern Hemisphere and the slight increase in temperature in the Southern Hemisphere (where human activity and human-generated particle pollution is lowest) (Figure 9–2) are cited as evidence that the CO_2 warming effect may be gradually overcoming cooling effects (Damon & Kunen 1976).

Possible Effects on Climate Why worry about all of this? At first thought a slightly warmer climate of 1° to 3°C might seem desirable, resulting in longer growing seasons

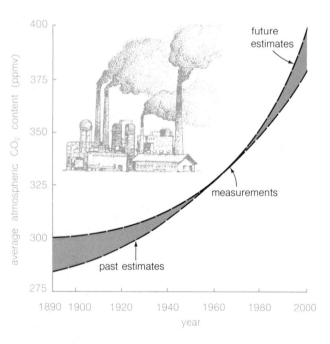
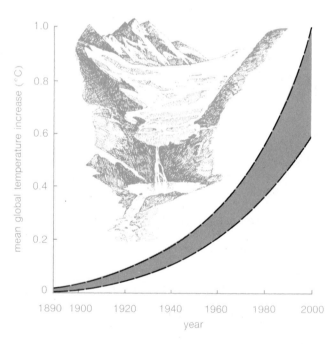

Figure 9–4 Estimated changes in atmospheric CO_2 content (left) and the resulting increase in mean atmospheric temperature (right) between 1890 and 2000. Width of shaded portions indicates the range of estimates. (Data from Keeling et al. 1976, Manabe & Wetherald 1975, National Academy of Sciences 1977a, Schneider 1975)

and milder winters that would save fuel. But unfortunately along with benefits for some parts of the world there could be serious consequences in other areas, especially if such a change took place fairly rapidly over a few decades (Baes et al. 1977, Kellogg 1977, 1978, McLean 1978, National Academy of Sciences 1977a, Schneider 1976a, Smith 1978, Wilcox 1976). No one knows exactly what would happen, but we can get some clues by looking at what happened during a period of slight warming (about 2°C) 4,000 to 8,000 years ago (Kellogg 1977, 1978, McLean 1978).

The major effect of a slight warming would be shifts in crop-growing regions plus changes and shifts in rainfall patterns, which make it difficult to know where to plant crops from year to year. Some arid regions, such as the Sahel area in Africa and the Sahara and Arabian deserts, might get more rain while the midwestern breadbasket in the United States might become drier. The U.S. wheat and corn belt in Iowa and Indiana might shift northward into Saskatchewan in Canada, where the soils are poorer and less productive. Fish populations might move northward so that New England's fishing fleet would find their cod off Greenland instead of Nova Scotia. Some nations might eventually be able to grow more food than they do today. But for several decades there would probably be a sharp drop in global food production and distribution because many of the new crop-growing areas would have poor soils and not be organized to farm, store, and distribute large amounts of grain.

The effects at the poles would be even more drastic, since a 2°C (3.6°F) rise in mean global temperature would result in a 4° to 10°C (7° to 18°F) rise there. Sea levels would rise about 1 meter (3.3 feet) because of the thermal expansion of warmer ocean water (National Academy of Sciences 1977a). Most, if not all, of the floating Arctic ice pack would probably melt, which would have the benefit of opening the northwest and northeast passages to ships through most of the year. Since this ice pack is afloat, its melting would not raise the water level in oceans—just as melting a floating ice cube in a glass of water does not raise the water level. But the absence of polar ice would change ocean currents and trigger unpredictable changes in the climate of the Northern Hemisphere. Some of the land-based Antarctic glacial ice might melt slowly, but the increased evaporation of ocean water could also increase snowfall, building up the snow accumulation at the pole. The resulting stresses could cause the edges of the ice cap to break off and slide into the ocean, raising the sea level about 5 meters (17 feet) in 300 years (National Academy of Sciences 1977a). Despite stories in the popular press predicting that the world's major coastal cities and flood plains (which produce most of the world's food) will soon be flooded, this melting process, if it occurred, would probably take place very slowly over hundreds of years. Over the next 50 years the more immediate threat to the world from a global warming is the shift in food-growing regions and

capacity during a time when the world's population is expected to at least double.

9–3 Particles in the Atmosphere: Is the Atmosphere Cooling?

Aerosols or particles of solids and liquids are constantly injected into the atmosphere in large quantities. Dust, soot, and other particles enter the atmosphere from active volcanoes, forest fires, dust storms, sea spray, and other natural sources. Humans also add particles by clearing land for agriculture and urbanization and through smokestack, chimney, and automobile emissions. Unlike CO_2, particles differ markedly in size and chemical makeup.

The huge quantity of particles spewed into the atmosphere from a major volcanic eruption can apparently cause regional and global cooling for several months to a year after the eruption (Dyer 1974, Impact Team 1977, Lamb 1972, Mitchell 1975, Pollack et al. 1976, SMIC 1971, Watt 1972b). Because there have been no major volcanic eruptions since 1940, it is hypothesized that some of the drop in mean atmospheric temperature in the Northern Hemisphere between 1940 and 1970 (Figure 9–4) was caused by increased atmospheric inputs of particles from human activities (Bolin & Charlson 1976, Bryson & Petersen 1968, Bryson 1974, Bryson & Murray 1977, Bryson & Wendland 1975, Mitchell 1975, Rasool & Schneider 1971, Watt 1972b, Yamamato & Tanaka 1972). These particles, especially those in the upper atmosphere, could reflect some of the incoming sunlight back into space and thus reduce the amount of solar heat reaching the earth's surface (Bryson 1974).

However, particles need not always decrease atmospheric temperature. They can either raise or lower atmospheric temperature depending on their size and upon their composition, reflective properties, altitude, and the reflectivity of the earth's surface below (Chylek & Coakley 1974, Kellogg 1977, Kellogg & Schneider 1974, Kellogg et al. 1975, Mitchell 1972, SMIC 1971, Weare et al. 1974). Over a dark surface, such as the ocean, particles tend to reflect incoming sunlight and cool the atmosphere (Bolin & Charlson 1976, Bryson 1974, Rasool & Schneider 1971). But over much of the land, which is lighter than the oceans, particles can absorb heat energy and radiate some of it back toward the earth, thus warming the atmosphere (Kellogg 1977, Kellogg et al. 1975, Landsberg 1970b). In the atmosphere both the cooling and warming processes take place, and the net effect depends on the strength of each process and the altitude of the dust layer. If the layer is high enough, the cooling process probably dominates (Bolin 1977b, SMIC 1971).

There is considerable evidence that the human input of atmospheric particles has increased over the past few decades, especially above cities and industrial regions in

Europe and the United States (Bolin & Charlson 1976, Bryson 1974, Dyer 1974, Machta & Telegadas 1974, Mitchell 1974, SMIC 1971). But we do not know whether human activities are a major source of this input compared with natural processes (Bolin 1977b). Estimates of the human production of atmospheric dust range from 5 to 50 percent of the total input each year (Bolin 1977b, SMIC 1971). Most large-particle emissions near the earth's surface have a residence time of days to a few weeks before they fall out or are washed out by rain. Although they can affect local weather patterns significantly, these particles are not a major factor in global climate. However, very small particles that rise in or are injected into the stratosphere have a residence time of 1 to 5 years and can affect global climate. It is argued that since most particles from human activities end up in the lower atmosphere, their climatic effects are primarily local. Thus, the overall effects of particles from natural and human sources on global climate are complex and still poorly understood (Bolin 1977b, Kellogg 1977, Kellogg & Schneider 1974).

9-4   Heat: The Ultimate Pollutant

Cities and Heat   Take a breath, raise your arm, turn on a light, drive a car, or heat or air condition your house or car, and you add heat to the atmosphere. According to the second law of energy (Section 2-3), whenever energy is used, some of it is degraded to heat energy, which flows into the atmosphere and eventually back into space (Figure 3-7). The earth can only radiate heat back into space at a certain rate. If human activities should produce energy faster than it can be radiated back into space, then the temperature of the atmosphere will rise—just as an auditorium heats up when it is filled with people. Thus, as more and more people try to use more and more energy, this direct input of heat could cause atmospheric warming, first on a local and regional level, and eventually on a global level (Budyko 1970, 1972, Harte & Socolow 1971, Holdren 1971b, Kellogg & Schneider 1974, Landsberg 1970a, 1970b, 1974b, Lowry 1967, MacDonald 1972, Petersen 1973, Schneider & Bennett 1975, Sellers 1970, 1973, SMIC 1971, Weinberg & Hammond 1972).

This heating effect is already occurring in large cities and urban areas (Bryson & Ross 1972, Landsberg 1970a, 1970b, 1974b, Lowry 1967, World Meteorological Organization 1970). Anyone who lives or works in a city knows that it is warmer there than in nearby suburbs or rural areas. Day in and day out, cities emit vast quantities of heat through home and building heating and air conditioning, industrial plants, and automobiles. Concrete and brick buildings and asphalt pavements absorb heat during the day and release it slowly at night. Tall, closely spaced buildings slow down wind near the ground and reduce the rate of heat loss. Water rapidly runs off the paved surfaces in cities, in contrast to rural areas where water soaks into the soil and then slowly evaporates to cool the surrounding air. Thus, it is not surprising that a dome of heat hovers over a city, creating what is called an *urban heat island* (Figure 9-5) (Bryson & Ross 1972, Landsberg 1970a). Not only is a city warmer than rural areas, but it typically has more clouds, more rain, more air pollution, less sun, less wind, and lower humidity (Table 9-2).

As urban areas grow and merge into vast urban regions, the heat domes from a number of cities can combine to form *regional heat islands,* which could affect regional climate (Bolin 1977b, Bornstein 1968, Lees 1970, Schneider & Bennett 1975). The prevailing winds that normally cleanse the center of the dome would already be polluted. In addition, summer heat levels in the center could become intolerable, and the use of millions of air conditioners would increase the chances of power brownouts and blackouts.

Global Heating   Because of the second energy law, each human on earth radiates heat into the atmosphere continuously at about the same rate as a 100-watt light bulb. When we add the other direct and indirect uses of energy, each person in the world imposes a continuous average heat load onto the atmosphere equal to that of 50 100-watt bulbs. In the United States average per capita energy use is so high that every American citizen injects a continuous average heat load equivalent to 125 100-watt bulbs. As world population and energy use continue to increase, the resultant heat load could eventually affect global climate. Today the human input of heat is only about 0.01 percent of the input of energy from the sun (Brown 1971, Holdren 1971b, Kellogg 1977, Kellogg & Schneider 1974, Weinberg & Hammond 1972). In other words, at present the sun's contribution to the atmospheric heat load is about 10,000 times that caused by human activities.

Global climate changes could occur when the human heat input reaches about 0.5 to 1.0 percent of that from the sun. If world energy use grows at about 5 percent a year, we could reach this level within 125 years (Budyko 1974, Holdren 1971b, Petersen 1973, Kellogg 1977, Weinberg & Hammond 1972). This could cause the mean atmospheric temperature to rise from 0.2° to 4.0°C, with 4 to 5 times this change at the earth's poles (Schneider & Bennett 1975). Although such human-induced changes in global climate are not an immediate problem, they could occur within 100 years or perhaps sooner from the combined effects of direct inputs of heat and carbon dioxide (Section 9-2) from human activities (Schneider & Bennett 1975).

9-5   Thermal Pollution of Rivers and Lakes

Huge quantities of heated water are being dumped into streams, lakes, and oceans by power and industrial plants.

Figure 9–5 The urban heat island.

About 75 percent of the U.S. industrial use of water—or 38 percent of all water used—is utilized just for cooling electric power plants (Murray & Reeves 1977). A single 1,000-megawatt nuclear power plant requires about 4.7 million cubic meters (1.23 billion gallons) of cooling water

Table 9–2 Comparison of Urban and Nearby Rural Climates

Variable	Urban Compared with Rural Levels
Temperature	
Annual mean	0.5 to 1.0°C higher
Winter average	1.0 to 2.0°C higher
Cloudiness and fog	
Cloud cover	5 to 10 percent more
Winter fog	100 percent more
Summer fog	30 percent more
Visibility	5 to 30 percent less
Pollutants	
Particulates	10 times more
Gases (sulfur dioxide, carbon dioxide, carbon monoxide)	5 to 25 times more
Precipitation	
Rain	5 to 10 percent more
Snow	5 to 15 percent less
Solar radiation	15 to 20 percent less
Wind speed	
Annual mean	20 to 30 percent less
Calms (stagnant air)	5 to 20 percent more
Relative humidity	
Winter	2 percent less
Summer	8 percent less

Source: Landsberg 1970a.

per day (National Water Commission 1973). Since use of electricity in the United States could triple between 1970 and 2000, heat output from power plants could also (National Water Commission 1973). It has been estimated that by 1980 one-sixth, and by 2000 one-fourth to one-third, of all the freshwater runoff in the United States will be used to cool power plants (Holcomb 1970). This percentage could double during the summer when water flow is low. However, these figures mask the fact that streams near urban areas will be intensely heated while isolated ones may not. Although average temperature increases may not be too large, most of the hot water will be discharged near the shoreline. In a lake the shoreline zone is where fish spawn and young fish spend their first few weeks; both activities are extremely susceptible to temperature increases.

We also have the problem of the threshold effect. One or several power plants may use a given body of water without serious damage, thus giving the misleading impression that others can be built. Then just one more plant can completely disrupt the system by causing the system's threshold level to be exceeded.

You can see why environmentalists are concerned about aquatic ecosystems receiving large amounts of heated water. But again we run into a controversy (Esch & McFarlane 1976, Schurr 1971). Some view waste heat as a potential water pollutant that can damage and disrupt aquatic ecosystems (Brown 1971, Cairns 1971, 1972, Clark 1969, Gibbons & Sharitz 1974, National Water Commission 1973, U.S. Department of the Interior 1968). But others talk about using heated water for beneficial purposes and speak of *thermal enrichment* rather than *thermal pollution* (Coutant 1976, Horne 1978). Let's look at the effects of heat in water.

Undesirable Effects Excess heat in an aquatic ecosystem can produce a number of harmful effects (Cairns 1971,

1972, Esch & McFarlane 1976, Gibbons & Sharitz 1974). These include the following:

1. Thermal shock (the sudden death of thermally sensitive aquatic life due to sharp changes in temperature). Thermal tolerance varies widely not only among species but also among stages of life. When a plant first operates, the shock might kill existing species. Then, when it shuts down for repair, the sudden temperature drop could kill the new heat-resistant species that have moved in.

2. Increased susceptibility of aquatic organisms to parasites, disease, and chemical toxins.

3. Disruption of fish migration patterns.

4. Lowered dissolved oxygen concentrations, although higher temperatures raise organisms' need for oxygen.

5. Fewer eggs and fewer surviving young for thermally sensitive species.

6. Reduction of species diversity by eliminating thermally sensitive organisms.

7. Shift of species composition (this may be beneficial or harmful, depending on the new species, but slime and undesirable blue-green algae thrive in heated water).

8. Disruption of food webs by loss of one or several key species, especially plankton, at lower levels of the food chain.

9. Delay of spring and fall lake turnover.

In addition to heat, there are other serious side effects from using water to cool plants (Coutant 1976). Large fish and invertebrates are often killed on intake screens, through which water is taken into the plant. Smaller organisms, particularly fish larvae, are mutilated or killed when they move through intake pumps, pipes, and plant heat-exchange condensers. In addition, some of the fish kills and other ecological damages once believed to be caused by heat may be caused by the chlorine or copper sulfate used to keep bacteria and other microbes from fouling the water-cooling pipes in power plants (Coutant 1976).

Desirable effects Heated water can also have some benefits:

1. Lengthening of commercial fishing season and larger catches by attracting warm-water species to heated areas.

2. Reduction in winter ice cover.

3. Increase in recreational use because of the warming of very cold water bodies.

4. Increased irrigation of croplands (Carter 1969).

5. Use of warm water for aquaculture, such as the cultivation of catfish, shrimp, lobsters, carp, oysters, and other human food species (Lee 1972).

6. Use of heated water to heat buildings, provide hot water, remove snow, desalt ocean and brackish water, and provide heat for some chemical and industrial processes. These uses, however, would require that fossil fuel and nuclear power plants be located near urban areas, which could increase air pollution and problems with radioactivity in these areas (Section 7–3).

Possible Solutions The sites of most existing and future fossil fuel and nuclear power plants prevent the beneficial use of their enormous outputs of hot water. Pumping water for long distances to croplands, aquaculture ponds, and buildings requires energy (and money) and in the process most of the heat is lost. Thus the best course is to reduce thermal water pollution as much as possible. This leaves us with several alternatives, which are summarized in Table 9–3.

Because of strict federal water pollution laws, more power plants are using cooling ponds, canals, or cooling towers (Figure 9–6) to prevent thermal overload of rivers and lakes. Perhaps the real question we should ask ourselves is whether we really need all of this electricity.

9–6 Needed: A Global Plan

By burning up the world's fossil fuels, cutting down the world's forests, and converting land to cropland, we appear to be carrying out a gigantic climate experiment with unknown and perhaps disastrous long-term results. Although we don't have an adequate understanding of global climate change, there may be a significant change, or at least unpredictable variations, over the next 20 to 100 years. Regardless of the causes of climate change, clearly one of the major tasks facing the world today is to develop plans for responding to either global heating or global cooling.

Because a major climate change would probably take place gradually over many years, there may be a dangerous tendency to delay planning and action. But to establish new food-growing regions and food distribution networks or to limit the burning of fossil fuels and forest clearing would take decades. Failure to make plans and to develop better models for predicting climate change could easily doom millions of people to a premature death in the future.

We may be able to use fossil fuels (primarily coal if we run out of oil and natural gas) for another 30 to 50 years without drastic effects on climate (National Academy of Sciences 1977a). But after that period we must either shift

Sacramento Municipal Utility District

Figure 9–6 Cooling towers for the Rancho Seco nuclear power plant near Sacramento, California. Compare the size of the towers with the power plant and automobiles. Each tower is over 122 meters (400 feet) high and could hold a football field in its base.

Table 9–3 Methods for Minimizing Thermal Water Pollution

Input Approach	Output Approach
Use less energy	Return heated water in a way that minimizes damage (for instance, away from the fragile shore zone)
Waste less energy	Dissipate some of the heat in cooling ponds or canals (in places where land is cheap enough)
Limit the number of power and industrial plants allowed to use a given body of water	Transfer heat to the air either by evaporation (wet cooling towers) or by conduction and convection (dry cooling towers). However, cooling towers may rise as high as a 30-story building and measure more than a block in diameter at the base (Figure 9–6). Wet cooling towers can cause mist, fog, and ice around them. Both kinds are expensive, but the dry kind costs 2 to 4 times as much as the wet.

to other energy sources, such as nuclear, solar, and wind power, that do not produce carbon dioxide or we must find ways to remove CO_2 from fossil fuel emissions (Baes et al. 1977, National Academy of Sciences 1977a, Schneider 1976b, Schneider & Bennett 1975). In addition, we must support a massive global research program, costing between $20 million and $100 million a year, (1) to find out more about the ability of the oceans and green plants to absorb CO_2 from the atmosphere, (2) to learn the extent of global deforestation, (3) to develop better models for predicting the effects of increased atmospheric CO_2, particles, heat, and cloudiness on global and regional climate, and (4) to develop alternative ecological, agricultural, economic, social, and political plans to adapt to possible climate changes (Baes et al. 1977, Bryson 1974, Bryson & Murray 1977, Central Intelligence Agency 1974b, Elliot & Machta 1977, Gribbin 1977, Kellogg 1977, 1978, Mitchell 1975, National Academy of Sciences 1975g, 1977a, Ponte 1976, Schneider 1976a, 1976b, Siegenthaler & Oeschger 1978,

Singer 1975a, Smith 1978, Wilcox 1976, Woodwell 1978, Woodwell et al. 1978).

Such research is crucial, but it will take decades—perhaps after long-term and potentially harmful changes have already occurred. Because of this uncertainty, climatologist Stephen H. Schneider (1976b), as discussed in his Guest Editorial at the end of this chapter, has urged the world to store up several years of food as insurance against climate change and variability. In the Book of Genesis the pharaoh heeded Joseph's advice to store up food for the lean years. Hopefully, we will be wise enough to adopt a similar "genesis strategy" (Schneider 1976b).

When you understand all about the sun and all about the atmosphere and all about the rotation of the earth, you may still miss the radiance of the sunset.

Alfred North Whitehead

Guest Editorial: Climate and the Human Predicament

Stephen H. Schneider

Stephen H. Schneider is deputy head of the Climate Project at the National Center for Atmospheric Research in Boulder, Colorado. He is editor of the interdisciplinary, international journal Climate Change. *He has testified before various congressional committees on the issues of climatic change, food production, energy use, water supply, and weather control, and has served on the Carter-Mondale task force on science policy and on the Colorado Drought Council, which coordinated responses to the emergency drought situation in Colorado in 1977. In addition to publishing scores of scientific articles, he is author (with L. E. Mesirow) of* The Genesis Strategy: Climate and Global Survival. *Stephen Schneider is one of the new breed of highly competent scientists who combine humane concern with the ability to tackle important interdisciplinary problems.*

Climatic change is an important component of the human predicament—the problems of food, population, resources, and environment. But what really is the climate problem and what should we be doing about it? Some talk about famine from climate change, while others speak of wheat gluts from good weather. Much has also been written recently about such conflicting possibilities as the melting of the ice caps due to the "greenhouse effect" caused by air pollution and the triggering of a new ice age from dust and smoke. All this climatic confusion makes it very difficult to sort out a real message.

However, there is no single underlying climatic problem or message, but a series of them. In the short term, the main problem is to be sure that our society is not too vulnerable to the fluctuations in climate that have wreaked havoc on our crops, water supply, and energy demand in the past. For example, in 1972 dramatic fluctuations in food prices and dwindling of food reserves took place because of a shortened monsoon season in India, failure of much of the Russian wheat harvest, and failure of the Peruvian anchovy catch. Again in 1974 we suffered from a severe reduction in U.S. food productivity and another shortened monsoon season in India. Food reserves were cut in half, and bloated bodies of spindly-legged children in Africa and India were pictured on the covers of major magazines in 1974.

Since 1974 some modest gains in food reserves—mostly in the United States—have led to talk of a "wheat glut." But it must be recognized that the way to cope with short-term variations in climate is to maintain adequate food reserves and an accompanying distribution system that can cope with several climatic "lean years." This is what I have called "the Genesis strategy," after the biblical story of Joseph's advice to the pharaoh to stockpile food after seven fat years as a margin of safety against the possibility of a coming food shortage. As with food, we also need sufficient water reserves to prevent the kind of rationing that occurred in much of the drought-stricken western United States in 1976 and 1977. Finally, adequate reserves of energy, in particular natural gas, are essential to prevent sharp jumps in temporary unemployment, such as occurred when industrial concerns in a number of states were forced to shut down for lack of natural gas during the winter of 1977.

Another climate problem relates to long-term trends. In particular, the use of fossil fuels—coal, oil, and natural gas—generates pollution by-products such as carbon dioxide (CO_2). For decades carbon dioxide has been building up in the atmosphere, and this buildup can be expected to accelerate over the next several decades as more and more people use more and more fossil fuels. What does this mean climatically? The well-known greenhouse effect would, according to theoretical models, lead to a planetary warming, which could be as great as any warming in the last 5,000 years. In the next century, this warming could move grain belts, redistribute rain patterns, and perhaps even change the volume of glacial ice, thus altering the sea level and changing the coastline geography.

The interesting question here is, How do we verify the predictions of the climatic models, which suggest such drastic outcomes? Since we have never before experienced such a carbon dioxide buildup, theoretical models are the only way we can estimate the potential effect of this unprecedented environmental insult. If the models are correct, then it seems urgent that we either slow down the growth rates of industrial society or shift away from fossil fuels to other energy supply systems (some of which have other problems, even if they prove to be economically feasible). Unfortunately, such drastic decisions rest uneasily on climatic models that are far from certain.

We face a difficult choice. We can proceed along the current path, merely collecting data by studying the events (as many scientists have suggested we should), or we can begin to implement hedging policies, such as dramatic curbs on the growth rate of energy, strong efforts to increase the efficiency of energy use, and a major attack on the engineering problems that hinder the rapid deployment of one of the safest energy sources, the sun. These are not just technical issues, but issues that involve value judgments of whether the risks inherent in present climatic trends are justified by the benefits of continuing to use fossil fuels. Clearly, these value judgments must travel through the political process—the choice of what to do in the face of these uncertainties must not be made by technical committees of scientific "experts" but by all those affected, which is everybody.

From this brief discussion, it is clear that our climate problems cannot be divorced from the other human problems of population, food, resources, and environment. The pressures to pollute and thus possibly to change the climate are in direct proportion to population size and life-style demands. The economic and social costs of suddenly slowed growth have to be weighed against the economic and social costs of accelerated growth, which leads to a degraded environment. Perhaps reduced economic growth in the richer countries and temporary economic expansions in the poorer ones—what I have referred to as the "global survival compromise" in *The Genesis Strategy* (1976b)—would be appropriate.

Whatever growth strategy is chosen, it must be recognized that solutions to the human predicament lie not in one discipline or in one approach. Instead, solutions require a massive interdisciplinary effort that examines global systems as an interconnected group of subsystems and subproblems. Certainly, specialization has its place. Knowledge cannot be integrated into a realistic interdisciplinary approach if that knowledge has not first been obtained from rigorous work by disciplinary experts. Yet the very institutions at the forefront of new knowledge, the universities and academic laboratories, have been among the most resistant to interdisciplinary efforts. While we all face grave potential dangers, we find too many of the very people to whom society often looks for intellectual leadership and nonpartisan advice squabbling over the purity of disciplinary originality rather than looking for ways out of the human predicament. In the meantime, it is my hope that those of you who will make up the next generation of scholars will get your priorities straight in time to make a difference.

Guest Editorial Discussion

1. Stephen Schneider urges that we stockpile large reserves of food to aid starving people in times of famine, while some other scientists argue that we should stop giving away food since it only encourages population growth that in the long run leads to even greater famines. Which of these opposing views do you support? Why?

2. Do you believe that we should shift away from fossil fuels and drastically curtail energy use in order to prevent the potential heating up of the atmosphere several decades from now? Why? How would this affect your life?

3. How would you change the educational process to prepare you to tackle interdisciplinary problems and still provide you with the disciplinary base needed to deal with such problems?

Discussion Topics

1. Trace all of the direct and indirect effects you had today on local and global climate. Classify these activities as essential, desirable, or frivolous.

2. Explain why most radiation returning to space has longer wavelengths (lower energy) than incoming solar radiation.

Does this mean that less energy flows back than reaches the earth? Explain.

3. Criticize the following statements:

   a. A new ice age could spread across the United States by the year 2050.

   b. Massive global flooding would occur if we melted the floating Arctic ice pack.

   c. Massive global flooding near seacoasts could occur by the year 2050.

4. Explain how particles, depending on their size and location, cause the atmosphere (a) to cool, (b) to heat up.

5. Criticize the statement "We shouldn't worry about the heating up of the atmosphere from increased carbon dioxide levels because a warmer climate is more desirable."

6. What effect on the climate might each of the following have: (a) oil spills, (b) increased land under cultivation, (c) driving an air conditioned automobile, (d) switching on a light, (e) air conditioning your home or place of work, (f) strip mining, (g) using an electric dryer to dry hair or clothing, (h) switching from oil and coal power plants to nuclear power plants, (i) switching from fossil fuel and nuclear power plants to solar energy power plants?

7. Are the climate changes in urban areas shown in Table 9-2 desirable or undesirable in terms of human comfort and energy use during the winter and summer? Explain.

8. Criticize the statement "Human actions will not affect global climate for 100 to 200 years, so we need not be concerned with the problem now."

9. Debate the idea that we should set up a world food bank to store several years' food as insurance against climate change. How would you decide who gets this food in times of stress?

10. Some studies (Levin et al. 1972, Merriman 1970) have shown that thermal outputs from nuclear and fossil fuel plants have had no major ecological consequences so far. Why should we be concerned?

Further Readings

Baes, C. F., Jr., et al. 1977. "Carbon Dioxide and Climate: The Uncontrolled Experiment." *American Scientist*, vol. 65, 310–320. Excellent overview of this important problem.

Bolin, Bert. 1977. "The Impact of Production and Use of Energy in Global Climate." In *Annual Review of Energy*. Vol. 2. Palo Alto, Calif.: Annual Reviews. Superb overview of potential effects of human activities on climate. Highly recommended.

Bryson, Reid A., and Thomas J. Murray. 1977. *Climates of Hunger: Mankind and the World's Changing Weather*. Madison: University of Wisconsin Press. Excellent summary of why the world may be cooling. Highly recommended.

Bryson, Reid A., and John E. Ross. 1972. "The Climate of the City." In Thomas R. Detwyler and Melvin G. Marcus, eds., *Urbanization and Environment*. North Scituate, Mass.: Duxbury. Superb summary of urban climate effects.

Cairns, John, Jr. 1971. "Thermal Pollution—A Cause for Concern." *Journal of the Water Pollution Control Federation*, vol. 43, no. 1, 55–66. Outstanding summary of problems and solutions.

Calder, Nigel. 1974. *The Weather Machine: How Our Weather Works and Why It Is Changing*. New York: Viking. Very readable overview with emphasis on global cooling.

Elliot, W. P., and L. Machta, eds. 1977. *Proceedings of ERDA Workshop on Environmental Effects of Carbon Dioxide from Fossil Fuel Combustion*. Washington, D.C.: U.S. Department of Energy. Very useful, technical overview.

Holdren, John P. 1971. "Global Thermal Pollution." In J. P. Holdren and P. R. Ehrlich, eds., *Global Ecology*. New York: Harcourt Brace Jovanovich. Very clear summary of the calculations and principles involved in predicting the effects of human heat inputs on climate.

Kellogg, William W. 1977. "Global Influences of Mankind on the Climate." In John Gribbin, ed., *Climatic Change*. Cambridge: Cambridge University Press. Outstanding overview with emphasis on global warming. Highly recommended.

Lamb, H. H. 1972. *Climate: Present, Past and Future*. Vol. 1. London: Methuen. Very useful discussion of climatic history. See also Lamb 1977 (vol. 2).

Landsberg, H. E. 1970. "Man-Made Climatic Changes." *Science*, vol. 170, 1265–1274. Outstanding balanced summary. Highly recommended. Good bibliography.

National Academy of Sciences. 1975. *Understanding Climatic Change: A Program For Action*. Washington, D.C.: National Academy of Sciences. Superb overview.

SCEP (Study of Critical Environmental Problems). 1970. *Man's Impact on the Global Environment*. Cambridge, Mass.: MIT Press. Very useful and authoritative source.

Schneider, Stephen H. 1976. *The Genesis Strategy: Climate and Global Survival*. New York: Plenum Press. Outstanding overview of possible effects of human activities on climate with a detailed plan for action. Try to read this important book.

Woodwell, George M. 1978. "The Carbon Dioxide Question." *Scientific American*, vol. 238, no. 1, 34–43. Superb overview with emphasis on effects of land-clearing activities.

10

What We Must Do!

10-1 Hope: The People Are Stirring

A New Dream   Present undesirable trends do not necessarily indicate where we are heading. As René Dubos reminds us, *"Trend is not destiny." We can say no!* We can alter catastrophic trends if we choose to accept the sacrifices that all important transitions require and the joy that they produce. Nobel Prize winning chemist Glenn T. Seaborg (1970) urges us to look at the present and future with new eyes: "What we are seeing today in all our social upheavals, in all our alarm and anguish over an environmental feedback and, in general, the apparent piling of crisis upon crisis to an almost intolerable degree, is not a forecast of doom. It is the birthpangs of a new world." Or as Samuel Beckett put it, "We are between a death and a difficult birth."

If human behavior and institutions change in the next 50 years half as significantly as they did during the past 50 years, we can make the transition to an earthmanship society. Adopting an earthmanship consciousness means that we can no longer expect clean air and still drive big cars with internal combustion engines; instead, we must develop efficient mass and para transportation. We can no longer justify using and wasting the world's mineral, energy, and food resources at a rate that literally means misery and death for other human beings. We cannot continue to talk about peace, honor, brotherhood and sisterhood, justice, freedom, and wars on poverty while wasting enormous amounts of money and scarce resources on armaments.

Some Hopeful Signs   Is the achievement of an earthmanship society over the next few decades a hopeless, idealistic goal? Fortunately, the answer to this important question is no. There are growing signs that we can make such a transition. *Fifteen years ago only a few specialists had ever heard of the words ecology, pollution, and environment. Today in affluent nations there is a sophisticated awareness of these problems, and this knowledge is spreading to poor nations.*

Even more important, this awareness has been translated into action (Brown 1978b, Council on Environmental Quality, *Environmental Quality,* 1977, Esfandiary 1970, Seaborg 1970, Ward 1976). Today there are over 3,000 organizations worldwide devoted to environmental issues (Christman 1977). Most affluent nations have passed laws designed to protect the air, water, land, and wildlife from abuse. Nations are also getting together to begin dealing with global environmental problems. Between 1965 and 1977, 50 U.S. rivers, lakes, and streams were cleaned up and levels of many air pollutants in most U.S. cities have decreased since 1968 (Council on Environmental Quality, *Environmental Quality,* 1977). Smog in London has decreased sharply since 1952, and the river Thames is returning to life (Ward 1976). *The amazing thing is not a lack of progress but that so much progress has been made in only 15 years.*

J. M. Stycos has observed that major social changes go through four stages:

Phase 1: no talk, no do
Phase 2: talk, no do
Phase 3: talk, do
Phase 4: no talk, do

During the short period between 1965 and today, most U.S. citizens became aware of and concerned about the environment (Harnik 1978). In April 1970 just after the first Earth Day, polls showed that reducing pollution was the second most important national problem. Today it is still an important concern (Staff report 1978c). On the pollution front the United States has already moved into phase 3, with real progress on several environmental problems and more progress expected during the next decade.

Since 1970 a number of strong environmental protection laws have been passed and billions have been spent on pollution control. Since 1968 levels of many air pollutants have decreased in most U.S. metropolitan areas, and they should be reduced to acceptable levels in all but a few urban areas by 1990 (Staff report 1978c). California has set an example for the rest of the United States and the world by establishing stricter air pollution standards than the federal government.

The United States is behind schedule in achieving the congressional goal of fishable and swimmable waters by 1983. But significant progress has been made since 1970 in reducing water pollution. Nationwide analyses show significant improvement in water quality in most areas, and already 50 U.S. lakes, rivers, and streams have been cleaned up through public and private efforts (Council on Environmental Quality, *Environmental Quality,* 1977). Oregon has set an example by its massive cleanup of the Willamette River, by being the first state to pass a law encouraging the use of returnable bottles instead of throwaway cans, and by discouraging growth.

With regard to population the United States has made some hopeful movements into phase 3. Zero population growth is probably at least 50 years away because of the momentum from the youthful age structure, but the birth rate and total fertility rate fell dramatically between 1968 and 1976, rising slightly in 1977 and 1978. If these low rates can be maintained, especially through 1987, the United States could have a stable population by 2020, and perhaps as early as 2010.

Nevertheless, we shouldn't get carried away with rosy optimism. With respect to the energy crises, we are still in phase 2—much talk, little action. We have only started to deal with the complex energy problems facing us, but we have made an important beginning. Nurturing this hope into a new earthmanship society requires that we avoid several traps that prevent people from becoming involved.

We can make the transition to an earthmanship society within the next 50 years, only if we avoid three traps: (1) the *blind technological optimism* of those who believe that science and technology will always save us, (2) the *gloom-and-doom pessimism* of those who have given up hope, and (3) *apathy* resulting from a fatalistic outlook or a naive view of reality.

Making the transition to an earthmanship society means we can't just sit around and moan about our problems. In the words of E. F. Schumacher (1974):

> What we need are what I would call optimistic pessimists who can see clearly that we can't continue as before, but who have enough vigor and joyfulness to say, all right, so we change course. I know it can be done and will be done if people are not paralyzed by either the technological optimists or the doom-watching pessimists.

10–2 The Four Levels of Environmental Awareness and Action

The First Level: Pollution There are four levels of awareness of the ecological crisis (see the accompanying box). At the first level we discover the symptom, *pollution.* In only a few years pollution has become a major issue for most U.S. citizens (Staff report 1978c). Although this is very encouraging, it is also dangerous. As soon as we discover a problem, we want to fix blame. We are still engaged in an unhealthy, counterproductive phase of the environmental crisis—a "pollution witch hunt." We blame industry, government, technology, and the poor—anyone but ourselves. Of course, we must point out and stop irresponsible acts of pollution by large and small organizations and resist being duped by slick corporate advertising. But we must at the same time change our own life-styles. We have all been drilling holes in the bottom of our boat. Arguing over who is drilling the biggest hole only diverts us from working together to keep the leaky boat from sinking.

Another danger in remaining at the pollution awareness level is that it leads people to see the crisis as a problem comparable to a "moon shot," and to look for a quick solution. Have technology fix us up, send me the bill at the end of the month, but don't ask me to change my way of

---

Four Levels of Environmental Awareness

First level: Pollution. Discovering the symptoms.

Second level: Overpopullution. Seeing that population times per capita consumption times environmental impact equals ecosystem disruption and pollution.

Third level: Spaceship earth. Seeing the problem as a complex mix of physical, social, political, and economic factors. Everything is connected to everything and our job is to run and preserve the ship by controlling everything and everybody.

Fourth level: Earthmanship. Seeing the problem as a complex mix of physical, social, political, economic, and ethical factors. Everyone and everything is interconnected, and our job is to preserve stability, diversity, and human dignity and freedom by cooperating with nature and by caring and sharing. Because we can never know how everything or even most things are interconnected, we must exercise restraint and humility as trustees of the earth—not as its masters.

living. Using technology and spending enormous amounts of money will be necessary, but they are not enough.

The problem at the pollution level is that individuals and industries see their own impacts as too tiny to matter. This is what human ecologist Garrett Hardin (1968) calls the *tragedy of the commons*. Individuals and industries tend to pollute common resources such as air and water that are not owned by anyone; laws must be passed and enforced to protect these resources from abuse.

The Second Level: Overpopullution Many have already moved to the second level of awareness, the *overpopullution* level. The cause of pollution is not just people but their level of consumption and the environmental impact of various types of production, especially in developed nations. At the overpopullution level the answers seem obvious. We must simultaneously reduce the number of passengers in both rich and poor nations and the levels of consumption in rich nations. We also need to change to less harmful and wasteful consumption patterns, especially in the industrialized nations, which, with less than 30 percent of the world's population, account for about 90 percent of the environmental pollution.

The Third Level: Spaceship Earth But these changes will not even start until a reasonable number of leaders and citizens move to a third plateau of awareness, the *spaceship earth* level. At this point we recognize that the earth has limits and that our life-support system is vulnerable. We are forced to recognize that all human beings depend on each other and on the same life-support system and that protecting and preserving the ecosphere that sustains all life must be our primary goal.

The danger of the spaceship earth level is following the astronaut model too closely (Richardson 1973). To protect astronauts and their life-support system, every natural function must be rigidly controlled in a programmed existence. Instead of novelty, spontaneity, joy, and freedom, the spaceship model is based on cultural homogenization, social regimentation, artificiality, monotony, sameness, and gadgetry. We must control and manage parts of the ecosphere, but using a spaceship crew as the ultimate model for solving problems poses a dire threat to individual human freedom and to the ecosphere.

The Fourth Level: Earthmanship Recognizing our finiteness and interdependence and moving from a frontier world view to a spaceship world view constitute an important step. But this step is not enough. Somehow we must move to the *earthmanship* level. At this level we finally see that the solution to our problems lies in collaborating with nature and in selectively controlling nature using ecological understanding. Earthmanship is based on an ethic of creative earth stewardship. The important differences between the spaceship and earthmanship views (Table 10–1) are the recognition of *freedom* (versus control), *humility* (versus the assumption of total knowledge and control), deliberate preservation of *diversity* (versus artificial simplification), and *sharing* (versus greed). Or to put it in the words of Mahatma Gandhi, "There is enough for everybody's need but not for anybody's greed."

Earthmanship means that affluent nations must build a conserver society—a society which emphasizes the reduced use and waste of matter and energy resources and the increased use of intermediate, decentralized technology. Rich nations must also help poor nations to become more self-reliant and to develop appropriate technology that avoids the heavy resource use and heavy pollution now found in affluent nations. For more details on the meaning and challenges of earthmanship, see the Guest Editorial at the end of this chapter by Richard A. Falk.

Some may see earthmanship as "going back to nature." But this attitude is based on an idealized and romanticized view that nature's ways are somehow always kind, beautiful, and gentle. Such people do not know nature's harsh realities, confusing a desire to feel close to nature with living close to nature. A mass return to natural living would also mean death for billions of human beings. Long ago we exceeded the population carrying capacity for a world living at a low technological level. This option is available to only a few in an overcrowded world that has lost its technological and social virginity.

But this does not mean we can't make our life-styles and our mind rhythms more harmonious with natural cycles and adopt a philosophy of enoughness. Important examples of low consumption, appropriate technology, and ecologically sane alternatives to growth mania can be seen in the myriad of fragile but crucial experiments now being carried out in America, western Europe, and some developing nations. These activities include rural and urban communes, extended families, experiments in organic farming and appropriate technology, alternative nonprofit cooperative marketing groups, countermedia (such as *Mother Earth News*, *CoEvolution Quarterly*, the *Whole Earth Catalog* and *Epilog*, and the *Journal of the New Alchemists*), voluntary simplicity, do-it-yourself neighborhood urban renewal, the global ecology and feminist movements, and free schools and clinics. From such attempts to break out of the conventional urban-industrial-high-technology trap will come diverse and meaningful alternatives (Elgin & Mitchell 1977, Henderson 1978c). As in any transition period, many of these experiments will fail. But by searching for new meaning, a few experiments will survive to show others the way (Roszak 1972, Schumacher 1973).

Table 10-1 Stages of Cultural and Ecological Evolution

Characteristic	Stage			
	Primitive	Frontier	Spaceship	Earthmanship
Human relationship to nature	Humans *in* nature, but controlled by nature	Humans *vs.* nature: increased control over nature	Humans *vs.* nature: attempt at complete control	Humans *and* nature: selective control
Individual goals	Survival	Survival, high quality of life for self	Survival, high quality of life for everyone	Survival, high quality of life for everyone
Method of reaching goals	Try to get enough food, clothes, and shelter to stay alive	Produce, use, acquire as much as possible	Complete technological and social control of nature and people to avoid exceeding the limits of the earth	Selective control based on ecological understanding, diversity, cooperation, and caring to avoid exceeding the limits of the earth
Social units	Individual, tribe	Family, community, corporation, nation	Family, community, earth	Family, community, earth
Reward	Staying alive	Profit, efficiency, power	Survival, comfort, power	Survival, joy, purpose to life
Population	Reproduction to survive	Reproduction determined by economic and social factors	Reproduction controlled by the state	Reproduction controlled by a combination of voluntary action, education, and mutually agreed upon laws
Environmental quality	Not always a meaningful idea	A free good to be used and abused at will	A basic concept of critical value	A basic concept of critical value
Sharing wealth and resources	Not always a meaningful idea	A poor idea; acquire as much as possible	Crucial for survival	Crucial for survival

10-3 Principles of an Energy Plan for the United States

Basic Principles of a U.S. Energy Plan We can use the energy concepts and the evaluation of the various energy alternatives to help us develop the basic principles of an energy plan that would allow the United States to make the transition to a new earthmanship energy era over the next 50 years.[1] The box on pp. 154-55 lists principles for such an energy plan.

One highly controversial aspect of these suggested principles is the deregulation of natural gas and oil prices. This principle, however, is a very important part of the strategy to encourage massive energy conservation (Lovins 1978a). Even with the price rises since the 1973 oil embargo, the U.S. government has kept energy prices at moderate levels by regulating the price of natural gas and by keeping domestic oil prices well below prices for imported oil. From an international standpoint energy prices in the United States are still very low, which partially explains why conservation efforts in the United States have lagged so far behind those in most other industrialized nations (Hayes 1976a).

Congress believes it is performing a valuable service to consumers and the national economy when it keeps energy prices down. This belief is based on the false ideas that cheap energy increases consumer buying power and that high rates of per capita energy consumption are necessary for a high rate of economic growth (Ross & Williams 1977a). In fact, when government keeps energy prices down, domestic consumption is encouraged and domestic exploration and production is discouraged because of low

[1]For more information on proposed energy plans, see the following: Anthrop 1974, Armstrong & Willis 1975, Auer 1974, Bohi & Russell 1975, Boshier 1978, Brookings Institution 1975, Brown 1978a, 1978b, Brubaker 1975, Carter 1975, Clark 1974a, Coomer 1977, Craig et al. 1976, David 1973, Davis 1974, Ehrlich et al. 1977, Energy Policy Project 1974, Energy Research and Development Administration 1976c, Executive Office of the President 1977, Federal Energy Administration 1974a, 1976, Freeman 1974, Goldstein 1978, Hammond 1973b, 1974b, Hannon 1977a, Harman 1975, Hayes 1976a, 1977, Henderson 1978a, 1978b, Kalter & Vogely 1976, League of Women Voters Education Fund 1977a, 1977b, Lovins 1974, 1975, 1976, 1977a, 1977c, 1978a, Mead 1977, Meador 1978, Naill 1977, 1978, Nash 1977, Office of Emergency Preparedness 1972, Policy Study Group of the M.I.T. Energy Laboratory 1974, Rose 1974a, Ruzic 1978, Sporn 1974, Tavoulareas & Kaysen 1977, Udall 1973, Udall et al. 1974, U.S. Atomic Energy Commission 1973a, White 1973, Willrich 1975a, 1976, Wilson 1972, 1977.

profit levels (Hannon 1977b). This leads to rapid depletion of domestic resources and a widening gap between domestic supply and demand that must be made up by importing foreign crude oil. This loss of capital to other nations leads to increased inflation, lower consumer buying power, a lower rate of economic growth, increased unemployment, increased crime (because of the unemployment), and an increase in the size and authority of government so that it can deal with all of these problems (Hannon 1977a, Ross & Williams 1977a).

Thus, allowing energy prices to rise would increase—not decrease—consumer buying power. To be equitable, however, it is essential that price rises be coupled with tax rebates, energy stamps, lifeline low rates, or other schemes to see that poor and middle class citizens do not bear the brunt of the price increases and to ensure that energy companies do not reap excessive profits.

Higher energy prices would also tend to raise employment rates and help decrease centralized economic and political power by large energy companies and the federal government (Hannon 1977b, McCaull 1976b). Rising prices increase spending on conservation and the development of solar, wind, and other renewable resources and decrease spending for new coal and nuclear power plants and other energy production activities. The energy-producing industries are the most capital-intensive and least labor-intensive sector of the U.S. economy (Ehrlich et al. 1977, Hayes 1976a). By contrast, conservation and renewable energy-source activities are more decentralized and employ more people per unit of energy saved or produced. Thus, shifting money to these activities will increase employment and consumer buying power (Hannon 1977a, Hayes 1976a, McCaull 1976b, Subcommittee on Energy of the Joint Economic Committee, Congress of the United States 1978). Since energy conservation and solar and wind power can be developed competitively at the local level by small companies, they can help decrease the influence of large, centralized energy companies and centralized federal control (Lovins 1978a).

Another controversial principle is the suggestion that the large energy companies be broken up. The purpose of this action is twofold. First, it would eliminate the possibility of *horizontal* monopolistic control of energy prices and supplies, which occurs when one company or a group of companies own large shares of normally competing energy sources (such as oil, coal, natural gas, and uranium). Second, it would prevent the possibility of *vertical* monopolistic control of the prices and supply of a single energy source (such as oil), which occurs when oil companies own everything from the well to the gasoline pump. There are four ultimate monopolies over people's lives—control of air, water, food, and energy. Regardless of whether one believes that energy companies have conspired directly or indirectly to control energy supplies and prices, the potential for such control is clear and could increase.

Vertical integration of many oil companies—the control of every step of oil production and distribution—already exists (Blair 1976, Netscheat 1971, Novick 1976a, Peach 1973, Rand 1976, Sampson 1976). But the real danger in the long run is horizontal integration of many big oil companies, which can be more accurately described as energy companies (Lovins 1974, Medvin 1974, Sampson 1976, Senate Energy Committee 1977). Government investigations (General Accounting Office 1977, Senate Energy Committee 1977) have revealed that the large oil companies (1) own at least 70 percent of the U.S. natural gas reserves, (2) own 47 percent of economically recoverable U.S. uranium reserves and 41 percent of the uranium-milling capacities, (3) own 12 percent of the nation's recoverable coal reserves and 20 percent of the annual coal production, and (4) are moving to lease much of the richest oil shale and geothermal energy reserves on federal lands and to dominate the newly emerging coal gasification industry (Lovins 1974). Horizontal divestiture of holdings in several energy resources could be required by federal law, and the federal government could control the companies that are allowed to lease the large government-owned reserves of coal, oil shale, and geothermal resources (Figure 8-8). A Federal Energy Administration economist estimates that a breakup of the 18 largest oil companies would save consumers $6 to $8 billion dollars (*Washington Post*, July 6, 1977).

Energy companies and other opponents of vertical and horizontal divestiture (Anderson 1976, Markham et al. 1978) argue the following: (1) The oil industry is highly competitive and is not a monopoly, with no one company dominating more than 10 percent of the nation's petroleum supply, refining capacity, and retail sales; (2) vertical integration is commonplace in many U.S. industries and increases efficiency and service; (3) if oil companies are broken up, energy costs will rise and the amount of energy available will decrease because large, integrated companies can raise the large amounts of capital needed for energy exploration and development more readily; (4) it is in the best interests of the nation for oil companies to use their expertise and capital to develop other energy resources; and (5) there is no danger of an energy monopoly, since the four largest oil companies control only about 18 percent of the total national energy output (Markham et al. 1978). Thus, American citizens must weigh the risk of decreasing the efficiency of national energy production against the risk of a group of large energy companies gradually controlling more and more of the national energy supply and prices and thus gaining even greater political influence and control over individual lives.

The Present U.S. Short-Term Energy Plan After the 1973 oil embargo, Congress was prodded to pass a number of laws, including the Energy Reorganization Act of 1974, the Federal Nonnuclear Energy Research and Development Act

Basic Principles of a U.S. Energy Plan

1. Have the newly created Department of Energy (DOE) develop a comprehensive national energy plan for the short term (1980 to 1990), intermediate term (1990 to 2005), and long term (2005 to 2030), and implement a massive program to educate the American public and members of Congress about the nature of the four energy crises (Section 1-1).

2. Require net useful energy analysis based on a standardized set of guidelines to be applied to all estimates of remaining supplies of nonrenewable energy resources and to all evaluations of which mix of energy alternatives should form the basis for a national energy strategy.

3. Place primary emphasis on a massive energy conservation program (see Chapter 5 for details) to reduce energy waste, match energy quality with energy needs, decrease the environmental impact of energy use, reduce dependence on oil imports, save money, decrease the total and average per capita use of energy, and buy time to develop and phase in a mix of other energy alternatives before fossil fuel supplies (especially oil and natural gas) are depleted. Devote more money to developing improved methods of conservation and to alternatives for the internal combustion engine.

4. Deregulate domestic oil and natural gas prices and allow them to rise to world price levels no later than 1985, rather than keeping them artificially low. This will stimulate energy conservation and energy exploration and give consumers a more realistic view of the four energy crises. Price rises, however, must be coupled with a program to ensure that poor and lower middle class citizens do not bear the brunt of price increases. This program might consist of one or more of the following methods: (a) tax rebates, (b) guaranteed low price for a basic "lifeline" energy supply, and (c) an energy stamp program (somewhat like the present food stamp program). Energy companies that don't devote a standardized portion of their increased profits to energy conservation, a search for new fossil fuel supplies, or development of other energy alternatives would have excessive profits taxed at a very high rate.

5. Encourage conservation by (a) using positive incentives such as tax credits for individuals and companies that insulate their homes or buildings or that install solar heating or other energy-saving devices and (b) changing building codes and money-lending policies that hinder energy conservation efforts.

6. Use positive financial incentives to stimulate the exploration for and development of additional domestic supplies of oil and natural gas while employing strict environmental controls. This should be done with the clear public understanding that new supplies will merely buy time to find energy alternatives and will not solve the nation's energy problems in the intermediate and long term.

7. Set aside a 1-year supply of emergency oil by 1985 (Executive Office of the President 1977, Federal Energy Administration 1974a, Odum 1973) and a 2-year supply by 1990 to prevent an oil embargo, to keep world oil prices from rising too rapidly, and to reduce chances of international conflict over remaining world oil supplies. Also, set aside 10 percent of all undeveloped oil and natural gas reserves to supply petrochemical industries in the future.

---

of 1974, the Energy Policy and Conservation Act of 1976, the Energy Conservation and Production Act of 1976, and finally, after almost 2 years of delay and vigorous debate, the National Energy Act of 1978. The acts passed prior to 1978 included some important steps, such as (1) establishing a national 88-kilometer-per-hour (55-mile-per-hour) speed limit, (2) requiring automobiles to get an average of 8.5 kilometers per liter (20 miles per gallon) by 1980 and 12 kilometers per liter (27.5 miles per gallon) by 1985, (3) providing funds to stockpile a 3-month supply of oil by 1985, (4) requiring all major appliances to have labels indicating energy efficiency or average annual operating cost, (5) significantly increasing budget allocations for energy research and development, and (6) establishing the Federal Energy Administration (FEA) to oversee national energy policy and the Energy Research and Development Administration (ERDA) to oversee research and development of energy alternatives. But despite these and other encouraging changes, none of the new laws represented a comprehensive short-, intermediate-, or long-term plan.

In April 1977 President Carter presented his National Energy Plan (Executive Office of the President 1977). The proposed plan represented the first major attempt to develop a comprehensive short-term energy plan (to 1985)

8. Prohibit any energy company, such as an oil company, from owning stock, reserves, or major patents in any other energy alternative. This should increase competition and reduce the possibility of horizontal monopolistic control of energy prices and supplies. The present practice of allowing oil companies to own and control oil from the well to the gas pump should also be prohibited in order to encourage competition and reduce the possibility of vertical monopolistic control of oil and gasoline prices and supplies.

9. Institute a massive crash program for net useful energy evaluation and the development and phasing in of a mix of decentralized energy alternatives based on renewable energy flows, such as sunlight, wind, and vegetation (biomass) (Lovins 1976, 1977c, 1978a).

10. Increase the use of coal to produce electricity for the short term (1980 to 1990) and perhaps for the intermediate term (1990 to 2005) in order to reduce dependence on imported oil. However, this use must employ strict environmental controls and be applied only to take up any slack not provided by massive energy conservation. Increase research and development on the more efficient burning of coal (fluidized beds and magnetohydrodynamic conversion) and on increased pollution control for coal-burning power plants. Also emphasize research and development of coal gasification, coal liquefaction, and oil shale, but phase these techniques in rapidly only if they are feasible from net useful energy, economic, and environmental standpoints.

11. Consider establishing a Federal Energy Company that would (a) store a 2-year supply of emergency oil by 1990, (b) evaluate and aid in the development of coal gasification, coal liquefaction, oil shale, and geothermal energy, (c) direct the crash program for evaluating and developing nonrenewable energy alternatives (sunlight, wind, and biomass) (Carr 1976).

12. Institute a moratorium on the building of any new conventional nuclear power plants and shelve plans to develop nuclear breeder reactors. The goal should be to phase out nuclear power by 2005 unless the crash program on renewable energy resources (principle 9) reveals that these sources cannot begin to replace fossil fuels by 2030. A successful energy conservation program (principle 3) should eliminate the need for any new nuclear power plants between 1980 and 2000. In effect, the rapidly escalating costs of nuclear power have already produced such a moratorium (see Section 7–1), and such a moratorium will not have any catastrophic effects on energy use between 1980 and 2010 (Institute for Energy Analysis 1976). Use nuclear energy research funds to (a) evaluate net useful energy yield for the entire system, (b) improve nuclear plant safety, (c) prevent shipments of nuclear materials from being hijacked to make atomic bombs, (d) develop a safe method for the long-term storage of radioactive wastes, and (e) develop and evaluate nuclear fusion.

13. Stabilize the U.S. population at about 250 million by 2015.

14. Carefully integrate energy plans with those for population control, land use, agriculture, nonfuel mineral resources, water resources, and pollution control.

and to include a careful balance of a number of the principles suggested in this section. The plan was built around the principles of (1) greatly increasing energy conservation by 1985, (2) increasing but not deregulating the prices of domestic oil and natural gas, (3) increasing the use of coal through 1985, (4) establishing a strategic oil reserve to meet needs for about 10 months by 1985, (5) shelving indefinitely plans to build a nuclear breeder demonstration reactor, (6) increasing funding for development of solar, wind, and biomass energy alternatives, and (7) creating a Department of Energy (DOE) to oversee national energy policy and energy research and development, replacing FEA and ERDA.[2]

As expected, many members of Congress, oil companies, and some economists, environmentalists, and other specialists criticized the plan (Goldstein 1978, Mead 1977, Naill 1977, Novick 1977, Wells 1977a). Oil companies and some economists complained that deregulation of energy prices was necessary to stimulate domestic exploration and production (Mead 1977), and some environmentalists argued that without deregulation energy conservation goals

[2] Actually the DOE was part of a separate reorganization plan submitted to Congress, but it was an important part of the president's national energy strategy.

could not be met (Lovins 1978a). Environmentalists applauded the emphasis on energy conservation (Lovins 1978a, Naill 1977) and the shelving of the potentially dangerous nuclear breeder reactor (Section 7–2). But some criticized the failure of the plan (1) to attempt reducing the amount of energy used each year rather than merely reducing the rate of growth of energy use by 1.5 percent between 1978 and 1985 (Hohenemser 1977), (2) to declare a moratorium on the further use of conventional nuclear power (Hohenemser 1977, Wells 1977a),[3] (3) to provide a massive crash program to develop solar, wind, and biomass energy alternatives (Lovins 1978a), and (4) to develop an intermediate- and long-term national energy strategy.

The proposed National Energy Plan was subjected to intense and often conflicting lobbying pressures from the oil industry, the coal industry, labor unions, environmental groups, and special consumer groups. As a result, the National Energy Act of 1978 which emerged from Congress after almost 2 years of intense debate bore only modest relationship to the original plan. Some efforts to encourage energy conservation remained, but many of the important measures were eliminated; one result is that the original 1985 conservation goals will not be met. Tax credits for homeowners who install insulation, solar heating, and energy-saving equipment were retained. Conservation of natural gas and stimulation of domestic production were encouraged by allowing prices to rise more than proposed in the original plan. Taxes on gas-guzzling cars not meeting specified mileage standards were retained, but vans, pickup trucks, and recreational vehicles were exempted from the tax. A proposed standby tax on gasoline to encourage conservation was not passed, but the federal income tax deduction for state and local taxes on gasoline was eliminated. A proposed federal requirement that utility rates be restructured to encourage conservation by having small users of electricity pay the lowest rather than the highest rates was not passed. The federal government, however, was given the right to intervene and exert pressure on state and local utility commissions to reform rates, and utilities will be required to buy excess power from industries that produce their own power from waste heat (cogeneration). The proposed wellhead tax on oil was eliminated so that wasteful use of oil and gasoline will continue and dangerous dependence on imports will not be reduced nearly enough by 1985. A tax credit was provided, however, for equipment used to produce synthetic oil from oil shale and synthetic natural gas from coal by using an underground (in situ) conversion process (Sec-

tion 6–2). The hopes of increasing the use of coal from 19 percent of all energy used in 1977 to 25 percent by 1985 were undermined. Industries that install energy-saving equipment and convert from oil or gas to coal will be given a tax credit (the carrot). But the proposal to impose strict penalties on industries not making such a switch (the stick) was eliminated, and burning oil and natural gas to generate electricity will not be banned until after 1990 except in special cases for environmental reasons. The controversial nuclear breeder demonstration reactor was shelved, but Congress voted funds to continue large-scale research on this project. Increased funding for research and development of energy alternatives was approved, but no crash program was instituted. In separate legislation the Department of Energy (DOE) was officially established.

Federal expenditures for energy research and development have increased sixfold since 1973. But as Table 10–2 reveals, total spending is still a drop in the bucket compared with the importance of energy to American society. *The total government energy research and development expenditure approved by Congress for 1979 was no more than the amount that the United States spends on the research and development needed to build three nuclear aircraft carriers.* Table 10–2 also reveals that despite official statements that nuclear energy should be downplayed, it still makes up the largest fraction (29 percent) of the total energy budget. About half of this amount is being used to develop the breeder reactor, which is supposed to have been shelved indefinitely. Environmentalists have become increasingly alarmed over this commitment to nuclear power at the expense of renewable solar, wind, and biomass alternatives. This fear was heightened by the fact that former Department of Energy Secretary James R. Schlesinger was once head of the now defunct Atomic Energy Commission and that in 1978 the Department of Energy had 1,700 employees involved in nuclear energy development work (1,300 field persons and 400 people at the Washington headquarters) compared with less than 50 people working on wind and solar energy research (Staff report 1978i).

10–4 What Can You Do?

Finally, it all comes down to what you and I are willing to do as individuals and in groups. Begin with yourself.

1. *You can sensitize yourself to your environment.* Stand up, look around, compare what is with what could and should be. Examine your room, your home, your school, your place of work, your street, and your city, state, nation, and world. What things around you really improve the quality of your life? What are your own environmental bad habits?

---

[3]Energy expert Amory Lovins (Staff report 1977f), however, has argued that the proposed plan amounts to a nuclear moratorium because it provides no government subsidies to bail the nuclear industry out of its present economic difficulties and because it encourages energy conservation and the increased use of coal, practices that would eliminate the need for any new nuclear power plants.

Table 10–2 Approved Federal Expenditures for Energy Research and Development for 1979

Program	Expenditure (millions of dollars)	Percentage of Total Energy Budget	Approximate Military Expenditure Equivalents
Nuclear energy	1,132	29	One missile-carrying submarine
Breeder fission	608	15	Two conventional submarines
Conventional fission	297	8	One conventional submarine
Fusion	227	6	Three long-range bombers
Conservation	792	20	One conventional aircraft carrier
Fossil fuel energy	577	15	Four destroyers
Basic energy research and technology development	338	9	Four long-range bombers
Solar energy	321	8.6	Three long-range bombers and one F-15 fighter plane
General science and research	307	8	Three B-1 bombers
Environmental research and development	186	5	Two long-range bombers
Geothermal energy	133	3	One destroyer
Wind energy	54	1.4	Four F-15 fighter planes
Biomass energy	24	0.5	Two F-15 fighter planes
Hydroelectric energy	23	0.5	Two F-15 fighter planes
Total	3,887	100	Three nuclear-powered aircraft carriers

Source: Staff report 1978h.

2. *You can become ecologically informed.* Give up your frontier, or linear, thinking and immerse yourself in earthmanship thinking. Don't fall into the "all growth is good" and "technology will save us" traps. Specialize in one particular area of the ecological crisis and pool your specialized knowledge with others. Everyone doesn't need to be an ecologist, but you do need to "ecologize" your particular profession or job.

3. *You can choose a simpler life-style, reducing your energy and matter consumption and waste and entropy (pollution) production.* Go on an energy, matter, and entropy diet. For every high-energy or high-entropy thing you do (having a child, buying a car, living or working in an air conditioned building), give up a number of other things. Where possible, use low or intermediate technology instead of high-level technology. Such a life-style will be cheaper, and it may add more joy as you learn how to break through the plastic, technological membrane that separates us from nature and from one another.

4. *You can remember that environment begins at home.* Before you start converting others, begin by changing your own living patterns. Move closer to work, ride a bicycle to the shopping center or to work, refuse to buy beer and soft drinks in throwaway cans and bottles. Be prepared for the fact that if you become an ecological activist, everyone will be looking for and pointing out your own ecological sins.

5. *You can avoid the extrapolation-to-infinity syndrome as an excuse for not doing anything*—the idea that if we can't change the entire world quickly, then we won't change any of it. While most people are talking about the difficulties of changing the system, others (such as Rachel Carson, Ralph Nader, and Martin Luther King) went ahead and changed it.

6. *You can become politically involved on local and national levels.* Start or join a local environmental group, and also join national organizations. Become the ecosphere citizen of your block or school. Use positive synergy to amplify your efforts. We would see major improvements in the environment if each of us made an annual donation to one or more politically active environmental organizations. In this way you are hiring professional lobbyists, lawyers, and experts to work for you. Better yet, volunteer your services to such organizations. Work to elect earthmanship leaders and to influence officials once they are elected.

7. *You can do the little things.*[4] Individual acts of consumption, litter, and so on, have contributed to the mess. When you are tempted to say this little bit won't hurt, multiply it by millions of others saying the same thing. Picking up a single beer can, not turning on a light, using a car pool, writing on both sides of a piece of paper, and not buying a grocery product with more packages inside of the outer package are all very significant acts. Each small act reminds us of ecological thinking and leads to other ecologically sound practices.

---

[4]For detailed lists, see the following: Cailiet et al. 1971, Fritsch et al. 1977, Koestner et al. 1971, Saltonstall 1971, Sickle 1971.

Start now, with a small concrete personal act and then expand your actions in ever widening circles. Little acts can be used to expand our awareness of the need for fundamental changes in our political, economic, and social systems over the next few decades. These acts also help us avoid psychological numbness when we realize the magnitude of the job to be done.

8. *You can work on the big polluters and big problems, primarily through political action.* Individual actions help reduce pollution, give us a sense of involvement, and help us develop a badly needed ecological consciousness. Our awareness must then expand to recognize that large-scale pollution and environmental disruption are caused by industries, municipalities, and big agriculture. Picking up a beer can is significant, but it does not mean we can allow uncontrolled strip mining of coal in South Dakota.

9. *You can start a counter J curve of awareness and action.* The world is changed by changing the two people next to you. For everything, big or little, that you decide to do, make it your primary goal to convince two others to do the same thing and persuade them in turn to convince two others. Carrying out this doubling process only 28 times would convince everyone in the United States. After 32 doublings everyone in the world would be convinced.

10. *Don't make people feel guilty.* If a couple has several children or if neighbors are overconsuming, don't make them feel bad. Instead, find the things that each individual is willing to do to help our environment. There is plenty to do and no one can do everything. Use positive rather than negative reinforcement (win-win rather than win-lose games). We need to nurture, reassure, and understand rather than threaten one another.

Begin at the individual level and work outward in ever widening circles. Join with others and amplify your actions. This is the way the world is changed. Envision the world as made up of all kinds of cycles and flows in an incredibly beautiful and diverse web of interrelationships and kaleidoscope of patterns and rhythms whose very complexity and multitude of potentials remind us that cooperation, honesty, humility, and love must be the guidelines for our behavior toward one another and the earth.

Indifference is the essence of inhumanity.

George Bernard Shaw

Guest Editorial: The Challenge of Earthmanship

Richard A. Falk

Richard A. Falk is Albert E. Milbank Professor of International Law and Practice at Princeton University. He is a Senior Fellow of the Institute of World Order and has served as Director of American participation in the World Order Models Project since its start in 1968. He has written hundreds of articles and a number of important books (Falk 1971a, 1971b, 1975, Falk & Mendlovitz 1966, 1967, 1973) emphasizing the need for world order and describing how we can make the transition to a world order society. He is an example of an outstanding earthmanship thinker and leader.

Barely noticed by Americans as yet, a remarkable development has occurred in the late 1970s. Throughout western Europe, Japan, and to a lesser extent North America, a militant struggle against reliance on nuclear energy has taken shape. This international opposition to nuclear power is virtually without precedent. The movement is growing in numbers and intensity. In West Germany, where as many as 15 million are actively associated with antinuclear citizens' groups, demonstrations have involved hundreds of thousands, have caused large-scale combat with the police, and have led to a virtual moratorium on the construction of new nuclear reactors. Two hundred thousand people took part in an antinuclear protest in Bilbao, Spain, during July 1977; weeks later in France, a demonstrator was killed in a clash with the police. The nuclear controversy is the first battleground on which the potency of earthmanship as a challenge to the prevailing order has been revealed.

Of course, there are many strong beliefs on both sides of the nuclear debate. A social movement reveals its character by the outlook of its most committed adherents. In essence, I believe the struggle over nuclear power pits the forces of system maintenance against the forces of system change. Advocates of nuclear power believe, by and large, that if this technological energy solution can take place without disruption, the stability and prosperity of industrial civilization can be sustained and gradually spread to the rest of the world. Opponents, while skeptical of these claims, rest their case mainly on the convictions that nuclear power is too sinister a technology to entrust to human institutions, that its deployment threatens the sanctity of life and prospects for humane governance, and that more benign energy alternatives exist.

In the wider setting of global policy, the nuclear issue is a microcosm of contending world views on the most momentous challenge that has ever confronted the human species: learning to cope with the emergent realities of an *inevitable* social, economic, political, cultural, and ecological order of *planetary scale.* Institutions don't learn, only people learn. Individuals, especially those whose attitudes are not shaped by the roles they play in the existing system, can learn to reshape their expectations and behavior—although it is difficult. Often young people and artists play critical roles in cultural innovation, which is why these groups are so quickly perceived as threatening to guardians of the established order.

Throughout the world this process of challenge to existing structures and resistance to demands for change is taking place. Only in the Western world do we associate the impulse to earthmanship with the antinuclear movement. Throughout Asia, Africa, and Latin America the impulse is associated with the struggle to create independent and fair national societies that are able to meet the basic needs of their people. In the Third World earthmanship means primarily struggling to establish social, economic, and political arrangements that allow the mass of a population to live free from misery and repression. It is not surprising that this struggle engenders powerful resistance from entrenched leaders eager to retain privileged positions of wealth and power. The realities of population growth make it seem impossible to keep the privileged sectors of society satisfied while binding the wounds of the poor. We witness, then, a strong tendency for moderate government to collapse and be replaced by authoritarianism of some form, whether it appeals to the left or right. The global rise of authoritarian government has an ominous bearing on the hopes for a new orientation toward reality—what we are calling earthmanship.

In America and some other liberal democracies, a series of discoveries are being made about the conditions for human development in our time. Such discoveries begin with individuals and communities. These include organic farming and eating, equality in social and economic relations, and planetary citizenship. The lure of voluntary simplicity (Elgin & Mitchell 1977) emerges to displace the lure of affluence;

global humanism supersedes traditional patriotism; decentralized images of organization with the emergence of appropriate technologies for human scale seize hold of the imagination.

Somewhere in this process belongs a utopian vision, to guide the transition to an earthmanship society. And utopias are born in creative, questing minds. Ursula Le Guin's fine book, *The Dispossessed,* exhibits the impulse to achieve such a cultural revolution. It also resists the temptation to depict a new Eden as an easy solution not beset by contradictions of its own; she has set forth, in her words, ''an ambiguous utopia.'' Others are beginning to design just world order systems for the future. Rearrangements of power and wealth are taking shape that embody what must be done to provide self-sustaining development paths for the poor of the world and for humanity as a whole. An undertaking such as the World Order Models Project has this as its central ambition, linking scholars from the major regimes and cultures of the world in a continuing search for new political forms to make human governance, and hence earthmanship, possible.

As in any period of transition the evidence points in both directions. Virtually everywhere state power is growing and assuming more control over lives and destiny. At the same time even political leaders speaking from the pinnacles of state power are beginning to acknowledge that fundamental changes are necessary, although their roles discourage any appropriate actions. In fact, promises of a new world order, of human rights, of satisfaction of basic needs for everyone, and of nonmaterialist priorities are being made to the peoples of the world while the old order perfects neutron bombs and finds more fiendish means to torture its opponents. The mystification and hypocrisy of this gap between promise and performance are beginning to cast doubts in many minds as to whether it is any longer possible to leave the future in the hands of government. An impulse to act grows stronger as the case for change becomes more imperative. The challenge of earthmanship is an invitation to join in the struggle to transform the values and institutions of this world so as to make us feel positive and joyful about the future of the planet and about our own gifted, tormented species.

Guest Editorial Discussion

1. What major global issues represent an attempt to come to grips with the concept of earthmanship?

2. Compare the concepts of earthmanship for developed and developing nations.

3. Do you agree that it may no longer be possible to leave the future in the hands of government? What are the alternatives?

Discussion Topics

1. As a class, list the rationalizations that we typically use to avoid thought, action, and responsibility.

2. Do you agree with the cartoon character Pogo that "we have met the enemy and he [or she] is us"? Why or why not? Criticize this statement from the viewpoint of the poor; from the viewpoint that large corporations and government are the really big polluters.

3. Distinguish carefully between the spaceship earth and earthmanship world views.

4. Do you agree with the characteristics of the human cultural and ecological stages summarized in Table 10–1? Can you add other characteristics?

5. Do you agree or disagree with the following propositions? Defend your choice.

   a. To conserve finite and dwindling supplies of oil and natural gas, the United States should shift back to coal and ease air pollution and strip mining regulations to make this possible.

   b. The energy crisis of the early 1970s was staged by the major oil companies to drive prices up, increase profits, and eliminate competition from independent gas stations.

   c. To conserve finite and dwindling supplies of oil and natural gas and to decrease reliance on imports, the United States should shift to nuclear power, especially the breeder reactor, as soon as possible.

   d. The price of electricity and domestic fossil fuels in the United States should be increased significantly in order to promote energy conservation and to reduce environmental impact of energy use.

   e. The United States should not be overly concerned about foreign oil imports because they improve international relationships and prevent the nation from depleting its own remaining oil and natural gas supplies.

   f. The United States uses far too much energy relative to its needs and should institute a program designed to cut average per capita energy use by at least 35 percent.

   g. The United States should declare a moratorium on the building and licensing of any new nuclear power plants until there is greater assurance of their safety and of the feasibility of safe transportation and long-term nuclear waste storage.

   h. A mandatory energy conservation program should form the basis of an energy policy for the United States.

   i. The vertical and horizontal structure of the major oil or energy companies should be broken up within the next 10 years.

   j. A National Energy Company, supported by taxes, should be established to develop and control about one-fourth to one-third of U.S. energy resources in competition with major energy companies in order to protect the consumer from rising prices.

   k. A National Energy Company should be created, but instead of competing directly with private energy companies, its mission should be to develop a 2-year reserve supply of oil and gas and to develop solar, wind, biomass, and geothermal energy.

   l. All we need to do to solve the energy crisis is to find more oil and natural gas.

   m. All we need to do to solve the energy crisis is to learn how to recycle energy.

Further Readings

See also the references for Chapters 1 and 4.

Cailiet, G., et al. 1971. *Everyman's Guide to Ecological Living.* New York: Macmillan. Superb summary of what you can do.

Caldwell, Lynton K., et al. 1976. *Citizens and the Environment: Case Studies of Popular Action.* Bloomington: Indiana University Press. The best available summary of what citizens can do to improve the environment. Highly recommended.

Callahan, Daniel. 1973. *The Tyranny of Survival.* New York: Macmillan. Magnificent analysis contrasting earthmanship ethics and spaceship earth ethics. Try to read this book.

Callenbach, Ernest. 1975. *Ecotopia.* Berkeley, Calif.: Banyan Tree Books. Stirring vision of what the world could be like in 1990 if we move to an earthmanship society. Highly recommended.

Elgin, Duane, and Arnold Mitchell. 1977. "Voluntary Simplicity (3)." *CoEvolution Quarterly,* Summer, pp. 4–27. Superb description of the trend toward an earthmanship life-style. Highly recommended.

Fritsch, Albert J., et al. 1977. *99 Ways to a Simple Lifestyle.* Bloomington: University of Indiana Press. Outstanding summary. Try to read this book and pass it on to others.

Fromm, Eric. 1968. *The Revolution of Hope: Toward a Humanized Technology.* New York: Harper & Row. Excellent analysis of hope, going beyond the typical superficial approach. Effective antidote to despair.

Gardner, John W. 1970. *The Recovery of Confidence.* New York: Norton. Hope is the driving force of human action. Highly recommended.

Hardin, Garrett. 1977. *The Limits of Altruism: An Ecologist's View of Survival.* Bloomington: University of Indiana Press. Superb and controversial discussion of environmental ethics. Highly recommended. See also Hardin 1968, 1974, 1976c, 1978.

Heilbroner, Robert L. 1974. *An Inquiry into the Human Prospect.* New York: Norton. A noted economist and thinker is very pessimistic about our future.

Henderson, Hazel. 1978. *Creating Alternative Futures.* New York: Berkley. Excellent description of exciting experiments and trends that could lead to an earthmanship society. Try to read this book.

Livingston, John A. 1973. *One Cosmic Instant.* Boston: Houghton Mifflin. Superb and readable summary of human cultural evolution and relationship to nature.

Miller, G. Tyler, Jr. 1979. *Living in the Environment.* 2nd ed. Belmont, Calif.: Wadsworth. My own more detailed text on major environmental problems and possible solutions to these problems.

Nicholson, Max. 1973. *The Big Change: After the Environmental Revolution.* New York: McGraw-Hill. Superb analysis of the major changes we must make within the next 50 years. Highly recommended.

Platt, John R. 1966. *The Step to Man.* New York: Wiley. An important and insightful book written by one of the most brilliant ecosphere thinkers on this planet. Try to read this important collection of essays.

Sickle, D. V. 1971. *The Ecological Citizen.* New York: Harper & Row. Excellent handbook of what you can do.

Stivers, Robert L. 1976. *The Sustainable Society.* Philadelphia: Westminster. Excellent discussion of environmental ethics and an earthmanship society.

Watt, Kenneth E. F. 1974. *The Titanic Effect: Planning for the Unthinkable.* Stamford, Conn.: Sinauer. Superb overview of our problems and their possible solutions. Highly recommended.

Epilogue

This book is based on nine deceptively simple theses:

1. The ecological crisis is not only more complex than we think but more complex than we can ever think.

2. In Garrett Hardin's terms, the basic principle of ecology is "that everything and everyone are all interconnected." Truly accepting this and trying to learn how things and people are connected will require a basic change in our patterns of living. But because we can never completely know how everything is connected, we must function in the ecosphere with a sense of humility and creative cooperation rather than blind domination.

3. On a closed spaceship there are no consumers, only users of materials. We can never really throw anything away. This is a threat to a frontier society, but an opportunity for reuse, recycling, and conservation of matter resources in an earthmanship society.

4. Because of the first law of thermodynamics, we can't get anything for nothing, and because of the second law of thermodynamics almost every action we take has some undesirable impact on our environment, or life-support system. As a result, there can be no completely technological solution to pollution on a spaceship, although technology can help. If the number of passengers and their wasteful use of energy and materials continue to increase, the quality of life can only decline, eventually threatening survival for many passengers.

5. Because we have rounded the bend on the J curves of population, resource and energy use, and pollution, we could now seriously disrupt our life-support system.

6. The implication of these ideas is that each of us, and particularly those in the affluent middle and upper classes, must now give up certain things and patterns in our lives to prevent a continuing decrease in freedom and in the quality of life for all.

7. Our primary task must be to move from simplistic, linear thinking to circular, cybernetic thinking that is harmonious with the ecological cycles that sustain us; we must form a dynamic, diverse, adaptable, steady state, earthmanship society that is in keeping with the fundamental rhythms of life.

8. Informed action based on hope rather than on pessimism, technological optimism, or apathy offers humankind its greatest opportunity to come closer to that elusive dream of peace, freedom, brotherhood, sisterhood, and justice for all.

9. It is not too late, if . . . . There is time—50 years—to deal with these complex problems if enough of us really care. It's not up to "them," but to "us." Don't wait.

References

References preceded by an asterisk (*) are recommended for a basic environmental library.

Abelson, Philip H. 1976. "Glamorous Nuclear Fusion," *Science*, vol. 193, 279.

Abelson, Philip H. 1978. "Five Years of Energy Paralysis," *Science*, vol. 201, 775.

*Abrahamson, Dean E. 1972. "Ecological Hazards from Nuclear Power Plants." In M. T. Farvar and J. P. Milton, eds. *The Careless Technology: Ecology and International Development.* Garden City, N.Y.: Natural History Press.

Ackerman, Adolph J. 1972. "Atomic Power: Fallacies and Facts," *IEEE Transactions on Aerospace and Electronic Systems*, vol. AES-8, no. 5, 576–582.

*Adams, Anthony. 1975. *Your Energy Efficient House.* Charlotte, Vt.: Garden Way.

*Adkins, Jan. 1974. "How To Cut Fat Out of Your Home Energy Budget," *Smithsonian*, March, pp. 54–64.

*Alfvén, Hannes. 1972. "Energy and Environment," *Bulletin of the Atomic Scientists*, May, pp. 5–7.

*Alfvén, Hannes. 1974. "Fission Energy and Other Sources of Energy," *Bulletin of the Atomic Scientists*, January, pp. 4–8.

*Allen, A. R. 1975. "Coping with the Oil Sands." In L. C. Ruedisili and M. W. Firebaugh, eds., *Perspectives on Energy.* New York: Oxford University Press.

Altshuler, Alan. 1977. "The Politics of Urban Transportation Innovation," *Technology Review*, May, pp. 51–58.

Alves, Ronald, and Charles Milligan. 1978. *Living with Energy: Alternative Sources in Your Home.* New York: Penguin.

American Assembly. 1976. *The Nuclear Power Controversy.* Englewood Cliffs, N.J.: Prentice-Hall.

*American Chemical Society. 1978. *Cleaning Our Environment: The Chemical Basis for Action*, 2nd ed. Washington, D.C.: American Chemical Society.

*American Nuclear Society. 1976. *Nuclear Power and the Environment.* Hinsdale, Ill.: American Nuclear Society.

*American Physical Society. 1975. *Efficient Use of Energy.* New York: American Institute of Physics.

*American Physical Society. 1979. *Principal Conclusions of the American Physical Society Study Group on Solar Photovoltaic Energy Conversion.* New York: American Physical Society.

Anderson, Earl V. 1976. "Divestiture Is a Four-Letter Word, to Some," *Chemical and Engineering News*, May 31, pp. 8–9.

*Anderson, Earl V. 1978. "Gasohol: Energy Mountain or Molehill?" *Chemical and Engineering News*, July, pp. 8–15.

*Anderson, Bruce N., and Michael Riordon. 1976. *The Solar Home Book.* (EARS) (TEA).

*Anderson, Bruce N., and Charles J. Michael. 1978. "Passive Solar Design." In Jack M. Hollander et al., eds., *Annual Review of Energy*, vol. 3. Palo Alto, Calif.: Annual Reviews.

*Anderson, E. W., et al. 1973. "Effect of Low-Level Carbon Monoxide Exposure on Onset and Duration of Angina Pectoris," *Annals of Internal Medicine*, vol. 73, 46–48.

*Anderson, C., et al. 1974. *An Assessment of U.S. Energy Options for Project Independence.* Livermore, Calif.: Lawrence Livermore Laboratory.

*Angino, Ernest E. 1977. "High-Level and Long-Lived Radioactive Waste Disposal," *Science*, vol. 198, 885–890.

Angrist, S. W., and L. G. Hepler. 1967. *Order and Chaos.* New York: Basic Books.

*Antal, M. J., Jr. 1976. "Tower Power: Producing Fuels from Solar Energy," *Bulletin of the Atomic Scientists*, May, pp. 69–72.

Anthrop, Donald F. 1974. "The Need for a Long-Term Policy," *Bulletin of the Atomic Scientists*, May, pp. 33–37.

*Anthrop, Donald F. 1978. "The Carter Energy Plan and the American West," *Bulletin of the Atomic Scientists*, January, pp. 27–32.

*Appel, J., and J. Mackenzie. 1974. "How Much Light Do We Really Need?" *Bulletin of the Atomic Scientists*, vol. 30, no. 10, 18–24.

Arehart-Treichel, Joan. 1973. "Manure: Something New to Swear By," *Science News*, vol. 103, 314–315.

*Armstead, H. C. H., ed. 1973. *Geothermal Energy.* Paris: UNESCO.

*Armstead, H. C. H., and H. Christopher, eds. 1973. *Geothermal Energy: A Review of Research and Development.* Park Ridge, N.J.: Noyes Data.

*Armstrong, Joe E., and Harman Willis. 1975. *Plausibility of a Restricted Energy Use Scenario.* Menlo Park, Calif.: Stanford Research Institute.

*Arrandale, Tom. 1978. "Western Land Policy," *Editorial Research Reports*, vol. 1, no. 5, 83–100.

*Askin, Bradley. 1978. *How Energy Affects the Economy.* Lexington, Mass.: Heath.

*Atlas, Ronald M. 1978. "Microorganisms and Petroleum Products," *BioScience*, vol. 28, 387–391.

Atwood, Genevieve. 1975. "The Strip-Mining of Western Coal," *Scientific American*, vol. 233, no. 6, 23–29.

*Auer, Peter L. 1974. "An Integrated National Energy Research and Development Program," *Science*, vol. 184, 295–301.

*Axtmann, R. 1975. "Environmental Impact of a Geothermal Power Plant," *Science*, vol. 187, 795–803.

Babcock, Lyndon R., Jr. 1970. "A Combined Pollution Index for Measurement of Total Air Pollution," *Journal of Air Pollution Control Association*, vol. 20, 653–659.

*Bacastrow, R., and C. D. Keeling. 1973. "Atmospheric Carbon Dioxide and Radiocarbon in the Natural Carbon Cycle." In George M. Woodwell and E. V. Pecan, eds., *Carbon and the Biosphere.* Springfield, Va.: National Technical Information Service.

*Bach, Wilfrid. 1972. *Atmospheric Pollution.* New York: McGraw-Hill.

*Baes, C. F., Jr., et al. 1977. "Carbon Dioxide and Climate: The Uncontrolled Experiment," *American Scientist*, vol. 65, 310–320.

Bair, W. J., and R. C. Thompson. 1974. "Plutonium: Biomedical Research," *Science*, vol. 183, 715–721.

*Bamberger, C., and J. Braunstein. 1975. "Hydrogen: A Versatile Element," *American Scientist*, vol. 63, 438–447.

*Barber Associates. 1975. *LDC Nuclear Power Prospects, 1975–1990: Commercial, Economic, and Security Implications.* Springfield, Va.: National Technical Information Service.

Barnea, J. 1972. "Geothermal Power," *Scientific American*, vol. 226, no. 1, 70.

*Basile, Paul S., and David Sternlight. 1977. "The Coming Energy Shortage: Oil Is Not Enough," *Technology Review*, June, pp. 41–49.

*Bebbington, William P. 1976. "The Reprocessing of Nuclear Fuels," *Scientific American*, December, pp. 30–41.

*Beckmann, Peter. 1976. *The Health Hazards of Not Going Nuclear.* Boulder, Colo.: Golem Press.

*Behrman, Daniel. 1976. *Solar Energy: The Awakening Science.* Boston: Little, Brown.

*Bell, Larry. 1978. "Mass Transit and Appropriate Technology," *The Futurist*, June, pp. 169–174.

*Bendixon, Terrence. 1975. *Without Wheels: Alternatives to the Private Car.* Bloomington: Indiana University Press.

*Benedict, H. M., et al. 1973. *Assessment of Economic Impact of Air Pollutants on Vegetation in the United States: 1969 and 1971.* Palo Alto, Calif.: Stanford Research Institute.

*Bent, Henry A. 1971. "Haste Makes Waste: Pollution and Entropy," *Chemistry*, vol. 44, 6–15.

*Bent, Henry A. 1977. "Entropy and the Energy Crisis," *Journal of Science Teaching*, vol. 4, no. 5, 25–29.

*Berg, Charles A. 1973a. "Energy Conservation through Effective Utilization," *Science*, vol. 181, 128–138.

*Berg, George G. 1973b. "Hot Wastes from Nuclear Power," *Environment*, vol. 15, no. 4, 36–44.

Berg, Charles A. 1974a. "Conservation in Industry," *Science*, vol. 184, 264–270.

*Berg, Charles A. 1974b. "A Technical Basis for Energy Conservation," *Technology Review*, February, pp. 15–23.

*Berg, Alan. 1975. "To Save the World from Lifeboats," *Natural History*, June/July, pp. 4–6.

*Berg, Charles A. 1976. "Potential for Energy Conservation in Industry." In Jack M. Hollander and Melvin K. Simmons, eds., *Annual Review of Energy*, vol. 1. Palo Alto, Calif.: Annual Reviews.

*Berg, Charles A. 1978. "Process Innovation and Changes in Industrial Energy Use," *Science*, vol. 199, 608–618.

*Berg, R. R., et al. 1974. "Prognosis for Expanded U.S. Production of Crude Oil," *Science*, vol. 184, 331–336.

Berg, George G., et al. 1976. *Nuclear Power Economics and the Environment.* New York: The Scientists' Institute for Public Information.

*Berger, John J. 1977. *Nuclear Power: The Unviable Option.* New York: Dell.

Berger, R., and W. F. Libby. 1969. "Equilibration of Carbon Dioxide with Sea Water," *Science,* vol. 164, 1395.

*Berkowitz, David A., and Arthur M. Squires, eds. 1971. *Power Generation and Environmental Change.* Cambridge, Mass.: MIT Press.

*Berman, Edward R. 1975. *Geothermal Energy.* Park Ridge, N.J.: Noyes Data.

*Berndt, Ernest R. 1978. "Aggregate Energy Efficiency and Productivity Measurement." In Jack M. Hollander et al., eds., *Annual Review of Energy,* vol. 3. Palo Alto, Calif.: Annual Reviews.

*Bernton, Hal. 1978. "Paving the Way for Alcohol Fuels," *Environmental Action,* vol. 10, no. 10, 4–7.

*Berry, Stephen R. 1970. "Perspectives on Polluted Air—1970," *Bulletin of the Atomic Scientists,* April, pp. 33–42.

*Berry, R. Stephen, and Margaret F. Fels. 1973. "The Energy Cost of Automobiles," *Bulletin of the Atomic Scientists,* December, pp. 11–60.

*Berry, Stephen R., and Hiro Makino. 1974. "Energy Thrift in Packaging and Marketing," *Technology Review,* February, pp. 33–43.

Berry, James W., et al. 1974. *Chemical Villains: A Biology of Pollution.* St. Louis: C. V. Mosby.

*Bethe, H. A. 1976. "The Necessity of Fission Power," *Scientific American,* vol. 234, no. 1, 21–32.

*Bethe, H. A. 1977. "The Need for Nuclear Power," *Bulletin of the Atomic Scientists,* March, pp. 59–63.

*Billings, W. D. 1970. *Plants, Man, and the Ecosystem.* 2nd ed. Belmont, Calif.: Wadsworth.

*Bishop, James, Jr. 1974. "Oil Shale," *National Wildlife,* vol. 12, no. 8, 11.

*Blair, John J. 1976. *The Control of Oil.* New York: Pantheon.

*Bliss, Raymond W. 1976. "Why Not Just Build the House Right in the First Place?" *Bulletin of the Atomic Scientists,* March, pp. 32–40.

*Blomeke, J., et al. 1974. *Projections of Radioactive Wastes To Be Generated by the U.S. Nuclear Industry.* Springfield, Va.: National Technical Information Service.

*Blot, W. J., and J. F. Fraumeni, Jr. 1975. "Arsenical Air Pollution and Lung Cancer," *Lancet,* July 26.

*Blumer, Max. 1971. "Scientific Aspects of the Oil Spill Problems," *Environmental Affairs,* vol. 1, 54–73.

*Bockris, J. O. 1971. "Electrochemistry: Key to a Clean Future," *Ecology Today,* September, pp. 15–17.

*Bockris, J. O. 1972. "A Hydrogen Economy," *Science,* vol. 176, 1326.

*Bockris, J. O. 1975. *Energy: The Solar Hydrogen Alternative.* New York: Halsted.

*Bodkin, L. D. 1974. "Carbon Monoxide and Smog," *Environment,* vol. 16, no. 4, 35–41.

*Boesche, Donald F., et al. 1974. *Oil Spills and the Marine Environment.* Cambridge, Mass.: Ballinger.

*Boffey, Philip M. 1976. "Plutonium: Its Morality Questioned by National Council of Churches," *Science,* vol. 192, 356–359.

*Bohi, Douglas R. and Milton Russell. 1975. *U.S. Energy Policy: Alternatives for Security.* Baltimore, Md.: Johns Hopkins University Press.

*Bolin, Bert. 1977a. "Changes of Land Biota and Their Importance for the Carbon Cycle," *Science,* vol. 196, 613–615.

*Bolin, Bert. 1977b. "The Impact of Production and Use of Energy in Global Climate," *Annual Review of Energy,* vol. 2. Palo Alto, Calif.: Annual Reviews, pp. 197–226.

*Bolin, Bert, and R. J. Charlson. 1976. "On the Role of the Trophospheric Sulfur Cycle in the Shortwave Radiative Climate of the Earth," *Ambio,* vol. 4, 65–74.

*Boretsky, Michael. 1977. "Opportunities and Strategies for Energy Conservation," *Technology Review,* July-August, pp. 57–61.

*Bormann, F. H. 1976. "An Inseparable Linkage: Conservation of Natural Ecosystems and the Conservation of Fossil Energy," *BioScience,* vol. 26, 754–760.

Bornstein, R. D. 1968. "Observation of the Urban Heat Island Effect in New York City," *Journal of Applied Meteorology,* vol. 2, 574.

*Boshier, John F. 1978. "Can We Save Energy by Taxing It?" *Technology Review,* August-September, pp. 62–70.

*Bossong, Ken. 1978. "Hazards of Solar Energy," *People and Energy,* vol. 4, no. 9, 5–6.

*Boulding, Kenneth E. 1964. *The Meaning of the Twentieth Century.* New York: Harper & Row.

*Boulding, Russell. 1976. "What Is Pure Coal?" *Environment,* vol. 18, no. 1, 13–36.

Boulding, Kenneth E. 1977. "The Poverty of Power Reviewed," *CoEvolution Quarterly,* Summer, pp. 36–38.

*Bourlag, Georg. 1977. "Challenging the World Food Crisis," *Intellect Magazine,* April, pp. 322–324.

*Boyd, J., and L. T. Silver. 1977. *United States Uranium Position.* Los Angeles: American Society of Nuclear Engineers.

Boyle, Thomas J. 1973. "Hope for the Technological Solution," *Nature,* vol. 246, 127–128.

Brand, Daniel. 1976. "Bringing Logic to Urban Transportation Innovation," *Technology Review,* January, pp. 39–45.

*Breckhoeft, J. D., et al. 1978. *Geologic Disposal of High-Level Radioactive Wastes—Earth Science Perspectives.* Arlington, Va.: U.S. Geological Survey.

*Bregman, Sandra E. 1978. "Solar Energy Comes of Age," *Environment,* vol. 20, no. 5, 25–31.

Brinkworth, B. J. 1974. *Solar Energy for Man.* New York: Halsted Press.

*Britton, Peter. 1979. "Geothermal Goes East," *Popular Science,* February, pp. 66–69.

*Broad, William J. 1978. "Small Hydro: Sleeping Giant," *Science News,* July, pp. 43–45.

*Brobst, D. A., and W. A. Pratt, eds. 1973. *United States Mineral Resources,* U.S. Geological Survey Paper 820. Washington, D.C.: Government Printing Office.

*Brodine, Virginia. 1972a. "Point of Damage," *Environment,* vol. 14, no. 4, 2–15.

*Brodine, Virginia. 1972b. "Running in Place," *Environment,* vol. 14, no. 1, 2–11, 52.

*Brodine, Virginia. 1973. *Air Pollution.* New York: Harcourt Brace Jovanovich.

*Brodine, Virginia. 1975. *Radioactive Contamination.* New York: Harcourt Brace Jovanovich.

*Broecker, W. S. 1975. "Climatic Change: Are We on Brink of a Pronounced Global Warning?" *Science,* vol. 189, 460–463.

Brookhaven National Laboratory. 1957. *Theoretical Possibilities and Consequences of Major Accidents in Large Nuclear Power Plants,* WASH-740. Washington, D.C.: Atomic Energy Commission, March.

*Brookhaven National Laboratory. 1977. Data given in "How To Save Energy," *Newsweek,* April 18, pp. 70–80.

*Brookings Institution. 1975. *Energy and U.S. Foreign Policy.* Cambridge, Mass.: Ballinger.

*Brown, Theodore L. 1971. *Energy and Environment.* Columbus, Ohio: Charles E. Merrill.

*Brown, Harrison. 1976a. "Energy in Our Future." In Jack M. Hollander and Melvin K. Simmons, eds., *Annual Review of Energy,* vol. 1. Palo Alto, Calif.: Annual Reviews.

*Brown, J. Martin. 1976b. "Linearity vs. Nonlinearity of Dose Response for Radiation Carcinogenosis," *Health Physics,* vol. 31, 231–245.

*Brown, Harrison. 1978a. *The Human Future Revisited.* New York: W. W. Norton.

*Brown, Lester R. 1978b. *The Twenty-Ninth Day: Accommodating Human Needs and Numbers to the Earth's Resources.* New York: W. W. Norton.

*Brown, Lester R. 1978c. "Global Economic Ills: The Worst May Be Yet to Come," *The Futurist,* June, pp. 157–168.

*Brown, Lester R. 1978d. *The Global Economic Prospect: New Sources of Economic Stress.* Washington, D.C.: Worldwatch Institute.

*Brubaker, Sterling. 1975. *In Command of Tomorrow.* Baltimore: Johns Hopkins University Press.

*Bruce-Briggs, B. 1976. "Mass Transportation and Minority Transportation," *The Public Interest,* Fall.

*Bryerton, Gene. 1970. *The Nuclear Dilemma.* New York: Ballantine.

*Bryson, R. A. 1974. "A Perspective on Climatic Change," *Science,* vol. 184, 753–759.

*Bryson, Reid A., and Thomas J. Murray. 1977. *Climates of Hunger: Mankind and the World's Changing Weather.* Madison: University of Wisconsin Press.

Bryson, R. A., and J. T. Petersen. 1968. "Atmospheric Aerosols: Increased Concentration during the Last Decade," *Science,* vol. 162, October 4.

*Bryson, R. A., and John E. Ross. 1972. "The Climate of the City." In Thomas A. Detwyler and Melvin G. Marcus, eds., *Urbanization and Environment.* North Scituate, Mass.: Duxbury Press, pp. 61–68.

*Bryson, Reid A., and W. M. Wendland. 1975. "Climatic Effects of Atmospheric Pollution." In S. Fred Singer, ed., *The Changing Global Environment.* Dordrecht, Netherlands: Reidel.

*Budnitz, Robert J., and John P. Holdren. 1976. "Social and Environmental Costs of Energy Systems." In Jack M. Hollander and Melvin E. Simmons, eds., *Annual Review of Energy,* vol. 1. Palo Alto, Calif.: Annual Reviews.

Budyko, M. J. 1969. "The Effect of Solar Radiation Variation on the Climate of the Earth," *Tellus,* vol. 21, 611–619.

Budyko, M. J. 1970. "Comments," *Journal of Applied Meteorology,* vol. 9, 310.

Budyko, M. J. 1972. "The Future Climate," *EOS, Transactions of the American Geophysical Union,* vol. 153, 868–874.

*Budyko, M. J. 1974. *Climate and Life.* New York: Academic Press.

*Buell, P., and J. E. Dunn. 1967. "Relative Impact of Smoking and Air Pollution on Lung Cancer," *Archives of Environmental Health,* September, pp. 138–148.

*Bull, C. 1975. "Radioactive Waste Disposal." *Science,* vol. 189, 596.

*Bupp, Irvin C., and Jean-Claude Derian. 1974. "The Breeder Reactor in the U.S.: A New Economic Analysis," *Technology Review,* July-August, pp. 26–36.

*Bupp, Irvin C., and Jean-Claude Derian. 1978. *Light Water: How the Nuclear Dream Dissolved.* New York: Basic Books.

*Bupp, Irvin C., et al. 1975. "The Economics of Nuclear Power," *Technology Review,* February, pp. 15–25.

*Bureau of Reclamation, Department of Interior. 1975. *Critical Water Problems Facing the Eleven Western States.* Washington, D.C.: Government Printing Office.

*Burke, Barbara L., and Robert N. Meroney. 1977. *Energy from the Wind,* Supplement I. Fort Collins, Colo.: Engineering Research Center.

*Burwell, C. C. 1978. "Solar Biomass Energy: An Overview of U.S. Potential," *Science,* vol. 199, 1041–1048.

*Cailiet, G., et al. 1971. *Everyman's Guide to Ecological Living.* New York: Macmillan.

*Cairns, John, Jr. 1971. "Thermal Pollution—A Cause for Concern," *Journal of the Water Pollution Control Federation*, vol. 43, 55–66.

*Cairns, John, Jr. 1972. "Coping with Heated Waste Water Discharges from Steam-Heated Electric Power Plants," *BioScience*, vol. 22, 411–419.

*Calder, Nigel. 1974. *The Weather Machine: How Our Weather Works and Why It Is Changing.* New York: Viking Press.

*Calder, Nigel. 1975. "In the Grip of a New Ice Age?" *International Wildlife*, July/August, pp. 33–35.

*Caldwell, Lynton K., et al. 1976. *Citizens and the Environment: Case Studies in Popular Action.* Bloomington: Indiana University Press.

*Calef, Charles E. 1976. "Not Out of the Woods," *Environment*, vol. 18, no. 7, 17–25.

*Callahan, Daniel. 1973. *The Tyranny of Survival.* New York: Macmillan.

*Callenbach, Ernest. 1975. *Ecotopia.* Berkeley: Banyan Tree Books.

Callendar, G. S. 1958. "On the Amount of Carbon Dioxide in the Atmosphere," *Tellus*, vol. 10, 243–248.

*Calvin, Melvin. 1974. "Solar Energy by Photosynthesis," *Science*, vol. 184, 375–381.

*Calvin, Melvin. 1976. "Photosynthesis as a Resource for Energy and Materials," *American Scientist*, vol. 64, no. 3, 270–278.

*Calvin, Melvin. 1978. "Green Factories," *Chemical and Engineering News*, March, pp. 30–36.

*Cambel, Ali B. 1970. "Impact of Energy Demands," *Physics Today*, December, pp. 38–45.

*Campbell, W. J., and S. Martin. 1974. "Oil Spills in the Arctic Ocean: Extent of Spreading and Possibility of Large-Scale Thermal Effects," *Science*, vol. 186, 843–846.

*Caputo, Richard S. 1977. "Solar Power Plants: Dark Horse in the Energy Stable," *Bulletin of the Atomic Scientists*, May, pp. 46–56.

*Carr, Donald E. 1976. *Energy and the Earth Machine.* New York: Norton.

Carruthers, W., et al. 1967. "L-2 Benzanthracene Derivatives in Kuwait Mineral Oil," *Nature*, vol. 213, 691–692.

Carter, Luther J. 1969. "Warm-water Irrigation: An Answer to Thermal Pollution," *Science*, vol. 165, 478–480.

*Carter, Luther J. 1974. "Floating Nuclear Plants: Power from the Assembly Line," *Science*, vol. 183, 1063–1065.

*Carter, Luther J. 1975. "Energy: A Strategic Oil Reserve as a Hedge against Embargoes," *Science*, vol. 189, 364–366.

*Carter, Luther J. 1978a. "A Bright Solar Prospect Seen by CEQ and OTA," *Science*, vol. 200, 627–630.

*Carter, Luther J. 1978b. "Peat for Fuel Development Pushed by Big Corporate Farm in Carolina," *Science*, vol. 199, 33–34.

*Carter, Luther J. 1978c. "NRC Panel Renders Mixed Verdict on Rasmussen Reactor Safety Study," *Science*, vol. 201, 1196–1197.

*Carter, Luther J. 1978d. "Nuclear Wastes: The Science of Geologic Disposal Seen as Weak," *Science*, vol. 200, 1134–1137.

Carter, Luther J. 1978e. "Sweetness and Light from Industry and Environmentalists on Coal," *Science*, vol. 203, 252–253.

Carter, Luther J. 1979. "Policy Review Boosts Solar as a New-Term Energy Option," *Science*, vol. 203, 252–253.

*Cassiday, Bruce. 1977. *The Complete Solar House.* New York: Dodd, Mead.

Caudill, Harry. 1971. *My Land is Dying.* New York: E. P. Dutton.

*Caudill, William W., et al. 1974. *A Bucket of Oil: The Humanistic Approach to Building Design for Energy Conservation.* New York: Cahners Books.

*Center for Science in the Public Interest. 1977. *99 Ways to a Simple Lifestyle.* New York: Doubleday.

*Central Intelligence Agency. 1974a. *A Study of Climatological Research as It Pertains to Intelligence Problems.* Washington, D.C.: Central Intelligence Agency.

*Central Intelligence Agency. 1974b. *Potential Implications of Trends in World Population, Food Production, and Climate.* Washington, D.C.: Central Intelligence Agency.

*Central Intelligence Agency. 1977. *The International Energy Situation: Outlook to 1985.* Washington, D.C.: Central Intelligence Agency.

*Chasan, Daniel J. 1973. "An Answer to City Traffic May Be a Horizontal Elevator," *Smithsonian*, vol. 4, no. 4, 47–52.

*Chase, Victor D. 1977. "Rusty Iron May Be the Key to Cheaper Gas from Coal," *Popular Science*, January, pp. 91–94.

*Chase, Victor D. 1978. "Coming: Super Windmills for Super Power," *Popular Mechanics*, May, pp. 114–287.

*Cheney, Eric S. 1974. "U.S. Energy Resources: Limits and Future Outlook," *American Scientist*, vol. 62, January/February, pp. 14–22.

*Cheremisinoff, Nicholas P. 1978. *Fundamentals of Wind Energy.* Ann Arbor, Mich.: Ann Arbor Science.

*Cheremisinoff, Paul N., and Angelo C. Morres. 1977. "Energy from Wood Wastes," *Environment*, vol. 19, no. 4, 25–31.

*Cheremisinoff, Paul N., and Thomas C. Regino. 1978. *Principles and Applications of Solar Energy.* Ann Arbor, Mich.: Ann Arbor Science.

*Chester, C. V. 1976. "Estimates of Threats to the Public from Terrorist Acts against Nuclear Facilities," *Nuclear Safety*, vol. 17, no. 6, 659–665.

*Chow, Brian G. 1975. *The Liquid Metal Fast Breeder Reactor: An Economic Analysis.* Washington, D.C.: American Enterprise Institute for Public Policy Research.

*Chow, Brian G. 1977. "The Economic Issues of the Fast Breeder Reactor Program," *Science*, vol. 195, 551–556.

*Christiansen, Bill, and Theodore H. Clark, Jr. 1976. "A Western Perspective on Energy: A Plan for Rational Energy Planning," *Science*, vol. 194, 578–584.

*Christman, Russell F. 1977. "The Environmentalist," *Environmental Science and Technology*, vol. 11, 537.

*Chylek, P., and J. Coakley. 1974. "Aerosols and Climate," *Science*, vol. 183, 75–77.

*Citizens' Advisory Committee on Environmental Quality. 1973. *Citizen Action Guide to Energy Conservation.* Washington, D.C.: Government Printing Office.

*City of Davis, Community Development Department. 1977. *Davis Energy Conservation Report: Practical Use of the Sun.* Davis, Calif.: City of Davis, Community Development Department.

*Clairborne, Robert. 1970. *Climate, Man, and History.* New York: W. W. Norton.

*Clapham, W. B., Jr. 1973. *Natural Ecosystems.* New York: Macmillan.

*Clark, John R. 1969. "Thermal Pollution and Aquatic Life," *Scientific American*, March.

*Clark, Wilson. 1973. "Interest in Wind is Picking Up as Fuels Dwindle," *Smithsonian*, vol. 4, no. 8, 70–78.

*Clark, Wilson. 1974a. *Energy for Survival: The Alternative to Extinction.* New York: Doubleday.

*Clark, Wilson. 1974b. "It Takes Energy to Get Energy: The Law of Diminishing Returns Is in Effect," *Smithsonian*, December, pp. 84–90.

*Clark, Wilson. 1974c. *The Case for a Nuclear Moratorium,* Washington, D.C.: Environmental Action Foundation.

Clarke, Robin, 1977. *Building for Self-Sufficiency.* New York: Universe Books.

*Clegg, Peter. 1975. *New Low-Cost Sources of Energy for the Home.* Charlotte, Vt.: Garden Way.

Coan, Eugene. 1971. "Oil Pollution," *Sierra Club Bulletin*, March, pp. 13–16.

*Cochran, Thomas B. 1974a. *The Liquid Metal Fast Breeder Reactor: An Economic and Environmental Critique,* Baltimore: Johns Hopkins University Press.

*Cochran, Thomas B. 1974b. "The Liquid Metal Fast Breeder Reactor," *Resources for the Future*, April, pp. 1–2.

*Cochran, Neal P. 1976. "Oil and Gas from Coal," *Scientific American*, vol. 234, no. 5, 24–30.

*Cochran, Thomas B., et al. 1975. "A Poor Buy," *Environment*, vol. 17, no. 4, 12–20.

Cohen, Bernard L. 1967. *The Heart of the Atom.* Garden City, N.Y.: Doubleday-Anchor.

*Cohen, Bernard L. 1974a. *Nuclear Science and Society.* New York: Anchor Books.

*Cohen, Bernard L. 1974b. "Perspectives on the Nuclear Debate," *Bulletin of the Atomic Scientists*, October, pp. 35–39.

*Cohen, Bernard L. 1976a. "Biological and Environmental Behavior of Plutonium," *Nuclear Engineering International*, November, pp. 1–10.

*Cohen, Bernard L. 1976b. "Hazards from Plutonium Toxicity," *Health Physics*, January, pp. 1–21.

*Cohen, Bernard L. 1976c. "Impact of the Nuclear Energy Industry on Human Health and Safety," *American Scientist*, vol. 64, 550–559.

*Cohen, Bernard L. 1977a. "Abundance of Nuclear Fuel," *Bulletin of the Atomic Scientists*, April, p. 2.

*Cohen, Bernard L. 1977b. "The Disposal of Radioactive Wastes from Fission Reactors," *Scientific American*, vol. 236, no. 6, 21–31.

*Cohen, Bernard L. 1977c. "High-Level Radioactive Waste from Lightwater Reactors," *Reviews of Modern Physics*, January, pp. 1–20.

*Cohen, Bernard L. 1977d. "The Potentialities of Terrorism," *Nuclear Engineering International*, February, pp. 1–10.

*Cohn, Charles E. 1975. "Improved Fuel Economy for Automobiles," *Technology Review*, February, pp. 45–52.

*Cole, Lamont C. 1958. "The Ecosphere," *Scientific American*, April, pp. 11–16.

*Cole, David E. 1972. "The Wankel Engine," *Scientific American*, vol. 227, no. 2, 14–23.

*Colinvaux, Paul. 1973. *Introduction to Ecology.* New York: John Wiley.

*Collie, M. J., ed. 1978. *Geothermal Energy—Recent Developments.* Park Ridge, N.J.: Noyes Data.

*Comar, C. L., and L. A. Sagan. 1976. "Health Effects of Energy Production and Conversion." In Jack M. Hollander and Melvin K. Simmons, eds., *Annual Review of Energy*, vol. 1. Palo Alto, Calif.: Annual Reviews.

*Comey, David D. 1975. "On Cooking Curves," *Bulletin of the Atomic Scientists*, October, pp. 40–42.

*Comey, David D. 1976. "The Perfect Trojan Horse," *Bulletin of the Atomic Scientists*, June, pp. 33–35.

*Committee on Interior and Insular Affairs, U.S. Senate. 1972. "Conservation of Energy," Serial No. 98–18. Washington, D.C.: Government Printing Office.

*Committee on Interior and Insular Affairs, U.S. Senate. 1973. "Report of the Cornell Workshop on Energy and the Environment." Washington, D.C.: Government Printing Office.

*Commoner, Barry. 1970a. "The Ecological Facts of Life." In H. D. Johnson, ed., *No Deposit—No Return.* Reading, Mass.: Addison-Wesley, pp. 18–35.

*Commoner, Barry. 1970b. "Nuclear Power: Benefits and Risks." In Harvey Foreman, ed., *Nuclear Power and the Public.* Minneapolis: University of Minnesota Press, pp. 224–239.

*Commoner, Barry. 1971. *The Closing Circle: Nature, Man and Technology.* New York: Knopf.

*Commoner, Barry. 1976. *The Poverty of Power: Energy and the Economic Crisis.* New York: Knopf.

Commoner, Barry. 1978. "The Solar Transition," *Environment*, vol. 20, no. 3, 6–15.

*Commoner, Barry, et al., eds. 1975. *Energy and Human Welfare*. 3 vols. New York: Macmillan.

*Connolly, C. H. 1972. *Air Pollution and Public Health*. New York: Dryden.

*Conover, Patrick W. 1973. "The Potential for an Alternate Society," *The Futurist*, June, pp. 111–116.

*Conservation Foundation. 1972. *CF Newsletter*, April.

*Consumer Guide editors. 1977. *Energy Savers Catalog*. New York: Putnam.

Consumer Reports. 1975. "Para Transit," April.

*Cook, Earl. 1971. "The Flow of Energy in an Industrial Society," *Scientific American*, September, pp. 83–91.

*Cook, Earl. 1972. "Energy for Millenium Three," *Technology Review*, December, pp. 16–23.

*Cook, Earl. 1975a. "The Depletion of Geologic Resources," *Technology Review*, June, pp. 15–27.

*Cook, Earl. 1975b. "Ionizing Radiation." In William W. Murdoch, ed., *Environment: Resources, Pollution and Society*, 2nd ed. Sunderland, Mass.: Sinauer.

*Cook, Earl. 1976a. "Limits to Exploitation of Nonrenewable Resources," *Science*, vol. 191, 677–682.

*Cook, Earl. 1976b. *Man, Energy, Society*. San Francisco: W. H. Freeman.

*Coomer, James C. 1977. "Solving the Energy Dilemma," *The Futurist*, August, pp. 228–230.

Coppi, Bruno, and Jan Rem. 1972. "The Tokamak Approach in Fusion Research," *Scientific American*, vol. 227, no. 1, 65.

*Cottrell, Fred. 1955. *Energy and Society*. New York: McGraw-Hill.

*Council on Environmental Quality. Annual. *Environmental Quality*. Washington, D.C.: Government Printing Office.

*Council on Environmental Quality. 1973. *Energy and the Environment*. Washington, D.C.: Government Printing Office.

*Council on Environmental Quality. 1976. *Environmental Impact Statements: An Analysis of Six Years Experience by Seventy Federal Agencies*. Springfield, Va.: National Technical Information Center.

Council on Environmental Quality. 1977. *The Food-People Problem: Can the Land's Capacity to Produce Food Be Sustained?* Washington, D.C.: Council on Environmental Quality.

*Council on Environmental Quality. 1978. *Solar Energy: Progress and Promise*. Washington, D.C.: Council on Environmental Quality.

*Cousins, Norman. 1974. "Hope and Practical Realities," *Saturday Review*, December 14, pp. 4–5.

*Cousteau, Jacques. 1974. "The Perils and Potentials of a Watery Planet," *Saturday Review*, August 24, pp. 6–7.

*Coutant, Charles C. 1976. "How to Put Waste Heat to Work," *Environmental Science and Technology*, vol. 10, 868–871.

*Cowell, E. B. 1976. "Oil Pollution of the Sea." In R. Johnston, ed., *Marine Pollution*. New York: Academic Press.

*Cowen, Robert. 1977. "Dirty Directions for Nuclear Fusion," *Technology Review*, March-April, pp. 8–9.

*Craig, Paul P., et al. 1976. "Social and Institutional Factors in Energy Conservation." In Jack M. Hollander and Melvin K. Simmons, eds., *Annual Review of Energy*, vol. 1. Palo Alto, Calif.: Annual Reviews.

*Creighton, Roger L. 1970. *Urban Transportation Planning*. Urbana: University of Illinois Press.

*Cuddihy, Richard G., et al. 1977. "Radiation Risks from Plutonium Recycle," *Environmental Science and Technology*, vol. 11, no. 13, 1160–1165.

*Cummings, Ronald G., et al. 1979. "Mining Earth's Heat: Hot Dry Rock Geothermal Energy," *Technology Review*, February, pp. 58–78.

*Cushing, D. H., and J. J. Walsh, eds. 1976. *The Ecology of the Seas*. Oxford: Blackwell.

*Dahlberg, Richard C. 1978. "Weapons Proliferation and Criteria for Evaluating Nuclear Fuel Cycles," *Bulletin of the Atomic Scientists*, January, pp. 38–42.

*Daly, Herman E. 1977. *Steady-State Economics*. San Francisco: W. H. Freeman.

*Damon, Paul E., and Steven M. Kunen. 1976. "Global Cooling," *Science*, vol. 193, 447–453.

*Daniels, Farrington. 1964. *Direct Use of the Sun's Energy*. New Haven: Yale University Press.

*Daniels, George. 1976. *Solar Homes and Sun Heating*. New York: Harper & Row.

*Dansgaard, W., et al. 1971. *The Late Cenozoic Glacial Ages*. New Haven: Yale University Press.

*Dark, Harris Edward. 1975. *Auto Engines of Tomorrow: Power Alternatives for Cars to Come*. Bloomington: Indiana University Press.

*Darling, Lois, and Louis Darling. 1968. *A Place in the Sun*. New York: Morrow.

*Darling, Frank F., and Raymond F. Dasmann. 1969. "The Ecosystem View of Human Society," *Impact of Science on Society*, vol. 19, 109–121.

*Darmstadter, Joel. 1971. *Energy in the World Economy*. Baltimore: Johns Hopkins University Press.

*Darmstadter, Joel. 1975. *Conserving Energy*. Baltimore: Johns Hopkins University Press.

*Darmstadter, Joel, et al. 1977. *How Industrial Societies Use Energy*. Baltimore: Johns Hopkins University Press.

*Darmstadter, Joel, et al. 1978. "International Variations in Energy Use: Findings from a Comparative Study." In Jack M. Hollander et al., eds., *Annual Review of Energy*, vol. 3. Palo Alto, Calif.: Annual Reviews.

*Darnell, Rezneat M. 1973. *Ecology and Man*. Dubuque, Iowa: Wm. C. Brown.

*Dasmann, Raymond F. 1970. "Ecological Diversity." In H. D. Johnson, ed., *No Deposit—No Return*. Reading, Mass.: Addison-Wesley, pp. 108–112.

*Dasmann, Raymond F. 1976. *Environmental Conservation*, 4th ed. New York: John Wiley.

*David, Edward E., Jr. 1973. "Energy: A Strategy of Diversity," *Technology Review*, June, pp. 26–31.

*Davidson, J., et al. 1974. "Trace Elements in Fly Ash: Dependence of Concentration on Particle Size," *Environmental Science and Technology*, vol. 8, 1107–1113.

*Davies, J. Clarence III, and Barbara S. Davies. 1975. *The Politics of Pollution*, 2nd ed. Indianapolis: Pegasus (Bobbs-Merrill).

*Davis, David H. 1974. *Energy Politics*. New York: St. Martin's.

*Day, M. C. 1975. "Nuclear Energy: A Second Round of Questions," *Bulletin of the Atomic Scientists*, December, pp. 52–60.

Deevey, Edward S., Jr. 1951. "Life in the Depths of a Pond," *Scientific American*, vol. 185, 68–72.

Demand and Conservation Panel of the Committee on Nuclear and Alternative Energy Systems, National Academy of Sciences. 1978. "U.S. Energy Demand: Some Low Energy Futures," *Science*, vol. 200, 142–152.

*de Marsily, G., et al. 1977. "Nuclear Waste Disposal: Can the Geologist Guarantee Isolation?" *Science*, vol. 197, 519–527.

*DeNike, L. Douglas. 1974. "Radioactive Malevolence," *Bulletin of the Atomic Scientists*, February, pp. 16–20.

*Dennis, Landt. 1976. *Catch the Wind*. New York: Four Winds.

DeRenzo, Dorothy. 1978. *Energy from Bioconversion of Waste Materials*. Park Ridge, N.J.: Noyes Data.

*Derven, Ronald. 1976. "Heat Pumps: Cheapest Cooling and Heating for Your Home?" *Popular Science*, September, pp. 92–95.

*Detwyler, Thomas R., and Melvin G. Marcus, eds. 1972. *Urbanization and Environment*. North Scituate, Mass.: Duxbury Press.

Devanney, John W., III. 1974. "Key Issues in Offshore Oil," *Technology Review*, January, pp. 21–25.

*Dials, G. E., and E. C. Moore. 1974. "The Cost of Coal," *Environment*, vol. 16, no. 7, 18–37.

Dickson, E. M. 1977. *The Hydrogen Energy Economy*. New York: Praeger Special Studies in U.S. Economic, Social, and Political Issues.

*Dickson, E. M., et al. 1976. *The Hydrogen Economy: A Preliminary Technology Assessment*. Menlo Park, Calif.: Stanford Research Institute.

*Dinneen, G. U., and G. L. Cook. 1974. "Oil Shale and the Energy Crisis," *Technology Review*, vol. 76, no. 3, 26–33.

Dole, Charles E. 1977. "Transportation for the 80's," *Christian Science Monitor*, August 18, pp. 14–15.

Domencick, Thomas A., and Gerald Kraft. 1970. *Free Transit*. Cambridge, Mass.: Charles Rivers Associates.

*Doolittle, Jesse S. 1978. *Energy: A Crisis—A Dilemma—Or Just Another Problem?* Champaign, Ill.: Matrix.

*Dorf, Richard C. 1978. *Energy, Resources, and Policy*. Reading, Mass.: Addison-Wesley.

*Douglas, John H. 1976a. "The Great Nuclear Power Debate," *Science News*, vol. 109, 44–45.

*Douglas, John H. 1976b. "The Great Nuclear Power Debate (2)," *Science News*, vol. 109, 59–61.

*Doyes, William S. 1976. *Strip Mining of Coal: Environmental Solutions*. Park Ridge, N.J.: Noyes Data.

Dreschhoff, Gisela, et al. 1974. "International High Level Nuclear Waste Management," *Bulletin of the Atomic Scientists*, January, pp. 28–33.

Dubin, F. S. 1972. "Energy Conservation Needs New Architecture and Engineering," *Public Power*, March/April.

*Duffie, John A., and William A. Beckman. 1976. "Solar Heating and Cooling," *Science*, vol. 191, 143–149.

*Duguay, M. A. 1977. "Solar Electricity: The Hybrid System Approach," *American Scientist*, vol. 65, 422–427.

Dunham, James T. 1974. "High-Sulfur Coal for Generating Electricity," *Science*, vol. 184, 346–350.

*Dupree, Walter G., Jr., and James A. West. 1972. *United States Energy through the Year 2000*. Washington, D.C.: Government Printing Office.

*Dyer, A. J. 1974. "The Effect of Volcanic Eruptions on Global Turbidity," *Quarterly Journal of the Royal Meteorological Society*, vol. 100, 563–571.

*Dyson, Freeman. 1971. "Energy in the Universe," *Scientific American*, vol. 224, no. 2, 50–57.

*Eccli, Eugene, ed. 1976. *Low Cost, Energy-Efficient Shelter*. Emmaus, Pa.: Rodale.

*Eckholm, Erik P. 1975. *The Other Energy Crisis: Firewood*. Washington, D.C.: Worldwatch Institute.

*Eckholm, Erik P. 1976. *Losing Ground: Environmental Stresses and World Food Prospects*. New York: W. W. Norton.

*Eckholm, Erik. 1977. *The Picture of Health: Environmental Sources of Disease*. New York: W. W. Norton.

*Edberg, Rolf. 1969. *On the Shred of a Cloud*. University: University of Alabama Press.

*Edelson, Edward. 1974. "Fusion Power: Is It All Coming Together?" *Popular Science*, August, pp. 52–59.

*Edsall, John T. 1976. "Toxicity of Plutonium and Some Other Actinides," *Bulletin of the Atomic Scientists*, September, pp. 27–28.

*Ehrenfeld, D. W. 1970. *Biological Conservation*. New York: Holt, Rinehart & Winston.

*Ehrlich, Paul R., et al. 1976. *Biology and Society*. New York: McGraw-Hill.

*Ehrlich, Paul R., et al. 1977. *Ecoscience: Population, Resources and Environment*. San Francisco: W. H. Freeman.

*Eldridge, Frank. 1976. *Wind Machines*. Washington, D.C.: Government Printing Office.

*Elgin, Duane, and Arnold Mitchell. 1977. "Voluntary Simplicity (3)," *The CoEvolution Quarterly*, Summer, pp. 4–27.

*Elipper, Alfred W. 1970. "Pollution Problems, Resource Policy, and the Scientist," *Science*, vol. 169, 11–15.

*Elliot, W. P., and L. Machta, eds. 1977. *Proceedings of ERDA Workshop on Environmental Effects of Carbon Dioxide from Fossil Fuel Combustion*. Washington, D.C.: U.S. Department of Energy.

*Ellis, A. J. 1975. "Geothermal Systems and Power Development," *American Scientist*, vol. 63, 501–521.

Emlen, J. M. 1973. *Ecology: An Evolutionary Approach*. Reading, Mass.: Addison-Wesley.

*Emmel, Thomas C. 1973. *An Introduction to Ecology and Population Biology*. New York: W. W. Norton.

*Emmett, John L., et al. 1974. "Fusion Power by Laser Implosion," *Scientific American*, vol. 230, no. 6, 24–37.

*Energy and Environment Subcommittee of the U.S. House of Representatives Government Operations Committee. 1978. *Nuclear Power Costs*. Springfield, Va.: National Technical Information Service.

*Energy Policy Project. 1974. *A Time to Choose: The Final Report of the Energy Policy Project of the Ford Foundation*. Cambridge, Mass.: Ballinger.

*Energy Research and Development Administration. 1975a. *Final Environmental Statement, Liquid Metal Fast Breeder Reactor Program*. 10 vols. Washington, D.C.: Energy Research and Development Administration.

*Energy Research and Development Administration. 1975b. *National Solar Energy Research, Development, and Demonstration Program: Definition Report*. Washington, D.C.: Energy Research and Development Program.

*Energy Research and Development Administration. 1975c. *Nuclear Fuel Cycle: A Report by the Fuel-Cycle Task Force*. Springfield, Va.: National Technical Information Service.

*Energy Research and Development Administration. 1976a. *Alternatives for Managing Wastes from Reactors and Post-Fission Operations in the LWR Fuel Cycle and Production*. Washington, D.C.: Energy Research and Development Administration.

*Energy Research and Development Administration. 1976b. *Energy from Coal: A State of the Art Review*. Arlington, Va.: Tetra Tech.

*Energy Research and Development Administration. 1976c. *A National Plan for Energy, Research, Development, and Demonstration: Creating Energy Choices for the Future*. Washington, D.C.: Government Printing Office.

*Energy Research and Development Administration. 1977a. *Shipping of Nuclear Wastes*. Washington, D.C.: Energy Research and Development Administration.

*Energy Research and Development Administration. 1977b. *Solar Energy in America's Future: A Preliminary Assessment*. Washington, D.C.: Government Printing Office.

Environmental Protection Agency. 1971. *Estimates of Ionizing Radiation Doses in the United States, 1959–2000*. Washington, D.C.: Government Printing Office.

Environmental Protection Agency. 1973. Testimony by John R. Quarles, Acting Deputy Administrator, before the Subcommittee on the Environment and the Subcommittee on Mines and Mining, Committee on Interior and Insular Affairs, U.S. House of Representatives, May 14.

*Environmental Protection Agency. 1974a. *The Bicycle vs. the Energy Crisis*. Washington, D.C.: Environmental Protection Agency.

*Environmental Protection Agency. 1974b. *Current Status of Alternative Automotive Power Systems and Fuels*. Washington, D.C.: Environmental Protection Agency.

*Environmental Protection Agency. 1974c. *Environmental Protection in Surface Mining of Coal*. Washington, D.C.: Government Printing Office.

*Environmental Protection Agency. 1974d. *Control of Environmental Impacts from Advanced Energy Sources*. Washington, D.C.: Environmental Protection Agency.

*Environmental Protection Agency. 1975a. *Oil Spills*. Washington, D.C.: Environmental Protection Agency.

*Environmental Protection Agency. 1975b. *A Study of Indoor Air Quality*. EPA-USO/4-74-02. Washington, D.C.: Environmental Protection Agency.

*Environmental Protection Agency. 1976a. *The Allegheny County Air Pollution Episode*. Washington, D.C.: Environmental Protection Agency.

*Environmental Protection Agency. 1976b. *Reactor Safety Study: A Review of the Draft Report*. Springfield, Va.: National Technical Information Service.

*Environmental Protection Agency. 1976c. *Radiological Quality of the Environment*. Washington, D.C.: Environmental Protection Agency.

*Environment Staff Report. 1973. "Natural Radiation," *Environment*, vol. 15, no. 10, 31–35.

*Epstein, S. S. 1974. "Environmental Determinants of Human Cancer," *Cancer Research*, vol. 34, 2425–2435.

*Epstein, S. S., and D. Hattis. 1975. "Pollution and Human Health." In William W. Murdoch, ed., *Environment: Resources, Pollution and Society*, 2nd ed. Sunderland, Mass.: Sinauer, pp. 195–219.

*Esch, Gerald W., and Robert W. McFarlane, eds. 1976. *Thermal Ecology*. Oak Ridge, Tenn.: Energy Research and Development Administration.

*Esfandiary, F. M. 1970. *Optimism One: The Emerging Radicalism*. New York: W. W. Norton.

*Eskridge, Nancy K. 1978. "Congress High on Alcohol Fuels," *Features and News*, vol. 28, no. 7, 469–470.

*Esposito, John, and Ralph Nader. 1970. *Vanishing Air: Task Force Report on Air Pollution*. New York: Grossman.

*Executive Office of the President. 1977. *The National Energy Plan*. Washington, D.C.: Government Printing Office.

*Exxon Company. 1976. *Energy Outlook—1975–1990*. Houston, Tex.: Exxon Company.

*Falk, Richard A. 1971a. "Adapting World Order to the Global Ecosystem." In John Harte and Robert H. Socolow, eds., *Patient Earth*. New York: Holt, Rinehart & Winston, pp. 245–257.

*Falk, Richard A. 1971b. *This Endangered Planet: Prospects and Proposals for Human Survival*. New York: Random House.

*Falk, Richard A. 1975. *A Study of Future Worlds*. New York: Free Press.

Falk, Richard A., and Saul H. Mendlovitz, eds. 1966, 1967, 1973. *The Strategy of World Order*. 4 vols. New York: World Law Fund.

*Farmer, F. R., ed. 1977. *Nuclear Reactor Safety*. New York: Academic Press.

*Farney, Dennis. 1974. "Ominous Problem: What to Do with Radioactive Waste," *Smithsonian*, vol. 5, no. 1, 20–26.

*Farrington, John W. 1977. "The Biogeochemistry of Oil in the Ocean," *Oceanus*, vol. 20, no. 4, 5–14.

F.A.S. 1978. "Voyage into the Sun?" *F.A.S. Public Interest Report*, vol. 31, no. 3, 1–7.

*Federal Energy Administration. 1974a. *Project Independence Report*. Washington, D.C.: Government Printing Office.

*Federal Energy Administration. 1974b. *Synthetic Fuels from Coal*. Washington, D.C.: Federal Energy Administration.

*Federal Energy Administration. 1974c. *Solar Energy Task Force Report*. Washington, D.C.: Government Printing Office.

*Federal Energy Administration. 1976. *National Energy Outlook*. Washington, D.C.: Government Printing Office.

*Federal Energy Administration. 1977a. *Tips for Energy Savers*. Washington, D.C.: Federal Energy Administration.

Federal Energy Administration. 1977b. *Monthly Petroleum Statistics*. Washington, D.C.: Federal Energy Administration.

*Feiveson, Harold A. 1978. "Proliferation Resistant Nuclear Fuel Cycles." In Jack M. Hollander et al., eds., *Annual Review of Energy*, vol. 3. Palo Alto, Calif.: Annual Reviews.

*Feiveson, Harold A., et al. 1979. "Fission Power: An Evolutionary Strategy," *Science*, vol. 203, 330–337.

*Feld, Bernard T. 1974. "The Menace of a Fission Power Economy," *Bulletin of the Atomic Scientists*, April, pp. 32–42.

*Feld, Bernard T. 1975. "Making the World Safe for Plutonium," *Bulletin of the Atomic Scientists*, May, pp. 5–6.

*Fennelly, Paul F. 1976. "The Origin and Influence of Airborne Particulates," *American Scientist*, vol. 64, 46–56.

Fenner, David, and Joseph Klarman. 1971. "Power from the Earth," *Environment*, vol. 13, no. 10, 19–34.

Ferguson, H. L. 1968. *Atmosphere*, vol. 6, 133.

Fisher, John C. 1974. *Energy Crises in Perspective*. New York: John Wiley.

*Fisher, Arthur. 1975a. "Wave Power," *Popular Science*, May, pp. 68–73.

*Fisher, Arthur. 1975b. "Energy from the Sea," *Popular Science*, June, pp. 78–83.

*Fisher, Arthur. 1978. "What Are We Going To Do about Nuclear Waste?" *Popular Science*, December, pp. 90–97.

*Fisher, J., et al. 1969. *Wildlife in Danger*. New York: Viking Press.

Fletcher, J. O. 1969. "Controlling the Planet's Climate," *Impact of Science on Society*, vol. 19, no. 2.

*Flood, Michael. 1976. "Nuclear Sabotage," *Bulletin of the Atomic Scientists*, October, pp. 29–36.

*Flower, Andrew R. 1978. "World Oil Production," *Scientific American*, vol. 238, no. 3, 42–49.

*Flowers, Brian, ed. 1976. *Nuclear Power and the Environment*, Sixth Report of the Royal Commission on Environmental Pollution. London: H. M. Stationery Office.

*Flowers, Brian. 1978. "Nuclear Power: A Perspective of the Risks, Benefits and Options," *Bulletin of the Atomic Scientists*, March, pp. 21–57.

*Foin, Theodore C., Jr. 1976. *Ecological Systems and the Environment*. Boston: Houghton Mifflin.

*Forbes, J. A., et al. 1972. "Cooling Water," *Environment*, vol. 14, no. 1, 41.

*Ford, Daniel F. 1977. *A History of Federal Nuclear Safety Assessment*. Cambridge, Mass.: Union of Concerned Scientists.

*Ford, D. F., and H. W. Kendall. 1972. "Nuclear Safety," *Environment*, vol. 14, no. 7.

*Ford, Daniel F., and Henry W. Kendall. 1975. "Nuclear Misinformation," *Environment*, vol. 17, no. 5, 17–27.

*Ford, Daniel F., et al. 1974. *The Nuclear Fuel Cycle*. Cambridge, Mass.: Union of Concerned Scientists.

*Foreman, Harvey, ed. 1971. *Nuclear Power and the Public*. Minneapolis: University of Minnesota Press.

*Foster, William M. 1976. *Homeowner's Guide to Solar Heating and Cooling*. New York: Tab Books.

*Fowler, John W. 1975a. *Energy and the Environment.* New York: McGraw-Hill.

*Fowler, John W. 1975b. *Energy-Environment Source Book.* 2 vols. Washington, D.C.: National Science Teachers Association.

*Fowler, T. A., and K. Z. Post. 1976. "Fusion Power and the Environment." In R. A. Karam and K. Z. Morgan, eds., *Energy and the Environment: Cost-Benefit Analysis.* New York: Pergamon.

*Fowler, John M., et al. 1978. "Power Plant Performance," *Environment,* vol. 20, no. 3, 25–32.

*Francis, John, and Paul Abrecht. 1976. *Facing Up to Nuclear Power.* Philadelphia: Westminster Press.

*Franta, Gregory E., and Kenneth R. Olson. 1978. *Solar Architecture.* Ann Arbor, Mich.: Ann Arbor Science.

*Freeman, S. David. 1974. *Energy: The New Era.* New York: Walker.

*French, J., et al. 1973. "The Effect of Sulfur Dioxide and Suspended Sulfates on Acute Respiratory Disease," *Archives of Environmental Health,* vol. 27, 129–133.

*Fritsch, Albert J. 1974. *The Constrasumers: A Citizens' Guide to Resource Conservation.* New York: Praeger.

*Fritsch, Albert J., et al. 1977. *99 Ways to a Simple Lifestyle.* Bloomington: Indiana University Press.

*Fromm, Erich. 1968. *The Revolution of Hope: Toward a Humanized Technology.* New York: Harper & Row.

*Fuller, John G. 1975. *We Almost Lost Detroit.* New York: Reader's Digest Press.

*Futures Group. 1977. *A Technology Assessment of Geothermal Energy Resource Development.* Washington, D.C.: Government Printing Office.

*Galveke, Clarence G., and P. H. McGavhey. 1976. "Waste Materials." In Jack M. Hollander and Melvin K. Simmons, eds., *Annual Review of Energy,* vol. 1. Palo Alto, Calif.: Annual Reviews.

*Gannon, Robert. 1974. "Shale Oil . . . How Soon?" *Popular Science,* September, pp. 78–114.

*Gardner, John W. 1970. *The Recovery of Confidence.* New York: W. W. Norton.

*Garnish, J. D. 1978. "Progress in Geothermal Energy," *Endeavour,* vol. 2, no. 2, 66–71.

*Garvey, Gerald. 1972. *Energy, Ecology, Economy.* New York: W. W. Norton.

*Gates, David M. 1971. "The Flow of Energy in the Biosphere," *Scientific American,* September.

*Gay, Larry. 1974. *The Complete Book of Heating with Wood.* Charlotte, Vt.: Garden Way.

*Geesaman, Donald P., and Dean E. Abrahamson. 1974. "The Dilemma of Fission Power," *Bulletin of the Atomic Scientists,* November, pp. 37–41.

General Accounting Office. 1971. "Progress and Problems in Programs for Managing High-Level Radioactive Wastes," B164052, *Report to Joint Committee on Atomic Energy.* January 29. Washington, D.C.: General Accounting Office.

*General Accounting Office. 1977. *The State of Competition in the Coal Industry.* Washington, D.C.: General Accounting Office.

George, Carl J., and Daniel McKinley. 1971. *Urban Ecology: In Search of an Asphalt Rose.* New York: McGraw-Hill.

*Georgescu-Roegen, Nicholas. 1971. *The Entropy Law and the Economic Process.* Cambridge, Mass.: Harvard University Press.

*Georgescu-Roegen, Nicholas. 1975. "Energy and Economic Myths," *Southern Economic Journal,* vol. 41, 347–381.

*Georgescu-Roegen, Nicholas. 1976. *Energy and Economic Myths.* New York: Pergamon.

*Georgescu-Roegen, Nicholas. 1977. "The Steady State and Ecological Salvation: A Thermodynamic Analysis," *BioScience,* vol. 27, 266–270.

*Georgia Conservancy. 1976. *The Wolfcreek Statement: Toward a Sustainable Energy Society.* Atlanta, Ga.: Georgia Conservancy.

*Geothermal Project et al. 1976. *Geothermal Handbook.* Washington, D.C.: ERDA/TIC.

*Gibbons, J. Whitfield, and Rebecca R. Sharitz. 1974. "Thermal Alteration of Aquatic Ecosystems," *American Scientist,* vol. 62, 660–670.

*Gibson, J. E. 1977. *Designing the New City: A Systematic Approach.* New York: Wiley.

*Gillette, Robert. 1973a. "Nuclear Safeguards: Holes in the Fence," *Science,* vol. 182, 1112–1114.

*Gillette, Robert. 1973b. "Radiation Spill at Hanford: The Anatomy of an Accident," *Science,* vol. 181, 728–730.

*Gillette, Robert. 1974a. "Plutonium (I): Questions of Health in a New Industry," *Science,* vol. 185, 1027–1032.

*Gillette, Robert. 1974b. "Plutonium (II): Watching and Waiting for Adverse Effects," *Science,* vol. 185, 1140–1144.

*Gilliland, Martha W. 1975. "Energy Analysis and Public Policy," *Science,* vol. 189, 1051–1056.

Gillinsky, Victor. 1971. "The Military Potential of Civil Nuclear Power." In Mason Willrich, ed., *Civil Nuclear Power and International Security.* New York: Praeger.

*Gillinsky, Victor. 1977. "Plutonium, Proliferation, and Policy," *Technology Review,* February, pp. 58–65.

*Gilmore, John S. 1976. "Boom Towns May Hinder Energy Resource Development," *Science,* vol. 191, 535–540.

*Gilmore, William R. 1977. *Radioactive Waste Disposal—Low and High Level.* Park Ridge, N.J.: Noyes Data.

*Gilmore, C. P. 1978. "Higher Efficiency with Solar-Assisted Heat Pumps," *Popular Science,* May, pp. 86–90.

*Global Atmospheric Research Program. 1975. *The Physical Basis of Climate Modeling.* Geneva, Switzerland: Global Atmospheric Research Program.

*Gofman, John W. 1975a. *The Cancer Hazard from Inhaled Plutonium.* Dublin, Calif.: Committee for Nuclear Responsibility.

*Gofman, John W. 1975b. *Estimated Production of Human Lung Cancers by Plutonium from Worldwide Fallout.* Dublin, Calif.: Committee for Nuclear Responsibility.

*Gofman, John W., and Arthur R. Tamplin. 1970a. "Low Dose Radiation and Cancer," *IEEE Transactions on Nuclear Science,* vol. N5-17, no. 1, 1–9.

*Gofman, John W., and Arthur R. Tamplin. 1970b. "Radiation: The Invisible Casualties," *Environment,* April, p. 12.

*Gofman, John W., and Arthur R. Tamplin. 1971. *Poisoned Power: The Case against Nuclear Power.* Emmaus, Pa.: Rodale Press.

Goldsmith, J. R., and S. A. Landaw. 1968. "Carbon Monoxide and Human Health," *Science,* vol. 162, 1352–1359.

*Goldstein, I. S. 1975. "Potential for Converting Wood into Plastics," *Science,* vol. 189, 847–852.

*Goldstein, Walter. 1978. "The Political Failure of U.S. Energy Policy," *Bulletin of the Atomic Scientists,* November, pp. 17–20.

*Goodenough, John B. 1976. "The Options for Using the Sun," *Technology Review,* October-November, pp. 63–71.

*Gordon, Richard L. 1978. "The Hobbling of Coal: Policy and Regulatory Uncertainties," *Science,* vol. 200, 153–158.

*Gordon, Howard, and Roy Meador, eds. 1977. *Perspectives on the Energy Crisis,* vol. 2. Ann Arbor, Mich.: Ann Arbor Science.

*Gosz, James R., et al. 1978. "The Flow of Energy in a Forest Ecosystem," *Scientific American,* vol. 238, no. 3, 93–103.

*Gough, William C., and Bernard J. Eastlund. 1971. "The Prospects of Fusion Power," *Scientific American,* February, pp. 56–64.

*Gouse, S. William, Jr. 1970. "Steam Cars," *Science Journal,* January, pp. 50–54.

*Grad, Frank, et al. 1975. *The Automobile and the Regulation of Its Impact on the Environment.* Norman: University of Oklahoma Press.

Graef, W., and C. Winter. 1968. "3,4 Benzopyrene in Erodel," *Archives of Hygiene,* vol. 152, no. 4, 289–293.

*Greenburg, William. 1973. "Chewing It Up at 200 Tons a Bite: Strip Mining," *Technology Review,* February, pp. 46–55.

*Greenwood, Ted, et al. 1977. *Nuclear Proliferation: Motivation, Capabilities, and Strategies for Control.* New York: McGraw-Hill.

*Gregory, Derek P. 1973. "The Hydrogen Economy," *Scientific American,* vol. 228, no. 1, 13–21.

*Gregory, D. P., and J. B. Pangborn. 1976. "Hydrogen Energy." In Jack M. Hollander and Melvin K. Simmons, eds., *Annual Review of Energy,* vol. 1. Palo Alto, Calif.: Annual Reviews.

*Grenon, M. 1977. "Global Energy Resources." In Jack M. Hollander et al., eds., *Annual Review of Energy,* vol. 2. Palo Alto, Calif.: Annual Reviews.

*Gribbin, John. 1976. *Forecasts, Famines and Freezes: Climate and Man's Future.* New York: Walker.

*Gribbin, John, ed. 1977. *Climatic Change.* Cambridge, England: Cambridge University Press.

*Griffith, Edward D., and Alan W. Clarke. 1979. "World Coal Production," *Scientific American,* vol. 240, no. 1, 38–47.

Griggin, W. C., Jr. 1965. "America's Airborne Garbage," *Saturday Review,* May 22, pp. 32–34, 95–96.

*Grossman, Richard, and Gail Daneker. 1977. *Jobs and Energy.* Washington, D.C.: Environmentalists for Full Employment.

*Grundlach, Erich R. 1977. "Oil Tanker Disasters," *Environment,* vol. 19, no. 9, 16–28.

*Gwynne, Peter. 1976. "Plutonium: 'Free' Fuel or Invitation to a Catastrophe?" *Smithsonian,* July, pp. 93–99.

*Gwynne, Peter, et al. 1976. "How Safe Is Nuclear Power?" *Newsweek,* April, pp. 70–75.

*Hackelman, Edwin C., Jr. 1977. "Is an Electric Vehicle in Your Future?" *Environmental Science and Technology,* vol. 2, 858–862.

*Häfele, Wolf. 1974. "A Systems Approach to Energy," *American Scientist,* vol. 62, 438–447.

*Häfele, Wolf, and W. Sassin. 1977. "The Global Energy System." In Jack M. Hollander et al., eds., *Annual Review of Energy,* vol. 2. Palo Alto, Calif.: Annual Reviews.

*Häfele, Wolf, et al. 1977. *Fusion and Fast Breeder Reactors.* Laxenburg, Austria: International Institute for Applied Systems Analysis.

*Hafemeister, David N. 1979. "Nonproliferation and Alternative Nuclear Technologies," *Technology Review,* December-January, pp. 58–62.

*Hagen, Arthur W. 1976. *Thermal Energy from the Sea.* Park Ridge, N.J.: Noyes Data.

*Halacy, D. S., Jr. 1973. *The Coming Age of Solar Energy.* 2nd ed. New York: Harper & Row.

*Halacy, D. S., Jr. 1975. *The Energy Trap.* New York: Four Winds Press.

*Halacy, D. S., Jr. 1977. *Earth, Water, Wind and Sun.* New York: Harper & Row.

*Halacy, D. S., Jr. 1978. *Ice or Fire? Surviving Climatic Change.* New York: Harper & Row.

*Hambleton, William W. 1972. "The Unsolved Problem of Nuclear Wastes," *Technology Review,* March/April, pp. 15–19.

*Hamer, John. 1976. "Solar Energy," *Editorial Research Reports,* vol. 2, no. 18, 825–842.

*Hamilton, W. F., II, and Dana K. Nance. 1969. "Systems Analysis of Urban Transportation," *Scientific American,* vol. 221, no. 1, 19–27.

*Hammond, A. L. 1972. "Conservation of Energy: The Potential for More Efficient Use," *Science*, vol. 178, 1079–1081.

*Hammond, A. L. 1973a. "Dry Geothermal Wells: Promising Experimental Results," *Science*, vol. 182, 43–44.

*Hammond, A. L. 1973b. "Energy and the Future: Research Priorities and National Policy," *Science*, vol. 179, 164–166.

*Hammond, A. L. 1973c. "Solar Energy: Proposal for a Major Research Program," *Science*, vol. 179, 1116. See also A. L. Hammond. 1972. "Solar Energy: The Largest Resource," *Science*, vol. 177, 1088–1090.

*Hammond, A. L. 1974a. "Individual Self-Sufficiency in Energy," *Science*, vol. 184, 278–282.

*Hammond, A. L. 1974b. "A Timetable for Expanded Energy Availability," *Science*, vol. 184, 367–369.

*Hammond, Allen L. 1975. "Solar Energy Reconsidered: ERDA Sees Bright Future," *Science*, vol. 189, 538–539.

*Hammond, Allen L. 1976a. "Coal Research (III): Liquefaction Has Far to Go," *Science*, vol. 193, 873–876.

*Hammond, Allen L. 1976b. "Uranium—Will There Be a Shortage or an Embarrassment of Enrichment?" *Science*, vol. 192, 866–867.

*Hammond, R. Philip. 1977a. "Nuclear Power Risks," *American Scientist*, vol. 62, 155–160.

*Hammond, Allen L. 1977b. "Alcohol: A Brazilian Answer to the Energy Crisis," *Science*, vol. 195, 564–567.

*Hammond, Allen L. 1977c. "Photosynthetic Solar Energy: Rediscovering Biomass Fuels," *Science*, vol. 197, 745–746.

*Hammond, Allen L. 1977d. "Photovoltaics: The Semiconductor Revolution Comes to Solar," *Science*, vol. 197, 445–447.

*Hammond, A. L., et al. 1973. *Energy and the Future*. Washington, D.C.: American Association for the Advancement of Science.

*Hammond, Ogden, and Robert E. Baron. 1976. "Synthetic Fuels: Prices, Prospects, and Priorities," *American Scientist*, vol. 64, 407–417.

*Hammond, Ogden, and Martin B. Zimmerman. 1975. "The Economics of Coal-Based Synthetic Gas," *Technology Review*, July-August, pp. 43–51.

*Hand, A. J. 1977. *Home Energy How To*. New York: Harper & Row.

*Hannon, Bruce M. 1974. "Options for Energy Conservation," *Technology Review*, February, pp. 24–31.

*Hannon, Bruce. 1975. "Energy Conservation and the Consumer," *Science*, vol. 189, no. 4197, 95–102.

*Hannon, Bruce. 1977a. "Economic Growth, Energy Use, and Altruism." In Dennis L. Meadows, ed., *Alternatives to Growth I*. Cambridge, Mass.: Ballinger.

*Hannon, Bruce. 1977b. "Energy, Labor, and the Conserver Society," *Technology Review*, March-April, pp. 47–53.

*Hannon, Bruce, and F. Puelo. 1974. *Transferring from Urban Cars to Buses: The Energy Employment Impacts*. Urbana: University of Illinois Press.

Hannon, Bruce, et al. 1978. "Energy and Labor in the Construction Sector," *Science*, vol. 202, 837–847.

*Hardin, Garrett. 1968. "The Tragedy of the Commons," *Science*, vol. 162, 1243–1248.

*Hardin, Garrett. 1974. "Living on a Lifeboat," *BioScience*, vol. 24, 561–568.

*Hardin, Garrett. 1975. "Gregg's Law," *BioScience*, vol. 25, 415.

*Hardin, Garrett. 1976a. "Living with the Faustian Bargain," *Bulletin of the Atomic Scientists*, November, pp. 25–28.

*Hardin, Garrett. 1976b. "Probable Results of Atomic Energy Dependency." In Colbert E. Cushing, Jr., ed., *Radioecological Problems Associated with the Development of Energy Sources*. London: Dowden, Hutchinson & Ross.

*Hardin, Garrett. 1976c. "Pejorism: The Middle Way," *The North American Review*, Summer, pp. 9–14.

*Hardin, Garrett. 1976d. "A Rapout of O'Neill's Dream," *The CoEvolution Quarterly*, Spring, pp. 28–29.

*Hardin, Garrett. 1977. *The Limits of Altruism: An Ecologist's View of Survival*. Bloomington: Indiana University Press.

*Hardin, Garrett. 1978. *Exploring New Ethics for Survival*, 2nd ed. New York: Viking Press.

*Harman, Willis W. 1975. "Changing Society to Cope with Scarcity," *Technology Review*, June, pp. 29–35.

*Harman, Willis W. 1977. "The Coming Transformation," *The Futurist*, February, pp. 4–11.

*Harnik, Peter. 1978. "How Strong Is the Movement?" *Environmental Action*, vol. 9, no. 24, 4–6.

*Hart, G. Kimball. 1978. *How to Cut Your Energy Cost: A Guide to Major Savings at Home and on the Road*. New York: Simon & Schuster.

*Harte, John, and Mohamed El-Gasseir. 1978. "Energy and Water," *Science*, vol. 199, 623–634.

*Harte, John, and Alan Jassby. 1978. "Energy Technologies and Natural Environments: The Search for Compatibility." In Jack M. Hollander et al., eds., *Annual Review of Energy*, vol. 3. Palo Alto, Calif.: Annual Reviews.

Harte, John, and Robert Socolow. 1971. *Patient Earth*. New York: Holt, Rinehart & Winston.

*Harvey, Douglas G., and W. R. Menchen. 1974. *The Automobile, Energy, and the Environment*. Columbia, Md.: Hittman Associates.

*Havlick, Spenser W. 1974. *The Urban Organism*. New York: Macmillan.

Hawley, Amos H. 1971. *Urban Society: An Ecological Approach*. New York: Ronald Press.

Hayes, Denis. 1976a. *Energy: The Case for Conservation*. Washington, D.C.: Worldwatch Institute.

*Hayes, Earl T. 1976b. "Energy Implications of Materials Processing," *Science*, vol. 191, 661–665.

*Hayes, Denis. 1976c. "Energy and Food," *Sierra Club Bulletin*, vol. 61, no. 5, 29–31.

*Hayes, Denis. 1976d. *Nuclear Power: The Fifth Horseman*. Washington, D.C.: Worldwatch Institute.

*Hayes, Denis. 1977. *Rays of Hope: The Transition to a Post-Petroleum World*. New York: Norton.

*Hayes, Denis. 1978a. *Repairs, Reuse, Recycling—First Steps toward a Sustainable Society*. Washington, D.C.: Worldwatch Institute.

*Hayes, Denis: 1978b. *The Solar Energy Timetable*. Washington, D.C.: Worldwatch Institute.

*Hayes, Earl T. 1979. "Energy Resources Available to the United States, 1985 to 2000," *Science*, vol. 203, 233–239.

*Hays, J. D., et al. 1976. "Variations in the Earth's Orbit: Pacemaker of the Ice Ages," *Science*, vol. 194, 1121–1132.

*Healy, Timothy J. 1974. *Energy, Electric Power and Man*. San Francisco: Boyd and Fraser.

*Healy, J. W., ed. 1976. *Plutonium: Health Implications for Man*. New York: Pergamon.

*Healy, Robert G., and Henry R. Hertzfeld. 1976. *Energy Conservation Strategies*. Washington, D.C.: Conservation Foundation.

Heilbroner, Robert L. 1974a. "The Human Prospect," *The New York Times Review*, January 24, pp. 21–34.

Heilbroner, Robert L. 1974b. *An Inquiry into the Human Prospect*. New York: W. W. Norton.

*Henahan, John F. 1974. "Geothermal Energy," *Popular Science*, November, pp. 96–143.

*Henderson, Carter. 1978a. *The Inevitability of Petroleum Rationing in the United States*. Princeton, N.J.: Princeton Center for Alternative Futures.

*Henderson, Carter. 1978b. "The Tragic Failure of Energy Planning," Bulletin of the Atomic Scientists, December, pp. 15–19.

*Henderson, Hazel. 1978c. *Creating Alternative Futures: The End of Economics*. New York: Berkley.

*Hendrie, J. M. 1976. "Safety of Nuclear Power." In Jack M. Hollander and Melvin K. Simmons, eds., *Annual Review of Energy*. Vol. 1. Palo Alto, Calif.: Annual Reviews.

*Herbert, Frank. 1976. *Dune*. New York: Ace.

*Heronemus, W. E. 1971. "Extraction of Pollution Free Energy from the Winds." Reprinted in *Congressional Record*, 92nd Congress, vol. 117, no. 190, pp. S. 20776–20780, December 7.

Heronemus, W. E. 1972a. "Power from Offshore Winds," proceedings of the 8th Annual Marine Technology Society Conference, Washington, D.C.

*Heronemus, W. E. 1972b. "The United Energy Crisis: Some Proposed Gentle Solutions." Paper presented at the joint meeting of the American Society of Mechanical Engineers and the Institute of Electrical and Electronics Engineers, West Springfield, Mass., January 12. Available from the author, University of Massachusetts, Amherst, Mass. 01002.

*Heronemus, W. E. 1975. "Wind Power: A Near-Term Partial Solution to the Energy Crisis." In L. C. Ruedisili and M. W. Firebaugh, eds., *Perspectives on Energy*. New York: Oxford University Press.

*Hesketh, H. E. 1974. *Understanding and Controlling Air Pollution*. Ann Arbor: Ann Arbor Science Publishers.

*Hess, W. N., ed. 1974. *Weather and Climate Modification*. New York: John Wiley.

*Hess, Hamilton. 1976. "Geothermal Energy Prospects and Limitations," *Sierra Club Bulletin*, vol. 61, no. 10, 9–12.

*Hexter, A. C., and J. R. Goldsmith. 1975. "Carbon Monoxide: Association of Community Air Pollution with Mortality," *Science*, vol. 172, 265–267.

*Hickel, Walter S., et al. 1972. *Geothermal Energy*. Fairbanks: University of Alaska.

*Higgins, I. T. T. 1974. *Epidemiology of Chronic Respiratory Disease: A Literature Review*. Washington, D.C.: Environmental Protection Agency.

*Hildebrant, Alvin F., and Lorin L. Vant-Hull. 1977. "Power with Heliostats," *Science*, vol. 197, 1139–1146.

*Hirst, Eric. 1973a. "The Energy Cost of Pollution Control," *Environment*, vol. 15, no. 8, 37–45.

*Hirst, Eric. 1973b. "Transportation, Energy Use and Conservation Potential," *Bulletin of the Atomic Scientists*, November, pp. 31–42.

*Hirst, Eric. 1974. "Food-Related Energy Requirements," *Science*, vol. 184, 134–138.

*Hirst, Eric. 1975a. "Energy Implications of Cleanup Operations," *Environmental Science and Technology*, vol. 9, no. 1, 25–28.

Hirst, Eric. 1975b. *Oak Ridge National Laboratory Report ORNL-NSF-EP-44*. Oak Ridge, Tenn.: Oak Ridge National Laboratory.

*Hirst, Eric. 1976a. "Residential Energy Use Alternatives: 1976 to 2000," *Science*, vol. 196, 1247–1252.

*Hirst, Eric. 1976b. "Transportation Energy Conservation Policies," *Science*, vol. 192, 15–20.

*Hirst, Eric, and Janet Carney. 1978. "Effects of Federal Residential Energy Conservation Programs," *Science*, vol. 199, 845–851.

*Hirst, Eric, and John C. Moyers. 1973. "Efficiency of Energy Use in the United States," *Science*, vol. 179, 1299–1304.

*Hirst, Eric, and Mayo S. Stuntz, Jr. 1976. "Urban Mass Transit Energy Use and Conservation Potential," *Energy Systems and Policy*, vol. 1, no. 4, 391–406.

Hobbs, P. V., et al. 1974. "Atmospheric Effects of Pollutants," *Science*, vol. 183, 909–914.

*Hodges, Laurent. 1977. *Environmental Pollution*, 2nd ed. New York: Holt, Rinehart & Winston.

*Hohenemser, Kurt H. 1975. "The Failsafe Risk," *Environment*, vol. 17, no. 1, 6–10.

*Hohenemser, Kurt H. 1977. "The National Energy Plan," *Environment,* vol. 19, no. 7, 4–5.

*Hohenemser, Christoph, and Robert Goble. 1978. "Statistical Analysis of Nuclear and Coal Power Plant Performance," *SIPI Scope,* vol. 6, no. 4, 1–57.

*Hohenemser, Christoph, et al. 1977. "The Distrust of Nuclear Power," *Science,* vol. 196, 25–34.

Holcomb, R. W. 1969. "Oil in the Ecosystem," *Science,* vol. 166, 204–206.

*Holcomb, R. W. 1970. "Radiation Risk: A Scientific Problem?" *Science,* vol. 167, 853–855.

*Holdren, John P. 1971a. "Adequacy of Lithium Supplies as a Fusion Energy Source." In U.S. Congress, Joint Committee on Atomic Energy, *Controlled Thermonuclear Research.* Washington, D.C.: Government Printing Office.

*Holdren, John P. 1971b. "Global Thermal Pollution." In J. P. Holdren and P. R. Ehrlich, eds., *Global Ecology.* New York: Harcourt Brace Jovanovich, pp. 85–88.

*Holdren, John P. 1974. "Hazards of the Nuclear Fuel Cycle," *Bulletin of the Atomic Scientists,* October, pp. 14–23.

*Holdren, John P. 1975a. "Energy Resources." In William W. Murdoch, ed., *Environment: Resources, Pollution and Society,* 2nd ed. Sunderland, Mass.: Sinauer.

*Holdren, John P. 1975b. "Uranium Availability and the Breeder Decision," *Energy Systems and Policy,* vol. 3, no. 3, 38.

*Holdren, John P. 1978. "Fusion Energy in Context: Its Fitness for the Long Term," *Science,* vol. 200, 168–180.

*Holdren, John P., and Philip Herrera. 1971. *Energy.* San Francisco: Sierra Club.

*Holland, W. W., ed. 1972. *Air Pollution and Respiratory Disease.* Westport, Conn.: Technomic.

*Holland, W. W., and D. D. Reid. 1965. "The Urban Factor in Chronic Bronchitis," *Lancet,* February 27, pp. 6–8.

*Hollander, Jack M., and Melvin K. Simmons, eds. 1976. *Annual Review of Energy,* vol. 1. Palo Alto, Calif.: Annual Reviews.

*Hollander, Jack M., et al., eds. 1977. *Annual Review of Energy,* vol. 2. Palo Alto, Calif.: Annual Reviews.

*Hollander, Jack M., et al., eds. 1978. *Annual Review of Energy,* vol. 3. Palo Alto, Calif.: Annual Reviews.

*Holling, C. S., and Gordon Orians. 1971. "Toward an Urban Ecology," *Ecological Society of America Bulletin,* vol. 52, no. 2, 2–6.

*Hollyer, Bill. 1977. "The Streetcar Dayton Desired," *Environmental Action,* vol. 9, no. 16, 4–7.

Holzman, David. 1978a. "Biomass Fuel: Fermenting Self-Sufficiency," *People and Energy,* February, pp. 10–11.

Holzman, David. 1978b. "Nuclear Fusion: Boon or Boondoggle?" *People and Energy,* July-August, pp. 4–6.

Holzman, David. 1978c. "Wood Fuel Makes Strong Come-back," *People and Energy,* May, pp. 5–6.

*Horne, R. A. 1978. *The Chemistry of Our Environment.* New York: Wiley-Interscience.

*Hottel, H. C., and J. B. Howard, 1972. *New Energy Technology: Some Facts and Assessments.* Cambridge, Mass.: MIT Press.

*Hoyle, Fred. 1977. *Energy or Extinction: The Case for Nuclear Energy.* New Hampshire: Heinemann Educational Books.

*Hubbert, M. King. 1962. *Energy Resources: A Report to the Committee on Natural Resources.* Publication 1000-D. Washington, D.C.: National Academy of Sciences.

*Hubbert, M. King. 1969a. "Energy Resources." In National Academy of Sciences, *Resources and Man.* San Francisco: W. H. Freeman.

*Hubbert, M. King. 1969b. "Tidal Power." In National Academy of Sciences, *Resources and Man.* San Francisco: W. H. Freeman.

*Hubbert, M. King. 1971. "The Energy Resources of the Earth," *Scientific American,* September.

*Hubbert, M. K. 1973. "Survey of World Energy Resources," *Canadian Mining and Metallurgical Bulletin,* vol. 66, no. 735, 37–54.

*Hubbert, M. K. 1974. *U.S. Energy Resources: A Review as of 1972.* Washington, D.C.: Senate Committee on Interior and Insular Affairs.

*Huettner, David A. 1976. "Net Energy Analysis: An Economic Assessment," *Science,* vol. 192, 101–104.

*Hull, Andrew P. 1971. "Radiation in Perspective: Some Comparisons of the Risks from Nuclear and Fossil Fueled Power Plants," *Nuclear Safety,* vol. 12, no. 3.

*Hutchinson, G. Evelyn. 1970. "The Biosphere," *Scientific American,* September. (Reprinted in Scientific American Editors, *The Biosphere,* San Francisco: W. H. Freeman, pp. 1–11.)

*Hyman, Barry I. 1973. *Initiatives in Energy Conservation.* Staff report prepared for the Committee on Commerce, U.S. Senate. Stock no. 5270-01960. Washington, D.C.: Government Printing Office.

*Iklé, Fred C. 1976. "Illusions and Realities about Nuclear Energy," *Bulletin of the Atomic Scientists,* October, pp. 14–17.

*Impact Team. 1977. *The Weather Conspiracy: The Coming of the New Ice Age.* New York: Ballantine.

*Inglis, David R. 1973. *Nuclear Energy: Its Physics and Social Challenge.* Reading, Mass.: Addison-Wesley.

*Inglis, David R. 1975. "Wind Power Now!" *Bulletin of the Atomic Scientists,* October, pp. 20–26.

*Inglis, David R. 1978. *Windpower and Other Energy Options.* Ann Arbor: University of Michigan Press.

*Institute for Energy Analysis. 1976. *Economic and Environmental Implications of a U.S. Nuclear Moratorium.* Oak Ridge, Tenn.: Institute for Energy Analysis.

*Institute for Energy Analysis. 1977. *The California Nuclear Initiative.* Palo Alto, Calif.: Stanford University.

*International Federation of Institutes for Advanced Study. 1974. *Energy Analysis Workshop on Methodology and Convention.* Stockholm: International Federation of Institutes for Advanced Study.

*Ishikawa, S., et al. 1969. "The Emphysema Profile in Two Midwestern Cities in North America," *Archives of Environmental Health,* April, pp. 132–138.

*IUCN. Published periodically. *Red Data Books.* Lausanne: IUCN.

*Jacoby, Henry D. 1977. "Uranium Dependence and the Proliferation Problem," *Technology Review,* June, pp. 19–29.

*Jakimo, Alan, and Irvin C. Bupp. 1978. "Nuclear Waste Disposal: Not in My Backyard," *Technology Review,* March-April, pp. 64–72.

Jamison, Andrew. 1970. *The Steam-Powered Automobile: An Answer to Air Pollution.* Bloomington: Indiana University Press.

*Jerome, John. 1972. *The Death of the Automobile.* New York: W. W. Norton.

*Jet Propulsion Laboratory. 1975. *Should We Have a New Engine?* 4 vols. Pasadena: California Institute of Technology.

*Jewell, William, et al. 1978. *Anaerobic Fermentation of Agricultural Residue.* Springfield, Va.: National Technical Information Service.

*Johnston, R., ed. 1976. *Marine Pollution.* New York: Academic Press.

*Joint Committee on Atomic Energy. 1973. *Understanding the National Energy Dilemma.* Washington, D.C.: Government Printing Office.

*Jones, Lawrence W. 1971. "Liquid Hydrogen as a Fuel for the Future," *Science,* vol. 174, 367–370.

*Kagawa, J., and T. Toyama. 1975. "Photochemical Air Pollution," *Archives of Environmental Health,* vol. 30, 117–122.

*Kalhammer, Fritz R., and Thomas R. Schneider. 1976. "Energy Storage." In Jack M. Hollander and Melvin K. Simmons, eds., *Annual Review of Energy,* vol. 1. Palo Alto, Calif.: Annual Reviews.

*Kalter, Robert J., and William A. Vogely. 1976. *Energy Supply and Public Policy.* Ithaca: Cornell University Press.

*Kane, D. N. 1976. "Bad Air for Children," *Environment,* vol. 18, no. 9, 26–34.

*Karam, R. A., and K. Z. Morgan, eds. 1976. *Energy and the Environment: Cost Benefit Analysis.* New York: Pergamon.

*Karnaky, Karl J., Jr. 1977. "Ocean Thermal Gradients—A Practical Source of Energy?" *Science,* vol. 195, 206–207.

Karsch, Robert F. 1970. "The Social Costs of Surface Mined Coal." In Alfred J. Van Tassel, ed., *Environmental Side Effects of Rising Industrial Output.* Lexington, Mass.: D. C. Heath.

*Kasper, William C. 1974. "Power from Trash," *Environment,* vol. 16, no. 2, 34–39.

*Keeling, C. D. 1973a. "Industrial Production of Carbon Dioxide from Fossil Fuels and Limestone," *Tellus,* vol. 25, 174–178.

*Keeling, C. D. 1973b. "The Carbon Dioxide Cycle: Reservoir Models to Depict the Exchange of Atmospheric Carbon Dioxide with the Oceans and Land Plants." In B. I. Rasool, ed., *Chemistry of the Lower Atmosphere.* New York: Plenum.

*Keeling, C. D. 1977. "Impact of Industrial Gases on Climate." In National Academy of Sciences, *Energy and Climate: Outer Limits to Growth.* Washington, D.C.: National Academy of Sciences.

*Keeling, C. D., et al. 1976. "Atmospheric Carbon Dioxide Variations at Mauna Loa Observatory, Hawaii," *Tellus,* vol. 20, 538–551.

*Keeny, Spurgeon M., Jr., ed. 1977. *Nuclear Power Issues and Choices.* Cambridge, Mass.: Ballinger.

*Keller, Eugenia. 1976. "Energy from the Earth," *Chemistry,* vol. 49, no. 4, 10–17.

*Kelley, J. H., and E. A. Laumann, eds. 1975. *Hydrogen Tomorrow: Demands and Technology Requirements.* Pasadena, Calif.: Jet Propulsion Laboratory.

*Kellogg, William W. 1977. "Global Influences of Mankind on the Climate." In John Gribbin, ed., *Climatic Change.* Cambridge, England: Cambridge University Press.

*Kellogg, William W. 1978. "Warming the Earth," *Bulletin of the Atomic Scientists,* February, pp. 11–19.

Kellogg, W. W., and G. D. Robinson, eds. 1971. *Man's Impact on Climate.* Cambridge, Mass.: MIT Press.

*Kellogg, W. W., and S. H. Schneider. 1974. "Climate Stabilization: For Better or for Worse," *Science,* vol. 186, 1163–1172.

*Kellogg, William W., et al. 1975. "Effect of Anthropogenic Aerosols on the Global Climate," *Proceedings of WMO/IAMAP Symposium on Long-Term Climatic Fluctuations.* Geneva: World Meteorological Organization.

*Kemp, Michael, and Melryn Cheslow. 1976. "Transportation." In William Gorham and Nathan Glazer, eds., *The Urban Predicament.* New York: Urban Institute, pp. 281–356.

*Kendall, H. W. 1975. *Nuclear Power Risks: A Review of the Report of the American Physical Society Study Group on Light Water Reactor Safety.* Cambridge, Mass.: Union of Concerned Scientists.

*Kendall, H. W., ed. 1977. *The Risks of Nuclear Power Reactors.* Washington, D.C.: Union of Concerned Scientists.

*Kennett, J. P., and P. Huddleston. 1972. "Abrupt Climatic Change at 90,000 Yr BP," *Quaternary Research,* vol. 2, 384–395.

*Kern, Ken. 1975. *The Owner Built Home*. New York: Scribner.

*Kerr, Richard A. 1977a. "Carbon Dioxide and Climate: Carbon Budget Still Unbalanced," *Science*, vol. 197, 1352–1353.

*Kerr, R. 1977b. "Oil in the Ocean: Circumstances Control Its Impact," *Science*, vol. 198, 1134–1136.

*Keyes, John. 1975. *Harnessing the Sun to Heat Your House*, 2nd ed. Dobbs Ferry, N.Y.: Morgan and Morgan.

*Keyfitz, Nathan. 1976. "World Resources and the World Middle Class," *Scientific American*, vol. 235, no. 1, 28–35.

*Kiefer, Irene. 1974. "Earth Boils Below While We Scratch the Surface for Fuel," *Smithsonian*, November, pp. 82–89.

*Kleeberg, Irene Cumming. 1977. *The Home Energy Saver: All the Facts You Need to Save Energy Dollars*. New York: Butterick.

*Knabe, W. 1976. "Effects of Sulfur Dioxide on Terrestrial Vegetation," *Ambio*, vol. 5, no. 5–6, 213–218.

*Kneese, Allen V. 1973. "The Faustian Bargain," *Resources*, no. 44, September, pp. 1–3.

*Knelman, Fred H. 1976. *Nuclear Energy: The Unforgiving Technology*. Edmonton, Alberta: Hurtig.

*Knowles, Ralph. 1975a. *Energy and Form: An Ecological Approach to Urban Growth*. Cambridge, Mass.: MIT Press.

*Knowles, Ruth S. 1975b. *America's Oil Famine*. New York: Knowles.

*Koestner, E. J., et al. 1971. *The Do-It-Yourself Environmental Handbook*. Boston: Little, Brown.

*Kohl, J. ed. 1976. *Energy from the Oceans, Fact or Fancy?* Springfield, Va.: National Technical Information Service.

*Komanoff, Charles. 1976. *Power Plant Performance*. New York: Council on Economic Priorities.

*Komanoff, Charles. 1977. *Comparative Economics of Nuclear and Fossil Fuel Generating Facilities*. New York: Komanoff Energy Associates.

*Koppenaal, David W., and Stanley E. Manahan. 1976. "Hazardous Chemicals from Coal Conversion Processes?" *Environmental Science and Technology*, vol. 10, no. 12, 1104–1107.

*Kormondy, Edward J. 1976. *Concepts of Ecology*, 2nd ed. Englewood Cliffs, N.J.: Prentice-Hall.

*Krebs, Charles T., and Kathryn A. Burns. 1977. "Long-Term Effects of an Oil Spill on Populations of the Salt-Marsh Crab *Uca pugnax*," *Science*, vol. 197, 484–487.

*Kreiger, David. 1975. "Terrorists and Nuclear Technology," *Bulletin of the Atomic Scientists*, June, pp. 28–34.

*Kruger, Paul. 1976. "Geothermal Energy." In Jack M. Hollander and Melvin K. Simmons, eds., *Annual Review of Energy*, vol. 1. Palo Alto, Calif.: Annual Reviews.

Kruger, P., and C. Otte, eds. 1972. *Geothermal Energy*. Stanford, Calif.: Stanford University Press.

*Kubo, Arthur S., and David J. Rose. 1973. "Disposal of Nuclear Wastes," *Science*, vol. 182, 1205–1211.

*Kukla, George J., and Helena J. Kukla. 1974. "Increasing Surface Albedo in the Northern Hemisphere," *Science*, vol. 183, 709–714.

*Kulcinski, G. L. 1974. "Fusion Power," *Energy Policy Journal*, vol. 2, no. 2, 104–125.

*Kulcinski, G. L., et al. 1979. "Energy for the Long Run: Fission or Fusion?" *American Scientist*, vol. 67, 78–89.

*Kuller, Lewis H., et al. 1975. "Carbon Monoxide and Heart Attacks," *Archives of Environmental Health*, vol. 30, 477–482.

*Ladurie, Emmanuel. 1973. *Times of Feast, Times of Famine*. London: Allen & Unwin.

*Lamb, H. H. 1972. *Climate: Present, Past, and Future*. London: Methuen.

*Lamb, H. H. 1977. *Climate: Present, Past, and Future*, vol. 2. New York: Barnes & Noble.

Lambert, P. M., and D. D. Reid. 1970. "Smoking, Air Pollution, and Health," *Lancet*, April 25.

Landis, John W. 1973. "Fusion Power," *Journal of Chemical Education*, vol. 50, no. 10, 658–662.

Landsberg, H. E. 1970a. "Climates and Urban Planning." In World Meteorological Organization, *Urban Climates*. Geneva: Secretariat of the World Meteorological Organization.

*Landsberg, H. E. 1970b. "Man-Made Climatic Changes," *Science*, vol. 170, 1265–1274.

*Landsberg, Hans H. 1974a. "Assessing the Materials Threat," *Resources*, no. 47, 1–3.

*Landsberg, Hans H. 1974b. "Low-Cost, Abundant Energy: Paradise Lost?" *Science*, vol. 184, 247–253.

*Landy, Marc K. 1976. *The Politics of Environmental Reform: Controlling Kentucky Strip Mining*. Baltimore: Johns Hopkins University Press.

*Lang, Jean M., and Dennis L. Fisher, eds. 1975. *Resources and Decisions*. Belmont, Calif.: Wadsworth (Duxbury).

Lanovette, William J. 1977. "Coal, a Beleaguered Savior," *National Observer*, May 9, p. 4.

*LaPorte, Todd R. 1978. "Nuclear Waste: Increasing Scale and Sociopolitical Impacts," *Science*, vol. 201, 22–28.

*Lapp, Ralph E. 1973a. *The Logarithmic Century*. Englewood Cliffs, N.J.: Prentice-Hall.

*Lapp, Ralph E. 1973b. "The Ultimate Blackmail," *New York Times Magazine*, February 4.

*Lapp, Ralph E. 1974. *The Nuclear Controversy*. Greenwich, Conn.: Fact Systems.

*Lappé, Frances M., and Joseph Collins. 1977. *Food First*. Boston: Houghton Mifflin.

*Large, David B. 1973. *Hidden Waste: Potentials for Energy Conservation*. Washington, D.C.: Conservation Foundation.

*Large, David B. 1976. *Hidden Waste*. Washington, D.C.: Conservation Foundation.

*Lave, Charles L. 1977a. *Transportation and Energy: Some Current Myths*. Irvine: Institute of Transportation Studies, University of California, Irvine.

Lave, Charles. 1977b. "Negative Energy Impact of Modern Rail Transit Systems," *Science*, vol. 195, 595–596.

*Lave, Lester B., and Eugene B. Seskin. 1970. "Air Pollution and Human Health," *Science*, vol. 169, 723–732.

*Lave, Lester B., and Eugene B. Seskin. 1977. *Air Pollution and Human Health*. Baltimore: Johns Hopkins University Press.

*Lave, L. B., and L. P. Silverman. 1976. "Economic Costs of Energy Related Environmental Pollution." In Jack M. Hollander and Melvin K. Simmons, eds., *Annual Review of Energy*. Palo Alto, Calif.: Annual Reviews.

*Laycock, G. 1970. *The Diligent Destroyers*. Garden City, N.Y.: Doubleday.

*Leachman, Robert B., and Phillip Althoff, eds. 1971. *Preventing Nuclear Theft: Guidelines for Industry and Government*. New York: Praeger.

*Leachman, Robert, and Glenn Seaborg, eds. 1977. *Preventing Nuclear Theft: Guidelines for Industry and Government*. New York: Irvington.

*League of Women Voters. 1970. *A Congregation of Vapors*. Washington, D.C.: League of Women Voters.

*League of Women Voters. 1977. "Are Jobs Really the Price of a Clean Environment?" *Current Focus*, publication no. 40, pp. 1–6.

*League of Women Voters Education Fund. 1977a. *Energy Dilemmas*. Washington, D.C.: League of Women Voters.

*League of Women Voters Education Fund. 1977b. *Energy Options*. Washington, D.C.: League of Women Voters.

*League of Women Voters Education Fund. 1977c. *Growth and Land Use: Shaping Future Patterns*. Washington, D.C.: League of Women Voters.

*Leavitt, Helen. 1970. *Superhighway—Superhoax*. New York: Doubleday.

*Leckle, Jim, et al. 1975. *Other Homes and Garbage: Designs for Self-Sufficient Living*. San Francisco: Sierra Club.

*Lee, William C. 1972. "Thermal Aquaculture: Engineering and Economics," *Environmental Science and Technology*, vol. 6, 232–237.

Lees, L. 1970. In Study of Critical Environmental Problems, *Man's Impact on the Global Environment*. Cambridge, Mass.: MIT Press, p. 63.

*Lehr, William E. 1973. "Marine Oil Pollution Control," *Technology Review*, February, pp. 13–22.

*Lenihan, John, and William W. Fletcher, eds. 1976. *Environment and Man*. Vol. 1: *Energy Resources and the Environment*. New York: Academic Press.

Leonard, R. R., Jr. 1973. "A Review of Fusion-Fission (Hybrid) Concepts," *Nuclear Technology*, vol. 10, 161–178.

*Lepkowski, Will. 1977. "Carbon Dioxide: A Problem of Producing Usable Data," *Chemical and Engineering News*, October 17, pp. 26–30.

Lepkowski, Will. 1979. "New Mexicans Debate Nuclear Waste Disposal," *Chemical and Engineering News*, January 1, pp. 20–24.

*Levin, A. A., et al. 1972. "Thermal Discharges: Ecological Effects," *Environmental Science and Technology*, vol. 6, 224–230.

*Lewis, Richard S. 1972. *The Nuclear Power Rebellion: Citizen vs. Atomic Industrial Establishment*. New York: Viking Press.

*Lewis, Harold, et al. 1978. *Risk Assessment Review Group Report to the U.S. Nuclear Regulatory Commission*. Washington, D.C.: Nuclear Regulatory Commission.

*Lidsky, Lawrence M. 1972. "The Quest for Fusion Power," *Technology Review*, January, pp. 10–21.

*Lieberman, M. A. 1976. "United States Uranium Resources: An Analysis of Historical Data," *Science*, vol. 192, 431–436.

*Lincoln, G. A. 1973. "Energy Conservation," *Science*, vol. 180, 155–162.

*Linden, O. 1975. "Acute Effects of Oil and Oil/Dispersant Mixture on Larvae of Baltic Herring," *Ambio*, vol. 4, no. 3, 130–133.

*Linden, H. R., et al. 1976. "Production of High-BTU Gas from Coal." In Jack M. Hollander and Melvin K. Simmons, eds., *Annual Review of Energy*, vol. 1. Palo Alto, Calif.: Annual Reviews.

Lindop, Patricia, and J. Rotblat. 1971. "Radiation Pollution of the Environment," *Bulletin of the Atomic Scientists*, September, pp. 17–24.

*Lindsley, E. F. 1975. "Storable, Renewable Hydrogen Power," *Popular Science*, March, pp. 88–145.

*Livingston, John A. 1973. *One Cosmic Instant*. Boston: Houghton Mifflin.

*Lockheed-California. 1978. *Wind Energy Mission Analysis*. Springfield, Va.: National Technical Information Service.

Lockwood, Arthur. 1969. *Diagrams*. New York: Watson-Guptill.

*Loftas, Tony. 1971. "The Unseen Dangers of Oil," *New Scientist*, February 4, p. 228.

*Loucks, Orie L. "Contaminants and Recycling in Relation to Biogeochemical Cycles." In John A. Behnke, ed., *Challenging Biological Problems*. New York: Oxford University Press, pp. 297–312.

*Love, Sam. 1975. "Houses Designed with Nature: Their Future Is at Hand," *Smithsonian*, vol. 6, no. 9, 46–53.

*Lovins, Amory B. 1973. "The Case against the Fast Breeder Reactor," *Bulletin of the Atomic Scientists*, March 1973, pp. 29–35.

*Lovins, Amory B. 1974. "World Energy Strategies, Parts 1 and 2," *Bulletin of the Atomic Scientists*, May and June, pp. 14–32.

*Lovins, Amory B. 1975. *World Energy Strategies: Facts, Issues, and Options*. Cambridge, Mass.: Ballinger.

*Lovins, Amory B. 1976. "Energy Strategy: The Road Not Taken," *Foreign Affairs*, October, pp. 55–96.

*Lovins, Amory B. 1977a. "Energy." In Hugh Nash, ed., *Progress As If Survival Mattered.* San Francisco: Friends of the Earth.

*Lovins, Amory B. 1977b. "Limits to Energy Conversion: The Case for Decentralized Technologies." In Dennis L. Meadows, ed., *Alternatives to Growth I.* Cambridge, Mass.: Ballinger.

*Lovins, Amory B. 1977c. *Soft Energy Paths.* Cambridge, Mass.: Ballinger.

*Lovins, Amory B. 1977d. "Epitaph for an Industry," *Not Man Apart,* November, pp. 14–15.

*Lovins, Amory B. 1978a. "Soft Energy Technologies." In Jack M. Hollander et al., eds., *Annual Review of Energy,* vol. 3. Palo Alto, Calif.: Annual Reviews.

Lovins, Amory B. 1978b. "Fission Not the Method," *Bulletin of the Atomic Scientists,* November, pp. 62–63.

*Lovins, Amory B. 1979. "Thorium Cycles and Proliferation," *Bulletin of the Atomic Scientists,* February, pp. 16–22.

*Lovins, Amory B., and John H. Price. 1975. *Non-Nuclear Futures: The Case for an Ethical Energy Strategy.* Cambridge, Mass.: Ballinger.

*Lowry, W. P. 1967. "The Climate of Cities," *Scientific American,* August.

Lubin, Moshe J., and Arthur P. Fraas. 1971. "Fusion by Lasers," *Scientific American,* vol. 224, no. 6, 21.

*Luten, Daniel B. 1971. "The Economic Geography of Energy," *Scientific American,* September.

*Lynn, David A. 1975. "Air Pollution." In William W. Murdoch, ed., *Environment: Resources, Pollution and Society.* Sunderland, Mass.: Sinauer, pp. 223–249.

*Lynn, David A. 1976. *Air Pollution—Threat and Response.* Reading, Mass.: Addison-Wesley.

*Lyons, Stephen, ed. 1978. *Sun! A Handbook for the Solar Decade.* San Francisco: Friends of the Earth.

*McBride, J. P., et al. 1978. "Radiological Impact of Airborne Effluents of Coal and Nuclear Power," *Science,* vol. 202, 1045–1050.

*McCaull, Julian, 1973. "Windmills," *Environment,* vol. 15, no. 1, 6–17.

*McCaull, Julian. 1974. "Wringing Out the West," *Environment,* vol. 16, no. 7, 10–17.

*McCaull, Julian. 1976a. "Energy and Jobs," *Environment,* vol. 18, no. 1, 18–20.

*McCaull, Julian. 1976b. "Storing the Sun," *Environment,* vol. 18, no. 5, 9–15.

*McDaniels, David K. 1979. *The Sun! Our Future Energy Source.* New York: Wiley.

MacDonald, Gordon J. 1972. "Energy in the Environment." In Sam H. Schurr, ed., *Energy, Economic Growth and Environment.* Baltimore: Johns Hopkins University Press, pp. 103–104.

*MacDonald, Gordon J. 1975. "Pollution, Weather and Climate." In W. W. Murdoch, ed., *Environment: Resources, Pollution and Society.* 2nd ed. Sunderland, Mass.: Sinauer.

*McGuigan, Dermot. 1978. *Harnessing the Wind for Home Energy.* Charlotte, Vt.: Garden Way.

*McGuigan, Dermot. 1979. *Harnessing Water Power for Home Energy.* Charlotte, Vt.: Garden Way.

*McHale, John. 1970. *The Ecological Context.* New York: George Braziller.

Machta, L. 1971. "The Role of the Oceans and the Biosphere in the Carbon Dioxide Cycle," *Nobel Symposium,* vol. 20, August.

*Machta, Lester. 1973. "Prediction of CO_2 in the Atmosphere." In George W. Woodwell and E. V. Pecan, eds., *Carbon and the Biosphere.* Springfield, Va.: National Technical Information Service.

*Machta, Lester, and K. Telegadas. 1974. "Inadvertent Large-Scale Weather Modification." In W. N. Hess, ed., *Weather and Climate Modification.* New York: John Wiley, pp. 687–726.

*McIntyre, Hugh C. 1975. "Natural-Uranium Heavy-Water Reactors," *Scientific American,* vol. 233, no. 4, pp. 17–27.

*McLean, J. G. 1972. *The United States Energy Outlook and Its Implications for National Policy.* Stamford, Conn.: Continental Oil Co.

*McLean, Dewey M. 1978. "A Terminal Mesozoic 'Greenhouse': Lessons from the Past," *Science,* vol. 201, 401–406.

*MacLeish, William H., et al. 1977. "High-Level Nuclear Wastes in the Seabed?" *Oceanus,* vol. 20, no. 1, 1–67.

*McMullan, J. T., et al. 1978. *Energy Resources.* New York: Halsted.

*McPhee, John. 1974. *The Curve of Binding Energy.* New York: Ballantine.

*McVeigh, J. C. 1977. *Sun Power: An Introduction to the Applications of Solar Energy.* New York: Pergamon.

*Maddox, John. 1975. *Beyond the Energy Crisis: A Global Perspective.* New York: McGraw-Hill.

*Makhijani, Arjun. 1976. "Solar Energy and Rural Development for the Third World," *Bulletin of the Atomic Scientists,* June, pp. 14–24.

*Makhijani, A. B., and A. J. Lichtenberg. 1972. "Energy and Well-Being," *Environment,* June, pp. 11–18.

*Malin, H. M. 1973. "Geothermal Heats Up," *Environmental Science and Technology,* vol. 7, no. 8, 680–681.

Manabe, S. 1971. "Estimate of Future Change of Climate Due to the Increase of Carbon Dioxide Concentration in the Air." In W. H. Matthews et al., eds., *Man's Impact on Climate.* Cambridge, Mass.: MIT Press, pp. 249–264.

Manabe, S., and K. Bryan. 1969. "Climate Calculations with a Combined Ocean Atmosphere Model," *Journal of Atmospheric Sciences,* vol. 26, 786.

Manabe, S., and R. T. Wetherald. 1967. "Thermal Equilibrium of the Atmosphere with a Given Distribution of Relative Humidity," *Journal of Atmospheric Sciences,* vol. 24, 241–259.

*Manabe, S., and R. F. Wetherald. 1975. "The Effects of Doubling the CO_2 Concentration on Climate of a General Circulation Model," *Journal of Atmospheric Sciences,* vol. 32, 3–15.

*Marcus, Henry S. 1973. "The U.S. Superport Controversy," *Technology Review,* March/April, pp. 49–57.

*Margen, Peter, and Sören Lindhe. 1975. "The Capacity of Nuclear Power Plants," *Bulletin of the Atomic Scientists,* October, pp. 38–40.

*Markham, Jesse W., et al. 1978. *Horizontal Divestiture and the Petroleum Industry.* Cambridge, Mass.: Ballinger.

*Marquis, Stewart. 1968. "Ecosystems, Societies, and Cities," *The American Behavioral Scientist,* July/August, pp. 11–15.

*Marston, Edwin H. 1975. *The Dynamic Environment: Water, Transportation, and Energy.* New York: John Wiley.

*Martin, S., and W. J. Campbell. 1974. "Oil Spills in the Arctic Ocean: Extent of Spreading and Possibility of Large-Scale Thermal Effects," *Science,* vol. 186, 843–846.

*Martin, William F., and Frank J. P. Pinto. 1978. "Energy for the Third World," *Technology Review,* July, pp. 46–56.

*Marx, Wesley. 1971. *Oilspill.* San Francisco: Sierra Club.

*Marx, J. L. 1975. "Air Pollution: Effects on Plants," *Science,* vol. 187, 731–733.

*Mason, Roy. 1976. "Underground Architecture," *The Futurist,* February, pp. 16–20.

*Mathias, David A. 1976. *Hydrogen Technology for Energy.* Park Ridge, N.J.: Noyes Data.

Maugh, Thomas H., II. 1972a. "Fuel Cells: Dispersed Generation of Electricity," *Science,* vol. 178, 1273–1274.

*Maugh, Thomas H., II. 1972b. "Fuel from Wastes: A Minor Energy Source," *Science,* vol. 178, 599–602.

*Maugh, Thomas H., II. 1972c. "Gasification: A Rediscovered Source of Clean Fuel," *Science,* vol. 178, 44–45.

*Maugh, Thomas H., II. 1972d. "Hydrogen: Synthetic Fuel of the Future," *Science,* vol. 178, 849–852.

*Maugh, Thomas H., II. 1976a. "Photochemical Smog: Is It Safe to Treat the Air?" *Science,* vol. 193, 871–873.

*Maugh, Thomas H., II. 1976b. "Rerefined Oil: An Option That Saves Oil, Minimizes Pollution," *Science,* vol. 193, 1108–1110.

*Maugh, Thomas H., II. 1976c. "Natural Gas: United States Has It If the Price is Right," *Science,* vol. 191, 549–550.

*Maugh, Thomas H., II. 1977a. "Sulfuric Acid from Cars: A Problem That Never Materialized," *Science,* vol. 198, 280–284.

*Maugh, Thomas H., II. 1977b. "Underground Gasification," *Science,* vol. 198, 1132–1136.

*Maugh, Thomas H., II. 1977c. "Oil Shale: Prospects on the Upswing . . . Again," *Science,* vol. 198, 1023–1028.

*Maugh, Thomas H., II. 1978. "Tar Sands: A New Fuels Industry Takes Shape," *Science,* vol. 199, 756–760.

*Maurer, Charles E. 1977. "How They're Extracting Oil from Tar Sands," *Popular Science,* May, pp. 80–83.

*Mazur, Allan, and Eugene Rosa. 1974. "Energy and Life-Style," *Science,* vol. 186, 607–610.

*Mead, Walter J. 1977. "An Economic Appraisal of President Carter's Energy Program," *Science,* vol. 197, 340–345.

*Meador, Roy. 1978. *Future Energy Alternatives: Energy Problems and Prospects.* Ann Arbor, Mich.: Ann Arbor Science.

*Meadows, Donella H., et al. 1972. *The Limits to Growth.* New York: Universe Books.

*Meadows, Dennis L., et al. 1974. *Dynamics of Growth in a Finite World.* Cambridge, Mass.: Wright-Allen.

*Medvin, Norman. 1974. *The Energy Cartel: Who Runs the American Oil Industry?* New York: Vintage.

*Meier, Richard L. 1974. *The Design of Resource-Conserving Cities.* Cambridge, Mass.: MIT Press.

*Meier, Richard L. 1976. "A Stable Urban Ecosystem," *Science,* vol. 192, 962–968.

*Meinel, Aden B., and Marjorie P. Meinel. 1971. "Is It Time for a New Look at Solar Energy?" *Bulletin of the Atomic Scientists,* October, pp. 32–37.

*Meinel, Aden B., and Marjorie P. Meinel. 1972. "Physics Looks at Solar Energy," *Physics Today,* vol. 25, no. 2, 44.

*Meinel, Aden B., and Marjorie P. Meinel. 1976. *Applied Solar Energy.* Reading, Mass.: Addison-Wesley.

*Menck, H. R., et al. 1974. "Industrial Air Pollution: Possible Effects on Lung Cancer," *Science,* vol. 183, 210–211.

*Merriam, Marshal F. 1977. "Wind Energy for Human Needs," *Technology Review,* January, pp. 29–39.

*Merriam, Marshal F. 1978. "Wind, Waves and Tides." In Jack M. Hollander et al., eds., *Annual Review of Energy,* vol. 3. Palo Alto, Calif.: Annual Reviews.

*Merriman, Daniel. 1970. "The Calefaction of a River," *Scientific American,* vol. 222, no. 5, 45–52.

*Mervine, K. E. 1974. *Urban Mass Transportation.* College Park: Department of Physics and Astronomy, University of Maryland.

*Mervine, Kathryn E., and Rebecca E. Cawley. 1975. *Energy-Environment Materials Guide.* Washington, D.C.: National Science Teachers Association.

*Metillo, Jerry M. 1972. *Ecology Primer.* West Haven, Conn.: Pendulum Press.

*Metz, William D. 1972a. "Laser Fusion: A New Approach to Thermonuclear Power," *Science,* vol. 177, 1180–1182.

*Metz, William D. 1972b. "Magnetic Containment Fusion: What Are the Prospects?" *Science*, vol. 178, 291–293.

*Metz, William D. 1973. "Ocean Temperature Gradients: Solar Power from the Sea," *Science*, vol. 180, 1266–1267.

*Metz, William D. 1975. "Energy Conservation: Better Living through Thermodynamics," *Science*, vol. 188, 820–821.

*Metz, William D. 1976a. "Fusion Research (I): What Is the Program Buying the Country?" *Science*, vol. 192, 1320–1323.

*Metz, William D. 1976b. "Fusion Research (II): Detailed Reactor Studies Identify More Problems," *Science*, vol. 193, 38–39.

*Metz, William D. 1976c. "Fusion Research (III): New Interest in Fusion-Assisted Breeders," *Science*, vol. 193, 307–309.

*Metz, William D. 1976d. "European Breeders (II): The Nuclear Parts Are Not the Problem." *Science*, vol. 191, 368–371.

*Metz, William D. 1977a. "Ocean Thermal Energy: The Biggest Gamble in Solar Power," *Science*, vol. 198, 178–180.

*Metz, William D. 1977b. "Reprocessing Alternatives: The Options Multiply," *Science*, vol. 196, 284–287.

*Metz, William D. 1977c. "Solar Thermal Electricity: Power Tower Dominates Research," *Science*, vol. 197, 353–356.

*Metz, William D. 1977d. "Wind Energy: Large and Small Systems Competing," *Science*, vol. 197, 971–973.

Metz, William D. 1977e. "Reprocessing: How Necessary Is It for the Near Term?" *Science*, vol. 196, 43–45.

*Metz, William D. 1978a. "Mexico: The Premier Oil Discovery in the Western Hemisphere," *Science*, vol. 202, 1261–1265.

*Metz, William D. 1978b. "Capturing Sunlight: A Revolution in Collector Design," *Science*, vol. 201, 36–39.

*Metz, William D. 1978c. "Energy Storage and Solar Power: An Exaggerated Problem," *Science*, vol. 200, 1471–1473.

*Metz, William D. 1978d. "New Review of Nuclear Waste Disposal Calls for Early Test in New Mexico," *Science*, vol. 199, 1422–1423.

*Metz, William D. 1978e. "Report of Fusion Breakthrough Proves to Be a Media Event," *Science*, vol. 201, 792–794.

*Metz, William D., and Allen M. Hammond. 1978. *Solar Energy in America*. Washington, D.C.: American Association for the Advancement of Science.

Metzger, H. Peter. 1972. *The Atomic Establishment*. New York: Simon & Schuster.

Meyer, Charles F., and David V. Todd. 1973. "Conserving Energy with Heat Storage Wells," *Environmental Science and Technology*, vol. 7, 512–516.

*Micklin, Philip P. 1974. "Environmental Hazards of Nuclear Wastes," *Science and Public Affairs*, April, pp. 36–42.

Mihursky, J. A. 1967. "On Possible Constructive Uses of Thermal Additions to Estuaries," *BioScience*, vol. 17, 698–702.

*Miles, Rufus E., Jr. 1976. *Awakening from the American Dream*. New York: Universe Books.

*Miller, G. Tyler, Jr. 1971. *Energetics, Kinetics and Life: An Ecological Approach*. Belmont, Calif.: Wadsworth.

*Miller, G. Tyler, Jr. 1972. *Replenish the Earth—A Primer in Human Ecology*. Belmont, Calif.: Wadsworth.

*Miller, Saunders, and Craig Severance. 1976. *The Economics of Nuclear and Coal Power*. New York: Praeger.

*Miller, Betty M., et al. 1975. *Geological Estimates of Undiscovered Oil and Gas Resources in the United States*. Reston, Va.: U.S. Geological Survey.

Mills, G. Alex. 1971. "Gas from Coal: Fuel of the Future," *Environmental Science and Technology*, vol. 5, no. 12, 1178–1182.

*Mills, G. Alex, et al. 1971. "Fuels Management in an Environmental Age," *Environmental Science and Technology*, vol. 5, no. 1, 30–38.

*Mines, Samuel. 1971. *The Last Days of Mankind*. New York: Simon & Schuster.

Mitchell, J. M., Jr. 1971. "The Effect of Atmospheric Aerosols on Climate with Special Reference to Temperature near the Earth's Surface," *Journal of Applied Meteorology*, vol. 11, 651–657.

*Mitchell, J. M., Jr. 1972. "The Natural Breakdown of the Present Interglacial and Its Possible Intervention by Human Activities," *Quaternary Research*, vol. 2, 436–445.

*Mitchell, J. M., Jr. 1974. "The Global Cooling Effect on Increasing Atmospheric Aerosols: Fact or Fiction?" In *Proceedings of IAMAP/WMO Symposium on Physical and Dynamic Climatology*. Leningrad: World Meteorological Organization.

*Mitchell, J. M., Jr. 1975. "A Reassessment of Atmospheric Pollution as a Cause of Long-Term Changes of Global Climate." In S. Fred Singer, ed., *The Changing Global Environment*. Dordrecht, Netherlands: Reidel.

*Mitchell, Edward J., ed. 1976. *The Question of Offshore Oil*. Washington, D.C.: American Enterprise Institute for Public Policy Research.

*Mitsui, Akira, et al., eds. 1977. *Biological Solar Energy Conversion*. New York: Academic Press.

*Montefiore, Hugh, and David Gosling, eds. 1977. *Nuclear Crisis: A Question of Breeding*. Dorchester, England: Prism.

*Moody, John O., and Robert E. Geiger. 1975. "Petroleum Resources: How Much Oil and Where?" *Technology Review*, March-April, pp. 39–49.

*Moore, Stephen F. 1976. "Offshore Oil Spills and the Marine Environment," *Technology Review*, February, pp. 61–67.

*Moore, John W., and Elizabeth A. Moore. 1976. *Environmental Chemistry*. New York: Academic Press.

*Moreland, Frank L., ed. 1975. *Alternatives in Energy Conservation: The Use of Earth Covered Buildings*. Washington, D.C.: Government Printing Office.

Morgan, Karl Z. 1971. "Never Do Harm," *Environment*, vol. 13, no. 1, 28–38.

*Morgan, Karl Z. 1975. "Suggested Reduction of Permissible Exposure to Plutonium and Other Transuranium Elements," *American Industrial Hygiene Association Journal*, August, pp. 567–575.

*Morgan, Richard. 1977. *Nuclear Power: The Bargain We Can't Afford*. Washington, D.C.: Environmental Action Foundation.

*Morgan, Karl Z. 1978a. "Cancer and Low Level Ionizing Radiation," *Bulletin of the Atomic Scientists*, September, pp. 30–41.

*Morgan, George B. 1978b. "Energy Resource Development: The Monitoring Component." *Environmental Science and Technology*, vol. 12, no. 1, 34–43.

Morgan, George B., et al. 1970. "Air Pollution Surveillance Systems," *Science*, vol. 170, 289–296.

Morrow, Walter E., Jr. 1973. "Solar Energy: Its Time Is Near," *Technology Review*, December, pp. 31–40.

*Morse, Frederick H., and Melvin K. Simmons. 1976. "Solar Energy." In Jack M. Hollander and Melvin K. Simmons, eds., *Annual Review of Energy*, vol. 1. Palo Alto, Calif.: Annual Reviews.

Moskin, J. Robert. 1973. "Life and Death in Your Automobile," *World*, March 13, pp. 14–20.

*Mostert, Noël. 1974. *Supership*. New York: Alfred A. Knopf.

Mother Earth News. 1974. *Handbook of Homemade Power: Some Concrete Answers to the Energy Crisis*. New York: Bantam.

*Mudd, J. B., and T. T. Kozlowski, eds. 1975. *Responses of Plants to Air Pollution*. New York: Academic Press.

Muffler, L. J. P. 1973. *U.S. Geological Survey Professional Paper No. 820*. Washington, D.C.: Government Printing Office.

Mulvihill, R. J., et al. 1965. *Analysis of United States Power Reactor Accident Probability*. Los Angeles: Planning Research Corporation.

*Mumford, Lewis. 1963. *The Highway and the City*. New York: Harcourt Brace Jovanovich.

*Murphy, P. M. 1972. "Future Possibilities in Nuclear Fuel Processing." In *Proceedings of Connecticut Clean Power Symposium*, St. Joseph College, West Hartford, Conn., May 13.

*Murphy, John A. 1976a. *The Homeowner's Energy Guide: How to Beat the Heating Game*. New York: Crowell.

*Murphy, Arthur W., ed. 1976b. *The Nuclear Power Controversy*. New York: American Assembly.

*Murray, C. R., and E. B. Reeves. 1977. *Estimated Use of Water in the United States in 1975*. U.S. Geological Survey Circular 765. Washington, D.C.: Government Printing Office.

*Myers, Phyllis. 1974. *So Goes Vermont*. Washington, D.C.: Conservation Foundation.

Myrup, L. O. 1969. "A Numerical Model of the Urban Heat Island," *Journal of Applied Meteorology*, vol. 8, 908–918.

*Nader, Ralph, and John Abbotts. 1977. *The Menace of Atomic Energy*. New York: Norton.

*Naill, Roger F. 1977. "Evaluating the National Energy Plan," *Technology Review*, July-August, pp. 51–56.

*Naill, Roger F. 1978. *Managing the Energy Transition*. Cambridge, Mass.: Ballinger.

*Naill, Roger F., et al. 1975. "The Transition to Coal," *Technology Review*, October-November, pp. 19–29.

*Najarian, Thomas. 1978. "The Controversy over the Health Effects of Radiation," *Technology Review*, November, pp. 78–82.

*Nash, Hugh, ed. 1977. *Progress as if Survival Mattered*. San Francisco: Friends of the Earth.

*National Academy of Sciences. 1969. *Resources and Man*. San Francisco: W. H. Freeman.

*National Academy of Sciences. 1972. *The Effects on Population of Low Levels of Ionizing Radiation*. Washington, D.C.: National Academy of Sciences.

*National Academy of Sciences. 1973. *Report by the Committee on Motor Vehicle Emissions*. Washington, D.C.: National Academy of Sciences.

*National Academy of Sciences. 1974a. *Materials and the Near Term Energy Program*. Washington, D.C.: National Academy of Sciences.

*National Academy of Sciences. 1974b. *More Water for Arid Land: Promising Technologies and Research Opportunities*. Washington, D.C.: National Academy of Sciences.

*National Academy of Sciences. 1974c. *Rehabilitation Potential of Western Coal Lands*. Cambridge, Mass.: Ballinger.

*National Academy of Sciences. 1975a. *Air Quality and Stationary-Source Emission Control*. Washington, D.C.: National Academy of Sciences.

*National Academy of Sciences. 1975b. *Mineral Resources and the Environment*. Washington, D.C.: National Academy of Sciences.

*National Academy of Sciences. 1975c. *National Materials Policy*. Washington, D.C.: National Academy of Sciences.

*National Academy of Sciences. 1975d. *Petroleum in the Marine Environment*. Washington, D.C.: National Academy of Sciences.

*National Academy of Sciences. 1975e. *Population and Food: Crucial Issues*. Washington, D.C.: National Academy of Sciences.

*National Academy of Sciences. 1975f. *Productivity of World Ecosystems*. Washington, D.C.: National Academy of Sciences.

*National Academy of Sciences. 1975g. *Understanding Climate Change: A Program of Action*. Washington, D.C.: National Academy of Sciences.

*National Academy of Sciences. 1976a. *Climate and Food*. Washington, D.C.: National Academy of Sciences.

*National Academy of Sciences. 1976b. *Energy for Rural Development: Renewable Resources and Alternative Technologies for Developing Countries*. Washington, D.C.: National Academy of Sciences.

*National Academy of Sciences. 1977a. *Energy and Climate: Outer Limits to Growth*. Washington, D.C.: National Academy of Sciences.

*National Academy of Sciences. 1977b. *Implications of Environmental Regulations for Energy Production and Consumption*. Washington, D.C.: National Academy of Sciences.

*National Academy of Sciences. 1977c. *Implications of Environmental Regulations for Energy Production and Consumption*. Washington, D.C.: National Academy of Sciences.

*National Academy of Sciences. 1977d. *Coal as an Energy Resource*. Washington, D.C.: National Academy of Sciences.

*National Academy of Sciences. 1978a. *Helium: A Public Policy Problem*. Washington, D.C.: National Academy of Sciences.

*National Academy of Sciences. 1978b. *Radioactive Wastes at the Hanford Reservation*. Washington, D.C.: National Academy of Sciences.

*National Council on Radiation Protection and Measurements. 1975. *Natural Background Radiation in the United States*. Washington, D.C.: National Council on Radiation Protection Publications.

*National Petroleum Council. 1972. *U.S. Energy Outlook*. Washington, D.C.: National Petroleum Council.

*National Tuberculosis and Respiratory Disease Association. 1969. *Air Pollution Primer*. New York: National Tuberculosis and Respiratory Disease Association.

*National Water Commission. 1973. *Water Policies for the Future*. Port Washington, N.Y.: Water Information Center.

*National Wildlife Federation. 1978. *The End of the Road: A Citizen's Guide to Transportation Problemsolving*. Washington, D.C.: National Wildlife Foundation and the Environmental Action Fund.

*Navickis, Roberta. 1978. "Biomass," *Science News*, vol. 113, no. 16, 258–259.

*Nelkin, Dorothy, and Susan Fallows. 1978. "The Evolution of the Nuclear Debate: The Role of Public Participation." In Jack M. Hollander et al., eds., *Annual Review of Energy*, vol. 3. Palo Alto, Calif.: Annual Reviews.

Nephew, E. A. 1973. "The Challenge and Promise of Coal," *Technology Review*, December, pp. 21–29.

*Nero, A. V., and Y. C. Wong. 1977. *Radiological Health and Related Standards for Nuclear Power Plants*. Berkeley: Lawrence Berkeley Laboratory, University of California.

*Netscheat, Bruce C. 1970. "The Economic Impact of Electric Vehicles: A Scenario," *Bulletin of the Atomic Scientists*, May, pp. 29–35.

*Netscheat, Bruce C. 1971. "The Energy Company: A Monopoly Trend in Energy Markets," *Bulletin of the Atomic Scientists*, October, pp. 13–19.

Newell, R. E. 1971. "The Global Circulation of Atmospheric Pollutants," *Scientific American*, vol. 224, 32.

Newman, John. 1974. "A Ride for Everyone," *Environment*, June, pp. 11–18.

*Newman, James E., and Robert C. Pickett. 1974. "World Climates and Food Supply Violations," *Science*, vol. 186, 877–881.

*Neyman, Jerzy. 1977. "Public Health Hazards from Electricity-Producing Plants," *Science*, vol. 195, 754–758.

*Niering, William A., and Richard H. Goodwin, eds. 1975. "Energy Conservation on the Home Grounds," *Connecticut Aboretum*, July, pp. 1–28.

*Nisbet, I. 1974. "Hydroelectric Power: A Nonrenewable Resource?" *Technology Review*, vol. 76, no. 7, 5.

*Norwine, Jim. 1977. "A Question of Climate," *Environment*, vol. 19, no. 8, 6–27.

*Novick, Sheldon. 1973a. "Looking Forward," *Environment*, vol. 15, no. 4, 4–15.

*Novick, Sheldon. 1973b. "Toward a Nuclear Power Precipice," *Environment*, vol. 15, no. 2, 32–41.

*Novick, Sheldon. 1974a. "Nuclear Breeders," *Environment*, vol. 16, no. 6, 6–15.

*Novick, Sheldon. 1974b. "Report Card on Nuclear Power," *Environment*, vol. 16, no. 10, 6–12.

*Novick, Sheldon. 1975. "A Troublesome Brew," *Environment*, vol. 17, no. 4, 8–11.

*Novik, Sheldon. 1976a. "The Fuel Industry," *Environment*, vol. 18, no. 8, 13–27.

*Novick, Sheldon. 1976b. *The Electric War: The Fight over Nuclear Power*. San Francisco: Sierra Club Books.

*Novick, Sheldon, 1977. "Special Report—Energy Roundup," *Environment*, vol. 19, no. 5, 29–33.

*Noyes, Robert, ed. 1978. *Coal Resources, Characteristics and Ownership in the U.S.A.* New York: Noyes Data.

*NSF/NASA Solar Energy Panel. 1973. *Solar Energy as a National Resource*. College Park: Department of Mechanical Engineering, University of Maryland.

*Nuclear Energy Policy Study Group. 1977. *Nuclear Power Issues and Choices*. Cambridge, Mass.: Ballinger.

*Nuclear Regulatory Commission. 1975. *Reactor Safety Study: An Assessment of Accident Risks in U.S. Commercial Nuclear Power Plants*. Springfield, Va.: National Technical Information Service.

*Nuclear Regulatory Commission. 1976a. *Alternative Processes for Managing Existing Commercial High Level Radioactive Wastes*. Washington, D.C.: Nuclear Regulatory Commission.

*Nuclear Regulatory Commission. 1976b. *Environmental Survey of the Reprocessing and Waste Management Portions of the LWR Fuel Cycle*. Washington, D.C.: Nuclear Regulatory Commission Report.

*Nye, Joseph S., Jr. 1979. "Balancing Nonproliferation and Energy Security," *Technology Review*, December-January, pp. 45–57.

Oakley, Donald T. 1972. *Natural Radiation Exposure in the United States*. Washington, D.C.: Environmental Protection Agency. (For a summary of this report see *Environment*, vol. 15, no. 10, 31–35.)

Oceanus. 1977. *Oceanus*, vol. 20, no. 4, entire issue.

Odum, Eugene P. 1962. "Relationships between Structure and Function in an Ecosystem," *Japanese Journal of Ecology*, vol. 12, 108–118.

*Odum, Eugene P. 1969. "The Strategy of Ecosystem Development," *Science*, vol. 164, 262–270.

*Odum, Howard T. 1971a. *Environment, Power and Society*. New York: Wiley-Interscience.

*Odum, Eugene P. 1971b. *Fundamentals of Ecology*. 3rd ed. Philadelphia: W. B. Saunders.

*Odum, Eugene P. 1972. "Ecosystem Theory in Relation to Man." In John A. Wiens, ed., *Ecosystem Structure and Function*. Corvallis: Oregon State University Press, pp. 11–24.

*Odum, H. T. 1973. "Energy, Ecology, and Economics," *Ambio*, vol. 2, no. 6, 1–8.

*Odum, Eugene P. 1975. *Ecology*. 2nd ed. New York: Holt, Rinehart & Winston.

*Odum, Howard T., and Elisabeth C. Odum. 1976. *Energy Basis for Man and Nature*. New York: McGraw-Hill.

*Office of Emergency Preparedness. 1972. *The Potential for Energy Conservation*. Stock No. 4102–00009. Washington, D.C.: Government Printing Office.

Office of Science and Technology. 1972. *Patterns of Energy Use in the United States*. Washington, D.C.: Government Printing Office.

*Office of Technology Assessment. 1977. *Application of Solar Technology to Today's Energy Needs*. Washington, D.C.: Office of Technology Assessment.

Olsen, Jack. 1971. *Slaughter the Animals, Poison the Earth*. New York: Simon & Schuster.

Olson, T. A., and F. J. Burgess, eds. 1967. *Pollution and Marine Ecology*. New York: Wiley-Interscience.

O'Neill, Gerard K. 1975. "Space Colonies and Energy Supply to the Earth," *Science*, vol. 190, no. 4218, 943–948.

*Ophuls, William. 1977. *Ecology and the Politics of Scarcity*. San Francisco: W. H. Freeman.

*Oregon Office of Energy Research Planning. 1975. *Transition: A Book on Future Energy—Nuclear or Solar?* Portland, Ore.: Prometheus Unbound.

*Organization for Economic Cooperation and Development. 1977. *World Energy Outlook*. Paris: Organization for Economic Cooperation and Development.

*ORNL–NSF Environment Program. 1974. *Energy Conservation and the Environment*. Oak Ridge, Tenn.: Oak Ridge National Laboratory.

*Orski, C. Kenneth. 1977. "Mass Transit versus Highways," *Science*, vol. 197, 7.

*Osborn, Elburt F. 1974. "Coal and the Present Energy Situation," *Science*, vol. 183, 477–481.

*O'Sullivan, Dermot A. 1978. "Western Europe Pushing Ahead To Develop First Breeder Reactor," *Chemical and Engineering News*, February 13, pp. 41–47.

Othmer, Donald F., and Oswald A. Roels. 1973. "Power, Fresh Water, and Food from Cold, Deep Sea Water," *Science*, vol. 182, 121–125.

*Ott, Henry C. 1976. "Net from Nuclear Power," *Chemical and Engineering News*, April, pp. 3, 55.

*Owen, Wilfred. 1972. *The Accessible City*. Washington, D.C.: Brookings Institution.

*Owen, Wilfred. 1976. *Transportation in Cities*. Washington, D.C.: Brookings Institution.

*Paehlke, Robert. 1976. "Canada Oil Sands and Oil Companies," *Environment*, vol. 18, no. 9, 2–4.

*Page, James K., Jr., and Wilson Clark. 1975. "The New Alchemy: How to Survive in Your Spare Time," *Smithsonian*, February, pp. 82–88.

*Palz, W. 1977. *Solar Electricity: An Economic Approach to Solar Energy*. Kent, England: Butterworth.

*Panel on Geothermal Energy Resources. 1972. *Assessment of Geothermal Energy Resources*. Washington, D.C.: Government Printing Office.

*Park, Charles F., Jr. 1975. *Earthbound: Minerals, Energy, and Man's Future*. San Francisco: Freeman, Cooper.

*Parkins, W. E. 1978. "Engineering Limitations of Fusion Power Plants," *Science*, vol. 199, 1403–1408.

*Patterson, Walter C. 1976. *Nuclear Power*. Great Britain: Cox & Wyman.

*Pauling, Linus. 1970. "Genetic and Somatic Effects of High Energy Radiation," *Bulletin of the Atomic Scientists*, September, pp. 3–7.

*Peach, W. N. 1973. *The Energy Outlook for the 1980's*. Stock No. 5270–02113. Washington, D.C.: Government Printing Office.

*Pelley, William E., et al. 1976. *The Energy Industry and the Capital Market*. In Jack M. Hollander and Melvin K. Simmons, eds., *Annual Review of Energy*, vol. 1. Palo Alto, Calif.: Annual Reviews.

*Perkins, H. C. 1974. *Air Pollution*. New York: McGraw-Hill.

*Perrini, Edward M. 1975. *Oil from Shale and Tar Sands*. New York: Vintage.

*Perry, Harry. 1974. "The Gasification of Coal," *Scientific American*, vol. 230, no. 3, 19–25.

*Perry, Harry, and Harold Berkson. 1971. "Must Fossil Fuels Pollute?" *Technology Review*, December, pp. 34–43.

*Petersen, J. T. 1969. "The Climate of Cities: A Survey of Recent Literature," Pub. AP-59. Raleigh, N.C.: National Air Pollution Control Administration.

*Petersen, J. T. 1973. "Energy and the Weather," *Environment*, vol. 15, no. 8, 4–9.

*Petroleum Economics Ltd. 1978. *Technical Analysis of the International Oil Market*. London: Petroleum Economics Ltd.

*Pfeffer, F. M. 1974. *Pollutional Problems and Research Needs for an Oil Shale Industry*. Washington, D.C.: Environmental Protection Agency.

*Phillips, John A., and David Michaelis. 1978. *Mushroom: The Story of the A-Bomb Kid*. New York: Morrow.

*Phillipson, John. 1966. *Ecological Energetics*. New York: St. Martin's Press.

*Pianka, E. R. 1974. *Evolutionary Ecology*. New York: Harper & Row.

*Pierce, John R. 1975. "The Fuel Consumption of Automobiles," *Scientific American*, vol. 232, no. 1, 34–44.

*Pierce, R. C., and Morris Katz. 1975. "Dependency of Polynuclear Aromatic Hydrocarbon Content on Size Distribution of Atmospheric Aerosols," *Environmental Science and Technology*, vol. 9, 347–353.

*Pigford, T. 1974. "Environmental Aspects of Nuclear Energy Production," *Annual Review of Nuclear Science*, vol. 24, 515–559.

*Pimental, D., et al. 1973. "Food Production and the Energy Crisis," *Science*, vol. 182, 443–449.

*Pimental, David, et al. 1975. "Energy and Land Constraints in Food Protein Production," *Science*, vol. 190, 754–761.

*Pimental, David, et al. 1976. "Land Degradation: Effects on Food and Energy Resources," *Science*, vol. 194, 149–155.

*Pimental, David, et al. 1978. "Biological Solar Energy Conversion and U.S. Energy Policy," *BioScience*, vol. 28, no. 6, 376–381.

*Pirages, Dennis C., and Paul R. Ehrlich. 1974. *Ark II: Social Response to Environmental Imperatives*. San Francisco: W. H. Freeman.

Plass, G. 1959. "Carbon Dioxide and Climate," *Scientific American*, vol. 201, 41.

Policy Study Group of the MIT Energy Laboratory. 1974. "Energy Self-Sufficiency: An Economic Evaluation," *Technology Review*, May, pp. 23–58.

*Pollack, J. B., et al. 1976. "Volcanic Explosions and Climatic Change: A Theoretical Assessment," *Journal of Geophysical Research*, vol. 81, 1071–1083.

*Pollard, Robert D. 1976a. *A Critique of the NRC Nuclear Plant Reactor Safety Review*. Cambridge, Mass.: Union of Concerned Scientists.

*Pollard, William G. 1976b. "The Long-Range Prospects for Solar-Derived Fuels," *American Scientist*, vol. 64, 509–513.

*Pollard, William G. 1976c. "The Long-Range Prospects for Solar Energy," *American Scientist*, vol. 64, 424–429.

*Ponte, Lowell. 1976. *The Cooling*. Englewood Cliffs, N.J.: Prentice-Hall.

*Poole, Alan D. 1976. "Flower Power: Prospects for Photosynthetic Energy," *Bulletin of the Atomic Scientists*, May, pp. 48–57.

Population Reference Bureau. 1977. "Energy: Increasing Consumption, Decreasing Resources," *Interchange*, vol. 6, no. 1, 1–3.

*Portola Institute. 1974. *Energy Primer: Solar, Water, Wind, and Biofuels*. Menlo Park, Calif.: Portola Institute.

*Post, R. F. 1976. "Nuclear Fusion." In Jack M. Hollander and Melvin K. Simmons, eds., *Annual Review of Energy*, vol. 1. Palo Alto, Calif.: Annual Reviews.

*Post, R. F., and F. L. Ribe. 1974. "Fusion Reactors as Future Energy Sources," *Science*, vol. 186, 397–406.

*Potter, Jeffrey. 1973. *Disaster by Oil*. New York: Macmillan.

*Pratt, Larry. 1975. *The Tar Sands: Syncrude and the Politics of Oil*. Edmonton, Alberta: Hurtig.

*Price, John. 1974. *Dynamic Energy Analysis and Nuclear Power*. London: Earth Resources Research.

*Price, Billy, and James Price. 1976. *Homeowner's Guide to Saving Energy*. Blue Ridge Summit, Pa.: Tab Books.

*Priest, Joseph. 1973. *Problems of Our Physical Environment: Energy, Transportation, Pollution*. Reading, Mass.: Addison-Wesley.

*Priest, Joseph. 1975. *Energy for a Technological Society*. Reading, Mass.: Addison-Wesley.

*Primack, Joel. 1975. "Nuclear Reactor Safety," *Bulletin of the Atomic Scientists*, September, pp. 15–41.

*Primack, Joel, and Frank von Hippel. 1974. "Nuclear Reactor Safety," *Bulletin of the Atomic Scientists*, October, pp. 5–12.

*Pryde, Lucy T. 1973. *Environmental Chemistry: An Introduction*. Menlo Park, Calif.: Benjamin Cummings.

*Public Interest Group. 1975. *A Citizen's Handbook on Solar Energy*. Washington, D.C.: Public Interest Group.

*Purdom, P. W., ed. 1971. *Environmental Health*. New York: Academic Press.

*Quarles, John. 1976. *Cleaning Up America*. Boston: Houghton Mifflin.

*Rabinowitch, Eugene. 1973. "Challenges of the Scientific Age," *Bulletin of the Atomic Scientists*, September, pp. 4–8.

Radcliffe, Donna, and Thomas A. Murphy. 1969. *Biological Effects of Oil Pollution—Bibliography*. Washington, D.C.: Federal Water Pollution Control Administration, Department of Interior.

*Rae, John B. 1972. "The Mythology of Urban Transportation," *Traffic Quarterly*, vol. 26, 85–98.

Rafalik, Dianne. 1974. "Architecture's Towering Energy Costs," *Environmental Action*, April 13, pp. 11–14.

*Rall, David P. 1974. "Review of Health Effects of Sulfur Oxides," *Environmental Health Perspectives*, August, pp. 97–99.

*Raloff, Janet. 1978a. "Catch the Sun," *Science News*, vol. 113, no. 16, 248–267.

*Raloff, Janet. 1978b. "Radiation Hazard: The Military Experience," *Science News*, vol. 113, no. 6, 92–93.

Raloff, Janet. 1979. "Radiation: Can a Little Hurt?" *Science News*, vol. 115, 44–45.

*Ramseir, René O. 1974. "Oil on Ice," *Environment*, vol. 16, no. 4, 6–14.

*Rand, Christopher T. 1976. "The World Oil Industry," *Environment*, vol. 18, no. 3, 13–26.

Rasool, S. I., and S. H. Schneider. 1971. "Atmospheric Carbon Dioxide and Aerosols: Effects of Large Increases on Global Climate," *Science*, vol. 173, 138–141.

*Rattien, Stephen. 1976. "Oil Shale: The Prospects and Problems of an Emerging Energy Industry." In Jack M. Hollander and Melvin K. Simmons, eds., *Annual Review of Energy*, vol. 1. Palo Alto, Calif.: Annual Reviews.

*Rechel, Ralph. 1976. *Transportation Policies and Energy Conservation*. Washington, D.C.: Conservation Foundation.

*Reddy, Kumar N. 1978. "Energy Options for the Third World," *Bulletin of the Atomic Scientists*, May, pp. 28–33.

Reed, C. B. 1975. *Fuels, Minerals, and Human Survival*. Ann Arbor: Ann Arbor Science.

*Reed, T. B., and R. M. Lerner. 1973. "Methanol: A Versatile Fuel for Immediate Use," *Science*, vol. 182, 1299–1304.

Reese, Alexander. 1977. "The Uncertain Outlook on Industrial Energy Conservation," *Inform News*, October, pp. 1–4.

*Reid, Keith. 1970. *Nature's Network*. Garden City, N.Y.: Natural History Press.

*Reisch, Diana. 1970. *Problems of Mass Transportation*. New York: H. W. Wilson.

*Reitze, Arnold W., Jr. 1977a. "An Otto for the Automobile," *Environment*, May, pp. 32–42.

*Reitze, Arnold W., Jr. 1977b. "Running Out of Steam," *Environment*, June/July, pp. 34–40.

*Resnikoff, Marvin. 1974. "Expensive Enrichment," *Environment*, vol. 17, no. 5, 26–35.

Resources for the Future. 1974. "Air Pollution and Human Health," *Annual Report, 1973*. Washington, D.C.: Resources for the Future, pp. 15–20.

*Revelle, Roger. 1976. "Energy Use in Rural India," *Science*, vol. 192, 969–975.

Rex, R. W. 1971. "Geothermal Energy: The Neglected Energy Option," *Bulletin of the Atomic Scientists*, vol. 27, no. 8, 52.

*Reynolds, John. 1970. *Windmills and Watermills*. New York: Praeger.

*Rice, Richard A. 1974. "Toward More Transportation with Less Energy," *Technology Review*, February, pp. 45–53.

*Richardson, R. A. 1973. "A Dissent from the Imagery of 'Spaceship Earth,'" *The North American Review*, Summer, pp. 3–7.

*Richardson, Francis W. 1975. *Oil from Coal*. Park Ridge, N.J.: Noyes Data.

*Richardson, Jonathan L. 1977. *Dimensions of Ecology*. Baltimore: Williams & Wilkins.

*Rickard, Corwin L., and Richard C. Dahlberg. 1978. "Nuclear Power: A Balanced Approach," *Science*, vol. 202, 581–584.

*Ricklefs, R. E. 1973. *Ecology*. Newton, Mass.: Chiron Press.

*Ricklefs, Robert E. 1976. *The Economy of Nature*. Portland: Chiron Press.

*Riesenberg, Laura Brunton. 1978. "Sun Day a Requiem for Gas, Coal, and Oil," *Chemistry*, vol. 51, no. 6, 12–19.

*Rimberg, David. 1974. *Utilization of Waste Heat from Power Plants*. Park Ridge, N.J.: Noyes Data.

*Robertson, Thomas A. 1975. "Systems of Energy and the Energy of Systems," *Sierra Club Bulletin*, vol. 60, no. 3, 21–23.

*Robertson, J. A. L. 1978. "The CANDU Reactor System: An Appropriate Technology," *Science*, vol. 199, 657–664.

*Robertson, James, and John Lewallen, eds. 1975. *The Grass Roots Primer: The Spare Time, Low Cost, At Home Guide to Environmental Action*. New York: Charles Scribner's.

*Robertson, D. E., et al. 1977. "Mercury-Emissions from Geothermal Power Plants," *Science*, vol. 196, 1094–1097.

*Robinette, Gary O. 1972. *Plants/People/and Environmental Quality*. Washington, D.C.: National Park Service, U.S. Department of the Interior.

*Robinson, E., and R. C. Robbins. 1971. *Emission Concentration and Fate of Particulate Atmospheric Pollutants*. Menlo Park, Calif.: Stanford Research Institute.

*Robson, Geoffrey R. 1974. "Geothermal Electricity Production," *Science*, vol. 184, 371–375.

*Rochlin, G. I. 1977. "Nuclear Waste Disposal: Two Social Criteria," *Science*, vol. 195, 23–31.

*Rodale, R. 1972. *Ecology and Luxury Living May Not Mix*. Emmaus, Pa.: Rodale Press.

Roos, Daniel. 1974. "Doorstop Transit," *Environment*, June, pp. 19–28.

Rose, David J. 1971. "Controlled Nuclear Fusion: Status and Outlook," *Science*, vol. 172, 797–808.

*Rose, David J. 1974a. "Energy Policy in the U.S.," *Scientific American*, vol. 230, no. 1, 20–29.

*Rose, David J. 1974b. "Nuclear Electric Power," *Science*, vol. 184, 351–359.

*Rose, David J. 1976. "The Prospect for Fusion," *Technology Review*, December, pp. 21–43.

*Rose, David J., and Richard K. Lester. 1978. "Nuclear Power, Nuclear Weapons and International Stability," *Scientific American*, vol. 238, 45–57.

*Rose, David J., et al. 1976. "Nuclear Power—Compared to What?" *American Scientists*, vol. 64, 291–299.

*Rosenthal, Barbara. 1977. "The Auto Option," *Environment*, vol. 19, no. 5, 18–25.

*Ross, Marc H., and Robert H. Williams. 1975. *Assessing the Potential for Energy Conservation*. Albany, N.Y.: Institute for Policy Alternatives.

*Ross, Marc H., and Robert H. Williams. 1976. "Energy Efficiency: Our Most Underrated Energy Resource," *Bulletin of the Atomic Scientists*, November, pp. 28–38.

*Ross, Marc H., and Robert H. Williams. 1977a. *Energy and Economic Growth*. Washington, D.C.: Government Printing Office.

*Ross, Marc H., and Robert H. Williams. 1977b. "The Potential for Fuel Conservation," *Technology Review*, February, pp. 49–56.

*Rossini, A. D., and T. A. Rieck. 1978. "Economics of Nuclear Power," *Science*, vol. 201, 582–589.

*Roszak, Theodore. 1972. *Where the Wasteland Ends*. New York: Doubleday.

*Rotblat, J. 1977. "Controlling Weapons-Grade Fissile Material," *Bulletin of the Atomic Scientists*, June, pp. 37–43.

*Rotblat, J. 1978. "The Risks for Radiation Workers," *Bulletin of the Atomic Scientists*, September, pp. 41–46.

*Rothchild, John, and Frank Tenny. 1978. *The Home Energy Guide: How to Cut Your Utility Bills*. New York: Ballantine.

*Rotty, R. M., and Alvin M. Weinberg. 1977. "How Long Is Coal's Future?" *Climatic Change*, vol. 1, 45–58.

*Rotty, R. M., et al. 1975. *Net Energy from Nuclear Power*. Oak Ridge, Tenn.: Institute for Energy Analysis.

*Rouse, Robert S., and Robert O. Smith. 1975. *Energy: Resource, Slave, Pollutant*. New York: Macmillan.

*Rubin, Milton D. 1974. "Plugging the Energy Sieve," *Bulletin of the Atomic Scientists*, December, pp. 7–17.

*Ruedisili, L. C., and M. W. Firebaugh, eds. 1975. *Perspectives on Energy*. New York: Oxford University Press.

*Ruzic, Neil P. 1978. "An International Decade of Energy Alternatives: Has the Time Come for This Idea?" *The Futurist*, February, pp. 27–33.

Sagan, L. A. 1972. "Human Costs of Nuclear Power," *Science*, vol. 177, 487–493.

*Sagan, Leonard A., ed. 1973. *Human and Ecologic Effects of Nuclear Power Plants*. Springfield, Ill.: Thomas.

Sagan, L. A., and Rolf Eliassen. 1974. *Human and Ecologic Effects of Nuclear Power Plants*. Springfield, Ill.: Thomas.

*Salisbury, David F. 1976. "Quarantining Plutonium," *Technology Review*, January, pp. 4–5.

Saltonstall, Richard. 1971. *Your Environment and What You Can Do about It*. New York: Walker.

*Saltzman, Arthur. 1973. "Para-Transit: Taking the Mass Out of Mass Transit," *Technology Review*, July/August, pp. 46–63.

*Sampson, Anthony. 1976. *The Seven Sisters: The Great Oil Companies and the World They Shaped*. New York: Bantam.

*Sanders, Howard L. 1977. "The West Falmouth Spill," *Oceanus*, vol. 20, no. 4, 15–24.

*Sarkanen, Kyosti V. 1976. "Renewable Resources for the Production of Fuels and Chemicals," *Science*, vol. 191, 773–776.

*Saunders, M. 1976. *The Economics of Nuclear and Coal Power*. New York: Praeger.

*Scalise, James W. 1975. *Earth-Integrated Architecture*. Tempe: College of Architecture, Arizona State University.

SCEP (Study of Critical Environmental Problems). 1970. *Man's Impact on the Global Environment*. Cambridge, Mass.: MIT Press.

*Schanz, John J. 1978. "Oil and Gas Resources—Welcome to Uncertainty," *Resources*, no. 58, 1–16.

*Schipper, Lee. 1976a. *Explaining Energy: A Manual of Non-Style for the Energy Outsider Who Wants In*. Springfield, Va.: National Technical and Information Service.

*Schipper, Lee. 1976b. "Raising the Productivity of Energy Utilization." In Jack M. Hollander and Melvin K. Simmons, eds., *Annual Review of Energy*, vol. 1. Palo Alto, Calif.: Annual Reviews.

*Schipper, Lee, and Allan J. Lichtenberg. 1976. "Efficient Energy Use and Well-Being: the Swedish Example," *Science*, vol. 194, 1001–1013.

*Schipper, Lee, and Joel Darmstadter. 1978. "The Logic of Energy Conservation," *Technology Review*, January, pp. 41–50.

*Schmidt, Richard A., and George R. Hill. 1976. "Coal: Energy Keystone." In Jack M. Hollander and Melvin K. Simmons, eds., *Annual Review of Energy*, vol. 1. Palo Alto, Calif.: Annual Reviews.

*Schmidt, Fred H., and David Bodarsky. 1977. *The Fight over Nuclear Energy*. Albion, Ohio: Albion.

*Schneider, K. R. 1971. *Autokind vs. Mankind*. New York: W. W. Norton.

*Schneider, Stephen H. 1975. "On Carbon Dioxide–Climate Confusion," *Journal of the Atmospheric Sciences*, vol. 32, 2060–2066.

*Schneider, Stephen H. 1976a. *Climate Change and the World Predicament: A Case Study for Interdisciplinary Research*. Boulder, Colo.: National Center for Atmospheric Research.

*Schneider, Stephen H. 1976b. *The Genesis Strategy: Climate and Global Survival*. New York: Plenum Press.

*Schneider, Hans K. 1977. "International Energy Trade: Recent History and Prospects." In Jack M. Hollander et al., eds., *Annual Review of Energy*, vol. 2. Palo Alto, Calif.: Annual Reviews.

*Schneider, Alan M. 1978. "A New Tax on Gasoline: Estimating Its Effect on Consumption," *Science*, vol. 202, 755–757.

*Schneider, Stephen H., and Roger D. Bennett. 1975. "Climatic Barriers to Long-Term Energy Growth," *Ambio*, vol. 4, no. 2, 65–74.

*Schneider, Stephen H., and R. E. Dickinson. 1974. "Climate Modelling," *Reviews of Geophysics and Space Physics*, vol. 12, 447–493.

*Schneider, Stephen H., and William W. Kellogg. 1973. "The Chemical Basis for Climate Change." In S. I. Rasool, ed., *Chemistry of the Lower Atmosphere*, New York: Plenum Press.

*Schneider, Stephen H., and Clifford Mass. 1975. "Volcanic Dust, Sunspots, and Temperature Trends," *Science*, vol. 190, 741–746.

*Schoen, Richard, et al. 1975. *New Energy Technologies for Buildings*. Cambridge, Mass.: Ballinger.

Schrenk, H. H., et al. 1949. "Air Pollution in Donora, Pennsylvania," *Public Health Service Bulletin No. 306*. Washington, D.C.: U.S. Public Health Service.

*Schultz, Mort. 1978. "Bold New Look at a Bright New Sun," *Popular Mechanics*, March, pp. 104–134.

*Schumacher, E. F. 1973. *Small Is Beautiful: Economics as if People Mattered*. New York: Harper & Row.

*Schumacher, E. F. 1974. "We Must Make Things Smaller and Simpler," *The Futurist*, December, pp. 281–284.

*Schurr, Sam H. 1971. *Energy Research Needs*. Washington, D.C.: Government Printing Office.

*Schurr, Sam H., ed. 1972. *Energy, Economic Growth, and Environment*. Baltimore: Johns Hopkins University Press.

*Science and Public Policy Program, University of Oklahoma. 1975. *Energy Alternatives: A Comparative Analysis*. Washington, D.C.: Government Printing Office.

*Scientific American. 1970. *The Biosphere*. San Francisco: W. H. Freeman.

*Scientific American. 1971. *Energy and Power*. San Francisco: W. H. Freeman.

*Scientists' Institute for Public Information. 1976a. *Congressional Seminar on the Potential for Solar and Wind Electric Power Generation*. New York: Scientists' Institute for Public Information.

Scientists' Institute for Public Information. 1976b. *The Economic Viability of Nuclear Energy*. New York: Scientists' Institute for Public Information.

*Seaborg, Glenn T. 1970. "The Birthpangs of a New World," *The Futurist*, December, p. 205.

*Seaborg, Glenn T., and Justin L. Bloom. 1970. "Fast Breeder Reactors," *Scientific American*, vol. 223, no. 5, 13–21.

*Seaborg, Glenn T., and William R. Corliss. 1971. *Man and Atom*. New York: E. P. Dutton.

*Selbin, Joel. 1975. "Uranium Supply Low," *Chemical and Engineering News*, July, p. 31.

*Selbin, Joel. 1977. "Unreal Thinking about Energy," *Bulletin of the Atomic Scientists*, September, pp. 54–56.

Sellers, William D. 1970. "A Global Climatic Model Based on the Energy Balance of the Earth-Atmosphere System," *Journal of Applied Meteorology*, vol. 8, 392–400.

Sellers, William D. 1973. "A New Global Climate Model," *Journal of Applied Meteorology*, vol. 12, no. 2, 241–254.

*Sellers, William D. 1974. "A Reassessment of the Effect of CO_2 Variations on a Simple Global Climatic Model," *Journal of Applied Meterology*, vol. 13, 831–833.

*Senate Energy Committee. 1977. *Petroleum Industry Involvement in Alternative Sources of Energy*. Washington, D.C.: U.S. Senate.

*Shapley, Deborah. 1977. "Reactor Safety: Independence of Rasmussen Study Doubted," *Science*, vol. 197, 29–31.

*Shea, Kevin P. 1976. "An Explosive Reactor Possibility," *Environment*, vol. 18, no. 1, 6–11.

*Shell Oil Company. 1973. "The National Energy Outlook." Available free from Shell Oil Company, Public Affairs, P.O. Box 2467, Houston, TX 77001.

*Shelton, Jay, and Andrew Shapiro. 1977. *The Woodburners Encyclopedia*. Waitsfield, Vt.: Vermont Crossroads.

*Sheridan, David. 1977. "A Second Coal Age Promises To Slow Our Dependence on Imported Oil," *Smithsonian*, September, pp. 31–37.

*Shettigrra, P., and R. W. Morgan. 1975. "Asbestos, Smoking, and Laryngenal Carcinoma," *Archives of Environmental Health*, vol. 30, 517–519.

Shinnar, Revel. 1972. "Systems Approach for Reducing Car Pollution," *Science*, vol. 175, 1357–1360.

*Shurcliff, William A. 1976. "Active-Type Solar Heating Systems for Houses: A Technology in Ferment," *Bulletin of the Atomic Scientists*, February, pp. 30–40.

*Shurcliff, William A. 1978. *Solar Heated Buildings of North America*. Harrisville, N.H.: Brick House Publishing.

*Shy, Carl M., and John F. Finklea. 1973. "Air Pollution Affects Community Health," *Environmental Science and Technology*, vol. 7, 204–208.

*Shy, C. M., et al. 1972. *Results of Studies in Cincinnati, Chattanooga, and New York*. Chicago: American Medical Association Conference.

*Sickle, D. V. 1971. *The Ecological Citizen*. New York: Harper & Row.

*Siegel, Sanford M., and Barbara Z. Siegel. 1975. "Geothermal Hazards: Mercury Emission," *Environmental Science and Technology*, vol. 9, no. 5, 473–474.

*Siegenthaler, U., and H. Oeschger. 1978. "Predicting Future Atmospheric Carbon Dioxide Levels," *Science*, vol. 199, 388–395.

*Simmons, Daniel M. 1975. *Wind Power*. Park Ridge, N.J.: Noyes Data.

*Simon, Noel, and Paul Geroudet. 1970. *Lost Survivors: The Natural History of Animals in Danger of Extinction*. New York: World.

Singer, S. Fred., ed. 1970. *Global Effects of Environmental Pollution*. New York: Springer-Verlag.

*Singer, S. Fred, ed. 1975a. *The Changing Global Environment*, Dordrecht, Netherlands: Reidel.

*Singer, S. F. 1975b. "Oil Resource Estimates," *Science*, vol. 188, 401.

*Skinner, Brian J. 1976. *Earth Resources*. 2nd ed. Englewood Cliffs, N.J.: Prentice-Hall.

*Skurka, Norma, and Jan Noor. 1976. *Design for a Limited Planet: Living with Natural Energy*. New York: Ballantine.

*Smagorinksy, J. 1974. "Global Atmospheric Modeling and Numerical Simulation of Climate." In W. N. Ness, ed., *Weather and Climate Modification*. New York: John Wiley, pp. 633–686.

*Smay, Elaine V. 1977. "Underground Houses—Low Fuel Bills, Low Maintenance, Privacy, Security," *Popular Science*, April, pp. 84–185.

SMIC (Study of Man's Impact on Climate). 1971. *Inadvertent Climate Modification*. Cambridge, Mass.: MIT Press.

*Smith, W. H. 1974a. "Air Pollution: Effects on the Structure and Function of the Temperate Forest Ecosystem," *Environmental Pollution*, vol. 6, 111–129.

*Smith, Robert L. 1974b. *Ecology and Field Biology*. 2nd ed. New York: Harper & Row.

*Smith, Robert Leo. 1976. *The Ecology of Man: An Ecosystem Approach*. 2nd ed. New York: Harper & Row.

*Smith, Irene. 1978. *Carbon Dioxide and the "Greenhouse Effect": An Unresolved Problem*. London, England: IEA Coal Research Technical Information Service.

*Snell, Jack E., et al. 1976. "Energy Conservation in New Housing Design," *Science*, vol. 192, 1305–1311.

*Socolow, Robert H. 1977. "The Coming Age of Conservation." In Jack M. Hollander et al., eds., *Annual Review of Energy*, vol. 2. Palo Alto, Calif.: Annual Reviews.

*Somers, Edward V., et al. 1976. "Advanced Energy Conversion." In Jack M. Hollander and Melvin K. Simmons, eds., *Annual Review of Energy*, vol. 1. Palo Alto, Calif.: Annual Reviews.

*Sørensen, Bert. 1975. "Energy and Resources," *Science*, vol. 189, 255–260.

*Sørensen, Bert. 1976. *Wind Energy, Bulletin of the Atomic Scientists*. September, pp. 39–45.

*Southwick, C. H. 1976. *Ecology and the Quality of the Environment*. 2nd ed. New York: Van Nostrand Reinhold.

*Speth, Gustave. 1978. "The Nuclear Recession," *Bulletin of the Atomic Scientists*, April, pp. 24–27.

*Speth, J. Gustave, et al. 1974a. "Plutonium Recycle: The Fateful Step," *Bulletin of the Atomic Scientists*, November, pp. 15–22.

*Speth, Gustave, et al. 1974b. "Plutonium: An Invitation to Disaster," *Environmental Action*, November, pp. 3–8.

*Speth, Gustave, et al. 1975. "Bypassing the Breeder," *Environmental Action*, April, pp. 10–13.

*Spinrad, Bernard I. 1973. "The Case for Nuclear Power," *Ambiente–Environment*, vol. 3, no. 2, 183–195.

*Spinrad, Bernard I. 1978. "Alternative Breeder Reactor Technologies." In Jack M. Hollander et al., eds., *Annual Review of Energy*, vol. 3. Palo Alto, Calif.: Annual Reviews.

*Sporn, Philip. 1974. "Multiple Failures of Public and Private Institutions," *Science*, vol. 184, 284–286.

*Squires, Arthur M. 1974. "Clean Fuels from Coal Gasification," *Science*, vol. 184, 340–346.

*Squires, Arthur M. 1976. "Chemicals from Coal," *Science*, vol. 191, 689–700.

Stacks, John F. 1972. *Stripping—The Surface Mining of America*. San Francisco: Sierra Club.

Staff report. 1970. "Canals Offer Vast Cooling Potential," *Environmental Science and Technology*, vol. 4, 287.

*Staff report. 1973a. "An Automobile Engine That May Be Cleaner," *Environmental Science and Technology*, vol. 7, 688–689.

Staff report. 1973b. "Canals Cool Hot Water for Reuse," *Environmental Science and Technology*, vol. 7, no. 1, 29–31.

Staff report. 1974a. "The New Math for Figuring Energy Costs," *Business Week*, June 8, pp. 42–43.

*Staff report. 1974b. *Oil Shale*. Grand Junction, Colo.: *The Daily Sentinel*.

Staff report. 1975. "Warning from the Rockies: Go Slow in Exploiting Our Fuel," *U.S. News and World Report*, December 22, pp. 41–43.

*Staff report. 1976a. "Energy: The Loss of Innocence," *Resources*, no. 51, p. 2.

Staff report. 1976b. "Superbulb," *Science News*, March 20, p. 185.

Staff report. 1976c. "Prospects for Substitute Fuels Look Poor," *Chemical and Engineering News*, October 18, pp. 36–39.

Staff report. 1976d. "Plenty of Water for Western Coal," *Technology Review*, July-August, p. 22.

*Staff report. 1977a. "Keeping Oil Out of the Marine Environment," *Environmental Science and Technology*, vol. 11, 1046–1048.

Staff report. 1977b. "Kitchen Smog," *Chemistry*, July/August, p. 5.

*Staff report. 1977c. News item in *Environmental Action*, July 16, p. 15.

Staff report. 1977d. "How to Save Energy," *Newsweek*, April 18, pp. 70–79.

*Staff report. 1977e. *Decentralized Energy Systems*. Washington, D.C.: Critical Mass Journal.

Staff report. 1977f. "Lovins Views Carter's Plan," *Not Man Apart*, Mid-July-August, p. 15.

*Staff report. 1977g. "Coal Burning Reignites Air Quality Battle," *Conservation Foundation Letter*, September, pp. 1–8.

Staff report. 1977h. "Outlook for Coal: Bright, But with Problems," *Chemical and Engineering News*, February 14, pp. 24–31.

*Staff report. 1977i. "Solar Energy: The Revolution Is Under Way," *Conservation Foundation Letter*, June, pp. 1–8.

Staff report. 1978a. "Dimensions of the Problem," *ZPG Reporter*, May, p. 7.

*Staff report. 1978b. *Environmental Action*, April 22, p. 15.

*Staff report. 1978c. "What the Public Thinks," *Resources*, January-March, pp. 1–2.

Staff report. 1978d. "Increased Use of Coal Deemed Safe through 1985," *Chemical and Engineering News*, January 30, pp. 22–24.

Staff report. 1978e. "MHD Power Outlook Remains Uncertain," *Chemical and Engineering News*, June 12, pp. 40–42.

*Staff report. 1978f. "Interview with James R. Schlesinger, U.S. Secretary of Energy," *U.S. News and World Report*, October 16, pp. 69–70.

Staff report. 1978g. "Carter Budget Brings Cheer to Environmentalists," *Conservation Foundation Letter*, February, pp. 1–8.

Staff report. 1978h. "Federal R & D Funding: Modest Gains in 1979," *Chemical and Engineering News*, October 23, pp. 16–17.

Staff report. 1978i. "Solar Slighted in New Budgets," *Not Man Apart*, Mid-March, p. 15.

Staff report. 1978j. "Passive Solar Retrofit," *People and Energy*, vol. 4, no. 6, 2–3.

Staff report. 1978k. "Sizing Up Solar Satellites," *People and Energy*, vol. 4, no. 5, 3–4.

Staff report. 1978l. "Breeders as Incinerators," *Scientific American*, May, pp. 81–82.

Staff report. 1979a. "Energy In, Energy Out," *Technology Review*, December-January, p. 21.

Staff report. 1979b. "Hydrocarbon Fuel Supplies," *Environmental Science and Technology*, vol. 13, no. 1, 27–30.

Staff report. 1979c. "Biomass Potential in 2000 Put at 7 Quads," *Chemical and Engineering News*, February 12, pp. 20–22.

Staff report. 1979d. "Energy Funding," *Chemical and Engineering News*, January 29, p. 23.

Staff report. 1979e. "New Analysis Finds Nuclear 60% More Expensive Than Coal," *Not Man Apart*, vol. 9, no. 2, 17.

*Stanford Research Institute. 1976. *The Hydrogen Economy*. Menlo Park, Calif.: Stanford Research Institute.

*Starr, Chauncey. 1971. "Energy and Power," *Scientific American*, September, pp. 3–15.

*Starr, Chauncey. 1973. "Realities of the Energy Crisis," *Bulletin of the Atomic Scientists*, September, pp. 15–20.

*Starr, Chauncey, and R. Philip Hammond. 1972. "Nuclear Waste Storage," *Science*, vol. 177, 744.

*Starr, Chauncey, et al. 1976. "Philosophical Basis for Risk Analysis," In Jack M. Hollander and Melvin K. Simmons, eds., *Annual Review of Energy*, vol. 1. Palo Alto, Calif.: Annual Reviews.

*Stauffer, T. R., et al. 1975. *An Assessment of the Economics Incentive for the Breeder Reactor*. Cambridge, Mass.: Harvard University Press.

*Steadman, Philip. 1975. *Energy, Environment and Building*. New York: Cambridge University Press.

*Stearns, Forest W., and Tom Montag. 1973. *The Urban Ecosystem: A Holistic Approach*. New York: Halsted (John Wiley).

*Stein, Richard G. 1972. "A Matter of Design," *Environment*, October, pp. 17–29.

*Stein, Charles, ed. 1976. *Critical Materials Problems in Energy Production*. New York: Academic Press.

*Stein, Richard G. 1977. *Architecture and Energy*. Garden City, N.Y.: Anchor Books.

*Steiner, Don. 1971. "The Radiological Impact of Fusion," *New Scientist*, December 16.

*Steiner, Don, and John F. Clarke. 1978. "The Tokamak: Model T Fusion Reactor," *Science*, vol. 199, 1395–1402.

*Steinhart, Carol E., and John S. Steinhart. 1972. *Blowout: A Case Study of the Santa Barbara Oil Spill*. North Scituate, Mass.: Duxbury Press.

*Steinhart, Carol E., and John S. Steinhart. 1974a. *Energy: Sources, Use and Role in Human Affairs*. North Scituate, Mass.: Duxbury Press.

*Steinhart, John S., and Carol E. Steinhart. 1974b. "Energy Use in the U.S. Food System," *Science*, vol. 184, 307–315.

*Stencel, Sandra. 1974. "Nuclear Safeguards," *Editorial Research Reports*, vol. 2, no. 19, 867–884.

*Stencel, Sandra. 1976. "Nuclear Waste Disposal," *Editorial Research Reports*, vol. 2, no. 21, 885–906.

Stern, A. C., ed. 1968. *Air Pollution*. 2nd ed. New York: Academic Press.

*Stern, A. C., et al. 1973. *Fundamentals of Air Pollution*. New York: Academic Press.

*Sternglass, Ernest. 1973. *Low Level Radiation*. San Francisco: Friends of the Earth.

*Stivers, Robert L. 1976. *The Sustainable Society*. Philadelphia: Westminister Press.

*Stoker, H. S., and Spencer L. Seager. 1976. *Environmental Chemistry: Air and Water Pollution*. 2nd ed. Chicago, Ill: Scott, Foresman.

*Stoker, H. Stephen, et al. 1975. *Energy: From Source to Use*. New York: Scott, Foresman.

*Stokinger, H. E. 1971. "Sanity in Research and

Evaluation of Environmental Health," *Science*, vol. 174, 662–665.

*Stone, Tabor R. 1971. *Beyond the Automobile.* Englewood Cliffs, N.J.: Prentice-Hall.

*Stoner, Carol. 1975. *Producing Your Own Power: How To Make Nature's Energy Sources Work for You.* New York: Vintage.

*Strange, James O. 1969. "The Urbanite's Interest in Rural Land Use Planning," *Journal of Soil and Water Conservation*, vol. 24, no. 5.

*Study Group on Technical Aspects of Efficient Energy Utilization. 1975. "Efficient Use of Energy," *Physics Today*, August, pp. 23–33.

*Stuiver, Minze. 1978. "Atmospheric Carbon Dioxide and Carbon Reservoir Changes," *Science*, vol. 199, 253–258.

*Stumm, Werner, ed. 1977. *Global Chemical Cycles and Their Alteration by Man.* Berlin: Dahlem Konferenzen.

*Subcommittee on Energy of the Joint Economic Committee, Congress of the United States. 1978. *Creating Jobs through Energy Policy.* Washington, D.C.: Government Printing Office.

*Sudia, Theodore W. 1971. *Man, Nature, City: The Urban Ecosystem.* National Park Service, Urban Ecology Series No. 1. Washington, D.C.: Government Printing Office.

*Sullivan, James B., and Paul A. Montgomery. 1972. "Surveying Highway Impact," *Environment*, vol. 14, no. 9, 12–20.

*Summers, Claude M. 1971. "The Conversion of Energy," *Scientific American*, September.

*Sunset Books editors. 1978. *Sunset Homeowner's Guide to Solar Heating.* Menlo Park, Calif.: Lane.

*Surface Mining Research Library. 1972. *Energy and the Environment: What's the Strip Mining Controversy All About?* Charleston, W. Va.: Surface Mining Research Library, 1218 Quarrier St., Charleston, WV 25301.

*Sutton, David B., and N. Paul Harmon. 1973. *Ecology: Selected Concepts.* New York: John Wiley.

*Swabb, L. E., Jr. 1978. "Liquid Fuels from Coal: From R & D to an Industry," *Science*, vol. 199, 619–629.

*Swann, Mark. 1976. "Power from the Sea," *Environment*, vol. 18, no. 4, 25–31.

*Swann, Mark. 1977. "Radioactive Waste Disposal: The Threat with No Solution," *Environment Action Bulletin*, vol. 8, no. 5, 1–8.

*Sweet, William. 1977. "The Opposition to Nuclear Power in Europe," *Bulletin of the Atomic Scientists*, December, pp. 40–47.

*Tamplin, Arthur R. 1973. "Solar Energy," *Environment*, vol. 15, no. 5, 16–34.

Tamplin, Arthur R., and T. B. Cochran. 1974. *Radiation Standards for Hot Particles.* Washington, D.C.: Natural Resources Defense Council.

*Tamplin, Arthur R., and John W. Gofman. 1970. *Biological Effects of Radiation—Population Control through Nuclear Pollution.* Chicago: Nelson-Hall.

*Tansley, A. G. 1935. "The Use and Abuse of Vegetational Concepts and Terms," *Ecology*, vol. 16, 284–307.

*Tardiff, R. C. 1975. "Transuranium Element Toxicity—Dose Response Relationships at Low Exposure Levels." In O. Nygaard et al., eds., *Radiation Research.* New York: Academic Press.

*Tavoulareas, William, and Carl Kaysen. 1977. *A Debate on "A Time To Choose."* Cambridge, Mass.: Ballinger.

*Taylor, T. B. 1975. "Nuclear Safeguards," *Annual Review of Nuclear Science*, vol. 25, 407–421.

*Technology Information Center. 1975. *Wind Energy Utilization.* Albuquerque: University of New Mexico.

*Technology Review. 1972. *Energy Technology in the Year 2000.* Cambridge, Mass.: Technology Review.

Teilhard de Chardin, Pierre. 1966. *Man's Place in Nature.* New York: Harper & Row.

*Theobald, P. K., et al. 1972. *Energy Resources of the United States.* U.S. Geological Survey Circular 650. Washington, D.C.: Government Printing Office.

*Thirring, Hans. 1958. *Energy for Man.* New York: Harper & Row.

*Thomson, L. M. 1975. "Weather Variability, Climatic Change, and Grain Production," *Science*, vol. 188, 535–541.

*Tillman, David A. 1976. "Status of Coal Gasification," *Environmental Science and Technology*, vol. 10, no. 1, 34–38.

*Tillman, David. 1978. *Wood as an Energy Resource.* New York: Academic Press.

*Todd, Nancy J., ed. 1977. *The Book of the New Alchemists.* New York: E. P. Dutton.

*Traffe, Edward J., and Howard L. Gauthier. 1973. *Geography of Transportation.* Englewood Cliffs, N.J.: Prentice-Hall.

*Train, Russell E. 1973. "Energy Problems and Environmental Concern," *Bulletin of the Atomic Scientists.* November, pp. 43–47.

*Transportation Research Board. 1976. *Paratransit.* Special Report 164. Washington, D.C.: Transportation Research Board.

*Turner, D. J. 1971. "Dams and Ecology: Can They Be Made Compatible?" *Civil Engineering–ASCE*, September, pp. 76–80.

*Tuve, George L. 1976. *Energy, Environment, Population, and Food: Four Interdependent Crises.* New York: John Wiley.

*Udall, Stewart L. 1973. "The Energy Crisis: A Radical Solution," *World*, May 8, pp. 34–36.

*Udall, Stewart, et al. 1974. *The Energy Balloon.* New York: McGraw-Hill.

*Union of Concerned Scientists. 1977. *The Risks of Nuclear Power Reactors.* Cambridge, Mass.: Union of Concerned Scientists.

*Union of Concerned Scientists. 1978. "Rasmussen Report Is Demolished by Union of Concerned Scientists," *The Nuclear Breakdown*, February, pp. 5–20.

*United Nations. 1976. *World Energy Supplies 1950–1974.* New York: United Nations.

U.S. Atomic Energy Commission. 1966. *The Genetic Effects of Radiation* (by Isaac Asimov and Theodosius Dobzhansky). Oak Ridge, Tenn.: USAEC Division of Technical Information Extension.

*U.S. Atomic Energy Commission. 1969a. *Atomic Fuel* (by John F. Hogerton). Oak Ridge, Tenn.: USAEC Division of Technical Information Extension.

U.S. Atomic Energy Commission. 1969b. *Wastes* (by Charles H. Fox). Oak Ridge, Tenn.: USAEC Division of Technical Information Extension.

*U.S. Atomic Energy Commission. 1973a. *The Nation's Energy Future.* Washington, D.C.: Government Printing Office.

U.S. Atomic Energy Commission. 1973b. "Nuclear Fuel Supply." USAEC Reports WASH 1242 and WASH 1243. Washington, D.C.: Atomic Energy Commission.

U.S. Atomic Energy Commission. 1973c. "Report on Investigation of 106T Tank Leak at Hanford Reservation, Richland, Washington." Washington, D.C.: Atomic Energy Commission (July).

*U.S. Atomic Energy Commission. 1974a. *Environmental Impact Statement on the Liquid Metal Fast Breeder Reactor Program.* Washington, D.C.: Government Printing Office.

*U.S. Atomic Energy Commission. 1974b. *High-Level Radioactive Waste Management Alternatives.* Springfield, Va.: National Technical Information Service.

*U.S. Atomic Energy Commission. 1974c. *Reactor Safety Study.* 12 vols. Washington, D.C.: Government Printing Office.

*U.S. Bureau of Mines. 1976a. *Mineral Facts and Problems.* Washington, D.C.: Government Printing Office. (Issued every 5 years.)

*U.S. Bureau of Mines. 1976b. *Mineral Trends and Forecasts.* Washington, D.C.: Government Printing Office.

*U.S. Department of Agriculture. 1978. *Gasohol from Grain—The Economic Issues.* Washington, D.C.: U.S. Department of Agriculture.

*U.S. Department of Energy. 1978. *Projections of Energy Supply and Demand and Their Impacts.* Washington, D.C.: Department of Energy.

*U.S. Department of Health, Education, and Welfare. 1968a. *Air Quality Criteria for Particulate Matter.* Pub. AP-49. Washington, D.C.: Government Printing Office.

U.S. Department of Health, Education, and Welfare. 1968b. *Air Quality Criteria for Sulfur Oxides.* Pub. AP-50. Washington, D.C.: Government Printing Office.

*U.S. Department of Health, Education, and Welfare. 1969a. *Control Techniques for Particulate Air Pollutants.* Pub. AP-51. Washington, D.C.: Government Printing Office.

U.S. Department of Health, Education, and Welfare. 1969b. *Control Techniques for Sulfur Oxide Air Pollutants.* Pub. AP-52. Washington, D.C.: Government Printing Office.

U.S. Department of Health, Education, and Welfare. 1970a. *Air Pollution Injury to Vegetation.* Pub. AP-71. Washington, D.C.: Government Printing Office.

*U.S. Department of Health, Education, and Welfare. 1970b. *Control Techniques for Carbon Monoxide, Nitrogen Oxide, and Hydrocarbon Emissions from Mobile Sources.* Pub. AP-66. Washington, D.C.: Government Printing Office.

U.S. Department of the Interior. 1968. *Industrial Waste Guide on Thermal Pollution.* Corvallis, Ore. Pacific Northwest Water Laboratory.

*U.S. Department of the Interior. 1975. *Energy Perspectives.* Washington, D.C.: Government Printing Office.

*U.S. Department of Transportation. 1973. *Highway Statistics.* Washington, D.C.: Government Printing Office.

U.S. House of Representatives. 1972. *Solar Energy Research: Staff Report of the Committee on Science and Astronautics.* Washington, D.C.: Government Printing Office.

*U.S. Senate. 1976. *Land Use and Energy: A Study of Interrelationships.* Washington, D.C.: Committee on Interior and Insular Affairs.

*U.S. Senate, Select Committee on Small Business and Committee on Interior and Insular Affairs. 1977. *Alternative Long-Range Energy Strategies.* 2 vols. Washington, D.C.: Government Printing Office.

*Utetz, George, and Donald L. Johnson. 1974. "Breaking the Web," *Environment*, vol. 16, no. 10, 31–39.

*Vale, Brenda, and Robert Vale. 1977. *The Autonomous House: Design and Planning for Self-Sufficiency.* New York: Universe Books.

*van Dam, André. 1978. "Growth without Pain," *Bulletin of the Atomic Scientists*, April, pp. 28–30.

*Van Loon, H., and J. Williams. 1976. "The Connection between Trends of Mean Temperature and Circulation at the Surface, Part I: Winter," *Monthly Weather Review*, vol. 114, 365–380.

*Vernberg, F. John, and Winona B. Vernberg. 1974. *Pollution and Physiology of Marine Organisms.* New York: Academic Press.

*Vitti, Joseph A., and William P. Staker. 1972. "The Breeder's Role in the Future Power Generation."

In *Proceedings of Connecticut Clean Power Symposium*, St. Joseph College, West Hartford, Conn., May 13.

*Vivian, John. 1976. *Wood Heat*. Emmaus, Pa.: Rodale.

*von Hippel, Frank. 1974. "Looking Back on the Rasmussen Report," *Bulletin of the Atomic Scientists*, February, pp. 42–47.

*von Hippel, Frank. 1977. "Toward a Solar Civilization," *Bulletin of the Atomic Scientists*, October, 12–15.

*von Hippel, Frank, and Robert H. Williams. 1975. "Solar Technologies," *Bulletin of the Atomic Scientists*, November, pp. 25–31.

*von Hippel, Frank, and Robert H. Williams. 1976. "Energy Waste and Nuclear Power Growth," *Bulletin of the Atomic Scientists*, December, pp. 18–21.

*Wade, Nicholas. 1974. "Windmills: The Resurrection of an Ancient Energy Technology," *Science*, vol. 184, 1055–1058.

*Wade, Alex, and Neal Ewenstein. 1977. *Thirty Energy-Efficient Houses You Can Build*. Emmaus, Pa.: Rodale.

*Waldbott, George L. 1978. *Health Effects of Environmental Pollutants*. 2nd ed. St. Louis: C. V. Mosby.

*Walker, Graham. 1973. "The Stirling Engine," *Scientific American*, vol. 229, no. 2, 80–87.

*Walsh, John. 1974. "Problems of Expanding Coal Production," *Science*, vol. 184, 336–339.

Walters, S. 1971. "Power in the Year 2001, Part 2—Thermal Sea Power," *Mechanical Engineering*, October, pp. 21–25.

*Walworth, David H. 1975. "Dial-a-Ride Reconsidered," *Environment*, vol. 7, no. 4, 2–3.

*Ward, Barbara. 1976. *The Home of Man*. New York: W. W. Norton.

*Warren, Betty. 1978. *The Energy and Environment Bibliography*. San Francisco: Friends of the Earth.

Washington, W. 1972. "Numerical Climatic Change Experiments: The Effect of Man's Production of Thermal Energy," *Journal of Applied Meteorology*, vol. 11, 768–772.

*Washington Center for Metropolitan Studies. 1976. *Capturing the Sun through Bioconversion*. Washington, D.C.: Washington Center for Metropolitan Studies.

*Watson, Donald. 1977. *Designing and Building a Solar Home: Your Place in the Sun*. Charlotte, Vt.: Garden Way.

*Watt, Kenneth E. F. 1972a. "Man's Efficient Rush toward Deadly Dullness," *Natural History*, vol. 81, 74–84.

*Watt, Kenneth E. F. 1972b. "Tambora and Krakatau: Volcanoes and the Cooling of the World," *Saturday Review*, December 23, pp. 43–44.

*Watt, Kenneth E. F. 1973. *Principles of Environmental Science*. New York: McGraw-Hill.

*Watt, Kenneth E. F. 1974. *The Titanic Effect: Planning for the Unthinkable*. Sunderland, Mass.: Sinauer.

*Watt, Kenneth E. F., et al. 1975. "A Simulation of the Use of Energy and Land at the National Level," *Simulation*, May, pp. 129–153.

*Watt, Kenneth E. F., et al. 1977. *The Unsteady State: Environmental Problems, Growth, and Culture*. Honolulu: University Press of Hawaii.

*Weare, B. C., et al. 1974. "Aerosol and Climate: Some Further Considerations," *Science*, vol. 186, 827–828.

*Webb, Richard E. 1976. *The Accident Hazard of Nuclear Power Plants*. Amherst: University of Massachusetts Press.

*Webber, Melvin. 1976. "The BART Experience," *The Public Interest*, Fall.

*Weinberg, A. M. 1972. "Social Institutions and Nuclear Energy," *Science*, vol. 177, 27–34.

*Weinberg, A. M. 1973. "Technology and Ecology— Is There a Need for Confrontation?" *BioScience*, vol. 23, 43.

*Weinberg, Alvin M. 1976. "The Maturity and Future of Nuclear Energy," *American Scientists*, vol. 64, 16–21.

*Weinberg, Alvin M. 1977. "Is Nuclear Energy Acceptable?" *Bulletin of the Atomic Scientists*, April, pp. 54–60.

*Weinberg, Alvin M. 1978. "Reflections on the Energy Wars," *American Scientist*, vol. 66, 153–158.

*Weinberg, A. M., and Philip R. Hammond. 1972. "Global Effects of Increased Energy Use," *Bulletin of the Atomic Scientists*, March, pp. 7–13.

*Weisz, John A. 1970. "The Environmental Effects of Surface Mining and Mineral Waste Generation." In Alfred J. Van Tassel, ed., *Environmental Side Effects of Industrial Output*. Lexington, Mass.: D. C. Heath.

*Wells, Malcolm B. 1973. "Confessions of a Gentle Architect," *Environmental Quality*, July, pp. 51–57.

*Wells, Malcolm. 1976. "Underground Architecture," *CoEvolution Quarterly*, Fall, pp. 85–94.

*Wells, Rick. 1977a. "Commoner Finds Pro-Nuclear Bias in Carter Energy Plan," *Environment Action Bulletin*, June 25, pp. 4–5.

*Wells, Malcolm. 1977b. *Underground Designs*. Available from the author, Box 1149, Brewster, Maine 02631.

*Wells, Malcolm, and Irwin Spetgang. 1978. *How To Buy Solar Heating and Cooling . . . Without Getting Burnt*. Emmaus, Pa.: Rodale.

*Whipple, D. Sawyer. 1976. "The Social Costs of Coal," *Environmental Action*, September, pp. 3–8.

*White, David C. 1973. "The Energy-Environment-Economic Triangle," *Technology Review*, December, pp. 11–19.

*White, D. E., and D. L. Williams, eds. 1975. *Assessment of Geothermal Resources of the United States*. Washington, D.C.: Government Printing Office.

*Whiting, Macauley. 1978. "Industry Saves Energy: Progress Report, 1977." In Jack M. Hollander et al., eds., *Annual Review of Energy*, vol. 3. Palo Alto, Calif.: Annual Reviews.

*Whitmore, William F. 1978. "OTEC: Electricity from the Ocean," *Technology Review*, October, pp. 58–63.

*Whittaker, Robert H. 1975. *Communities and Ecosystems*. 2nd ed. New York: Macmillan.

*Whittemore, F. Case. 1973. "How Much in Reserve?" *Environment*, vol. 15, no. 7, 16–37.

*Widmer, Thomas F., and Elias P. Gyftopoulos. 1977. "Energy Conservation and a Healthy Economy," *Technology Review*, June, pp. 31–40.

*Wiens, John A., ed. 1972. *Ecosystem Structure and Function*. Corvallis: Oregon State University Press.

*Wigg, E. E. 1974. "Methanol as a Gasoline Extender: A Critique," *Science*, vol. 186, 785–790.

*Wilcox, Howard A. 1976. *Hothouse Earth*. New York: Praeger.

*Wildhorn, Sorrell. 1975. *How To Save Gasoline: Public Policy Alternatives for the Automobile*. Cambridge, Mass.: Ballinger.

*Willett, H. C., and J. T. Prohaska. 1977. *Patterns, Possible Causes and Predictive Significance of Recent Climatic Trends of the Northern Hemisphere*. Cambridge, Mass.: Solar Climatic Research Institute.

*Williams, J. Richard. 1974. *Solar Energy Technology and Applications*. Ann Arbor, Mich.: Ann Arbor Science.

*Williams, Robert H., ed. 1975. *The Energy Conservation Papers*. Cambridge, Mass.: Ballinger.

*Williams, Robert H. 1978. "Industrial Cogeneration." In Jack M. Hollander et al., eds., *Annual Review of Energy*, vol. 3. Palo Alto, Calif.: Annual Reviews.

*Williamson, Samuel J. 1973. *Fundamentals of Air Pollution*. Reading, Mass.: Addison-Wesley.

*Willrich, Mason. 1975a. *Energy and World Politics*. New York: Free Press.

Willrich, Mason. 1975b. "Terrorists Keep Out," *Bulletin of the Atomic Scientists*, May, pp. 12–16.

*Willrich, Mason. 1976. "International Energy Issues and Options." In Jack M. Hollander and Melvin K. Simmons, eds., *Annual Review of Energy*, vol. 1. Palo Alto, Calif.: Annual Reviews.

*Willrich, Mason, and Theodore B. Taylor. 1974a. *Exploring Energy Choices*. Energy Policy Project, P.O. Box 23212. Washington, D.C. 20024.

*Willrich, Mason, and Theodore B. Taylor. 1974b. *Nuclear Thefts: Risks and Safeguards*. Cambridge, Mass.: Ballinger.

*Wilson, Thomas W., Jr. 1972. *World Energy, the Environment and Political Action*. New York: International Institute for Environmental Affairs.

*Wilson, Carroll L., ed. 1977. *Energy: Global Prospects 1985–2000*. New York: McGraw-Hill.

*Wilson, David G. 1978. "Alternative Automobile Engines," *Scientific American*, vol. 239, no. 1, 39–49.

*Wilson, W., and R. Jones. 1974. *Energy, Ecology and the Environment*. New York: Academic Press.

*Wilson, E. Milton, and Harry M. Freeman. 1976. "Processing Energy from Wastes," *Environmental Science and Technology*, vol. 10, no. 5, 430–435.

Wilson, R. D., et al. 1974. "Natural Marine Oil Seepage," *Science*, vol. 184, 858–865.

*Winkelstein, W., and R. Gay. 1971. "Suspended Particulate Air Pollution," *Archives of Environmental Health*, January, pp. 174–177.

*Winsche, W. E., et al. 1973. "Hydrogen: Its Future Role in the Nation's Energy Economy," *Science*, vol. 180, 1321–1332.

*Wishart, Ronald S. 1978. "Industrial Energy in Transition: A Petrochemical Perspective," *Science*, vol. 199, 614–618.

*Wolf, Martin. 1974. "Solar Energy Utilization by Physical Methods," *Science*, vol. 184, 382–386.

*Wolman, Abel. 1965. "The Metabolism of Cities," *Scientific American*, March, pp. 179–190.

Wood, Lowell, and John Nuckolls. 1972. "Fusion Power," *Environment*, vol. 14, no. 4, 29–33.

*Woodwell, G. M. 1970a. "Effects of Pollution on the Structure and Physiology of Ecosystems," *Science*, vol. 168, 429–433.

*Woodwell, G. M. 1970b. "The Energy Cycle of the Biosphere," *Scientific American*, September. (Reprinted in Scientific American Editors, *The Biosphere*. San Francisco: W. H. Freeman, pp. 25–36.)

*Woodwell, G. M. 1974. "Success, Succession and Adam Smith," *BioScience*, vol. 24, 81–87.

*Woodwell, George M. 1978. "The Carbon Dioxide Question," *Scientific American*, vol. 238, no. 1, 34–43.

*Woodwell, George M., and E. V. Pecan, eds. 1973. *Carbon and the Biosphere*. Springfield, Va.: National Technical Information Service.

*Woodwell, George M., et al. 1978. "The Biota and the World Carbon Budget," *Science*, vol. 199, 141–146.

World Meteorological Organization. 1970. *Urban Climates*. WMO Technical Note No. 108. Geneva: World Meteorological Organization.

Wouk, Victor. 1971. "Electric Cars: The Battery Problem," *Bulletin of the Atomic Scientists*, April, pp. 19–22.

*Wright, John, and John Syrett. 1975. "Energy Analysis of Nuclear Power," *New Scientist*, vol. 65, 66–67.

*Wright, G. S., et al. 1975. "Carbon Monoxide in the Urban Atmosphere," *Archives of Environmental Health*, vol. 30, 123–129.

*Yamamato, G., and M. Tanaka. 1972. "Increase of Global Albedo Due to Air Pollution," *Journal of Atmospheric Science*, vol. 29, 1405–1412.

*Yaverbaum, Lee. 1977. *Fluidized Bed Combustion of Coal and Waste Materials*. Park Ridge, N.J.: Noyes Data.

*Yegge, J., et al. 1974. *Citizens' Energy Workbook*. Oak Ridge, Tenn.: Oak Ridge Associated Universities.

*Yonas, Gerald. 1978. "Fusion Power with Particle Beams," *Scientific American*, vol. 239, no. 5, 50–61.

*Zebroski, E., and M. Levenson. 1976. "The Nuclear Fuel Cycle." In Jack M. Hollander and Melvin K. Simmons, eds., *Annual Review of Energy*, vol. 1. Palo Alto, Calif.: Annual Reviews.

*Zelby, Leon W. 1976. "Don't Get Swept Away by Wind Power Hopes," *Bulletin of the Atomic Scientists*, March, p. 59.

*Zelitch, Israel. 1975. "Improving the Efficiency of Photosynthesis," *Science*, vol. 188, 626–633.

Zener, Clarence. 1973. "Solar Sea Power," *Physics Today*, vol. 26, no. 1, 48.

*Zener, Clarence. 1976. "Solar Sea Power," *Bulletin of the Atomic Scientists*, January, pp. 17–24.

*Zinberg, Dorothy. 1979. "The Public and Nuclear Waste Management," *Bulletin of the Atomic Scientists*, January, pp. 34–39.

Index

Boldface numbers indicate pages on which terms are defined;
italic page numbers refer to figures and tables.